Olympic Opening Ceremony

SWITZERLAND

U.S.S.R.

United States Olympic Book 1980

VIII
Pan American
Games
San Juan
Puerto Rico

XIII Olympic
Winter Games
Lake Placid
USA

The Games
of the
XXII Olympiad
Moscow
USSR

United States Olympic Book
1980

Publisher　United States Olympic Committee
Colorado Springs, Colorado
in cooperation with
Sport & Culture U.S.A., Inc./proSport
Salt Lake City, Utah

**United States
Olympic Committee**　F. Don Miller
Executive Director

C. Robert Paul, Jr.
Director, Communications

R. Michael Moran
Assistant Director
Communications,

**Sport & Culture
U.S.A./proSport**　Roland Wolf

Karl Wadosch
International Management

Erwin Roth
Management

Edith Lake
Executive Assistant

Prof. Parry D. Sorensen
Managing Editor

Dietrich Steinhorst
Editing Consultant

Ernst Haas
Rainer Martini
Erwin Fieger
Lorenz Baader
Hans Rauchensteiner
Wilfried Witters
Exclusive Color Photography

Heribert J.A. Wuehr
Photo-Editor

Production　Bailey-Montague & Associates
Graphic Design

Publishers Press,
Salt Lake City, Utah
Under supervision of
Busche, Dortmund,
West Germany
Printing

Accu-Type
Salt Lake City,. Utah
Typesetting

Mountain States Bindery
Salt Lake City, Utah
Binding

Simpson Paper-Company
Basis 80 Tahoe Gloss White
S.D. Warren Company, a division
of the Scott Paper Company
Basis 80 LOE Cream

Cover Photo　Royden Hobson

Table of Contents

This 1980 United States Olympic Book is dedicated in admiration of the competitors in the VIII Pan American Games, the XIII Olympic Winter Games, and the 461 athletes who earned places on the 1980 Olympic Summer Team.

The last four years have been busy and productive, ending in profound frustration but with our U. S. Olympic banner held high. The USA Summer Team, on demonstrated performance, was the most talented in history and was bountifully prepared to meet the best amateur athletes from the rest of the world in the XXII Olympiad had it been able to be at Moscow.

It was bountifully prepared because of the many advancements made by the United States Olympic Committee in the period 1977-1980, such as:

—Establishment of the National Sports Festival, a summer sports extravaganza for 3,000 athletes meeting in competitions in all the sports on the programs of the Olympic and Pan American Games, under Olympic conditions.

—Implementation of the National Training Center concept, offering opportunities for our National Sports Governing Bodies to identify, train, and polish their potential Olympians, at all levels of ability and at all ages, under optimum training conditions.

—Development of a sophisticated sports medicine program designed to maximize the skills of all athletes selected to use the facilities of the National Training Centers at Colorado Springs and Squaw Valley.

—Establishment of a Job Opportunities Program designed to provide career employment opportunities for the mature athlete, enabling him to work and to continue his training on a regular basis without a loss in pay.

In addition there were these accomplishments:

—Offering National Sports Governing Bodies the opportunity to establish their administrative offices on the site of the head-quarters Olympic House at Colorado Springs. Fourteen are now there and others are to follow.

—Increased support of the annual National Olympic Academy for educators, members of the school college community, and volunteers and believers in the Olympic movement to gather for seminars on a myriad of topics concerned with a greater awareness of the world-wide Olympic movement.

—Enlarging on an ambitious program of providing Broken Time reimbursement pay to compensate athletes with a hardship during the periods they are training for and competing in the Olympic Games. In addition, working closely with State Govern-ments to adopt legislation to compensate their employees who are selected for Olympic and Pan American teams, during their period of training and competition. Thus far, 13 states have adopted such legislation.

—Bringing the Olympic Summer Games to Los Angeles in 1984 in partnership with a private group of California residents.

Amateur athletics are served better as a result of the adoption of the Amateur Sports Acts of 1978 in the closing hours of the 95th Session of the Congress of the United States. For the first time, regulatory criteria have been adopted for the operations of our 33 national sports governing bodies; the rights of athletes have been recognized and ensured, and the Congress established the United States Olympic Committee as the coordinating agency for amateur sports in our country.

No record of the United States Olympic Committee history for the last four years would be complete without mention of the special recognition accorded members of the 1980 Summer Olympic Team in Washington, D. C., July 25-30. One of the highlights of this Honors Program was the presentation of Congressional gold medals by the officers of the Olympic Committee on the steps of the Capitol. On this day too, the President of the United States praised the achievements of the athletes for having been chosen for the Team and expressed his thanks for the sacrifice they were asked to make. The program concluded with a buffet dinner on the lawn of the White House and an evening of entertainment at the Kennedy Center of the Performing Arts. It was a memorable occasion.

Notwithstanding the wrenching hurt of not taking part in the Summer Games, I do believe the Olympic movement in this country has been left with a splendid legacy. The exploits of the Winter Olympic Team at Lake Placid and the Pan-American Team at Puerto Rico and the courage, grace, and dignity demonstrated by the disappointed Summer athletes will be remembered with pride. I shall always be grateful to them and to those who served in the National Governing bodies and those on the USOC Executive Board and in the House of Delegates, and most notably to the members of the staff, for their devotion and educated talents.

It has been an honor for me to serve with you.

Robert J. Kane
President,
United States Olympic Committee

Heiden and Hockey Will Make Us
Remember the 1980 Olympics

By C. Robert Paul, Jr.

The XIII Olympic Winter Games, from the point of view of the United States populace, will be long remembered for the heroics of the young U.S. ice hockey team winning the gold against what were regarded as insurmountable odds and the superb performance of an All-American youngster, Eric Heiden, who defied the schedule-makers and won all five gold medals in the men's speed skating events.

Unlike recent Olympic Games and Olympic Winter Games, for once we had Games without serious disputes or official protests involving the competition. As expected, and as always, there were major dis-agreements in the judgments of the figure skating officials, and there may be real merit in making radical changes, although a certain amount of the acri-mony is bestirred by the media — print and electronic.

For the first time in three sets of Olympic Winter Games· the USA men outscored the ladies in competition. The USA men were 6-0 in gold medals (the ice hockey medals only count a total of one), in silver medals it was 1-3, and in the bronze it was one for the ladies and one for the men.

Overall, speedskating, expec-tedly, and ice hockey, most surprisingly, rallied the nation and brought them closer together than at any time since Neil Armstrong's stroll as first man on the moon.

Figure skating brought two medals to the U.S.A., and· perhaps a third was forfeited with the withdrawal of Tai

Mr. Paul is Director
of Communications for the U.S.
Olympic Committee

U.S. Team marches in the opening ceremony.

Babilonia and Randy Gardner from the pairs skating event following Randy's serious groin injury which may have written "finis" to their careers as amateur skaters.

Alpine skiing is an unpre-dictable sport, although all but one of the gold medalists were big names on the World Cup circuit. Again, the U.S.A. had to content itself with a silver medal — by Phil Mahre, the "gutsiest" Alpine specialist in the Olympic competition. He was skiing the same slope where he was seriously injured one year earlier. Solace for Phil Mahre was the gold medal from the International Ski Federation

for the "world championship combined events" title. Medals are awarded by the international federation at every Olympic Winter Games for the top three finish placers combining per-formances for the three Alpine disciplines.

Also, Cynthia Nelson, a bronze medalist four years ago in the downhill, failed to win a medal in any of the three events, but she was one of six women completing all three events. Marc Hodler, presi-dent of the international ski group, presented her with the silver medal for the "world com-bined championship" (she had won the bronze at Innsbruck). The gold medal, of course, was earned by the Queen of the Games, Hanni Wenzel of the tiny principality of Liechtenstein, who won two golds and a single silver in the three Alpine races. She equalled the record of West Germany's Rosi Mittermaier at Innsbruck in 1976.

The tone of the Olympic Winter Games before 23,000 chilled spectators in the temporary stands at the Horse Show Grounds was set during the Opening Ceremony. All the chills running up and down the spines on that day of February 13th were not attributed to the windy blasts. Staged by Tommy Walker of the Walt Disney organization, it was typically American. Vice President Walter Mondale pinch-hit for President Carter who was confined to Washington because of the pressure of the world situation. However, the President did catch the Olympic Fever and made personal phone calls to hockey coach Herb Brooks and speedskater Eric Heiden prior to entertaining the U.S. Olympic delegation at an elegant White House reception which attracted cabinet members, governors, and key Congressional leaders whose constituents were members of the U.S.A. team. It was Heiden's first visit with a President, as well as his first visit to the nation's capital.

And now to get back to the typically American opening. The U.S.A. delegation outfitted by the Levi Strauss Company of San Francisco were dressed in typically American clothing, topped off with glistening bright white "ten gallon" hats.

The U.S.A. standard bearer was figure skater Scott Hamilton, selected by the ten U.S.A. team captains. Taking the oath to participate in the games fairly was Eric Heiden, and for the officials was a former Olympic speedskating champion, Terry McDermott, winner of the 500 meters at Innsbruck in 1964.

Almost unnoticed among the spectators were two great '32 heroes, Jack Shea (now the burgomeister for the North Elba Park District which embraces the Village of Lake Placid) and Irving Jaffee, retired and living in San Diego. In 1932 each had won two gold medals as the U.S.A. swept the four golds in speedskating. Thus, the only two times the U.S. has come even close to sweeping the men's gold in speedskating was on the friendly ice rink at Lake Placid.

It was typically an American celebration of the quadrennial winter sports extravaganza, including ticket and other prices which some considered out-of-line. Yet, the ticket prices were in line with those of Innsbruck four years earlier except for a modest ten percent boost plus the State of New York tax.

Sure, there were major/minor dislocations caused by the lack of a transportation system for spectators and the press. However, the Lake Placid Olympic Games Organizing Committee did provide above average transportation for the athletes, getting them to and from practice and competition sessions with little or no interruption. However, even Eric Heiden had to walk back (with many other stars of the Games) from the Opening Ceremony because of the inadequacies of transportation — buses piled up in parking lots waiting for someone to tell

them the Party Was Over and the athletes wanted to proceed back to their quarters in the Olympic Village.

Before the Games much had been written about the inadequacies of the Olympic Village because of its designated "after use" as a medium security federal prison. The following quotation is from Sports Illustrated and is supported by the writer who slept, ate, and worked in an office within the Olympic Village for 21 days during the Games.

". . . Even the incipient prison that is the Village drew rave reviews from most of the occupants. Despite last year's complaints by various National Olympic Committees over the tiny cells and bleak institutional atmosphere of the lodgings, once the 1,400 athletes had actually moved in, everyone was happy. The hit of the Village was a psychedelic room full of blinking electronic game machines, which could make Lake Placid live in memory as the Pinball Olympics. And even the French and Swiss said that the food was at least passing good."

Long after the transportation debacle for spectators, the lobster thermidor in the athletes' cafeteria, the $3 hot dogs in the Olympic Fieldhouse, the apple strudel offered on Main Street, the attractively garbed "team hostesses" looking similar to the Innsbruck team hostesses of four years earlier, the songs of Dionne Warwick in the athletes' theater, the farewell party for athletes in the Olympic Arena sponsored by the AAU and a fast-food chain and Eric

Buses everywhere, but never enough of them.

Heiden carrying the Stars and Stripes of the U.S. in the Closing Ceremony are forgotten, Sports Illustrated's words will become a part of American folklore in encapsulating the moment of euphoria when the U.S. ice hockey team defeated the U.S.S.R. And we quote directly:

"For millions of people, their single, lasting image of the Lake Placid Games will be the infectious joy displayed by the U.S. hockey team following its 4-3 victory over the Soviet Union. It was an Olympian moment, the kind the creators of the Games must have had in mind, one that said: Here is something bigger than any of you. It was bizarre, it was beautiful.

Upflung sticks slowly cartwheeled into the rafters. The American players — in pairs rather than in one great glop — hugged and danced and rolled on one another."

Never in history have the biathletes and lugers received so much attention from the American print and electronic media. The young men and young ladies presented a different "picture" to the media who loved the refreshing frankness of these athletes whose sports are little understood at best by the media. Certainly, this exposure to the big-time sportswriters should prove a boom to future sports activity for athletes looking for real competitive challenges with no opportunity

for post-Olympic monetary rewards.

Who were the ten most exciting athletes in the XIII Olympic Winter Games? Rather than striving to list these athletes in order of preference, let's jot down the names in alphabetical order and trust that their accomplishments will be chronicled in the following pages. If their achievements are omitted, for one reason or another, they will be noted here:

Robin Cousins, Great Britain, men's figure skating champion.

Jim Craig, U.S.A., goalie, ice hockey.

Eric Heiden, U.S.A. speed skating.

U.S. Hockey champs meet the press after their final victory.

Anton Innauer, Austria, ski jumping.

Mark Johnson, U.S.A., ice hockey.

Annemarie Moser-Proell, Austria, skiing.

Meinhard Nehmer, German Democratic Republic, bob-sledding.

Ingemar Stenmark, Sweden, millionaire Alpine Slalom winner.

Ulrich Wehling, German Democratic Republic, three-time Nordic Combined champ.

Hanni Wenzel, Liechtenstein, skiing, Queen of the Ball Game.

Lake Placid had coined a phrase in November or December, "Welcome World — We're Ready" which may have been preferable as a rhetorical question. But the competition facilities were, as advertised, "fantastic, best in the world". The Bunny Sheffield Memorial Skating Oval helped produce the fastest "times" in the history of Olympic speedskating.

Eric Heiden, of course, made Olympic Games' history by sweeping all five men's speed-skating races. Those living within the confines of the Olympic Village became a part of Heidenmania which sprung up. The icing on the cake for the likeable pre-medical school student at the University of Wisconsin was a personal call from the President of the United States, the morning after his fabulous fifth, and a meeting with Vice President Mondale between the second and third periods of the final hockey game, U.S.A. vs. Finland.

The list of medal winners to be enshrined in the coming years in a special memorial atop Pikes Peak should be em-blazoned in something special because these athletes provided the American people with new hopes in the troubled inter-national theatre.

But forever Pikes Peak will carry the names of the 20 members of the ice hockey team led so nobly by Mike Eruzione, the oldest player; Eric Heiden, fellow speedskaters Leah Mueller and Eric's younger sister, Beth; skier Phil Mahre, and figure skaters Linda Fratianne and Charlie Tickner.

Who can rightfully say what was the biggest single moment of the XIII Olympic Winter Games? Here are some great sports moments which will be long preserved in our memory:

* The Victory of the U.S.A. ice hockey team over the U.S.S.R., 4-3, in the first game of the final round.

* Any victory of Eric Heiden. Five Olympic records and a world mark in his final race, the 10,000 meters.

* The crushing 7-3 ice hockey triumph over Czechoslovakia in the preliminary round — The U.S.A. team was on its way after that game.

* Charlie Tickner's free skating routine that placed him third.

* The return of Rodnina and Zaitsev after a year's vacation from figure skating.

* Meinhard Nehmer, German Democratic Republic, driving the 4-man bobsled to a first-ever sub-one-minute run on the new Mt. Van Hoevenberg refrigerated run. He won his third Olympic gold medal in bobsledding.

* Hanni Wenzel, Liechtenstein, winning both women's slaloms and placing second to the non-pareil Annemarie Moser-Proell in the downhill.

* Ulrich Wehling, German Democratic Republic, winning his third consecutive Nordic Combined Olympic title.

Superhero Heiden on the victory stand.

* Jeff Davis' 91-meter leap during the 70m special jumping event. This was probably the single greatest jump ever by one of our jumpers. It was disallowed by startled officials who ruled out the jump and caused the entire competition to be restarted even though Jeff was No. 9 off the in-run. Previously, Davis gained negative fame at the 1978 world championships when he took a nasty spill that was a favorite among the re-runs of America's No. 1 sports television network.

* The jubilation of the U.S.A. ice hockey team and 11,000 frenetic spectators following the medal-clinching triumph over Finland. It was a case of the hockey team appreciating the support of the American rooters and the American rooters loving the hockey players for their heard-round-the-world achievement of winning gold.

That's the XIII Olympic Winter Games Decalogue. But there were other inspiring moments, achievements, and memories which must not go unrecorded, nor unrecognized.

Leah Poulos Mueller, the second U.S.A. ladies skater to skate in three Olympic Games, closed out her 21-year career by winning her 2nd and 3rd silver medals. The sport is a better one because of skaters like Leah.

Linda Fratianne battling what proved to be insurmountable odds (low ratings by *unkind* judges in the compulsory figures) to finish runner-up to Ms. Poetzch.

Walter Malmquist's jumping in the Nordic Combined event which made possible a 12th-place finish, highest ever for the U.S.A. in this event.

Lisa-Marie Allen's emerald green costume in the ladies figure skating.

The German Democratic Republic's winning 4 x 5 kilometer cross country relay team. The anchorperson, Barbara Petzold, upon crossing the finish line, proudly announced she was abandoning skiing to concentrate on her medical studies.

Jim Denney, ace U.S.A. ski jumper, after an early-season filled with doubts and uncertainties, attributed his rousing 8th place finish (also the highest ever for the U.S.A. in ski jumping since 1924) to his deep abiding faith in the Almighty.

Leonhard Stock, Austria, won the downhill race in a distinct upset. He was a last-minute addition to the team and he replaced the 1979 World Cup Downhill champion, Sepp Walcher. One source said Stock is assured a six-figure income for the rest of his life after the triumph. What would the late Pierre de Coubertin think of such shenanigans?

There were 38 nations included among the entries, eleven won gold medals and 19 were included among the medal winners.

In closing, the Organizing Committee came up with innovative Award Ceremonies each evening at Mirror Lake. No admission was charged and thousands of Villagers and fans gathered for one final look at the medalists.

Lake Placid in 1932 and 1980 Is a Study in Contrasts

By Parry D. Sorensen

Opening ceremony — Lake Placid — 1932.

Turning the pages of history back to 1932 is a study in contrasts for the Winter Olympics.

When the games were held at Lake Placid 48 years ago the world was in the midst of the Great Depression. Only 16 nations sent a total of 330 athletes to compete, and more than half of them were from the United States and Canada. They competed in only 14 events.

This year there were more than 1500 athletes representing 38 countries competing in 38 events.

The total budget for the 1932 games, including all construction, was $1.1 million. The 1980 budget was about $150 million.

Ticket sales in 1932 totalled $96,000. This year they came to $13 million.

A couple of dozen writers and a half a dozen radio men covered those games of 48 years ago. In 1980 the press, radio and TV contingent far outnumbered the competitors.

In contrast to these astronomical increases there is one decrease to report. The population of Lake Placid has declined in 48 years from 2,930 to 2,731.

How did the Winter Olympics come to be held in such a small village in the first place? It was the practice in those days to hold the Winter and Summer games in the same country. So when Los Angeles was designated as the site for the Summer Olympics the International Olympic Committee could choose from among seven

U.S. locations that wanted to stage the games in the ice and snow. They included Lake Tahoe and Yosemite Valley in California, Minneapolis and Duluth, Minnesota; Bear Mountain, New York; Denver, Colorado; and Lake Placid.

The Lake Placid boosters who presented their bid to the I.O.C. were confident they would succeed. After all, their town was known, in the east at least, as the winter sports capital of the country, and proclaimed itself to be the "St. Moritz of America".

Situated on Mirror Lake and with the Adirondack Mountains as a backdrop, the little town was famous before the turn of the century as a summer retreat for the upper class from the New

---

Mr. Sorensen is professor of communication at the University of Utah.

York City area. This fame was enhanced by the founding and construction of the Lake Placid Club by Melvil Dewey, the same man who devised the Dewey Decimal System for classifying library books. By the mid-1920's the Club was among the grandest and most exclusive of the Adirondack resort hotels.

In 1904 Dewey decided that the club should be a winter, as well as summer, resort. So he imported 40 pairs of hickory skis from Norway and encouraged club members to ski and toboggan on the mountain slopes and to skate on the frozen surface of the lake. Getting the Games to Lake Placid was climax of his long love affair with the area. Appropriately enough, it was his son, Dr. Godfrey Dewey, who headed the delegation that appeared before the I.O.C. and convinced that body that Lake Placid was the place.

Ironically, Melvil Dewey didn't live to see his dream fulfilled. He died on Christmas Day, 1931, a scant six weeks before the Games began.

The 14 events of the 1932 games did not include the Alpine ski events. There was ice hockey, figure skating, men's speed skating and the only Nordic competition was in jumping and cross country.

Jack Shea

Speed skating was held in the same place as this year, right in front of the High School on Main Street. Some of the hockey matches were played on the outdoor rink, the others in the Olympic Field House which was refurbished and used this year as an adjunct to the new arena.

For the first and only time in Olympic history the United States "won" the Winter Games by winning gold medals in six of the 14 events, plus four silver and one bronze. Three of the golds were won by Lake Placid residents.

Jack Shea, 21-year-old son of a local grocer, who had learned to skate on Mirror Lake, won the gold medal in both the 500 and 1500 meter speed skating races. The two-man bobsled winners were the Stevens brothers, Hubert and Curtis, who, in contrast to Shea, represented the Lake Placid patrician establishment. Their family owned the elegant Stevens House, a rambling hotel situated on a hill

overlooking the town and the lake.

Two of the other gold medals were won by Irving Jaffe in the 5,000 and 10,000 meter skating events. The sixth gold went to the U.S. four-man bobsled team.

Star of the Norwegian team was their 19-year-old figure skating queen, Sonja Henie, who had won at St. Moritz when she was 15. She won again in 1936 at Garmisch-Partenkirchen. No other skater has ever dominated the sport like Sonja Henie. She won the World Championship in 1927 and kept winning it every year through 1936. Ten World Titles and three Olympic gold medals is a record that will probably never be broken.

Following her 1936 triumphs, Sonja turned professional, skated in ice shows, became a movie star, and married, among others, an American millionaire sportsman, Dan Topping.

Between the two of them, Shea and Jaffe duplicated Eric Heiden's feat of winning all of the men's speed skating events. Shea, a student at Dartmouth College, had the honor of taking the Olympic oath on behalf of all the participants, as did Eric Heiden in 1980. Then he put on his skates and on the same day won the 500 meter race, beating the favorite, Bernt Evenson of Norway. Shea's victory was doubly sweet because the 500 gold medal in the 1924 Winter games at Chamonix, France had been won by Charley Jewtraw, also of Lake Placid, who had been Shea's boyhood idol.

That same afternoon of opening day saw the U.S. winning its second gold when Irving Jaffe, who had learned his skating on the frozen pond of New York's Central Park, won the 5,000 meter race and teammate Ed Murphy took the silver medal. On that first day of competition the Yanks picked up as many medals as they had won in the entire 1924 Games.

Next day Shea easily won the 1,500 meter race and three days later Jaffe completed the sweep by taking the 10,000 meter event.

Those 1932 Games marked the first and last time the "pack" format was used for speed skating. In the short races Shea went against five other finalists, while Jaffe had to jostle and jockey for position with more than a dozen others in the longer races.

Before that, and ever since, the skating events have matched two skaters racing in pairs against the clock and observing strict rules on lanes and cross-overs.

Shea is now 69 years old and is supervisor (chief executive officer) of North Elba, the governmental jurisdiction which includes the village of Lake Placid. From his office window he can see the rink where he enjoyed what he describes as "the most glorious day of my life".

"You have no idea what it felt like," he told reporters just before this year's games, "to see the American flag raised, the pride — in a way it was the culmination of a community project. Lake Placid and I had been pointing toward that

moment since I was three years old."

To win the gold medal in the two-man bobsled, the Stevens brothers had to outrace the Swiss team which had set a new record on their last run. The Americans beat the Swiss record by two full seconds on their final run down the mile and a half course. They had to do it, because their cumulative time for their four runs was less than two seconds better than the Swiss.

The American victory in the four-man bobsled was almost anti-climactic. Rain and warm weather had turned the bob run into slush and they had to wait until the day after the closing ceremonies to finish the event.

Eddie Eagan, who won the light-heavyweight boxing title at the 1920 Games was a member of the four-man team, and thus is the only man to win a gold medal in both the Summer and Winter Olympics.

The only ski events in 1932 were the 90 meter jump and two cross country races. Norway, Sweden and Finland and shared the honors in those events.

Birge Rudd, an 18-year-old daredevil from Norway won the jumping gold on snow that was trucked to the site because a thaw and rain had left the hill practically bare. Rudd repeated his win at Garmisch in 1936 and finished second by a scant two feet in 1948 at St. Moritz when he was 34 years old. Norwegians won the jumping gold medals in every Olympics from 1920 through 1952.

The combined cross country-ski jump medal was won by Rudd's fellow countryman, Johan Grottumsbraaten. Winner of the 18 kilometer race was Sven Utterstrom of Sweden,

while Finland's Veli Saarinen won the gold medal in the 50 kilometers.

Canada won the hockey championship by beating the U.S. 2-1 in an overtime. Only four countries entered the competition, the two others being Germany, who finished third, and Poland. It was the Canadians' fourth straight Olympic championship. Their string was broken when they lost to Great Britain in 1936, but resumed again with gold medals in 1952 and 1956. Ironically, most of the members of Britain's 1936 champions were Canadians who had become naturalized British citizens a short time before the Games.

Eric Heiden's five gold medals assure him a permanent place in Olympic record books, as well as the opportunity to capitalize on his fame financially.

Jack Shea returned to Dartmouth after his double triumph and was too busy with his studies to compete in the World Championships in Norway that year.

Irving Jaffe went back to New York City, couldn't find a job during the Depression, and ended up pawning his gold medals, along with 400 others won in skating competition, for $2,000. He had a year to reclaim them from the pawn shop, but before the year was up the building was torn down and he never saw the medals again.

All Jaffe could say was "Hero today, gone tomorrow."

America's Young Hockey Team
And The Impossible Dream

By Michael Shalin

It was only an hour after the United States Olympic hockey team had completed its miracle run to the gold medal. Outside, on the streets of Lake Placid the people were running through the streets, waving American flags, crying and shouting as if the country had won a war instead of a hockey game. Inside, Herb Brooks, the maestro who had written the music for the victory, tried to put things in proper perspective.

"You people are watching a group of people who startled the athletic world — not the hockey world, the athletic world," Brooks told the gathered media. "Whatever you choose to write — and I don't mean for you to be our cheerleaders — these people are deserving of so much in view of their age and the things they had to accomplish over a very short period of time.

"As a father, you have to kick your son in the butt a lot. As you know, you fathers and mothers that have to do it — you love your children as I love this hockey team."

To fully understand the success of this American team, we must go back and follow the gold-filled road to glory that ran from Colorado to the tiny hamlet in upstate New York.

Brooks, who led the University of Minnesota to three NCAA championships in his seven years at the school, decided a rigorous exhibition schedule was the way to get the most out of a young team. The club played 62 exhibition games in all kinds of cities all over the world. There was a new system to be learned — a European

Mr. Shalin is a writer for
United Press International
in New York City.

Adoring fans greet U.S. hockey team

system — and the coach felt his players needed playing time to learn it. He was right.

The schedule started with a 10-game series in Europe. Playing against the Dutch, Finns and Norwegians, the Americans ran up a 7-2-1 record. Upon returning home, the U.S. team lost four straight to National Hockey League competition before embarking on an "easier" schedule.

Brooks' troops toured the Central Hockey League, played

some colleges, sampled the American League and played other national teams. The U.S. club then went into the final five weeks of training, and it was here that Brooks experienced his first real motivational problems.

The "dog-days" of January saw the club's performance fall off. The Americans were still winning, but Brooks noticed a letdown as the Winter Games approached. Then came what may have turned out to be the turning point — a game against the Soviets at Madison Square Garden on the final weekend before the Olympics.

Two days before that game, Brooks attended a Garden press conference and surprised observers by declaring that what his team probably needed most was a good "butt-kicking". Brooks' team got its collective "butts" kicked by a 10-3 score that Saturday afternoon as the Soviets put on a clinic for the crowd of about 11,000.

"It was a good lesson for us," he said. "Our players learned a lot from the game. That picture was worth a thousand words. We're not demoralized. Sometimes a good kicking is good for you.

"I'm not worried about the Russians, they're gonna run away and hide at the Olympics anyway. We have to worry about the Swedes and the Czechs — our first two opponents next week. We have to beat one of those teams to have a shot at a medal and that's what we'll be shooting for."

Brooks' reference to the Russians "running away and hiding" seemed to be the one constant that followed this team through its journey to immortality. No one gave anybody a chance at beating the Soviets.

After all, the Russians had invaded that same Madison Square Garden exactly a year earlier and left as proud owners of the first NHL Challenge Cup. They had taken two out of three games from a talented group of NHL All-Stars and won the finale by a whopping 6-0 score with backup goaltender Vladimir Myshkin in goal. They were truly the world powers, and everyone else would be playing for the silver and bronze medals at Lake Placid.

"Obviously, the Russians have to be favored," said goalie Jim Craig, still a virtual no-name at the time. "Realistically, they are the team to beat. We're just trying to go in there and play up to our capabilities. If we can do that, we should come home with a medal. We'll just try and play the best we possibly can, do our best and see what happens. I'm not writing us off yet. We've got quite a few NHL draft picks here and I think we can be a factor at Placid.

"I'd be thrilled to get a gold but very satisfied with a silver or bronze. It will be in this order — thrilled, happy, satisfied, disappointed."

When Brooks and assistant coach Craig Patrick brought the road show to New York City for its match with the Soviets, the New York fans really didn't know what to expect. They knew they would go out there and root hard for the Americans, mainly because they were playing the Soviets during a time in history where the two countries weren't exactly holding hands.

Before Jim Craig could say Nikita Kruschev, he had surrendered four first-period goals and the Soviets were on their way to their merry romp. It was a great performance, even under high Russian standards, and left the Garden crowd stunned. Surprisingly, it didn't seem to bother the young Americans.

"This will help us out and will motivate us for sure against Sweden," said Mark Johnson, looking ahead to the Tuesday meeting with the Swedes.

Another person who didn't take too much stock in the exhibition rout was Soviet Coach Viktor Tikhonov, who said that both coaches were "holding back" in the Garden game.

"I think that this team (the U.S.) has a very good future," said Tikhonov, unaware of his statement's prophetic nature. "Both coaches took this as a practice game for the Olympics. The Olympic tournament is special because the games always have a lot of surprises." Tikhonov's words would prove true. The Olympic tournament would hold many surprises.

As the club left for what would be its fateful two weeks, there was excitement and eager anticipation. No one really knew what was in store, but all but Buzz Schneider — a 1976 Olympian — knew one thing for sure — they would be playing in what probably would be their only Olympic Games.

Mikko Leinonen scores for Finland in final game.

"If you can't get the adrenaline going in that kind of situation, then you're not much of a hockey player," said Mark Johnson. "It's gonna be easy to get motivated for that. Hopefully, though, we won't be too sky-high for the game. The Olympics are what we've been waiting for and those 60 training games are way in the back of my mind. All I can think about is Tuesday night."

On to Lake Placid.

Monday, Feb. 11.

Game No. 1 was just over 24 hours away, and the young Americans wanted to get started. They had heard a lot about the Swedes and their ability to stay close in big games against the powers. They were aware that the power of the Swedish team had been diminished by numerous losses to the NHL. The Swedes would be tough, and the Americans would have to try and overcome that and whatever overanxiousness they were sure to encounter to win the opener and get a running start at that medal.

Tuesday, Feb. 12.

Everyone in the U.S. contingent is aware of the importance of the first two games of the tounament. The Americans are forced to open their Blue Division schedule against Sweden and Czechoslovakia and losses to these two fine clubs would knock the U.S. out of any chance at a medal. It could all be over by late Thursday night.

The first period ends with Sweden leading 1-0 and holding a 16-7 shot advantage. At this point, Brooks felt it was time to relay a message to his young players.

Buzz Schneider's shot is blocked by three Finns.

"There were too many bleeps in there for me to repeat it," Brooks would say afterward. "But basically I said, 'If you want to play this game effectively, you'd better report to the game with a hard hat and lunch pail. If you don't, then you might as well go watch a couple of old guys ice fish.' "

The coach's message seemed to rally his players, who came out playing a more poised style of hockey. They spent the second period trying to get the equalizer, but the Swedes were stubborn.

The period enters its final minute with Sweden still ahead 1-0. Craig makes a save on Per Lundqvist and, on the ensuing play, Dave Silk and Johnson break into the Swedes' zone. Silk finishes off with a 10-footer to the glove side. The Americans outshoot the Swedes 12-11 in the period and game is even after two.

The Americans get the first big scoring opportunity of the third period. Johnson steals the puck from Mats Waltin and hits the post behind Lindbergh. The crowd is waiting for the U.S. to score the winning goal, but instead, just 30 seconds after

Johnson's chance, Thomas Eriksson taps a pass from Harald Luckner past Craig. Sweden leads with 15:15 remaining.

The period continues and the Americans keep missing scoring chances, failing on two power-play opportunities. The game enters its final minute and Brooks pulls Craig in favor of a sixth attacker. The strategy pays off, with Bill Baker beating Lindbergh with just 27 seconds showing on the clock.

The tie allowed the Americans to think of their long-range chances. They had escaped with a point against a very tough team and were mathematically alive. A loss would have been disastrous, but a tie? . . .

"When you tie a good hockey team in the last minute, you have to be both lucky and grateful," said Brooks. "We've got to consider ourselves lucky. They could have quit and just accepted the loss. We're very happy."

But the Czechs were waiting. Having beaten Norway 11-0 in their opener earlier in the day, they were the only team at Lake Placid given even the remotest of chances at beating the Russians for the gold.

Looking ahead at the Czechs, Brooks said, "They're awfully poised, awfully smart. They're bigger but not better skaters. We have played some good hockey and still can play even better hockey.

Brooks was right. His club was capable of playing "better hockey". It's not likely he knew just how right he was.

Thursday, Feb. 14

The Winter Games had officially opened the day before and the Americans were ready to play the final game of Day 2 of the hockey competition.

It takes the Czechs only 2:23 to get on the scoreboard. The crowd, much larger than in the opening game, is hushed by the goal. Could the bubble be bursting? No, because the Americans will come right back.

A little over two minutes later, Mike Eruzione, the team captain sends an angled 25-footer past Jiri Kralik to tie the score.

John Harrington, the young man who kept the official notebook of "Brooksisms", which consisted of the quaint sayings and slogans of the head coach, draws an assist as Schneider and Pavelich combine to score the go-ahead goal.

The Americans score four unanswered goals in 24 minutes as the game turns into a rout and the final is 7-3 for the U.S. The young Americans had earned three of a possible four points against its two most formidable opponents.

Saturday, Feb. 16

To the disappointment of several thousand U.S. fans, the Americans play the third game of the Olympic tournament in the smaller Olympic Arena, which holds only about 1,000 people. Norway comes into the game having lost twice by a combined score of 21-4. It was the perfect time for a U.S. letdown.

Norway, outshot 16-9 in the period, led 1-0 after one. But, the Norwegians had scored their only goal of the snowy afternoon.

The Americans get a power play 25 seconds into the second period, and cash in to tie the game. Christian's shot from the point is rebounded by Eruzione, who stuffs it into the net at 0.41. It marks the beginning of total domination by the U.S. squad that would turn the game into a laugher, 5-1.

Tom Eriksson puts Sweden ahead temporarily, 2-1.

Now, the brash young members of the U.S. team were able to start thinking ahead to a possible gold medal confrontation with the Soviets — and maybe even a repeat of the Miracle of Squaw Valley in 1960. Victories over Romania and West Germany would put the Americans in the medals round and give them their shot at the Soviets.

"We would have to play a perfect game and they would have to come out very flat,"

"I think we'll be a better hockey club against Romania," said Brooks, "but I'm scared to death of the West Germans. If you look back at the record books of United States hockey, you'll see that the Americans always lost the key game to the West Germans. But we're in a good position now to be seeded No. 1 going into the finals. We're tied with Sweden but they have that big game with the Czechs coming up."

Schneider said when asked about the Russians. "When you play the Soviets, it's like a high school team playing a team from the National Hockey League. They're that good."

But before the U.S. could think that far ahead, the club had to dispose of Romania and West Germany.

Monday, Feb. 18

The Americans open the game against Romania experiencing much of the same frustration they went through against Norway. The puck simply wouldn't go into the net and the contest remains scoreless through 12 minutes. Then, the U.S. strikes and, for the only time in their seven-game trip through the tournament, the Americans take a 1-0 lead, and end up with an easy 7-2 victory.

Wednesday, Feb. 20

Before they take the ice against West Germany the Americans are again bolstered by a Soviet near-miss. The Russians rally for four goals to post a 6-4 victory over Canada, but it's becoming more and more apparent that this team isn't quite as unbeatable as people, including Brooks, thought entering the tournament.

Things don't start very well for the Americans. With the game just 110 seconds old, Horst-Peter Kretchmer's 70-footer from center ice eludes Craig low on the glove side and the West Germans are ahead 1-0.

The West Germans, 1-3 coming into the game, took just four seconds to score again on a 4-on-3 power play and the Americans were in trouble.

But, the U.S. came back and tied it up in the second period on goals by Rob McClanahan and Neal Broten. The momentum had swung, and the Americans didn't wait long in the third period before settling the issue.

McClanahan, scored again just 77 seconds into the third period. Exactly three minutes later, Verchota tipped in a shot by Christian and the Americans had a 4-2 victory, a 4-0-1 record and a trip to the medals round.

The triumph left the U.S. tied with Sweden for first place in the Blue standings. By virtue of the tie-breaking category known as "goal differential", the Swedes finished first and the Americans second.

Over in the Red Division, the Soviets, despite their two scares, finished 5-0 and in first place. Finland polished off Holland 10-3 on the final day and entered the medals' round with a 3-2 record.

Even though they had to struggle to get by the West Germans and into the medals' round, the young Americans were happy — very happy — to be where they were.

"I don't think we looked ahead," said Harrington. "We knew we had to win to go undefeated and that's all we wanted to do. Hey, the West Germans didn't come here to just pack up and leave. They always play tough against us and tonight was no exception."

As far as Craig was concerned, the players had very little to do with the final outcome. It was all in the cards.

"I don't lie in bed worrying anymore because it's already been decided," he said. "Just wait for Sunday and tell me who won because that's what's gonna happen anyway."

Since Craig believed the whole thing had already been decided, would he like to know how it is going to come out?

"No, No, it would be no fun," he answered. "It's like getting a Christmas gift and opening it on the 22nd. It's getting nervous and waiting for your report card and waiting for your grade. All year long we've worked hard and if we keep working hard, someone's gonna give us a grade at the end of the tournament — either gold, silver or bronze. You get what you deserve."

Friday, Feb. 22

It really couldn't have been more patriotic. It was the ultimate "us" against "them", the good guys against the bad guys and all that. A lot was at stake, especially in light of the strained relations between the United States and Soviet Union. It was almost fitting that it would be played on George Washington's birthday.

The game began at 5:06 p.m. with the capacity crowd of over 8,500 chanting the now-familiar "USA, USA". The Soviets began the game by putting pressure on Craig, and the Americans found themselves in their customary position, one goal down. Vladimir Krutov, the youngest player on the Soviet lineup, deflected the puck past Craig on the glove side and it was 1-0 at 9:12.

But the Americans, who would be outshot 39-16 overall, needed less than five minutes to tie the score. Schneider, taking a pass from Pavelich, drilled a 40-footer past Tretiak for his fifth goal of the tournament.

The Soviets took a 2-1 lead with 2:26 left in the period when Sergei Markarov fired a 25-footer past Craig. The crowd booed lustily on the play because McClanahan had been pinned down by Alekse Kasatonov at the other end of the rink and was unable to get back into the play.

Captain Mike Eruzione scores the winning goal against Russia.

Then came the play — perhaps the strangest in the history of the game — that turned the contest and the tournament around in favor of the United States.

With the period's final seconds ticking off, Christian picked up a free puck in his own zone, moved up over the blue line and fired the puck at Tretiak from 100 feet away. What followed left the crowd — and the Soviets — shocked.

Christian's shot struck Tretiak on the pads (it should have been gloved but Tretiak has a notoriously weak glove hand) and bounced out some 30 feet in front. Johnson, seeing the Russian defense pair acting as if the period had ended, picked up the loose puck, walked in on Tretiak, and slid the puck past the startled goaltender, with one second left on the clock.

When the teams came out for the second period, Myshkin had replaced the embarrassed Tretiak in goal, and it took the Soviets only 2:18 to reclaim the lead on Aleksandr Maltsev's goal.

But, midway through the third period, Johnson and Eruzione would score goals 81 seconds apart to provide the margin in what may turn out to be the biggest upset in the history of hockey.

The turning point of the period came at 6:47, when Krutov senselessly cracked Broten over the head with his stick. With just eight seconds left on the power play, Johnson tied the game.

Tenacious forechecking by Pavelich and Harrington paved the way for Eruzione's game-winner. Eruzione picked up a loose puck, skated between the faceoff circles and fired a 30-foot screened drive past Myshkin. The goal came at 10 minutes of the period and the U.S. finally had the lead.

The Americans held their lead behind the solid goaltending of Craig, who had foiled both Markarov and Victor Zhluktov moments before the two-goal rally. As the clock ran out and with the crowd shouting in delirious glee, the American players mobbed Craig and many of them threw their sticks up in the air in a victory salute as the Soviets stood stunned at their own blue line.

Outside the Olympic Fieldhouse, fans honked horns, rang bells and screamed in delight. It was like something you'd expect after a war victory. The American people had themselves some genuine heroes — and they wanted to celebrate.

Brooks, who refused to meet with the press following the victories over Romania and West Germany, arrived at the post-game news conference at the high school and was greeted by the applause of the gathered media.

Brooks, whose players sang ''God Bless America'' in the dressing room, was asked if he would divulge the pre-game speech he gave his players before sending them into the lion's den.

"We had a noon meeting to discuss tactics and X's and O's," he said. "Then, prior to the game, I said (he quoted directly from his notes) 'You're born to be a player and you're meant to be here. This moment is yours. You're meant to be here at this moment. So let's have poise and possession of ourselves at this time.' "

"We went into the game feeling we could beat them and we just went out and did it," said Christian. "We worked hard for the whole game and played 60 minutes. That's the key."

Eruzione, who had become somewhat famous for his lengthy answers to rather simple questions, summed it up succinctly.

"When it was over, all I could think was, 'We beat the Russians, We beat the Russians.' "

Hours after the game, the people still celebrated in the streets. Many of the players walked around and joined in the fun, but there was still a game to be won.

Sunday, Feb. 24

The Americans begin against Finland as if they are intent on giving the whole thing away.

Craig makes saves on Esa Peltonen and Jari Kurri in the first 2:40 of the game and the Americans waste a penalty on Hannu Koskinen. They have their chances, but balding goaltender Jorma Valtonen is equal to the task.

Then, with the game in its 10th minute, Porvari's shot from inside the right point found its way over the right shoulder of Craig and the U.S. — as it had been for five of the first six games of the tournament — trailed 1-0.

Christoff stole the puck, and walked to within 20 feet of Valtonen before sending an off-speed back-hander past the surprised goalie. Christoff would later say he thought the goaltender was "out to lunch or something". The game was tied 1-1.

By the 6:05 mark of the third period however, the Americans had grabbed a 3-2 lead and the gold was in sight.

The Americans win the game 4-2, and the gold medal is theirs. The game ends and the players go through a similar on-ice celebration to the one they went through after the Soviet victory. Craig wound up with an American flag draped around his shoulders. It was pure pandemonium.

"To me, it's just unbelievable," Johnson said just after Brooks made his closing "father-son" remarks. "I never thought we'd even be this close. I'm sure the 20 guys here can't believe it. And they'll probably wake up tomorrow and still not be able to believe it."

The players and Brooks attended the post-tournament press conference as winners. There was no more speculation. There was no more talk of a possible upset. The whole thing had become so very real in such a short time that it all seemed to be the way it was supposed to be. The glory fit this bunch of young players, and they wore it so well. But, they never lost their youthful innocence.

The highlight of the conference was provided by Harrington, the official keeper of the "Brooksisms". Harrington, who chronicled his coach's remarks in a notebook, was asked if there was an appropriate Brooksism to put the whole thing in perspective.

"Well, we're damned if we did and we're damned if we didn't," he said to the uproarious laughter of the crowd.

There was also a touch of seriousness on this fateful afternoon.

"The saddest thing right now is that after we see the president tomorrow, we just go. We go different ways and who knows if I'll ever see John Harrington or David Christian again," said Eruzione.

"We came together as a team six months ago from all parts of the United States," he went on. "All different kinds of backgrounds and all kinds of ethnic beliefs. We jelled into a team and I don't think there's a coach or anybody in the country right now that can say they've experienced the kind of thing we have right here. This has just been such a thrill."

The awards presentation was something out of a fairy tale. The young Americans accepted their medals and many of them cried during the playing of the Star Spangled Banner. After the song ended, they took a "victory lap" around the arena, shaking hands, kissing adoring fans and waving. It was something of a dream. They had come all the way. If the sports world had ever seen a more remarkable story, there weren't too many people talking about it this Sunday in Lake Placid.

The struggle of giants reduced to a two-man tussle. Vladmimar Petrov, an old warrior of the Soviet team, against young Bill Baker of the U.S.A. Youth, vitality, and a fighting spirit which was not shaken by anything brought the U.S. a 4-3 victory that stunned the hockey world.

Feelings ran high when the Americans and Russians clashed in their hockey "summit" match. Officials had to work hard to maintain control. They are shown separating Steve Christoff and a Soviet opponent. U.S. Teammates Bob McClanahan, Eric Strobel, Phil Verchota, and Mike Ramsey watch from the reserve box.

One of the most exciting matches of the round-robin hockey competition was Canada's near upset of Russia. The wearers of the Maple Leaf led the Soviets 4-3 after the first two periods, but eventually lost, 6-4. Cheering Canadians are shown in the foreground as the scoreboard records the 1-1 first period tie.

Somewhere under the pile of American and Russian hockey players is the puck that U.S. Goalie Jim Craig kept out of the net. The Soviets had 39 shots during the match, but Craig blocked all but three. In contrast, the U.S. had only 16 shots but made four of them in the astounding 4-3 triumph.

Victory!
The picture speaks for itself. The United States hockey team has just achieved the near-impossible with a dramatic 4-3 victory over the highly favored Russians. It was a time for hugging, backslapping, and happy smiles. The spectators in the stands were just as excited as the players.

These photos are small reproductions of full color pictures on the following pages. The captions for the photos are alongside each reproduction.

Six Months of Blood, Sweat and Tears Finally Comes Down to 60 Minutes

By Frank Dolson

For six months they had worked. For six months, since the day they assembled in Bloomington, Minn., 20 young Americans had devoted their lives to putting together an ice hockey team good enough to challenge the world's best in the Olympic Games. And now those six months of blood, sweat and tears had come down to 60 minutes of hockey.

For Mike Eruzione, the gung-ho captain from the low minor leagues; for Jim Craig, the cool-as-ice, fast-talking, instantly likeable goaltender; for Mark Johnson, the short, slender kid with the big league moves; for Mike Ramsey, the hard-as-a-rock, 19-year-old defenseman with the dangerous habit of throwing his 190-pound body in front of enemy shots; for John Harrington, the winger from Minnesota with the wonderful knack of bringing laughter into the most pressure-packed situation; for all of those amazingly dedicated, beautifully emotional kids, this was it: the 60 minutes that would put the crowning touch on the last six months . . . if they could beat Finland on the final day of hockey competition in the Lake Placid Olympic Games.

Two weeks before, it had been little more than an impossible dream. No way these American amateurs, these kids of mostly college age, could reasonably be expected to challenge the Finns, the Swedes, the Czechs and, above all, the Russians for an Olympic gold medal.

A medal seemed within reach, if everything went right.

Mr. Dolson is a sports writer for the Philadelphia Inquirer.

Mark Johnson clinches the 4-2 victory over Finland.

But a GOLD medal? The Russians had won four straight Olympic golds. They were so strong, so talented, so awesome that not even the National Hockey League All-Stars had been able to keep up with them the year before, losing the rubber game of a three-game series, 6-0, on a National Hockey League rink with a National Hockey League referee.

And then there was that pre-Olympic meeting between the American kids and the Russian superstars at Madison Square Garden. Before the game the U.S. locker room was filled with gallows humor. "We sat around and we kinda joked around a little bit," said backup goalie Steve Janaszak. "(We said things like), 'Let's go out there and not lose by more than 10.'"

Turned out, they lost by seven. Well, why not? The best players in the NHL had lost to the Russians by six on the same ice. Nobody really expected these American kids to be in a class with the Russians.

And yet now here they were, two weeks later, one victory away from a gold medal. Thirteen days after getting clobbered, 10-3, in that final, pre-Olympic tuneup they had come from behind three times and finally beaten the Russians, 4-3, on a third-period goal by Eruzione with precisely 10 minutes to go. God, those last 10 minutes had taken a lifetime to play, but they had held the Russians at bay as an emotional, flag-waving, standing-room crowd at the Olympic Field House had chanted, "U.S.A... U.S.A.", and when the final horn sounded these incredible kids had hurled their hockey sticks in the air and danced for joy and tumbled along the ice in triumphant embraces that were at once jubilant and tearful.

It was, surely, one of the great sports upsets of our time, a truth-is-stranger-than-fiction epic if ever there was one. And yet it wasn't enough. Now, 39 hours after that physically and emotionally draining win over the Russians, they had to come back — at 11 o'clock on a Sunday morning — and find the strength and the spirit to do it once more. A loss to the Finns would destroy much of what they had accomplished two days before; a loss to the Finns and Russia would skate off with the gold medal, after all.

"Last night we all talked," Eruzione said, "and we realized what was ahead of us."

"I think in the back of everybody's mind (was the thought) that this 60 minutes was the end of our season, the end of togetherness," said Johnson, whose goal in the final split second of the first period had tied the Russians, 2-2, and kayoed their No. 1 goaltender.

U.S.A. 4, Russia 3.

"This was the last (game) for us and we knew we wouldn't ever be in this situation again. . . ."

So out they went, determined to make the most of their once-in-a-lifetime opportunity.

Eleven o'clock on a Sunday morning. What a brutal time to play a hockey game! What a brutal time to play the biggest game of your lives!

Maybe that's why the game started slowly. Or maybe it was the tension, the pressure that seemed to hang heavy over the rink in the early going as the defensive-minded Finns and the Americans sparred for an advantage.

Both the players and the spectators seemed strangely subdued at first. From the opening faceoff of the Russian game, you could feel the tension, the electricity. On this historic Sunday morning the tension was surely there, but the electricity wasn't. The Americans seemed tentative; the crowd seemed apprehensive. It was as if 11 o'clock on a Sunday morning in Lake Placid was too early to pull the switch.

The noise, the rooting, the chanting, the flag-waving had started in the opening minute against the Russians. Now the silence was almost eerie at times as the Americans and the Finns skated back and forth on the blue-white ice, probing, waiting...

Five minutes had elapsed before the first chant, "U.S.A... U.S.A.," rattled off the rafters, and even then it lacked the intensity of the chant that filled the place two nights before, quickly fading away into another round of nervous, apprehensive silence.

"I thought from the first shift of the game that there was no way they could skate with us," Eruzione would say later, but after the first period the score was Finland 1, the American kids 0. Six months had come down to 40 minutes.

The tying goal, by Steve Christoff, aroused the crowd, set the flags to waving, the spectators to chanting, but less than two minutes later the Finns scored on a power play and the apprehension, the nervousness returned.

The Finns weren't playing the Russian style of hockey. They weren't forechecking relentlessly. They weren't attacking in waves, setting up scoring thrusts with slick, fast passes. The Finns were sitting on that one-goal lead, repeatedly banging the puck off the boards into the center-ice zone or, when successful in gaining possession at center ice, dumping it into the American end. It wasn't pretty. It wasn't exciting but it WAS effective. After the second period the score was Finland 2, the American kids 1. Six months had come down to 20 minutes.

This was it. The crowd knew it. The players knew it. As the U.S. team took the ice dozens, then hundreds, then thousands of Americans stood up, began chanting, "U.S.A.... U.S.A....," and waving flags.

Mike Eruzione gets hugs from Christian and McClanahan.

There was no electric message board in the Olympic Field House to trigger the sudden emotional charge, and none was needed. These emotions came from the heart, not from a computerized scoreboard. They raised pulse rates across an entire nation, gripping people who were watching an ice hockey game for one of the few times in their lives. You didn't have to like hockey, you didn't have to know a blue line from a penalty box to get caught up in the drama, to find yourself hoping against hope that these American kids could do it one more time.

They had spent two weeks doing the near-impossible. They had tied the Swedes in their very first Olympic game on a goal by Bill Baker with 27 seconds to go and Craig pulled for an extra skater. They had spotted the Czechs a stunningly quick goal, then bounced back to beat them decisively. They had been forced to come from behind game after game, and now they would try to do it one more time.

Twenty minutes remained in the life of the 1980 U.S. hockey team . . . and the electricity in the Olympic Field House had been turned on again.

The kids were charging now, attacking relentlessly, making their final, all-out drive for gold medals nobody — not even they — seriously thought they had a chance to win when these Olympic Games began.

It was, after all, Brooks who had put together this most youthful, most unlikely of Olympic gold-medal contenderrs. He had snarled and threatened and cajoled; he had played the countless "mind games" he used to motivate his athletes; he had praised them and knocked them; he had tried everything he knew . . . and now, as the American kids stayed on the attack and the building exploded with noise no one could deny that his coaching tactics had worked.

They were flying now, the 20 survivors of this six-month push for gold. A tie wasn't enough. A tie and they'd have to await the outcome of the Russia-Sweden game and, of all things, root for the Russians.

Only a victory over the Finns could guarantee a gold medal at this moment. Only a victory over the Finns would be a fitting way for this Olympic team to say goodbye.

For 40 minutes you wondered if they could get it. Now, as the noise level kept growing and those incredible kids kept skating, kept digging, kept shooting, you knew they were going to get it.

It didn't take long. Mark Johnson, the slickest of all the U.S. stick-handlers, saw to that. A quiet kid, he can do wonderful things with a hockey puck and now, as the scoreboard clock ran past 14:00 to go, he did one of them, setting up Rob McClanahan for the go-ahead goal.

U.S. Coach Herb Brooks

Phil Verchota, one of the Minnesota boys, scored the tying goal and, after the initial cheering subsided a new chant rumbled across the rink: "Go for gold . . . Go for gold," and somebody sitting in the section across the ice from Vice-President Mondale held up a big sign that read, "Herb Brooks for President."

Mark Johnson makes it 2-2 with one second left in first period.

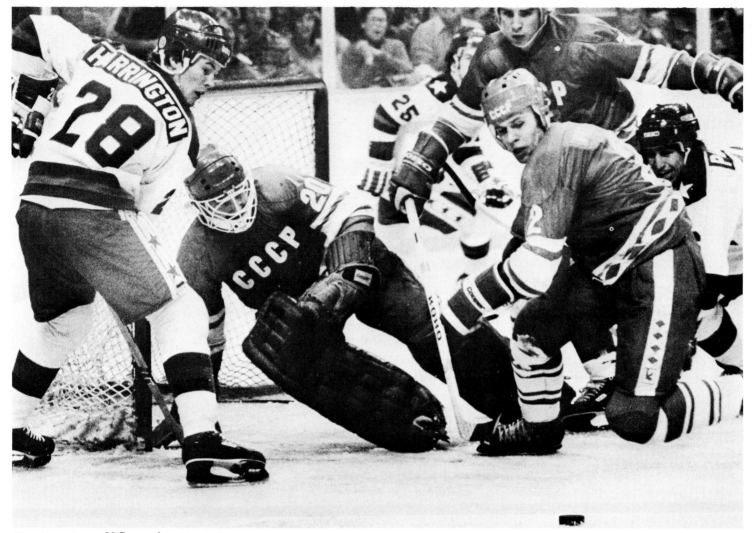

Russians stop a U.S. scoring attempt.

"Once we got up, there was no way (they were going to catch us)," Capt. Eruzione said.

He was right. Not even back-to-back penalties could turn this game around now. Craig was simply unbeatable. Somehow, he got his body in front of a smash by Jari Kurri from the left point, got his stick on a shot by Seppo Suoraniemi from the right point, and his glove on a drive by Jukka Porvari from the right circle.

It was clock-watching time again. The flashing numbers dipped below 8:00, below 7:00, below 6:00, below 5:00. Five minutes to go. Six months had come down to five minutes.

They were getting over-anxious now. Kids do that. Verchota checked a Finnish defenseman in the corner. They got tangled up. He hit him again. Two minutes for roughing; the Finn derisively waved him to the penalty box.

The Americans were a man down with 4:15 to go, but you wouldn't have known it to watch them. Brooks had Neal Broten, Christoff, Ramsey and Ken Morrow kill the penalty, and they did it by carrying the play to the Finns, by swarming around the Finnish net.

Exhausted, Broten took himself off and Johnson jumped off the bench to take his place. Christoff, still battling in the corner, got the puck to him near the blue line. It took a lot of doing, but Johnson controlled the erratically bouncing puck and fired a backhander at the net. Jorma Valtonen, the 33-year-old Finnish goaltender, stopped it, but Johnson was there for the rebound . . . and the field house became a mad house.

The last 3 minutes and 35 seconds didn't crawl by, the way they had in the Russian game. This time they were fun. The American kids knew they had it won now. They savored those final minutes even as they would savor the memories of the last six months. The game hadn't officially ended; their six months still had a few ticks of the clock to go, but they were Olympic champions, and they knew it.

The final seconds wound down and these kids got more and more revved up. Forty seconds to go and John Harrington leaned over the bench and banged his stick against the boards, again and again and again, and David Silk raised his hockey stick high over his head and waved it in triumph. Ten seconds to go and the crowd began counting, "Nine . . . eight . . . seven . . . six . . ."

John O'Callahan, the irrepresible, 22-year-old defenseman from Massachusetts, and Ramsey sought out assistant coach Craig Patrick on the bench and wrapped him in a bear hug as sub goalie Janaszak planted a big, wet kiss on Patrick's cheek.

"Five . . . four . . . three . . ."

Phil Verchota had his hockey stick in both hands now, holding it as high as he could; then, spotting Mark Johnson, he dropped the stick and hugged him.

"Two . . . one . . ." Zero hour.

The six months were history. The gold was theirs. The impossible dream had become reality. Mike Eruzione slammed his stick on the ice. David Christian hurled his as hard as he could against the corner boards, then embraced Broten and the two of them whirled

Guess who won?

in a wild victory dance at center ice, finally falling down near the boards, where they rolled over and over. McClanahan and Eruzione appropriated a large American flag from one of the fans who had come tumbling out of the stands and held it high for all to see. Silk and O'Callahan fell into each other's arms and began jumping for joy as one.

The standing-room crowd would never forget this moment. Neither would the millions of television viewers across the nation, nor the 20 kids who made it all happen, who made these Winter Olympic Games throb with life and emotion and togetherness.

Outside the field house strangers were embracing and dancing and singing; a band was playing. It didn't matter that a wet snow was falling. It didn't matter that the Russians were

about to roll up nine goals against the Swedes. The six months were up . . . and the American kids had won Olympic gold medals.

"The feeling right now?" Mark Johnson said. "I don't even know how to describe it. It's just unbelievable. I just sit here in awe."

When it all began, they had been in awe of the Russians. Now it was over and they were in awe of their own accomplishments.

"We came together six months ago from all parts of the United States," Mike Eruzione said. "We jelled into a team. I don't think there's a coach or anybody in the country right now that can say they've experienced the type of season we've had."

People Make the Olympics
A Major Happening

By Ray Grass

It was the people . . . tall and short, draped in furs or down, wearing the red and white of Austria or the sheepskin jackets of the USA, walking, running, cheering and crying . . . it was the people that made the Lake Placid Olympics what they were — a major happening.

A record number of athletes (1,567) were tested and tried by a record number of officials in a record number of events (38) before huge numbers of spectators and a record viewing audience.

For 13 days, the small up-state community of Lake Placid (population 2,700) was taken from its laid back lifestyle and dropped into the eye of the hurricane . . . the world's greatest spectacle.

Stories were told about the athletes and the officials. Winners and losers were notified and reported. The "how comes" and "what fors" went out over the airways, the phone lines and by postman. But then there were the people . . . the fans and the sightseers and the shoppers.

What of them? Well, as one Olympic official put it, "They were the best of all." For the most part, the fans took hardships in stride and met problems with patient and, sometimes, humor.

About the transportation, for example, one New Yorker said to a bus driver after a long, cold wait, "So this is what they mean by the agony of 'da-feet.'" Then there was the suggestion of a new Olympic event, "busing."

Mr. Grass is a writer on the staff of the Deseret News in Salt Lake City, Utah.

It was expected that as many as 50,000 spectators a day would be busing in for Olympic events. It was never felt that the number was ever reached although many a day, especially near the last, it was close. And, despite late or missing buses, it was obvious to the nearly 3,000 media representatives that nothing was going to stop the people from their planned task — to see the Olympics.

At the alpine events on White Face Mountain, about 15 miles from downtown Lake Placid, spectators began arriving hours before the events in hopes of getting prime seats, or standing room. They walked up the slopes, a 15-minute hike to the finish line, alone, in the cold and sometimes amid blowing wind and snow. The Russians in their furs, the Americans in their 'moon boots', the Austrians with their flags and the Japanese with their cameras. Some days the temperature was as cold as 14 below centigrade and the winds from 25 to 40 miles per hour. Still they waited . . . patiently.

At the luge and bobsled events it was the same. Thousands arrived early, waited hours in the cold to protect their "territory" and for a chance at a fleeting glimpse of a competitor on the course. They smiled and they joked. And they waited.

The closing ceremony was a "happy affair."

At the biathlon and cross-country events there were stadiums and seats — cold, hard bleachers, but nonetheless, seats. The tickets allowed spectators rights to see the start and finish of the cross-country and they got a bonus in the biathlon by being able to watch the shooting.

Conditions were better for the skating events. Unlike the other out-of-doors events, though, seating was limited. A ticket was good for one seat, and no more. The hockey and figure skating were indoors.

Sometimes it took a battle to get tickets and then a long wait for the arena to open, but it was inside and warm and also expensive. Ticket prices ranged from $22.50, for the speed skating, all the way up to $67.20, for one of the figure skating sessions.

But everywhere you go, people will be people and at the Lake Placid Olympics, people were no different than at previous Olympics. Which, of course, meant that trading between countries — pins — was one of the most popular events and certainly one of the most participated in.

At every venue, on every street, before every event, pins were on the trading block. "Sorry, no money please." "You got a pin or medal to trade?" "Knet." "No, please." "Oka-a-a," and "Thank you." were all the business talk a trader needed.

Captain Mike Eruzione on the victory stand.

Successful traders wore their pins like medals of honor on the fronts of their jackets. Novice traders wore them on their hats, lapels or kept their wares hidden.

Probably the most obvious nature of the crowd, though, was one of no boundaries.

Russians shook hands with Americans, and even had pictures taken together, and both were happy to do so. Language barriers were often jumped by a hand shake and a small smile, but most evident was the applause and the cheers, no matter the finishers' country, in appreciation for a performance well done.

And then there were the hockey games. Here there were definite lines of patriotism and, of course, the expected cross-overs. The traditional rooting for the underdog. Like when Japan played the Russians. No contest! The Japanese played well. They were hittin' on both cylinders. Trouble was the Russians, in traditional fashion, were hittin' on all 12 cylinders. The economy-minded Japanese were rolled over, 16-0. For every cheer the Russians received for a goal, the Japanese team received a louder one from the supportive crowd for a good pass.

For the most part, though, the French cheered for France's team, Germans for Germany's team, the Russians for Russia's team and the Americans for the "U. . . S. . . A."

U.S. and Russian teams in the traditional handshake.

"What so proudly we hailed . . ."

At no time during the Olympics, though, was the competitive fever so high among the fans — on both sides — as for the USA-Russian game, especially for the final 10 minutes when signs of the outcome first became visible. The fans cheered, clapped and cried . . . and when it was over, they cried some more. Some for joy and others for sorrow.

When the game ended, the benches cleared, but the center didn't. State police worked for over a half hour to get the cheering, flag-waving fans to leave. They sang and they cheered, they held fingers signifying "No. 1" high and they sang out choruses of "U.S.A." All were not signs of joy, though. One trooper near the Soviet bench went over to the Soviet captain and gave him his American flag lapel pin . . . a

gesture of friendship. The Soviet was in tears; probably the worst moment in his life. But, he managed to smile and said: "Thank you very much."

One hockey fan summed up the participation of the crowd when he said, "I felt as if I had played the game. I'm tired and I'm sweaty. But, believe me, it's great."

Command Performance
At the White House

By Richard P. Sorensen

Olympians at the White House.

It is Monday, February 25, the early afternoon of a cold and damp late winter day in Washington, D.C. Herb Brooks, Coach of the U.S. Olympic Hockey Team, is standing in the State Dining Room at the White House shaking his head in amazement. Brooks has just chatted with the President of the United States, and now he is mingling with Senators, Congressmen, Cabinet Secretaries, and members of the White House staff. Brooks is amazed

Richard P. Sorensen is a
free-lance writer based in
Washington, D.C.

because everyone in the room knows who he is, and all these important national leaders are asking for his autograph.

Brooks is talking with Chris Matthews, a speech writer for President Carter. Matthews mentions the topic that is still foremost on everyone's minds: the 4-3 win Friday night over the Russian Hockey Team. He tells Brooks, "It was great to see you going up and down the

bench, saying to your players, 'Play your game, play your game.' " Brooks shakes his head again, and says, "How did you know that? How did you know that's what I said? I can't believe it."

It hasn't fully dawned upon Brooks that in the past days the members of his team have become known in every corner of the nation. Through the miracle of television, millions of people have watched the American Hockey Team defeat first the Russians and then the Finns to win the gold medal. Overnight they have become national heroes. One Congressman has compared their victory over the Soviet team to Charles Lindbergh's solo flight over the Atlantic.

If anything, the triumph over the Russians was far more unexpected than Lindbergh's successful landing in Paris. As news of the win flashed across the country on Friday evening, the initial reaction was euphoria mixed with utter astonishment. There is a drinking establishment on Pennsylvania Avenue in Washington known as the Hawk and Dove, and a sense of mild satisfaction settled upon the Friday evening crowd when the bartender announced the first period score of 2-2. At least the Americans were keeping it close. As the score was announced every 10 minutes for the next hour, astonishment began to grow and pride began to swell. The announcement of the final score was greeted with happy shouts, hugs, and handshakes.

Everyone would watch the delayed telecast later that night, to bask in reflected glory and to make certain it had actually happened.

Inevitably, the U.S. win would take on political coloring. The victory had been achieved against a team that was not only the best in the world, but also the source of great national pride in the Soviet Union. Two months earlier, Soviet soldiers had invaded Afghanistan and now President Carter and other U.S.

Mrs. Carter, the President, and Eric Heiden.

Congratulations from the President.

political leaders were talking about a boycott of the Summer Olympics in Moscow. In the closing ceremonies at Lake Placid, Lord Killanin of Ireland had spoken of the Olympic ideals, which transcend narrow political ends: "The Olympics proved we can do something to improve mutual understanding in the world. . . . If we could all come together, it would be a better world."

In Washington, however, House Speaker Thomas P. "Tip" O'Neill, Jr., an Irish-American politician struck a different note: "[The Hockey Team's victory] is a great lift to the American people, and it goes beyond that. There is nothing the Soviet's appreciate more than sports — it is their one area of freedom — and their biggest sport is hockey. And

now with the United States boycott you can believe me heads will roll in Russia." The day following the upset of the Russians, the U.S. aircraft Nimitz in the Indian Ocean signaled a message to a Soviet intelligence ship cruising nearby: "Olympic hockey, United States 4, Soviet Union 3."

On Sunday President Carter dispatched three Air Force jets to Lake Placid to bring all the American Olympians to Washington the next morning. A crowd of more than 1,000, many of them waving American flags, greets the team when it arrives at Andrews Air Force Base. When the buses carrying the athletes roll into the White House grounds, the crowd of 2,500 government officials, who had gathered on the south lawn, begins to cheer. Many of the television people have stuck small American flags into their cameras and sound equipment. The Marine Band plays John Philip Sousa marches, "God Bless America," and "This is My Country."

President Carter addresses the Olympians from the Truman balcony. The athletes, dressed in red, white and blue, some wearing white Stetsons, flank the President on either side, standing on the steps that lead up to the balcony. The President says, "The U.S. Hockey Team — their victory was one of the most breathtaking upsets, not only in Olympic history, but in the entire history of sports." Speaking of all the athletes, he says, "We often hear it said that there are no more heroes. We are all supposed to be too sophisticated for the recognition of heroes. But our Olympic athletes are heroes. They endure long and brutal training schedules, they make hard sacrifices, and so do their families and their coaches. They do it to reach their greatest for themselves and their country." The jubilant scene is muted only by the President's statement that it would be necessary for the United States to boycott the summer games in Moscow. Other American athletes who have trained as long and as hard as these have, and who have shared the same hopes and anticipation, would not get the chance to compete.

President Carter admires Steve Janaszak's Gold Medal.

"We're proud of you . . ."

Following the President's remarks, the winter Olympians move inside for a reception and buffet lunch in the State Dining Room. Jim Craig, the goalie who fended off shot after shot so magnificently in the past three days, is suddenly aware of how much the hockey team's achievement has meant to his country. He says "Winning the gold medal is like going to the moon or something." Considering the way the nation has responded to their victory, it is only a slight exaggeration.

Craig bounds across the room to embrace Herb Brooks, and then begins to seek out each of his teammates. The team has been together for six months, and now they have played together for the last time. What a time it was.

The start of the Heiden show.
Driven forward by his muscular
legs, the skates pound the
ice until he is into his stride.
Then Heiden glides and nobody
can stop him. He won all five
possible gold medals.

A study of the Winter olympic
king. Arms behind his back
to give the chest more room
to breathe. Concentration
in his face. The upperbody
is resolutely bent forward
to maintain the optimal gravita-
tional axis at every second.

Nobody ran as elegantly, nobody
jumped the three jumps easier
and more assuredly. Robin
Cousins, the Englishman trained
in America. Gold for the ice
skater for whom the word
"art" stands in the foreground
despite all the technical ability
needed.

Flying people. The american
Charles Tickner (Bronze)
and his fellow American Linda
Fratianne (Silver) doing the
butterfley. Two who are very
happy: The winner Anett
Poetzsch from the GDR and
the bronze medal winner Dagmar Lurz from Dortmund.

The girl who brought the spectators to ecstatic applause
with her acrobatic ability.
Denise Biellmann from Switzerland. She did not win a medal
but she gave this figure her
name: the "Denise pirouette".

These photos are small reproductions of full color pictures
on the following pages. The captions for the photos
are alongside each reproduction.

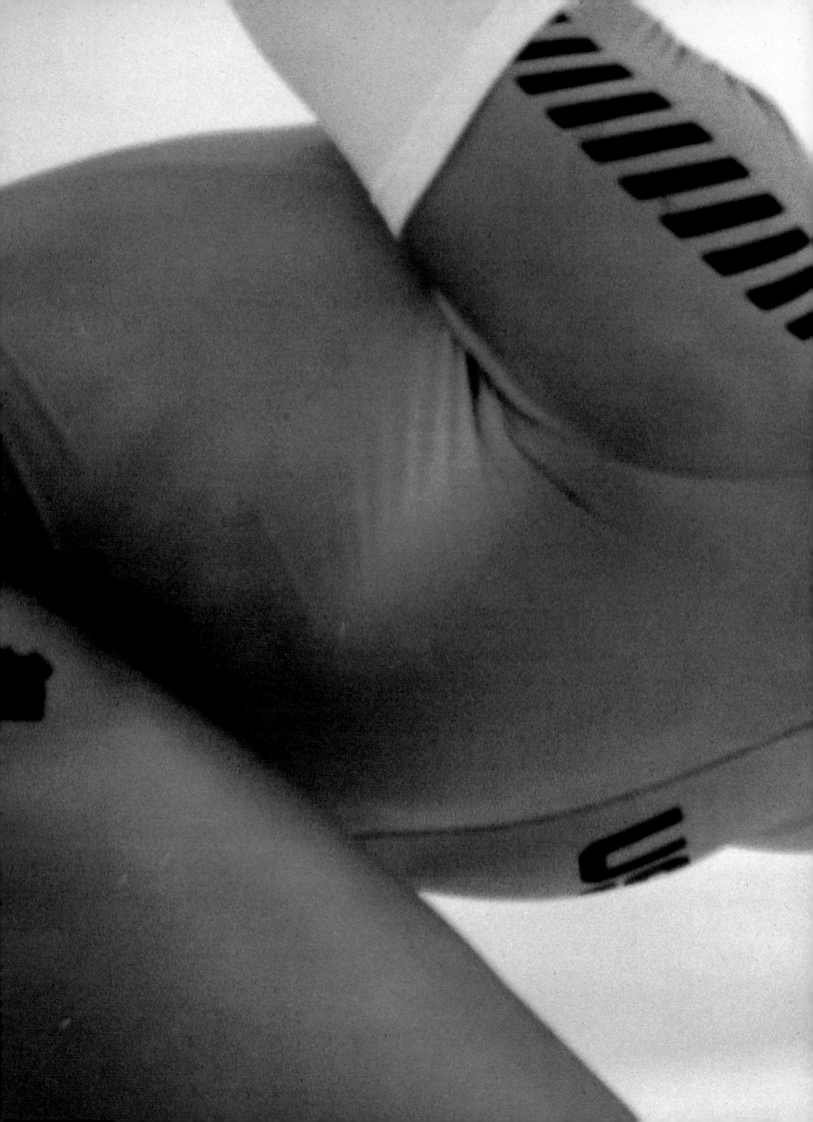

Five Golds Make Heiden An Authentic Hero

By Chris Jenkins

Eric Heiden and five golds.

The wool cap, pulled down almost to eyebrow level in a futile attempt to cover a shock of dark hair, had no great symbolic purpose. Nor did it provide its handsome occupant any great inspiration. And with its glaring rings of yellows and reds and heaven knows how

Mr. Jenkins is a writer for the Colorado Springs Gazette Telegraph in Colorado Springs, Colorado.

many other bright colors, it wasn't even particularly flattering.

The cap was, however, much-needed evidence that Eric Heiden was a mortal man.

"My girl friend gave it to me," said the 21-year-old speed-skating sensation from Madison, Wisc., answering what to him must have seemed only one of the more absurd of the zillions of questions fired his way at

the XIII Olympic Winter Games. "I think she'd get mad at me if I didn't wear it."

The likelihood of that was virtually nonexistent. Heiden didn't make a wrong move in the two weeks he spent in these Adirondacks. He placated his lady Cecelie, a pretty lass from Norway, by wearing the rainbow cap she knitted everywhere but on the Olympic Oval. He even had occasion to wear it on the uppermost step of the awards stand a time or five.

Five gold medals, Olympic variety. In the lexicon of Heiden's generation, unreal.

At the outset and throughout each of his five races, some of us called Heiden's historic quest the Olympic Sport of Heiden Seek. Heiden himself called it The Great Whoopee. He spoke of the Great Whoopee with something less than enthusiasm. Oh, Heiden liked winning as much as anybody, and he had the same dream as every Olympian. But his own excitement was tempered by the excitement of others, the millions of others who noted Heiden's accomplishment with awe. Time and again, occasionally with tongue firmly planted in cheek, Heiden made it all sound like much ado about nothing. Cases in point:

Upon claiming his fifth gold medal with an easy victory in the 10,000 meters, Heiden obliged photographers for the Spitzesque shot of the winner with his harvest. Then Heiden was asked what he'd do with all that gold. "They'll probably sit in the same place where all the rest of my medals sit — in my mother's dresser drawer. They'll just collect dust like all the others have.

"I'll never take them out and look at them again. You really can't do much with them. Oh well, maybe they'll be worth something someday."

No man or woman has ever done what Heiden did at Lake Placid. Sixteen years before, Lydia Skoblikova of the Soviet Union had won four gold medals in speedskating. Just four. Mark Spitz? Spitz can claim four with an asterisk, since three of his seven gold medals came in relay events. Yet Heiden remained unimpressed by himself. On the contrary, he said, he was more impressed the night before when the United States Hockey Team, a scrappy bunch of collegians who captivated the fancy of America and was placed on the same pedestal as Heiden, stunned the powerful Soviet Union 4-3 enroute to the gold medal. "Did you see that?" Heiden asked, the excitement rising in his voice. "Boy, that was great, the biggest accom-

plishment I've ever seen. I screamed my lungs out."

(Informed of Heiden's statement, U.S. Hockey Coach Herb Brooks declared Heiden's endeavors "the most amazing thing" he'd ever seen. "The only thing that scares me," said Brooks, who coached the University of Minnesota at the NCAA level, "is that Heiden might turn in his speed-skates and go play hockey for the University of Wisconsin." Brooks was only half-joking. Bob Johnson, the Wisconsin coach who was on hand to watch his son Mark play on the Olympic Hockey Team and who is an old friend of the Heiden family, was indeed prepared to offer Eric a scholarship on the spot.)

Heiden was a national celebrity before he ever arrived in Lake Placid. The United States had never won more than a dozen medals in any one Winter Olympiad, but Heiden alone was expected to win five—

and all of these gold. America badly needed just such a hero. The covers of publications like *Time* and *Sports Illustrated* made him just that, and he hadn't even laced on his skates yet. Not that Heiden put much stock in what he read about himself. "All the time I've been out here," he would say later, "I've been skating for myself. I don't care what you guys write. If I skate well I'll be happy. If I skate poorly I'll be upset. It doesn't matter if I win or lose, as long as I skate well. As for all the (attention) after a race, I'd just as soon be watching '2001: A Space Odyssey.' That's on right now (at the local Olympic Village moviehouse) and I'd like to see it."

And that's about as spacy as this kid ever got. Perhaps the most striking thing about Heiden was the way he kept his head when all others were losing their heads over him. The only time he admitted to anything approaching nervousness was after his first race. That was the 500, which was supposed to be Heiden's weakest event, if such a thing really existed. His opening-day jitters were hardly apparent, though, as Heiden dispatched the 500 field — a field that included world-record holder Yevgeny Kulikov of the Soviet Union. That completed, Heiden returned to his same old unfazed self. He just wanted to keep it simple. Indeed, he made it look simple.

The next day it was the 5,000. Tom Erik Oxholm of Norway was in the first pair and finished in a threatening time of 7:05.59. Heiden was in the second pair, matched against Hilbert van der Dulm of the

Beth Heiden won the 3000 meter bronze and Bjoerg Eva Jensen the gold.

Netherlands. van der Dulm saw nothing but the hind side of Heiden's gold racing suit once the starting gun sounded. Nevertheless, Heiden was keeping a pace deemed too slow to beat Oxholm's time. At one point in the early going, the race announcer (Jim Hawkins) subtly mentioned that Heiden was trailing Oxholm's pace by more than four seconds. Then it was three seconds. Then less than two seconds. With a little more than 1,000 meters in Heiden's one-man race, Oxholm bowed his head. Heiden had drawn even. He wasn't about to slow down, either. Urged on by the sound of thousands of pairs of clapping mittens — a sound not unlike that of a rampaging buffalo herd — Heiden blew across the finish line in 7:02.29. No world record or anything, but hey . . . two down, three to go.

Heiden had two days to contemplate the 1,000 meters, which was to be followed two days later by the 1,500. And for the first time, he was talking not about Oxholm or Kulikov but of a more challenging opponent. That is, pain.

"Now that I've got some time, I'll think about skating the perfect race," Heiden said. "But I have to let myself know that the race is going to hurt, and that's something I have to overcome. In the 1,000 and the 1,500, you feel the pain with a lap to go. It isn't too bad during the race until that last lap, but afterward you really hurt. You have a burning in your mouth and throat for another 30 minutes and you're

coughing up things for a few days, which is a drag."

No doubt. Heiden seemed to be suffering from neither of the symptoms, however, as he stepped onto the awards stand to receive his fourth gold. The 1,000 had been a breeze. The 1,500 had been likewise until Heiden's inside skate caught a rut in the ice and he appeared headed for a fall — in more ways than one. But Heiden needed only the assistance of one hand to regain his balance and, incredibly, went on to beat the field by almost a second-and-a-half. All he had left to pull out of Cecelie's hat was the 10,000.

The 10,000 is the marathon of speedskating, a grueling bit of monotony covering 25 laps, all skated at approximately the same pace. It is, by Heiden's admission, all rather boring. The only salvation, Heiden joked, is that "sometimes it's kind of fun to go out and get dizzy." Tell that to the thighs. Now, Heiden's thighs were as big as beer kegs— 29 inches round, in fact — but keep in mind they had already carried him through four races amounting to 8,000 meters.

This raises a point that makes Heiden's ensuing feat all the more remarkable. Like track and field, speedskating is a sport of specialists. Lake Placid was flooded with the world's best specialists. Specializing in everything, Heiden beat their slick racing suits off them. And that, curiously enough, is what seemed to give Heiden his greatest satisfaction.

"This was the best race I could've won," Heiden said after rounding out his clean sweep with a time of 14:28.13. "I think the 10,000 is neat to win

because it's a race that takes training to get good at. A race like the 500 is a race for sprinters, and I don't think sprinters have to train that much. Believe me, you have to train for the 10,000."

We believe. We believe. When it was all over, though, Heiden still had people wondering about something. With his All-America looks and his lode of gold, would Heiden go the way of Spitz and Bruce Jenner? America thrives on its Olympic heroes, and both Madison Avenue and Hollywood know it. Many, in fact, were the talent agents who came to the Adirondacks to convince Heiden of his own marketability. Publicly, though, Heiden said he wanted none of it.

"I hope I can stay away from all that stuff," said Heiden, whose immediate plans were to return to his pre-med studies at the University of Wisconsin with the hope of someday working in the sports medicine field. "I don't want to sell myself like a lot of people have. All I want after this is to just be the way I am. I don't want people sticking me on a pedestal. That'd bum me out. I just want to be Eric Heiden."

And Leah Poulos Mueller is quite content to be Leah Poulos Mueller, thank you. The silver medalist in the 1,000 meters four years before at Innsbruck, Mueller was almost an ignored commodity when she came to

Lake Placid, the thunder she merited having gone to Eric's younger sister, Beth Heiden. But it was Mueller and not Beth who emerged with the medals, winning silvers in both the 500 and the 1,000. Beth Heiden, as it turned out, offered a sad contrast to the performances of her brother. While he had done everything expected of him, she had fallen drastically short. The pre-Olympic favorite in three of the four events (in the callous American press), Beth finished seventh, seventh and fifth in her first three races, whereupon she took the press to task for having made her out to be something she wasn't. Adhering to the family motto of skating one's best and being happy with that, Beth said, "For a time I found myself skating not for myself but for the press. Well, the hell with you guys." Even Mueller came to Beth's defense, saying "I haven't been overshadowed by Beth. She's done well in her own right. She got a lot of publicity because she's Eric's sister, but she deserves it in her own right."

At which point Beth went out and took the bronze medal in the 3,000, giving the U.S. Speedskating Team eight medals, fully two-thirds of the entire American total. Beth couldn't get off that easy, though. As if the press hadn't emphasized her shortcomings enough, Beth got a backhanded shot from Soviet star Natalia Petruseva who had won the 1,000 meters and as the winner had to submit to a blood-doping test that seemed to take forever. "I was so excited about beating Beth Heiden for the *third* time,"

Eric Heiden and Yevgeny Kulikow in their classic 500 meter race.

Petruseva explained with a blush, "that I couldn't do what they asked me to do for the test."

Imagine, then, the excitement of Annie Borckink of the Netherlands. Having never placed in the top three at any previous international competition, Borckink went head-to-head with Heiden in the 1,500 meters and emerged a gold-medalist. Also imagine the delight of East Germany's Karin Enke, a teenager who had turned to speedskating a few years before only because her promising figure-skating career had been cut short by an injury. Figure-skating's loss meant a gold-medal gain by Enke, who clocked a 41.78 seconds in the 500 to beat the veteran Mueller. The gold in the 3,000 belonged to Norway's Bjorg Eva Jensen, who happened to be running in the same two-woman pairing as Beth Heiden.

Heiden. There's that name again. It circulated daily throughout the Adirondacks, in agony and in victory. With every victory, too, one of the Heidens came closer and closer to immortal status. That is, until word reached him.

"When people say things like that about me," Eric Heiden said, "it just goes in one ear and out the other."

But it has to get through that wool cap, first.

No Golds This Time For U.S. Figure Skaters

By Dan Hruby

That the U.S. win an Olympic gold medal in figure skating has never been compulsory. Usually, it just happened.

But compulsory became more than simply a word on the indoor ice at Lake Placid. Linda Fratianne missed the gold because she started off with disappointing marks in compulsory figures and the dynamic pairs team of Tai Babilonia and Randy Gardner failed because it still is compulsory to compete. In a tragic scenario, the tandem from California had to bow out at the last moment because of an injury to Gardner.

There probably isn't an event in the winter or summer Olympic Games where judging is more subjective and arbitrary and where the competitors expose the sour sides of their personalities than in figure skating. When the gold is on the line, the warmth and friendships nutured by

Mr. Hruby is a member of the sports staff of the San Jose (California) Mercury News.

Linda Fratianne

skaters in hours on the practice rink and even at world championships wane quickly. Maybe it's because the cost in money and sacrifice envelops entire families and communities and an untoward fierceness emerges at predictable moments.

U.S. figure skaters cradled notions of two golds, maybe three, as they entered competition. Fratianne, Charlie Tickner and Babilonia-Gardner all had won world championships. The opposition would be formidable, but this was home ice and friendly crowds in the past have pulled athletes to mighty performances. And, of course, influenced judges.

Fratianne came in saying she was unperturbed by her shaky showing while defending her national title a month earlier in Atlanta ("I had a bad attitude there."). But Anett Poetzsch took a commanding lead in school figures, putting the 19-year-old, doll-like California brunette in third place and in a serious bind.

With the compulsories counting 30 percent of the final score (the short program is 20 and the long, 50), the setback was critical to Linda's chances.

But Fratianne's courage and poise surfaced in the short program as she leaped past Dagmar Lurz of West Germany into second place.

In the end, the 5-0, 95-pound Fratianne had lost by only seven-tenths of a point. Poetzsch had 11 ordinals and 189.00 points and Fratianne 16 and 188.30. Lurz wound up third and Switzerland's Denise Biellman, who was the subject of a lot of flak over whether the U.S. team hairdresser should do her hair before the short program, came in fourth. Striking blonde Lisa-

Charles Tickner

Marie Allen of Colorado Springs finished fifth.

The Soviets had had Olympic pairs skating to themselves for almost 30 years and the USA, with Babilonia and Gardner, was primed to alter the pattern.

"Good luck, Randy and Tai," a banner on a Main Street restaurant proclaimed as the Games began. The matchup with Russians Irina Rodnina and Aleksandr Zaitsev had ABC-TV drooling as it looked to weekend ratings.

But it proved all academic when a groin injury Gardner had incurred two weeks earlier in practice in Los Angeles acted up. He had pulled the abductor muscle high on his right thigh while doing a routine move. Then, on the semi-final workout prior to the opening short program, Gardner reinjured himself. And he pulled another groin muscle besides. Reports of the setback flew around the Olympic Village.

A sad Randy Gardner and Tai Babilonia meet the press.

Doctors quietly tried ice packs and deep massage in the final minutes before Gardner left for the arena. There, a physician administered lidocaine, a pain killer permitted by Olympic doping rules, to numb the muscles. But Gardner fell three times during warmups. And, in a final test, he tried a simple lift at Coach John Nicks' request. He staggered through it, but almost dropped Babilonia. Once, years before, he had dropped her, badly bruising her face and loosening some teeth.

Gardner fell one more time and that was it — Nicks pulled them off the ice. They were broken-hearted. Tears flowed. Randy felt he had let Tai down. Tai wept because she believed she had let her friends and country down. And some of the nation sniffled at the thought of two youngsters working so hard for so long and then seeing a dream die aborning because of the cruel vagaries of the sport.

Rodnina, 30, and Zaitsev, 27, the pressure off, waltzed to the gold. The Soviets took the silver, too, and the East Germans the bronze. Americans Peter and Caitlin Carruthers finished fifth and Sheryl Franks and Michael Botticelli seventh.

The rhythmic and balletic Robin Cousins kept the gold medal in the British Isles, manifesting every bit as much power and grace as his Olympic predecessor at Innsbruck, John Curry.

Cousins had moved to Denver and enlisted Carlo Fassi, who had handled Dorothy Hamill and Curry, as his coach. Some experts called him the "finest free skater in the world," a ranking that ticked off friends of Tickner, who also called Denver home.

Cousins had the reputation of floundering in the figures, and he did have a problem in Lake Placid. Fassi even called him "chicken" over his casual approach to the first phase of the competition. He was in fourth place going into the short program, which requires seven mandatory moves. The U.S. camp was delighted at the prospects — Cousins was fourth and the former Russian world titlist, Victor Kovalev, had flopped in the figures and withdrawn. The USA's David Santee, crediting sports psychologist Bruce Ogilvie of San Jose, California, for buoying his confidence, stood third behind East German Jan Hoffman and Tickner. Hoffman was famous for fast starts and slow finishes.

Lisa-Marie Allen

The final tally was 13 ordinals and 189.72 points for Cousins and 15 and 187.86 for the German, an amazingly close windup for the men's event. An altered vote by a single judge could have made Hoffman the winner.

Tickner picked up the bronze. Santee took fourth, barely edging a fellow American, wee Scott Hamilton of Haverford, Pa. Hamilton had rebounded from a childhood disease that stopped his growth for four years.

It was form all the way in ice dancing, the Russians winning their second gold in the event since it was introduced at Innsbruck in 1976. Natalia Linichuk and Gennadi Karponosov wowed the judges but bored a crowd of 8,500 with their rather stodgy performance.

But disaster smote Tickner, 26, the "old man" of the U.S. team, in the short program. He muffed a combination spin and his overall performance was deemed too conservative to impress the judges. Hoffman held his lead, but Cousins vaulted into second to set up a dramatic finale.

Cousins, 22, nipped Hoffman, 24, on the artistic-impression phase of his five-minute free skating routine. On technical merit, both skaters were awarded 5.8 and 5.9 from the nine judges.

But then eight judges scored the high-leaping Cousins at 5.9 and one at 5.8 for artistic impression. Hoffman's best marks were three 5.8's. One judge, Sally Scapleford of Great Britain, hit him with a 5.5.

"I love the chance to show off a little and give of myself to the crowd," bubbled Cousins, who skated to a combination of popular, classical and disco music.

Franks and Botticelli

An almost symbolic picture: Ingemar Stenmark on his way to the top. At the peak of his career the Swede retrieved what he let slip in Innsbruck and won two gold medals – in the giant slalom and in the slalom. What is there left for him to achieve?

Stenmark always tries to find the shortest and quickest way to the finish. The photograph shows this: he touches the giant slalom pole with his shoulder without slowing down. The snow hardly dusts up when Stenmark digs in the edges of his kis.

The Queen of Lake Placid. Hanni Wenzel, the girl from Liechtenstein. has never looked more relaxed or happy. No wonder. Gold in the giant slalom and slalom, silver in the downhill event. The success of an imperturbable self-confident character.

Two photographs, one family. Hanni Wenzel skis to victory as though on rails, relaxed yet aggressive, courageous and technically perfect. And Andreas Wenzel, her brother, is also happy especially as he won his own silver medal in the giant slalom.

The victory pose which says everything. The photograph shows it all: Joy, pride, satisfaction. Leonhard Stock came as a reserve to Lake Placid and went home a winner. The downhill event was the Austrians' domaine. Annemarie Moser underlined this superiority.

The best in their team. Mariarosa Quariò from Italy was fourth in the slalom event, but just missed a bronze medal by one hundredth of a second. Phil Mahre, silver for America in the slalom event. And as an additional satisfaction: the world championship in the combination.

Bold and aggressive as always. Piero Gros, the Italien Olympic winner in the 1976 slalom event risked everything – but it was not enough to earn him a place among the medals. But his dynamic runs were well worth seeing.

Annemarie Moser, née Pröll, her dream come true. After a long career of fame and triumph she won at Lake Placid what she most passionately wanted. The gold medal in the downhill event.

This face under the goggles shows the absolute will to give of one's best. Doris de Agostino tries very hard to get into the best downhill posture even after her "crash" due to a rut in the ground.

These photos are small reproductions of full color pictures on the following pages. The captions for the photos are alongside each reproduction.

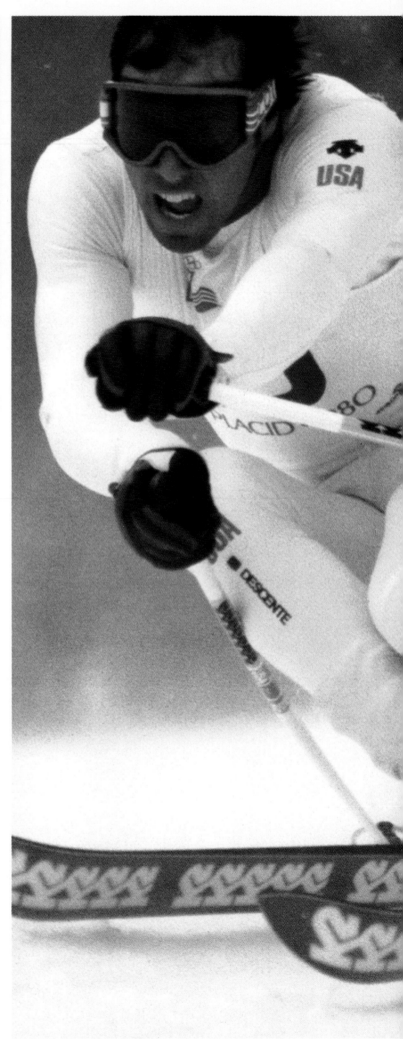

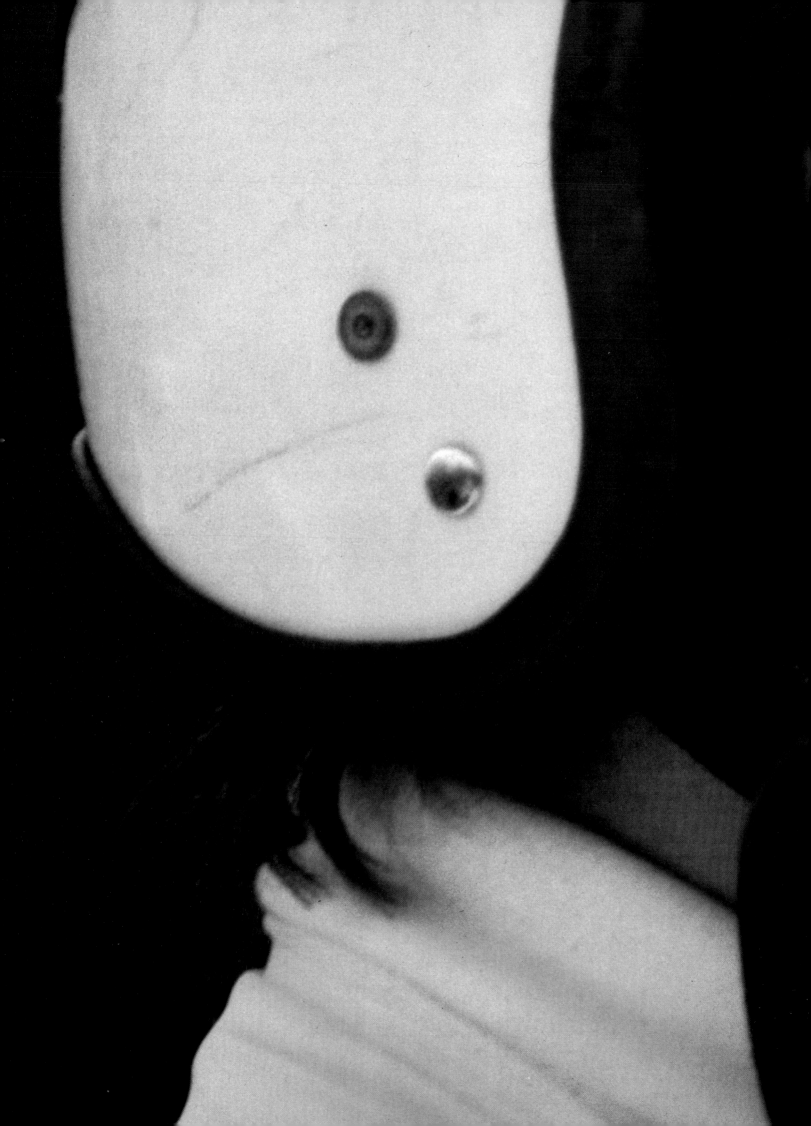

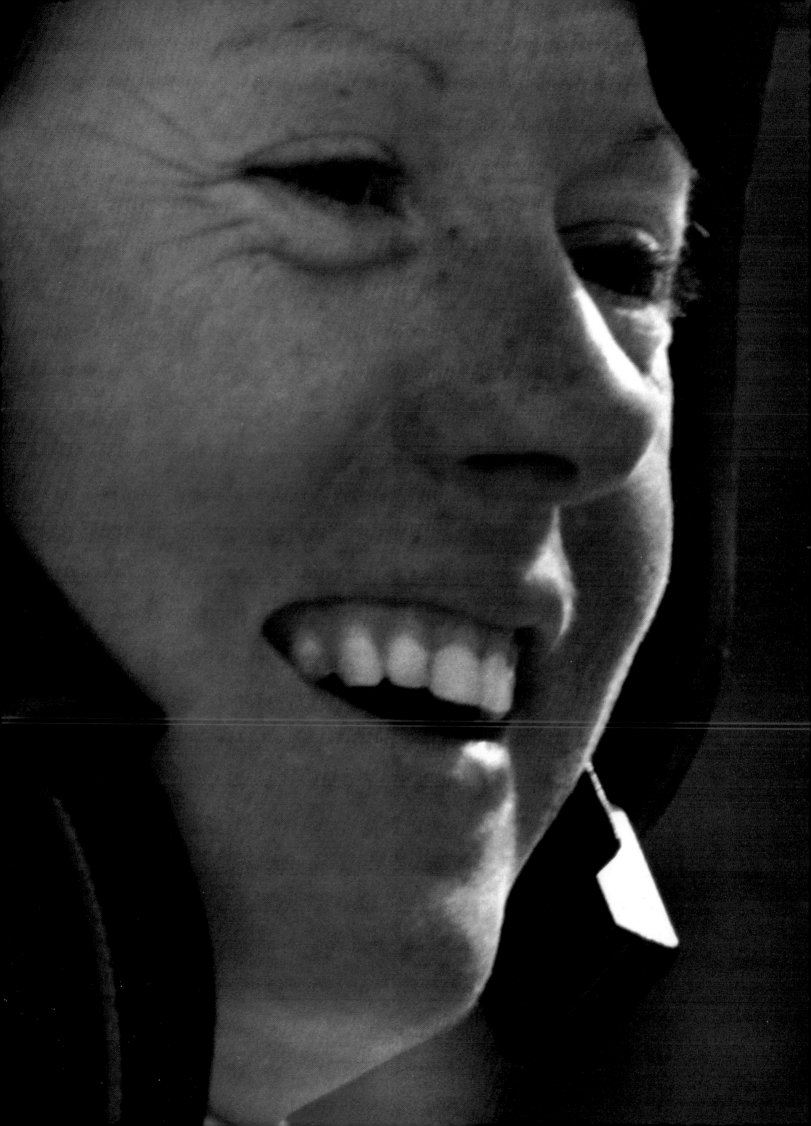

Superstars Come Through
On the Alpine Slopes

By Charlie Meyers

Forget about all the recent escalation on the international market. The medals are mostly silver anyway; only the outside plate is gold.

When they lined up to start the Olympic alpine events on Lake Placid's Whiteface Mountain, the lusting was for the medal, not the metal.

There was none of the usual blather, prevalent at the previous two Games, about how the Olympics really didn't mean that much; how the real alpine prize was the World Cup; how the true test of skiing greatness was over the long haul, not some flash-in-the-pan dash of a fleeting few seconds — even if there was gold at the bottom.

The reasons were easy to fathom, requiring only a brief look at recent Olympic history. The trick was not to notice who won gold medals over the last eight years, but rather who didn't. The missing names read like skiing's who's who, including the two greatest women racers of all time and the man who might reasonably make the same claim.

Indeed, one does have to look it up to believe that Annemarie Moser (She made it plain she has dropped her maiden name, Proell, for the married one.) had never won an Olympic gold in a career going all the way back to 1969 when she burst upon the scene as a precocious 14-year-old.

The same was true of Hanni Wenzel, the Liechtenstein lass who has picked up just about everything that escaped Moser

Mr. Meyers is a writer for the Denver Post in Denver, Colorado.

over the years. For her third — and last — Olympics, only gold would do.

But the greatest pressure of all fell on Ingemar Stenmark, whose 46 World Cup victories were far and away the most by any male skier.

The Swede's almost total dominance over the years in slalom and giant slalom had prompted the World Cup rules makers to change the game again and again until, finally, he no longer could win in 1979 despite

a record 14 individual race victories. No matter. Despite all this success, Ingemar had been castigated as an Olympic failure, with only a bronze in giant slalom to show for his 1976 efforts.

A pleasant, yet taciturn man from Sweden's Arctic frontier, Stenmark perhaps is the most single-minded person ever to buckle up a pair of ski boots. And he came to Lake Placid even more determined than ever and, like Moser, having spent

Phil Mahre

Phil Mahre and Ingemar Stenmark

months pointing solely for the moment.

Prior to the start of the season, when skiers gather on the glaciers of the high Alps for their serious training, there was Stenmark with, of all things, several pairs of downhill skis. If the World Cup fathers had deemed it essential to ski down- hill to win the championship, so be it.

But after several promising training runs, there came those eggbeater falls at high speed which prompts an involun- tary sucking of breath among all those watching. After Ingemar had been helicoptered to a hospital and his head

cleared of concussion, he made a firm decision. He would hedge his chance at the World Cup and go for the gold.

Moser faced no such trauma. From the time she grew from a skinny prodigy of a woman- child what seems like centuries ago to the broad-beamed ski kaiserin, she has been a down- hiller. The consummate woman downhiller. The only woman who could ski like a man, who could hold her tuck through the steepest, most difficult turns.

Haughty, imperious, dis- dainful, she came to Lake Placid with 65 World Cup victories and six overall championships, five of them in a row. As the

flagship of Austrian skiing, she had made a career of steam- rolling her opponents, destroying them both in mind and body.

Yet her previous Olympic experience at Sapporo in 1972 had been one of heartbreak. Twice she finished as runnerup to her Swiss rival, Marie-Theres Nadig, both in downhill and giant slalom. Then she spent the 1976 Innsbruck Games at the bedside of her ailing father during a 22-month self-imposed retirement, the culmination of travel fatigue, her recent marriage and Josef Proell's failing health.

Her own lagging finances brought her back a year later and

now, at age 26, she was set for her last season and Olympics. Honing her conditioning with almost computer precision following an early ankle injury, she dismissed December and January losses to Nadig.

"I will be ready at Lake Placid. I have just one goal left, to win a gold medal."

But Moser's personal drama could not match that swirling around the Austrian men's team, a group charged with upholding the awesome tradition of Toni Sailer, Egon Zimmerman and Karl Schranz and that startling run by Franz Klammer four years earlier.

Klammer had been left home, the victim, some said, of too much success. Others hinted he had lost his nerve. In his place had come a group which had not won a single downhill all season: Peter Wirnsberger, Walter Grissman, Harti Weirather, Josef Walcher and a last-minute alternate, Leonhard Stock.

But when Stock consistently turned in the best training times, Austria's coaches elevated him to the starting four and forced a do-or-die run-off among Grissman, Wirnsberger and Walcher for two open positions, Walcher was forced out and the reverberations threatened to split the team as well as the equally competitive Austrian ski manufactuers who supply it.

Still another element in this heady brew is the nature of Whiteface Mountain itself — frightfully steep at the top, agonizingly flat at the bottom. The requisite clearly was for a most talented skier, one who could carve perfect turns at high speed on the steep and twisting upper section, then ride a flat, fast ski to the finish.

Many thought this would be Peter Mueller of Switzerland, the 1979 World Cup downhill champion or Ken Read, chief hope for the first Alpine ski medal ever by a Canadian man.

Cindy Nelson

Then there was the saga of Phil Mahre and a United States team under the glare of a white-hot spotlight of expectation on its home soil.

Slightly less than a year before, Mahre had taken a fall on Whiteface just as it seemed he was about to achieve what

no American had ever done — win an overall World Cup championship. Worse, the entire room of his ankle joint had been shattered into fragments of splintered bone.

In agony, Mahre was flown by private jet to the South Lake Tahoe, Calif., office of orthopedic surgeon Richard Steadman. After Steadman inserted a steel plate and seven screws to bond the broken bones back together, there was doubt that Mahre could ever walk in normal fashion, let alone return to racing.

Rosi Mittermaier and an exhausted Leonhard Stock

Yet here he was, a consistent high finisher in early-season races and America's best hope for a medal, eager to erase the excruciating disappointment of the previous season on this same hill.

There was added irony for a United States team for whom the timing of this Olympics scarcely could have been worse. Two other team veterans also had suffered serious injury on Whiteface — Pete Patterson a broken leg in 1978 and Abbi Fisher torn ligaments in both knees in the same 1979 race, which put Mahre down.

Mahre no longer was a contender in the more physically demanding giant slalom and twin brother Steve was braced and bandaged from knee surgery compounded by a severe ankle injury only a month before the Games.

Cindy Nelson, a bronze medalist in downhill at Innsbruck, was in poor form and the remainder of the team was young and unproven. Still, the thought persisted among the domestic media that the team would give an inspired performance at home and, indeed, Alpine Director Bill Marolt had devised a grand, perhaps desperate, scheme to mitigate these handicaps.

Marolt sequestered his team at Killington, just across the Vermont border and, using a unique helicopter shuttle, ferried his skiers back and forth for downhill training on Whiteface and slalom work at Killington.

Seldom in Olympic history had there been such motivation for so many to succeed.

Two Gold Medals For "Mr. Slalom"

By Jacques Hereng

His nick-name is "Mr. Slalom" and it's a title he rightfully deserves. Sweden's Ingemar Stenmark hasn't lost a race since March, 1978. Coming into the Olympics he'd won 14 consecutive races in world class competition.

But he'd won an Olympic gold medal. At Innsbruck in 1976 Stenmark won a bronze in the giant slalom, finishing behind Heini Hemmi and Ernst Good of Switzerland.

After the first run of the giant slalom Ingemar was in third place behind Andreas Wenzel and Hans Enn of West Germany.

When reporters asked him about his chances of winning the next day he replied, "It's always the same. You people always ask me what went wrong if I don't come in first. Tomorrow will be different. The second run will be more direct, much steeper and more selective."

Stenmark dominated the second run and put Wenzel and Enn in second and third places.

"It did not matter that I was held in high regard when I arrived at the Olympic Village," he admitted after his giant slalom victory. "I felt the pressure mounting and had a hard time fighting it. It took a lot of effort to regain my peace of mind. It is easy to say that one race is the same as the other but that just is not true. The psychological climate of the Games is exceptional."

Three days later the Swedish superstar won the slalom. Again, he had to come from behind on the second run to beat Phil Mahre by half a second. Stenmark became the first man to win more than one Alpine medal since 1968, when Jean-Claude Killy of France won all three gold medals.

Ingemar Stenmark and Yugoslavia Bojan Kriszaj.

Three Medals Make Hanni
The Queen of Lake Placid

By Jacques Hereng

For the first time in history Liechtenstein made the honor roll of Olympic medal winners. The tiny principality nestled high in the Alps between West Germany and Switzerland made it in style with two golds and two silvers in the Alpine events. And they were won by a remarkable sister-brother team — Hanni and Andreas Wenzel.

Hanni won the first of the four medals by placing second to Austria's Annemarie Moser in the downhill. In winning the silver she was less than a second behind

Moser. Their respective times were 1:37.52 and 1:38.33.

Then it was brother Andreas's turn to go for a medal. He made the fastest run of the first day in the giant slalom by zig-zagging through the 56 gates on the 1,354 meter course .32 of a second faster than the favored Ingemar Stenmark. But the great Swede made the second run in 1:20.25 to edge Wenzel by .75 of a second.

The two silver medals were two more than Liechtenstein had ever won in Olympic history, but

Hanni added two golds with her victories in the slaloms. She equalled the record of West Germany's Rosi Mittermaier, who won two golds and a silver at the Innsbruck Games in 1976.

Rosi was not surprised, because after Hanni's second in the downhill, she said, "The hottest slalom skier right now is Hanni Wenzel. She is the one everyone is looking to to measure their times."

Hanni held a half-second lead over Irene Epple of West Germany after the first giant

Hanni Wenzel

slalom run, with Moser in seventh place. She maintained the margin the next day with a combined time of 2:41.66 to Epple's 2:42.12. Annemarie was sixth.

"I think yesterday's run was better," said Wenzel, but I also made no mistakes today. I was not going to lose."

With a gold and silver already won, Hanni was the picture of relaxation as she danced down the slalom course to record a two-run total of 1:25.09, nearly 1.5 seconds ahead of West Germany's Christa Kinshofer.

After receiving a kiss from her brother, Hanni said, "I really didn't count on winning both slaloms. I would have been happy with any of the medals. But today I won because I had no problems. Winning three medals is fantastic. I didn't think I had any chance for a downhill medal. I was just lucky there. But in the slaloms I made no mistakes. I was skiing very good."

The Queen of Lake Placid doesn't talk about retiring. She is only 23 years old. "I love skiing so much that I plan to continue for at least two more seasons," she said.

Those who watched her three-medal performance think that Hanni could win three more at the 1984 Olympics if she decides to go for them.

Two Wenzels, two golds, two silvers

The face of a tragic hero:
Juha Mieto, Finland. He ran
15 km to the point of exhaustion –
then missed the gold medal by
one hundredth of a second.
The curse of merciless technical
science which knows no
pardon measuring the mental
and physical achievement by
positions of a decimal point.

Thomas Wassberg from Sweden
has overtaken the Norwegian
Ove Aunli who started before
him. He takes lenghty strides
towards the finish in a race
against the clock. His hunt
brings him the gold medal
over 15 kilometres.

Toni Innauer – the man who,
with a combination of endless
energy and the will to prove
himself,recovered from a serious
injury, in order to climb to
the ranks of the world elite.
In Lake Placid he achieved
his goal: a gold medal. A just
reward for a sportsman who
won a fight with himself.

Zimyatov (Russia) and his
Finnish rival Mieto take a
slope in an almost "alpine"
downhill posture. Time to
breathe hard; and time to
gather strength again for the
slopes ahead

Powerful double stick start,
lengthy stride. Every metre
of the course must be conquered
by employing the most practical
technique for the surface.
The Russian biathlon fighter
Aljabiev, a master in distributing
his strenght

These photos are small reproductions of full color pictures
on the following pages. The captions for the photos
are alongside each reproduction.

Superstar Wehling Wins
His Third Nordic Gold

By Nicholas Thomas

If anyone could be given a gold medal for jumping into the Olympic history books, it must be Ulrich Wehling. The young GDR physical education teacher collected his third successive gold in the Nordic combined, a truly remarkable record for a man who is still just 27. As was the case in Sapporo 1972 and Innsbruck 1976 it was his skill at the 70 meter jump, which held him in good stead when put alongside his poorer performance in the 15 kilometers cross country. It was a bitterly cold day around the Intervale jump when 19,000 heavily clad spectators stood to watch the first section of the arduous combined event.

Wehling, from the University of Leipzig, showed from the start that he intended to capture that marvelous third gold when he soared out for a first jump of 80 meters. Others followed and landed a short way further down the white slope. But on the second jump Wehling recorded 85 meters, the best distance of the day. He watched out for his main rivals. Jouko Karjalainen of Finland could only manage best jumps of 79 and 81 meters which left him in seventh place overnight, while Wehling's GDR teammate Konrad Winkler did slightly better with 81 meters and 83.5.

That night Wehling, a tall, rangy man went to bed in the Olympic Village happy with his lead on 227.2 points. In second place was a surprised American, Walter Malmquist, with 221.8 points after two best jumps of 80 and 84 meters. Germany's Hubert Schwarz filled the third slot with 219.6 points after leaps of 81 and 84.5 meters.

Next day the same competitors were out on the 15 kilometer course at Mt. Van Hoevenberg. The Russian Fedor Kolchin set a scorching pace over the section, covering the first 5 kilometers in 15:19.6. German hopes rose when Urban Hettich was timed at 15:24.5. Then it was the turn for the strong Karjalainen to put on the pressure. Third fastest over the first 5 he spurted on to cover the 10 kilometers in 29:23.9, while Kolchin and Hettich appeared to be losing wind. Ulrich Wehling, with a wealth of experience behind him, was meanwhile pacing himself in masterly fashion. His 5 kilometer time was 15.54.1, the tenth fastest, while at 10 kilometers he was in ninth position with 30:23.8. At the back of his mind he knew that he had those 227.2 points from the jump up his sleeve.

At the end it was Karjalainen who had completed the course in the fastest time, 47:44.5, to collect 220 points. He now had a total of 429.500 points. Was that enough to win, and spoil Wehling's chances of becoming the first man ever to win the same skiing event at three Winter Olympics? Wehling finally crossed the line in 49:24.5 which gave him 10th place in the cross country and 205 points — a grand total of 432.200 and the coveted gold medal. Karjalainen had to be satisfied with the silver, while Konrad Winkler took 210.820 points for his 48:45.7 cross country, awarding him the bronze medal with a total of 425.320 points. Walter Malmquist did not live up to his earlier

Mr. Thomas is a British free-lance writer.

Thomas Wassberg, gold medalist

hopes with a slow cross country in 52.54.5. This was the third slowest which meant he finished 12th overall.

That is the end of Olympic record breaking for Ulrich Wehling, for he announced his retirement immediately after he had crossed the finishing line. His achievement will head the list of Nordic combined records for many years to come.

Nikolai Zimyatov, a 24-year-old Moscow student, powered his way to victories in the 30 kilometers, 50 kilometers and helped his Russian team win the 4 x 10 kilometers relay. In the first event, the 30 kilometers, he did not allow any of his opponents the slightest chance of thinking they may be heading towards the gold medal. Zimyatov was the fastest over each of the three laps and covered the course in 1.27:02.80, almost 32 seconds faster than his teammate Vasili Rochev, who skied home for the silver.

Ivan Lebanov of Bulgaria took the bronze in 1.28:03.87, his country's only medal of the Lake Placid Olympics. Lebanov's surprise success pushed the fancied Scandinavians from the medal list. Thomas Wassberg of Sweden was fourth, while the giant from Finland, Juha Mieto, was seventh. But these two were to fight out the closest drama of the Olympics later. This came in the 15 kilometer race when the same set of faces assembled at the cold Mt. Van Hoevenberg start.

Barbara Petzold

Wassberg, starting nine places behind Mieto knew what he had to beat. His Swedish teammates were along the track cheering him on. He completed the 5 kilometers in 13:22.08 to put him slightly ahead. He had the fastest time of 25:47.14 at the 10k mark, but could he keep up the pace? As the seconds ticked away on the bottom corner of television screens and it became obvious that Wassberg did have the strength to perhaps marginally capture the gold, all typewriters stopped clattering in the writing room of the downtown Press Center. All eyes watched the finishing line and the clock stopped at 41:57.63. The Swede had done it, by one hundredth of a second.

What a race, and as usual the first man to congratulate Wassberg was Mieto, probably the most popular man on the cross country circuit.

Zimyatov's next gold came in the 4 x 10 kilometers relay when he skied on the last leg and recorded the second fastest time for the distance, 28:27.70. The fastest time went to guess who — Juha Mieto. It soon became apparent that the Russian team had used their wax more expertly on what turned out to be the warmest day of the Olympics. The temperature at the start was just on zero centigrade but by the time the last leg men were on their way had risen to 7 degrees. First away for the Soviet squad was Vasili Rochev who gave his teammates a few heart murmurs shortly after the start when he tangled with another skier and fell down.

Rochev scrambled up quickly and was soon setting such a hot pace again that he handed a clear 24 second lead to Nikolai Bazhukov. This was soon wiped out by the second Norwegian Per Knut Aaland who put his country in the lead with a leg time of 29:26.77. Ove Aunli set out to try to keep Norway in front but soon he heard the sound of approaching skies and Russia's third man Evseny Beliaev went past him. He passed on to Zimyatov and the result was in doubt no longer. His fast time allowed the Russians a total time of 1.57:03.46.

The Norwegians held on to the silver medal with 1.58:45.77, while Finland took the bronze thanks to a last leg of 28:16.64 which stopped their total time at just 0.18 of a second over two hours. Mieto's phenomenal speed pushed a disappointed German quartet into fourth place and a trip home without a medal.

This was not the end for Zimyatov or Mieto as they had yet to meet over 50 kilometers.

Juha Mieto went off to a great cheer at number 38 among 47 starters, ninety seconds ahead of Zimyatov. At the halfway point Mieto was lying eighth and people in the know began talking of how he was better suited to the shorter races. Over the last 15 kilometers he bored through the woodland like a steam train to take his second silver medal of the Games. Zimyatov had finished in an unbeatable 2.27:24.60, while Mieto had taken revenge on the young Russian for his disappointing defeat by Wassberg earlier in the week.

For those who remember the women's Nordic events at Innsbruck 1976 there appeared to be a "here we go again" message when the 5 kilometers got underway. All the familiar names and medal winners were at the starting line — Russians Raisa Smetanina, Galina Kulakova and Nina Baldicheva, with their old rival from Finland, Helena Takalo. In the end it was Smetanina who took the gold medal in 15:06.92, just compensation for having to accept the silver four years earlier. On that occasion she finished behind Takalo, but this time she narrowly beat another Finn, Hikka Riihivuori, who clocked 15:11.96. The other big names were pushed away from medal places by young Kveta Jeriova from Czechoslovakia with a time of 15:23.44.

In the 10 kilometer event the older stars all finished among the first six but this time just Helena Takalo took a medal, winning the bronze behind her Finnish teammate Riihivuori who took her silver tally to two. The winner was Barbara Petzold from the DDR with a time of 30:31.54. Riihivuori finished in 30:35.05 while Takalo took 30:45.25. The three Russians had to be content with also-ran tags. Then came the 4 x 5 kilometers relay and this time the old hands from Russia, and Finland were given a sound beating by the young girls from the GDR. The foursome of Marlies Rostock, Carola Anding, Veronika Hesse and Barbara Petzold was so fast that each member turned in the fastest time over her leg. Their winning total was 1.02:11.10.

The more experienced Russian squad of Baldicheva, Rocheva, Kulakova and Smetanina held on for the silver in 1.03:18.30 while the young Norwegians (Brit Pettersen, Anette Boe, Marit Myrmael, Berit Anuli) sneaked in with a time of 1.04:13.50 to win the bronze medal. The experienced Finnish team was fifth.

Over on the 70-meter ski jump at Intervale again there was further drama when American jumper Jeff Davis could not believe his luck when he recorded 91 meters with his first attempt, much to the delight of the thousands huddled together in the cold at the bottom. The judges took one look at his success and decided that the starting gate would have to be moved to a lower point as there was the danger that the expert jumpers and probable medal winners to follow might soar on into the food tent at the bottom. So Davis's moment of glory was short-lived and the first set of jumpers ordered to start again.

In the end it was Austrian Anton Innauer who deservedly collected the gold medal with jumps of 89 and 90 meters and total points of 266.3. This gold would be added to the silver medal he won in the 90-meter event in his native Innsbruck four years earlier. There was an unexpected battle for the second spot which resulted in Manfred Deckert (GDR) and Hirokazu Yagi (Japan) tying with 249.2 points. Deckert jumped 85 and

88 meters, while Yagi recorded 87 and 83.5. They both received silver medals and no bronze was awarded. In the more spectacular 90-meter event, Anton Innauer was unable to improve his medal record when he met two Finnish jumpers in top form. Young Jouko Tormanen opened with a 114.5 leap, then astounded all the experts with a gold medal winning jump of 117 meters. Hubert Neuper (Austria) produced consistent 113 and 114.5 distances but his points tally of 262.4 could not touch Tormanen's 271. A second Finn, Jari Puikkonen, made it a great day for his country by taking the bronze medal with jumps of 110.5 and 108.5 and total points of 248.5. Innauer finished fourth with 245.7. Tormanen's triumph brought Finland its only gold medal of the Olympics

and delighted teammates threw him so far in the air with glee he almost needed skis to bring him down safely.

In the biathlon events, eight of the nine medals were shared by the Soviet Union and the GDR. The relay, as has been the custom for the past three Olympics, was won by the Russians and in the team was 33-year-old Alexander Tikhonov who in turn picked up his fourth gold medal. Superior shooting once again brought success to the Soviet Quartet, made up this time of old man Tikhonov and three newcomers Vladimir Alikin, Vladimir Barnaschov and Anatoli Aljabiev. Their total time was 1.34:03.27. Not far behind came the GDR group of Mathias Jung, Klaus Siebert, Frank Ullrich and Eberhard Rosch with a time of 1.34:56.99. Then to

finally break the Eastern bloc domination of the biathlon events came the German team, Franz Bernreiter, Hansi Estner, Peter Angerer and Gerd Winkler, with a time of 1.37:30.26. In the individual events the starts were Frank Ullrich (GDR) and Anatoli Aljabiev (Soviet Union). Ullrich won the 10 kilometer event with a time of 32:10.69 with Aljabiev taking the bronze. His Russian teammate Vladimir Alikin collected the silver with 32:53.10. In the 20 kilometer event the honors were reversed. Aljabiev won the gold with a time of 1.08:16.31 and no penalties. Ullrich grabbed the silver with a time of 1.08:27.79 and three penalties, while Eberhard Rosch of the GDR took the bronze in 1.11:11.73.

Biathlon rifle shooting

Not a Sport For The Weak of Heart

By Ray Grass

It was expected that Switzerland and East Germany would do well in the two bobsledding events . . . and they did. The two technically neighboring countries took home all the medals — gold, silver and bronze. They beat a course some called dangerous, others called unquestionably the fastest in the world. They left nothing in their path but some small chips of ice, a rush of air and a few unanswered questions . . . namely, should the United States have, in fact, made last-minute changes in its four-man bobsled teams?

The Swiss won the two-man gold and the East Germans the silver and bronze. The East Germans won the four-man gold and bronze and the Swiss the silver. The United States finished five and six in the two-man and 12th and 13th in the four-man. West Germany, thought at first to be on the same level as the Swiss and the East Germans, could do no better than a 10th in the two-man and a 9th in the four-man.

Bobsledding is not a sport for the weak of heart, especially on the modernized and artificially refrigerated track at Mt. Van Hoevenberg. Nor, as the U.S. was to find out, is it a sport where history counts for much but talk.

In the 1932 Olympics at Lake Placid, the U.S. went 1-2 in the four-man and won the two-man on a track at the very site — Mt. Van Hoevenberg. It was also the year Eddie Eagan became the first man to win gold medals in both the Winter and Summer Games. In 1920 he won the

Mr. Grass is a writer on the staff of the Deseret News in Salt Lake City,Utah.

Swiss two-man bobsled champions

Pushing off in the four-man bobsled run.

light heavyweight boxing title gold and in 1932 he was a member of the winning four-man bobsled team.

For the XIII Olympiad, the U.S. was running on home ice, so to speak, had raced well on the course before the Olympics and had in its fold Willie Davenport, who along with bobsled teammate Jeffrey Gadley represented the first black Americans in the Olympic Winter Games. Davenport also happened to be going for Eagan's record. Davenport won a gold medal in the 1968 Summer Games in the 110-meter hurdles.

For a short time, it looked as if the U.S. team might medal and Davenport would realize his goal to win a second gold. In pre-Olympic trials on the Lake Placid course, which happens to be the only bobsled course in the Western Hemisphere, the American team in "USA I" set

a new course record of 1:01.17. Members of the team included captain and driver Robert Hickey, Davenport, Gadley and Jeffrey Jordan. Things were doing well . . . everything was going just as planned. The year 1932 was about to be relived.

But then things started to go wrong. First off, Erich Schaerer, driver, and Josef Benz of Switzerland, set a course record, under cloudy, threatening skies, on their first of four runs, for the two-man, a 1:01.87 (time differences between the two-man and the four-man sleds was about two seconds). The team went on to win the gold with a combined time of 4:09.36.

The East German team of Bernhard Germeshausen and Hans Jurgen Gerhardt finished second in 4:10.93.

U.S. driver Howard Siler and passenger Dick Nalley finished four runs in 4:11.73 for fifth and the best finish by a U.S. team since 1956. That finish prompted Siler, a bruising 6-foot, 200-pound man, to say, "We're coming on. We're not going to stop until we have the flag-up. We're going to medal in the four-man." A sixth-place finish by U.S. driver Brent Rushlaw and rider Joseph Tyler had people wondering, at least. A fifth and sixth of 20 teams, after all, wasn't that bad.

Then the trouble started. Days before teams were to have begun their runs for the gold, controversy of a very large magnitude slapped the U.S. sledders right in the face. It was reported that in an earlier interview Davenport had made reference to the idea that bobsled racing was a, "Rich, white man's sport." The next day bobsled coach Gary Sheffield called for tryouts. For what reason? Sheffield said because the two U.S. teams might be juggled around, "in hopes of making up some of the time we're losing to the Swiss and the Germans." Others, close to the situation, said Davenport's remarks had caused some dissension and that Sheffield thought it best to replace him.

Hickey, though, ordered his team, Davenport included, not to report to the tryouts and told Sheffield that his team was solid, that he wouldn't make any changes. In Davenport's defense, he said that he was tired of all the fuss. "Here it is the 1980 Winter Games and I pick up a paper this morning and read, 'Davenport causes controversy.' There ain't no controversy. There never has been . . . a reporter asked me if I didn't think bobsleding was a sport for rich whites. I simply answered back, 'I'm in it.' That's all I said." He went on to say that the controversy, to him, was disheartening. "Here it is, the 1980 Olympics, and suddenly the competition is not important. What I said a month ago is suddenly so important." So was there dissension on the team? Davenport said no! Hickey said no! Sheffield said yes!

Then suddenly a new twist was thrown into the boiling pot. Just one day before the four-man competition was to have begun, both U.S. teams opted to use new sleds. Both teams were still running a second behind the Swiss and the German sleds and so they thought new sleds might do the trick. "I was against it," said Sheffield. "I told them I thought it was a mistake. They wanted to go with

Bobsledders, Jeff Jordan of Canada and Jeff Gadley and Willie Davenport of the USA.

the new sleds, though, so — they went."

From the first run on, the Americans were a second late and a few hundred feet short. The winning East German team set a new course record on their very first run, a :59.86. Hickey's team could only manage a 1:01.49 and Siler's team, in USA II sled, could only match the time, a 1:01.49. From that point on the days became warmer and the times slower.

It was a disappointing finish, needless to say, for the Americans.

Did the new sleds hurt the U.S. times? "I don't think they helped," said Sheffield. Did the Davenport problem hurt the U.S. times? "I'd rather not comment on that," said Sheffield. Could the U.S. have done better? "Yes," he concluded.

As for the course itself, it was called by the American teams, "fast and dangerous." It had an average incline of 9.5 percent over its 1,557.87 meters and 16 curves, two considered monuments to the skill and

daring of those who survived them.

The two curves, where many drivers agreed the races were won or lost, were "Shady" and "Zig-Zag." Shady is an almost 180-degree hairpin curve that had to be negotiated at speeds up to 90 miles per hour. Zig-Zag is a treacherous, G-pulling (some say at most four G's, or one more G than the maximum allowed by NASA for crew members on a space shot), breath-taking, "S-Turn." Teams were required to practice a minimum of five days before the start of each event to get the feel of these two turns.

As one driver put it, "This one is a driver's course. Anybody can run it — but doing it correctly is something else. If you come off Shady thinking ahead to Zig-Zag instead of the Little-S turn that comes in between, then you're in trouble."

Erich Schaerer from Switzerland is reckoned to be the best bob pilot in the world. Nobody pilots his bob more exactly or more professionally through bumpy straights and steep walls. The ideal complement to pilot Schaerer is his brake man Josef Benz.

Only a four man bob in complete harmony with itself can go faster than its rivals. The perspective in this photograph shows how difficult it is to keep in line behind the pilot at a speed of 130 and a pressure of more than 49.

Two silver medals for Italy in toboganning. Second place for Hildgartner in the single-seater competition. Haspinger (photo below) fell and missed gold on the last metres of the fourth run. Silver for Gschnitzer and Brunner – reward for their experience and preparation.

The photograph which gives one an impression of how fast the tobogganists steer their toboggan down the ice channel. There is always the danger of a fall on the Lake Placid course. It all depends on the reaction speed in the bends which rush so quickly.

Made it. Bob USA II just a few metres from the finish. The bob, that was one of the great attractions for the spectators in Lake Placid. Titillation of the nerves, they like that more than anything. And the bobhunt with speeds of around 140 km/h offers something of this.

These photos are small reproductions of full color pictures on the following pages. The captions for the photos are alongside each reproduction.

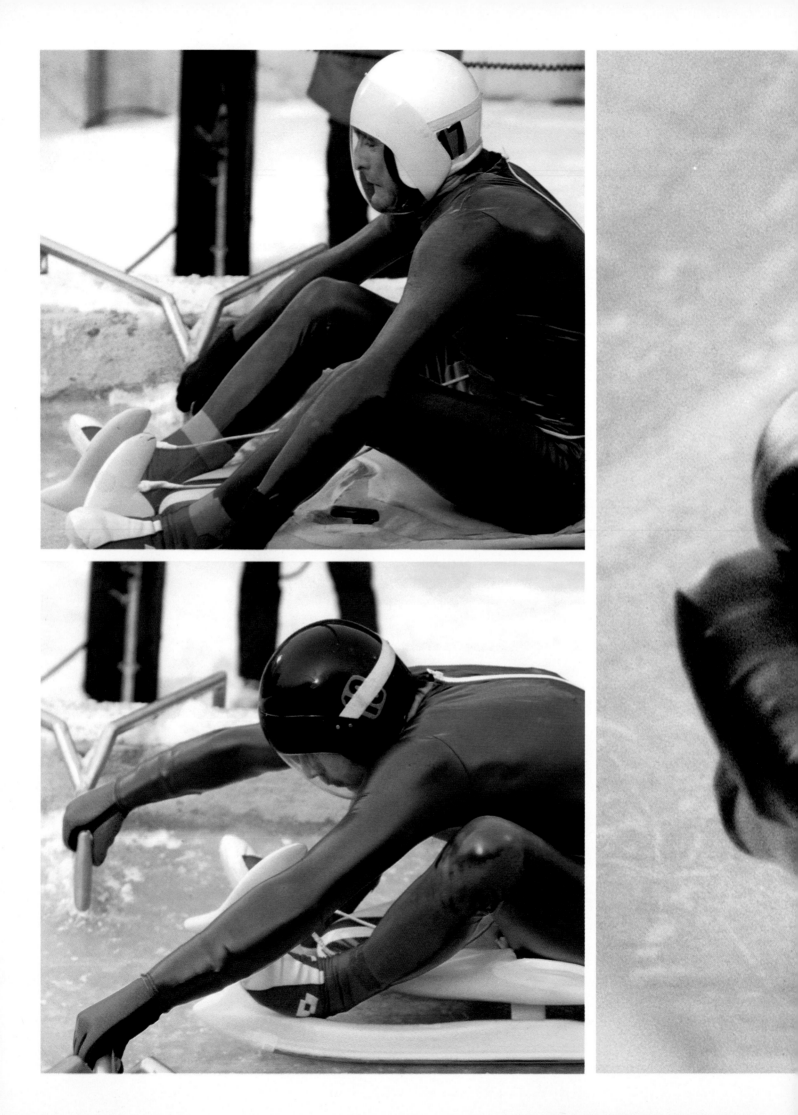

The Games of the XXII Olympiad Moscow USSR

July 19 - August 3, 1980

Russian Hosts Win A Record 80 Gold Medals at '80 Games

By C. Robert Paul, Jr.

The Games of the XXII Olympiad made history all along the competition front. For the first time in Olympic History at Montreal four years earlier, the host nation failed to have a single gold medalist. At Moscow, the U.S.S.R. won more gold medals (80) than any previous host, or participating nation.

In a closing telecast by the National Broadcasting Company on August 3, a commentator for the British Broadcasting Company almost whispered to the USA televiewers, "The United States was missed at the Games."

The unwarranted incursion of Soviet troops in Afghanistan left its mark on the Games. It has been reported that up to 36 countries didn't participate, many because of the Soviets' disturbing invasion of a friendly, defenseless nation. Ten of the 81 participating nations failed to take part in the Opening Ceremony, indicating an extreme distaste for the Soviet disturbance of world-wide peace while serving as host of the single strongest social force dedicated to peace, good fellowship, and a developer of better understanding among the nations of the world. It has been also reported that six nations marched in the Opening Ceremony behind the International Olympic Flag (rather than their national ensigns) reflecting their own displeasure with the Soviet posture against Afghanistan.

The worst fears of the detractors of the Olympic Games really *never* materialized. From the point of view of superb performances on the field of competition, the Games of the XXII Olympiad can be ranked with the best of the previous

Games. This rating has been merited in spite of the absence of such countries as the United States of America, Canada, Japan, Norway, Kenya, West Germany, the Republic of China (Taiwan) and the People's Republic of China.

The host organizing Committee reported entries had been made for 5,928 athletes, compared to 6,152 at Montreal and a record 8,144 at Munich in 1972. With 80 participating National Olympic Committees (see page 129 for a list of the countries) this was the smallest number since 67 NOCs sent athletes to Melbourne 24 years ago.

The print media dutifully reported there were 35 world records established, opposed to 38 at Montreal. The number of records, was also favorable for Olympic records set in track and field, swimming, shooting, archery and weightlifting compared to Montreal.

At no previous Olympic Games since World War I have two countries dominated the competitions to the same extent as did the host nation and the Democratic Republic of Germany (East Germany). An analysis of each of the sports on the program indicates almost total success for the U.S.S.R. (placing first or second in all individual

Misha, mascot of the games

The Opening Ceremony was awe-inspiring.

sports and placing either first, second or third in *every* men's and women's team sport). It is doubtful that this performance record will ever be equaled should the Games in the future witness entries from a full complement of National Olympic Committees.

One of the key issues concerning the Olympic movement was "nationalism." The International Olympic Committee at Lake Placid had adopted legislation permitting nations to use the IOC's five interlaced rings' flag in place of their own ensigns on all occasions, including victory ceremonies. Probably a dozen Western European NOCs chose to use the IOC flag.

When the winners of the 4,000 meter individual pursuit cycling competition were honored, three Olympic flags were hoisted as the gold, silver and bronze medals were awarded. In place of the national anthem of Switzerland, in honor of champion Robert Dill-Bundi, the band played the Olympic hymn. The media reported laconically, "While the Olympic hymn was played it was much to the displeasure of the Soviet crowd."

By any measuring stick, the Opening Ceremony was awe-inspiring. Those who were privileged to join the throng of about 100,000 acclaimed the Opening Ceremony as the most impressive in the history of the Games. Quoted below are a few lines penned from Lenin Stadium by veteran sportswriter Will Grimsley of *The Associated Press.*

"Take the Super Bowl, the Radio City Rockettes, Ringling Brothers Circus, and the Bolshoi Ballet, multiply them by 1,000 and you have a rough idea of the dazzling Opening Ceremony of the Games of the XXII Olympiad.

"Yet despite its vast scope and artistry, involving some 8,000 of the Soviet Union's most talented youths honed by months of rehearsals, there was a rancorous note to these festivities, hailing the start of sport's greatest event.

"Oldtimers who had seen every Olympics since Adolph Hitler's Nazi Games in 1936, agreed that there had never been another opening ceremony to match it.

"It probably was the best of any sports event ever."

Introduced by veteran IOC member, Count Jean de Beaumont of France, at Lake Placid in February, the powerful international group adopted a by-law permitting nations to use the Olympic flag and the Olympic anthem at award ceremonies, in place of their flags and anthems. The move was viewed not only as an Afghanistan-related protest but also an experiment in denationalizing future Games.

The Stars and Stripes was unfurled in the stands at the Opening Ceremony.

How successful was the move for denationalization? Writing in the *Los Angeles Times,* Kenneth Reich commented,

"But judging from reactions here — not so much among the Soviets as among the foreign tourists and the teams and Olympic officials from the Western countries involved — it is an experiment that is *not* catching on.

"In recent days, British, French, Dutch and Italian Olympic officials have all expressed hope that at the Los Angeles Games in 1984, they will be able to reinstate the national flags and anthems.

"The ongoing IOC president, Lord Killanin of Ireland, has said here in recent days that he counts himself among those who have 'always felt there is too much flag-raising and anthem-playing' at the Olympics.

"But this apparently remains a minority view within the IOC. Ashwini Kumar, an IOC executive board member from India, said that he sees no prospect of further moves to drop nationalistic symbols."

A minor flap was avoided during the closing ceremony. IOC Protocol dictates that the flag of the next host nation be raised, along with those of Greece and the current host. The IOC accepted a strongly worded but friendly request from President Carter's legal counsel that the Stars-and-Stripes *not* be raised. In its place, the flag of the City of Los Angeles was hoisted alongside those of the U.S.S.R. and Greece, the original host country.

As at all Olympic Games there were charges and counter-charges, speculations, allegations, and emotional displays perhaps overplayed by the mass media. Judging in gymnastics and measurements in a couple of field events in the athletics competition drew the ire of writers and sportscasters.

For example, Mexico City police protected the U.S.S.R. embassy there the day following the disqualification of the defending champion in the 20-kilometer race walk. Bautista of Mexico was disqualified about two-kilometers (1-1/4 miles) from the finish line. It is still difficult to believe that the Soviet state television cut away from the U.S.S.R.-Yugoslavia basketball game, with several minutes yet to be played, simply because the Yugoslavs were winning. (It is even more incongrous that a newscast was substituted.) The Soviet team then knotted the cout at 81-81 in the closing moments and lost 101-91 in the five-minute overtime period. At the conclusion of the newscast it was reported the state television whispered, "we lost." There were no further comments.

Television coverage in the United States was minimal. Apparently the Soviet Union and the Organizing Committee invoked IOC regulations prohibiting extensive TV coverage (other than footage supplied by the host organizing committee), except for NBC which retained its rights to televise as much as they wanted to televise. NBC, on closing day, presented a 90-minute program with many delightful highlights from swimming, track and field and gymnastics.

In rapid-fire order here are happenings which are etched in one's mind reflecting on the 1980 Olympic Games:

• Sebastian Coe-Steve Ovett confrontations in the 800m and 1,500m races in track and field. These two British middle distance runners each won a race, with the underdog prevailing in each of the classic races. Ovett scored a major upset in the 800m and Coe came back to score a triumph in the 1,500m.

• Daley Thompson, Great Britain, four days shy of 22, became the youngest decathlon champion since Bob Mathias, USA. He said he'll stick around and defend his title at Los Angeles . . . and he told Mathias that he would try for 3 gold medals.

• Miruts Yifter, Ethiopia, missed the starting line for the 5,000 meters at Munich and was forced to leave the Montreal Olympic Village when his team was called home. But at Moscow the "ageless" Ethiopian soldier was a convincing winner of the 5,000 and 10,000 meter races.

• Allan Wells, the reformed Scottish long jumper, caught Cuba's Silvio Leonard at the tape and was awarded the gold medal in the 100 meters.

• The second longest long jump in history (exceeded only by Bob Beamon's 29-2 leap in the rarified atmosphere at Mexico City) was credited to Lutz Dombrowski, East Germany, 28 feet 1/4 inch. Lutz had been on the doubtful list until he exhibited "healthiness" in a special meet to test him under "game conditions."

• The Soviet men and the East German women completely dominated the swimming events. The East German women placed 1, 2, 3 in six events and won 11 of 13; Vladimir Salnikov, U.S.S.R., broke the 15-minute barrier in winning the 1,500 meter freestyle race.

• The East Germans were wonderful in both men's and women's rowing. In the eight-race men's regatta, the East Germans won seven events and placed third in the other one, single sculls. In the women's regatta, the East Germans won four, placed second in one and third in the other in the six races.

• Although the U.S.S.R. placed first, second or third in all men's and women's team sports, the biggest setback of the Games, to the home fans, was the Soviets placing no higher than third in men's basketball. They lost to Italy and Yugoslavia in consecutive games in the preliminary round.

• A tip of the hat to two '76 victors who successfully defended their titles at Moscow: East Germany's Waldemar Cierpinski in the marathon (Abebe Bikila of Ethiopia with victories in 1960 and 1964, is the only other double marathon champion) and Tatyana Kazankina defeating East Germany's Christiane Wartenberg in the 1,500 meters.

• Lothar Thoms, East Germany, eclipsed a 16-year-old world record in winning the one-kilometer time trial in cycling.

• Cuba dominated the boxing. Teofilo Stevenson, 28, won his third straight heavyweight title and stretched his Olympic victory skein to 12 (unparalleled in Olympic boxing history, although Hungary's Lazlo Papp had won three gold medals in two different weight classes). In retrospect, the Cubanos won six gold medals (the USA twice had won five, including 1976), two silver and two bronze in the eleven weight classes.

• No world records were set in the men's running events, but three new marks were produced in the field events, by as many European countries. Hammer thrower Yuri Sedykh was credited with a toss of 268 feet, 4 inches; East Germany's Gerd Wessig high-jumped 7 feet, 8-3/4 inches; and, perhaps the most fetching of all was the winning vault of Poland's Wladyslaw Kozakiewicz, 18 feet, 11-1/4 inches.

• Zimbabwe (formerly known as Rhodesia and absent from the last three Olympic Games by dictate of the IOC) had its new National Olympic Committee "recognized" for competition about five weeks prior to the opening of the Games. Its women's field hockey team won the first-ever women's tournament. However, the five strongest nations had decided, prior to the Games, to pursue a policy of non-participation.

• In the Soviet Union, the No. 1 sports hero for almost a decade has been super heavyweight lifter, Vasily Alexeev. In the last two years Vasily has been beset by a series of injuries and indispositions. He failed to make his "opening" snatch lift of 396 pounds and was disqualified.

Alexeev's "shadow" proved himself a worthy successor when he equaled Alexeev's Olympic record for the combined lifts, 790 pounds. The new champion is Sultan Rakhmanov who weighed in at 319 pounds prior to the competition.

• Soviet sailor Valentin Mankin won the only gold medal for his country in the waters off Tallinn. This was his third, having previously won the Finn Class at Mexico's Alcapulco course in 1968, and then capturing the brass ring in the Tornado class at Kiel, West Germany. He also medaled in the Tornado class at Kingston, Ontario, four years ago.

• The host country dominated both men's and women's gymnastics for the first time. There was no real successor to Olga Korbut ('72) and Nadia Comaneci ('76) among the women, but the all-around champion was one of the lesser-known Soviet gymnasts — 18-year-old Yelena Davydova. With Japan absent, the well-balanced Soviet team walked off with team and individual honors in the men's division. All-time record: '79 all-around world champion, Alexandr Ditiatin, won eight (maximum) medals, including three gold, three silver, and two bronze.

The Los Angeles Flag replaced the American at the Closing Ceremony

• The French fencers finished No. 1 in all men's and women's competition. France won three of the four team titles (failing to place in the sabre competition won by the U.S.S.R.), and garnering gold in the women's foil (Pascale Trinquet), along with one second and one third in the other individual competitions.

• Blood is thicker than water: In the rowing events ten pairs of brothers (four of them twins) participated in the regatta. The Landvoigts of East Germany retained their laurels in the pairs without coxswain. They edged the Pimenov twins of the U.S.S.R. for the gold. The other twins were the Stockers of Switzerland in the fours with coxswain, and the Trzcinskis of Poland in the fours without coxswain. Brothers were also in the Austrian, Dutch and Brzilian quadruple sculls and the fours with coxswain from East Germany and the U.S.S.R. The final set of brothers rowed in the Hungarian eight.

SMILES (1) When asked for his opinion about the Soviet basketball coach Alexander Gomelsky's charge that the officials botched a call that could have given his team a win against Yugoslavia in a preliminary round game, the official scorer, Leon Wandel was reported to have commented:

"Mr. Gomelsky can say what he wants to. It's a free country."

(2) The first question asked of Miruts Yifter, the balding Eithiopian distance runner (he's father of five children) after winning the 10,000-meter race was "How do you pronounce your name?"

The Dutch journalist who made the inquiry knows how annoying mispronunciations of names can be. His name is Niko Vanderszweetslotenmacher.

•

Frustrations Cast Aside: The Tanzanian field hockey team in the men's tournament (added late because of defections of certain of the powers) lost its first two games by the combined score of 30-0. The coach cooly announced that he was sticking with the same goalie, Leopold Gracias.

Boxers from the tiny African nation of Benin had to get their kicks and thrills from merely competing. Two of them were in the ring less than 2½ minutes.

In the decathlon, Columba Blanco, Sierra Leone, put the 16-pound shot a mere 30 feet and tossed the javelin only 118 feet and finished the ten events with 5,080 points — more than 3,400 points behind the winner, Daley Thompson, Great Britain.

Libya, a last-minute addition to the men's volleyball tournament, got their games over in a hurry and didn't come close to winning a single set. When the real powers meet on the court the games can last 90 minutes; the Libyans usually were showering within 30 minutes after the opening serve.

•

In addition to some 36 nations that decided not to participate, there were additional instances of defections by strong entries in certain sports. What sports were most affected by the defections?

Certainly, the equestrian sports and rowing were crippled. Among the team sports, men's and women's field hockey and men's and women's volleyball had sub-par fields. As a result of the missing teams in the two field hockey tournaments the U.S.S.R. surprisingly snared bronze medals in each.

•

A warm salute to the youngest athlete in the Games — North Korea's Jong Sil Choe. She gracefully executed one of the more daring maneuvers in women's gymnastics by doing a 2½-somersault off the vault — the only woman to attempt the move.

The Future Is Here

On the first ballot, members of the International Olympic Committee elected Juan Antonio Samaranch (one day short of his 60th birthday) its seventh president since 1896. He has been serving as the Spanish Ambassador to the Soviet Union. He has relinquished his ambassadorial post and announced that in the fall of the year he will make the IOC headquarters in Lausanne his headquarters.

He will serve an eight-year term and is eligible for re-election for terms of four years each.

Samaranch's initial sports association, according to Neil Amdur of *The New York Times,* was as president of the Spanish Roller Skating Federation, a sport which is not on the Olympic Games' program, but one which was introduced to the Pan American Games at San Juan last summer.

In his first formal press conference upon taking over as *Numero Uno* the day after the close of the Games, President Samaranch promised additional studies would be undertaken by the IOC Eligibility Commission.

Note: The Games of the XXIII Olympiad are scheduled to open in Los Angeles, July 28, 1984.

PARTICIPATING NOCs

Prior to the opening of the competition on July 19, the International Olympic Committee announced that the following National Olympic Committees had filed entry blanks for athletes to compete in the Games of the XXII Olympiad:

Afghanistan, Algeria, Andorra, Angola, Australia, Austria, Belgium, Benin, Burma, Botswana, Brazil, Bulgaria, Cameroon, Cyprus, Colombia, Congo, Costa Rica, Cuba, Czechoslovakia.

Denmark, Dominican Republic, Ecuador, East Germany, Ethiopia, Finland, France, Great Britain, Greece, Guatemala, Guinea, Guyana, Hungary, Iceland, India, Iraq, Ireland, Italy.

Jamaica, Jordan, Kuwait, Laos, Lesotho, Lebanon, Libya, Luxembourg, Madegascar, Mali, Malta, Mexico, Mongolia, Mozambique, Nepal, Netherlands, Nicarauga, Nigeria, New Zealand, North Korea.

Peru, Poland, Puerto Rico, Portugal, Romania, San Marino, Senegal, Seychelles, Sierra Leone, Sri Lanka, Spain, Sweden, Switzerland, Syria, Tanzania, Trinidad and Tobago, Uganda, U.S.S.R., Venezuela, Vietnam, Yugoslavia, Zambia, Zimbabwe.

Total: 80 National Olympic Committees had athletes participating in the Games.

Farewell until 1984.

Moscow Diary: Superb Pageantry and Performances

By Peter Diamond
and
Linda Passudettie

Misha was present in many forms.

MOSCOW DIARY

For all but a few citizens of the United States, the games of the XXII Olympiad were "The Forgotten Olympics". Expected to be the biggest and most widely publicized games in history, the 1980 Olympics were, in fact, given relatively little attention in the U.S., as a result of the Western boycott. Still, despite the absence of the United States, Kenya, Japan, West Germany, Canada and the People's Republic of China, among others, the Moscow Olympics were held in first-rate facilities and a good deal of the competition was also first rate. A chronicle from two Americans who attended games:

Saturday, July 19 — Eighty nations marched in the Opening Ceremonies, 16 staging a protest by carrying Olympic flags, rather than their national flags. The pageantry was spectacular as 17,000 Soviets performed on the field, while a card section of 5,000 soldiers provided 174 different backgrounds. The soldiers had been practicing one year for this day, and in order to compose the various "human pictures", each man had nine colored flags, three balloons, two fans, six tunics and five hats. Three-time Olympic triple jump champion Viktor Saneev carried the Olympic flame into the stadium and passed it to 1972 basketball gold medalist Sergei Belov for the lighting of the Olympic flame. Belov climbed to the cauldron on a human stairway of 154 boards, held by the soldiers in the card section.

Sunday, July 20 — Competition began today with men's gymnastics and swimming the major events. In gymnastics the Soviets looked invincible in the men's compulsories and moved to a commanding lead. One wonders how the Americans — Kurt Thomas, Bart Conner and the rest — would have done. It was also a big day for the Soviets at the pool as Sergei Fesenko won his country's first men's swimming gold medal ever. The big disappointment was University of California-trained Par Arvidsson of Sweden, the pre-race favorite, who finished seventh. After the race he was philosophical: "I just didn't swim very well. I have no excuse. There's still the 100 'fly on the 23rd, and that's my best event."

Monday, July 21 — Women's gymnastics started today, and even though Nadia Comaneci is four inches taller and 15 pounds heavier than in Montreal, she still earned a 10 on the first day of competition, just as she did four years ago. But her perfect score on the balance beam was matched by Natalia Shaposhnikova of the Soviet Union, who earned a 10 in the vault. The Romanian women unseated the Soviets as world team champions in 1979, but this year it looks as if the Soviets will retake the gold. Four years ago Barbara Krause of East Germany was one of the world's top freestylers, but just before the start of the Montreal Games, she became seriously ill and missed an opportunity to gain a near-certain gold medal. Now, she is one of the veterans of the East German team, and tonight she won her first individual gold, setting a world record in the 100 freestyle.

Tuesday, July 22 — The Soviets clinched their ever first team title in men's gymnastics, and the only question now is which man will get the first 10 in Olympic history. Aleksandr Ditiatin's rings exercise received a 9.95, and he looks ready. Swimming history was made as Vladimir Salnikov of the Soviet Union became the first man to swim 1500 meters in under 15 minutes. Brian Goodell of the U.S. had missed "the barrier" by 2.40 seconds in Montreal and their confrontation in Moscow would have been one of the highlights of the Games. Two men — breaststroker Duncan Goodhew of Great Britain who attends North Carolina State and trapshooter Luciano Giavannetti of Italy became the first men to have the Olympic flag raised at their victory ceremonies.

Wednesday, July 23 — Today is the day that Comaneci proved she is not invincible. Thought the Soviets were on their way to another team title, Comaneci was leading in the individual all-around phase of the competition until she mounted the uneven bars . . . and fell off. Her score of 9.5 means that it will be extremely difficult for her to retain her individual all-around title. There was also controversy at the diving pool as Soviet Aleksandr Portnov, the eventual gold medalist, was granted a re-dive on his eighth dive following a disturbance on his original attempt. Protests by both the silver and bronze medalists, Carlos Giron of Mexico and Franco Cagnotto of Italy, and

Three-time champion Viktor Saneev carries the Olympic Flame into the stadium.

East Germany's Falk Hoffmann were disallowed. In swimming, Par Arvidsson finally got his gold medal, edging Roger Pyttel of East Germany by two hundredths of a second in the 100 'fly.

Thursday, July 24 — The gymnastics started quietly at the Luzhniki Palace of Sports as Ditiatin convincingly won the men's individual all-around title in the afternoon. In second place was his teammate, Nikolai Andrianov, who won seven medals in Montreal, but had performed unevenly over the past four years. Some had written him off completely. The women's all-around ended with Elena Davydova of the Soviet Union as the somewhat surprising winner, and Nadia Comaneci as a furious co-silver medalist with Maxi Gnauck of East Germany. In her last exercise of the evening Comaneci needed a 9.95 on the balance beam to retain the gold medal she had won in Montreal, but the judges awarded her only a 9.85. A furious protest from Bela Karolyi, Comaneci's coach, and Mme. Simionescu, the Romanian head judge on the balance beam, ensued and finally, after nearly 30 minutes of argument, Mme, Berger of East Germany, the head of the FIG's women's technical committee, entered the 9.85 into the computer and made the results official. The rest of the day — including four world records in the clean and jerk portion of the 165-pound class weightlifting by Assen Zlatev of Bulgaria and Aleksandr Pervy of the Soviet Union — seemed quiet.

Friday, July 25 — There's a new world's fastest human, and for the first time since Harold Abrahams in 1924, he's a representative of Great Britain. His name is Allan Wells, he doesn't like to use starting blocks (the rules require that he does), and he beat Silvio Leonard of Cuba by one inch. The race aftermath was bizarre, as all the photographers crowded around Leonard, while Wells took a victory lap, unnoticed by most of the spectators. It wasn't until the replay was shown on the stadium scoreboard that some people, including Wells' wife Margot, began to think that he had won. Daley Thompson of Great Britain finished today's five decathlon events on world record pace. Aleksandr Ditiatin won a medal in every one of the six gymnastics finals to bring his total to eight medals — three gold, four silver and one bronze — the most ever by an athlete in one Olympics. The women's gymnastics was quieter than last night even though there was a demonstration over Natalia Shaposhnikova's score on the balance beam, and Nelli Kim had to share the gold medal in the floor exercise with Nadia Comaneci. Comaneci's score was raised so that she tied Kim, but there was never an adequate explanation of why she received the extra .05. It was touching to see the gymnastics competition end with Comaneci and Kim together on the victory stand, certainly the last time we'll have the privilege of seeing them in Olympic competition. The triple jump had everything — a great performance by a great champion, Soviet Jack Uudmae; a valiant effort by one of the sport's all-time greats, Viktor

Saneev, who missed his fourth gold medal by only 11 centimeters . . . and controversy. Australia's Ian Campbell, who attends Washington State, had a lengthy jump called "foul." He complained bitterly, but it did no good.

Saturday, July 26 — Ever since the 1978 European Championships in Prague, the track world has been awaiting the rematch of Great Britain's Steve Ovett and Sebastian Coe. After the world records of 1979 and 1980, their confrontation became the most eagerly-awaited of the entire Olympics. Today's 800-meter race was exciting — Ovett won by three yards in 1:45.9 — but it was also disappointing, due to the slow time and the foolish tactics by Coe, who spent much of the race at the back of the pack. Said the world recordholder's father, Peter Coe, "Seb ran a stupid race." Daley Thompson won the decathlon easily. The weather was less then perfect and he failed to break either the world or Olympic record. He ran the final event, the 1500, just fast enough to insure victory rather than in the all-out fashion of Bruce Jenner's 1976 triumph. Thompson later explained that he wasn't running to gain a big commercial endorsement, but rather, he said, "I plan to stay around and win in Los Angeles." (He even sent a postcard to Bob Mathias, 1948 and 1952 champion, saying he was going to be back in 1984 and 1988.) Still, Thompson will reportedly have his own television show in London this fall. Vladimir Lapitsky, a Soviet fencer, was pierced through the chest by Adam Robak of Poland in a near-fatal accident, and the Soviets suffered another setback when its basketball team was upset by Italy. The Russians, obviously disappointed at the U.S. team's absence, are now in grave danger of losing the gold medal. In the 181.5-pound class weightlifter Yurik Vardanyan, a piano-playing Armenian representing the USSR, became the lightest lifter ever to hoist 400 kilograms (880 pounds) in the two-lift Olympic competition. The crusade of Puerto Rico's flyweight boxer Alberto Mercado ended in sadness tonight as he was cut in the first round of his first fight and the match was stopped at 1:32.

Sunday, July 27 — If Alexandr Ditiatin was the top gymnast of the Games, then there can be little doubt that Rica Reinisch, a 15-year-old East German, was the top swimmer of these Olympics. Tonight she won the 200-meter backstroke for her third gold medal and third world record. Miruts Yifter, the ageless Ethiopian, finally won his first Olympic gold medal. In 1972, he won a bronze medal in the 10,000 but missed his heat of the 5,000 by showing up too late for the race. In 1976, he was denied a chance to compete because of the African boycott. But this time, he won a gripping 10,000 that pitted three Ethiopians against two Finns, including Lasse Viren. Yifter won with his famous, last-lap surge, and the British delighted in calling him "Yifter the Shifter." The Olympic jinx once again struck Soviet weight-

Lutz Dombrowski

lifter David Rigert. In 1972 he entered the Games as the favorite and bombed out. He won a gold in 1976, but this year he lost 20 pounds in the three weeks before the Games in order to lift in the 90-kilo (198-pound) class and strengthen the overall Soviet lineup. The weakened world recordholder failed to snatch his starting weight.

Monday, July 28 — The discus turned out to be a sub-par competition, as unheralded Soviet, Victor Rasshchupkim, took the gold. Wolfgang Schmidt of East Germany, the heavy pre-event favorite, was reportedly injured and finished fourth. Like some of the other competitors here,

Schmidt seemed to lack inspiration with his American rivals not competing. World recordholder Pietro Mennea of Italy made up for his poor performance in the 100 by winning the 200 over an obviously tired Allan Wells. The margin of victory was five inches. East German Lutz Dombrowski leaped into the record books with the first 28-foot jump in history. Back home, American champion Larry Myricks said, "Dombrowski is lucky. If I'd been there, he'd have been the first man in history to jump 28 feet and lose."

Tuesday, July 29 — A traditional quiet day as there are no track and field events, but a group of American runners did stage their own race in Lenin Hills, near the Olympic Stadium. There were more members of the Soviet media than runners in attendance.

Wednesday, July 30 — Plenty of action, including a high-tension pole vault competition ending with a world record by Poland's Wladyslaw Kozakiewicz. Emotions between the Soviet fans of co-silver medalist Konstantin Volkov and the Polish fans ran so high that Kozak bounded from the pit on his winning jump with his own "special" salute to the crowd. The reign of Cuba's Alberto Juantorena is over. The double Olympic champion of 1976 never fully recovered from his latest achilles tendon operation and finished a well-beaten fourth in the 400 meters, the only one of his two titles he chose to defend.

The winner was Viktor Markin, a virtual unknown from the Soviet Union who set a European record. Yugoslavia won the men's basketball tournament as the Soviets took the bronze medal game. The Soviet women, led by their seven-foot center Uliana Semenova, easily won their second consecutive gold medal. For the first Olympics since 1968 the world's strongest man is not Vasili Alexeev. After a nearly two-year hiatus from competition, Alexeev returned, but was unable to lift his opening weight. He was roundly booed by the Soviet crowd. His successor is a gentle, middle Asian named Sultan Rakhmanov.

Thursday, July 31 — The Zimbabwe women's hockey team, invited to Moscow at the last minute following the boycott of most of the world's top teams, won the first gold medal ever for that infant nation. Filbert Bayi of Tanzania tried to run away with the 3000-meter steeplechase, as he has done with 1500-meter races in the past, but he was caught by the indomitable Pole, Bronislaw Malinowski, who won his first gold medal in three tries. One can only feel sorry for Poland's long jumper Anna Wlodarczyk, who jumped into second place with a leap of 22-9 3/4 in the last round, yet was passed by two subsequent 23-foot jumps to finish out of the medals in the greatest long jump competition in history. Soslan Andiev, a man regularly defeated by 350-pound Jimmy Jackson of the United States, won the super heavyweight freestyle wrestling.

Friday, August 1 — Sebastian Coe (3:38.4) got his revenge, beating Steve Ovett (3:39.0) and Jurgen Straub (3:38.8) in the 1500. Though the times were slow, the race was a classic with all three medalists running the last 800 meters in under 1:50. As the race ended, Coe knelt on the track, while Ovett's post-race behavior showed him to be the most gracious of losers. Tatyana Kazankina, who had taken time off to become a mother, defended her Olympic 1500 meter title, while "Yifter the Shifter" added the 5000 to his victory in the 10,000. Waldemar Cierpinski of East Germany duplicated the feat of Abebe Bikila by winning his second consecutive Olympic marathon. Though Rodolfo Gomez of Mexico made a valiant effort to steal the race, leading from the 13th through the 22nd mile. Cierpinski was as fresh at the end of this race as he was in Montreal, where he ran an extra lap in the stadium. Certainly, this mysterious man will be a formidable contender again in 1984.

Saturday, August 2 — Four years ago the boxing finals brought so much joy to the Americans with their five victories. Today it was the Cubans who won six of their eight matches in the finals. In the most-anticipated match, at least among boxing afficionados, Jose Gomez, a Leon Spinks-type brawler from Cuba, easily out-pointed the Soviets' hard punching Viktor Savchenko in

the middleweight final. Teofilo Stevenson won his third Olympic gold, joining Laszlo Papp of Hungary as the only man in history to do so, with a majority decision over the Soviet's Pyotr Zaev. Prior to the Games, Zaev, who sparred with Muhammad Ali when "The Greatest" visited the Soviet Union, was not considered the Soviets' best heavyweight. But with his tight, crouching style, Zaev was considered the man with the best shot at outpointing Stevenson. He came close to doing it, and at the announcement of the 4-1 verdict for the Cuban, the Soviet crowd booed lustily. The Teofilo Stevenson in Moscow was not the man we've been seeing for the past eight years.

Sunday, August 3 — Jan Kowalczyk of Poland won the 1980's final event, individual show jumping, and the closing ceremony was as magnificent as the opening. the card section formed a gigantic Misha the Bear, the mascot of the Games, and as the ceremony ended, he shed a tear.

It might well have been a tear for the athletes who had departed there, as well as for those who were there.

•

(Mr. Diamond and Miss Passudettie are ubiquitous followers of amateur sports competitions the world over and recognized authorities of sports history. Mr. Diamond has one of the most complete sports libraries in the USA. Miss Passudettie, by choice, pursues various aspects of higher mathematics.

Track and Field Honors Go To U.S.S.R., East Germany and Britain

Track and field has always been regarded as the classic sport on the program for the Olympic Games (outside of Soccer-crazy Europe and South America). With the absence of the USA from the 1980 Games, there was an opportunity for the first time for another nation to run off with top men's honors.

It has been coming for the last three Olympic Games — a switch from the West to the East in men's track; Eastern Europe has dominated the women's sport for the last three Olympic Games. Unfortunately there was no opportunity for the USA men's team to put forth the most successful performance for the 19th consecutive time.

Very quickly here's what an analysis of the first three placings in each event showed — for the men the Soviets won 23 medals including eight gold; East Germany garnered 14, including six gold; Great Britain (with its greatest performance in more than 20 years) totaled eight, four of which were gold, and Poland five, two of which were gold.

Among the women it was another U.S.S.R. — East Germany dual meet. In total medals it was the Soviets by one (17-16), in gold it was the Soviets by two (7-5). Other gold medals went to Italy and Cuba. The Socialist countries captured all but four of the 42 available medals.

Even without the USA and West Germany the track and field competition results compare favorably with those of previous Olympics.

• Record-wise (the lifeblood of statisticians the world over) the results may have been slightly down. Among the men, in 24 events three world records were established (all in the field events) and one additional Olympic record was set for a total of four when added to the world marks.

• In addition to three world marks, the women hung up nine Olympic records. Only the 4 x 400-meter relay and the 100m standards escaped unscathed.

• The Games produced new heroes and heroines for the mythical Olympic Games' Hall of Fame. Only three women, all married, (discus thrower, Evelin Schlaak Jahl, East Germany; Barbel Eckert Wockel, East Germany, 200m, and Tatyana Kazankina, U.S.S.R., 1,500m) retained their '76 tiaras. The only repeaters among the men were marathon victor Waldemar Cierpinski, East Germany and the Soviet's new world recordholder in the hammer throw, Yuri Sedykh.

• Persistence is rewarded: Poland's Bronislaw Malinowski won the steeplechase race. Previously he had garnered a silver in his specialty.

• A tip of the fedora to the four British Olympic champions — Allan Wells, 100m; Steve Ovett, 800m; Sebastian Coe, 1,500m; and Daley Thompson, decathlon.

• A salute to a pair of dedicated Italian champions — Pietro Mennea, 200m and Sara Simeoni, high jump. Both struggled inwardly to overcome their personal objections to U.S.S.R. activity in Afghanistan. Mennea won the 200m running from the dreaded outside lane (he was 4th in '76); Simeoni, a disciple of the Fosbury Flop, unseated the

defending champion from East Germany, Rosemarie Ackermann, a devotee of the old-style straddle technique. Sara had been runner-up in '76.

• In the men's competition the U.S.S.R. scored the only 1, 2, 3, sweep of the meet in the hammer throw. The Soviets also

Gerd Wessig

Wladyslaw Kozakiewicz

swept the pentathlon and 800 meters in the women's competition.

The greatest interest in the West was centered around a pair of British middle distance runners, Sebastian Coe and Steve Ovett. It is only fair to acknowledge that the results produced a dead heat. Ovett won the first round by scoring a tactical victory over Coe in the 800 meters. The second round was all Coe as he raced to victory in the classic 1,500m on the closing day of track and field. Coe broke a skein of 28 straight for Ovett in the metric–mile. His last previous defeat was three years ago to Steve Scott, USA, at Kingston, Jamaica.

After losing to Ovett in the 800m, Coe philosophized, "Some days you run well and some days you don't. I didn't run well today." Seven days later he let his performance speak for itself — victory in the metric-mile.

The most interesting of the gold medalists was Ethiopia's Myruts Yifter. A year ago he was victor in both the 5,000m and 10,000m races in World Cup II and at the Spartakiade dress rehearsal in Lenin Stadium.

The 10,000m race will go down in track history as one of the classic distance races of all times. It was "a team race" involving the Ethiopians and the Finns. The key figures were Yifter and Lasse Viren, winner of the race at the last two Olympic Games.

Yifter and Viren have one thing in common off the running rack. Yifter is a some-time policeman in his country's air force; Viren is constable in his hometown.

During the last nine laps of the 25-lap race the top five runners (all from the two countries) jockeyed back and forth. The computer-like "running brains" of all five, spewed out the same data: If Yifter was to be taken, he must be "out of the race" before the final 400m. It was known that no one would be able to keep pace with the ageless Yifter over the final lap. But Yifter's great finish kick brought him home in the van.

Sara Simeoni

The 5,000m race proved equally exciting. But again Yifter scored a narrow victory, by about four meters, over Suleiman Nyambui, a Tanzanian student at the University of Texas at El Paso. Viren was fifth.

In the sprints the victors were Allan Wells of Scotland (wearing the colors of Great Britain) who won a "slow" 100m and Italy's Pietro Mennea who may have capped a successful career with his victory in the 200m (after being eliminated in the heats of the 100m). Wells ran second in the 200m (in the lane adjoining Mennea) and was clocked two one-hundredths of a second slower.

Daley Thompson, just four days short of his 22nd birthday, is the offspring of a Nigerian mother and a Scottish father. He had trained all last winter in San Diego to escape Britain's cold and damp weather. It was in California where he worked hard to improve his throwing performances (shotput, discus and javelin). They are still his weak events. But his time in the 100m

still would have been good enough for a bronze medal behind Wells and Cuba's Silvio Leonard.

Statistically the most satisfying results were in the field events. Perhaps overshadowing the two world records plus an additional Olympic record was the splendid series of five jumps by Lutz Dombrowski, East Germany, in winning long jump honors. He had the second longest leap in history, 28 feet 1/4 inch. He "passed" one attempt and his other five jumps ranged from his winning effort of 28-0¼ down to 26-9 (all under legal wind conditions). The *cognoscenti* glowed with the information that Lutz had achieved the best "five–jump series" in the long history of the event.

Yuri Sedykh set a world record in the hammer throw by throwing the 16-pound-ball-and-chain an incredible 268-5 to defeat his teammate Sergei Litvinov who earlier in the year had etched his name in the world record-book with a throw of 267-11.

In the pole vault Wladyslaw Kozakiewicz of Poland has been flirting with world records for several years. He was at the top of his game and came within one-half inch of cracking the 19-foot barrier. The defending champion, Poland's Tadeusz Slusarski, tied Konstantin Volkov, U.S.S.R. for the silver medal at 18-8½, also better than the previous Olympic record.

The final world record was produced in the high jump when East Germany's Gerd Wessig cleared 7-8 3/4. It was the third time this year the world high jump standard has been "upped."

Vladimir Kiselyov, U.S.S.R., was credited with an Olympic record in the shotput, 70 feet 1/2 inch. Surprisingly, the defending champion, Udo Beyer, finished out of the money in fourth place.

The least likely among the gold medal winners in the field events was Viktor Rasschchupkin,

Pietro Mennea

U.S.S.R. His winning discus throw of 218-7 was considerably short of Mac Wilkins' elegant Olympic record of 224-0 set in the 1976 qualifying round. Viktor had not been ranked among the top 20 in the world in '79.

"Shocked" best described the immediate reaction to Wolfgang Schmidt, East Germany, current world record-holder and runner-up to Wilkins at Montreal, who finished fourth.

Schmidt had briefly taken over the lead on his fourth of six attempts and then Rasshchupkin, 29, unloaded his winning throw three feet three inches better than Schmidt's longest throw of 215-4.

Before leaving a discussion of the men's portion of the program one final note: Filbert Bayi, the converted metric–miler from Tanzania, won the first ever track and field medal for his country by finishing runner-up to Malinowski in the steeplechase. One other runner-up also earned the first ever men's track and field award for his country: The Netherlands' marathoner Gerard Nijboer pushed Cierpinski to the East German's second gold medal.

Make no mistake about it, the performances in the women's track and field events showed the "most progress" of any single *measurable* sport on the program at Moscow.

At Montreal the women were credited with nine Olympic records of which four were also recognized as world records. In the 14-event program for women at Moscow there were 12 new marks for Olympic competition, of which three were also world records.

Nadezhda Tkachenko, U.S.S.R., hung up the final world record of all time in the women's pentathlon with a superb performance of 5,083 points (the first ever to surpass the 5,000 point barrier). Starting next year the "pentathlon" will become the "heptathlon." Following the Europa Cup a year ago Nadezhda had been suspended when her test for doping substances came up "positive." By action of the International Amateur Athletic Federation, world governing

body, which had suspended her, she was forgiven and permitted to compete.

And speaking of the pentathlon, the U.S.S.R. did sweep both the pentathlon and the 800 meters. Another Nadezhda, Mrs. Olizarenko, also set a world record by scampering over the two laps in 1:53.5. Mrs. Olizarenko is the wife of a Soviet steeplechaser who advanced as far as

Allan Wells

the semi-finals. They frequently train together.

Olizarenko's winning margin of 1.6 seconds was even more impressive than Tatyana Kazankina, also U.S.S.R., becoming the first "repeater" in the 1,500m. Tatyana's margin of victory over East Germany's Christina Wartenberg was 1.2 seconds. The bronze medalist was scarcely identified in the public prints. She was Mrs. Olizarenko whose clocking of 3:59.6 equals the American record held by Mary Decker.

The best ever 100m sprint for women found Ludmila Kondratseva, U.S.S.R., "leaning" at

the finish tape to score the narrowest of victories over peerless Marlies Gohr, East Germany, the pre-Games' favorite. Kondrateva's 11.06 clocking was not an Olympic mark. At Montreal, Annegret Richter, the Dortmund housewife, set a world and Olympic record of 11.01 in the semi-final heat.

Another world recordholder who missed out for a medal was Poland's Grazyna Rabsztyn in the 100m hurdles. Grzyna's victory over '76 champion Johanna Schaller Klier, in the semi-final, was a cause for great joy in the Polish rooting section. But in the final it was strictly a race between Klier and the eventual winner, Vera Komisova, U.S.S.R., who took over the lead after clearing the fifth of ten hurdles. Komisova set an Olympic record of 12.56 seconds. Rabsztyn was fifth in 12.74, her same placing at Montreal.

Perhaps the most convincing victory in the running events was chalked up by Marita Koch, East Germany, in the 400m. She led almost all the way in winning over Jarmila Kratochvilova, Czechoslovakia, with an Olympic-record performance of 48.88 seconds. Marita had been spotlighted by one track and field publication as Women's Track and Field Athlete of the Year in both 1978 and 1979.

A parting note: Pietro Mennea, who had certain misgivings about competing, after his victory in the 200m said that he did not want to see the Olympic Games destroyed. He was quoted as saying, "I had a lot of doubts, but I wanted to see the games continue. I thought my presence here would help."

C. Robert Paul, Jr.

It Was Russia All The Way in Gymnastics

By C. Robert Paul Jr.

With Japan and the United States declining to participate it was expected that the U.S.S.R. would have a relatively easy path to gold in the men's division and would be capable of subduing Romania and East Germany in the ladies events.

What was also expected was the dissatisfaction with the judging. How much dissatisfaction was legitimate is hard to discern because such protestations are common.

What was disturbing was the apparent lack of a standing-room-only crowd at the individual exercise finals.

It is doubtful if gymnasts, gymnastics coaches, spectators, journalists and television commentators will ever come close to agreement. In the past there has been evidence of judges "manipulating" scoring for gymnasts. There was no reason to believe that it would be any better for Moscow.

Through the medium of television, Olga Korbut after the Munich competition and Nadia Comaneci after Montreal were known the world over for their derring-do and ballet-like expertise on the apparatus. Even without television in the United States it is doubtful if Moscow came up with a worthy successor to earn the plaudits of the sports world.

Being objective, would it be wrong to name the Soviet's Alexandr Ditiatin, 22, reigning world champion and winner of the maximum eight medals, as the "most noteworthy performer" during the entire sports competition at Moscow? No one had ever won eight medals in a single Olympic Games. But Ditiatin

Nadia Comeneci's famous tumble

took a giant step forward among the *all-time* gymnastics heroes by medalling in all six individual events, winning the combined exercise all-around diadem, and leading the Soviet men to their first-ever team championship.

Gymnasts, since the introduction of live Olympic television coverage (1968), and subsequent broader coverage by the print media, have captured the imagination of the writers, commentators and, alas, the general public. It would be difficult to point to any other group of athletes as talented and well-conditioned as the men gymnasts.

Since the International Gymnastics Federation introduced "bonus points" for ROV (Risk, Originality, and Virtuosity) in scoring optional exercises the men gymnasts have been throwing even greater moves to attract higher scores.

On the sidelines it has been difficult to accept the difference in scoring men's and women's performances. "Gadzooks," Ditiatin was given the first ever "ten" accorded a man in Olympic gymnastics. Since Comaneci cracked the "ten barrier" at Montreal, perfect ten scores have been the order of the day (cheaper by the dozen, perhaps) in the major women's competitions.

Not to be lost in a welter of statistics from the gymnastics floor were the Moscow achievements of the veteran Soviet ace, Nikolai Andrianov and the sport's *nonpareil* on the pommel horse, Hungary's Zoltan Magyar, who won his second straight gold in perhaps the most difficult and entertaining apparatus work in the sport.

Andrianov, '76 all-around champion and winner of four gold medals there, yielded the combined exercise all-around crown to his teammate, Ditaitin, 118.650 to 118.225 (out of a possible 120).

Too often in the past the battle for individual exercises medals developed into a two-country dual meet, or even one country might dominate with five of six entrants. A well-reasoned rule was adopted by the International Gymnastics Federation prior to the 1976 Olympic Games.

Yelena Davydova

Now a country may not qualify (by placing in the all-around) more than two gymnasts in each of the individual event exercises. Surprisingly enough the U.S.S.R. never "threw its weight around" to block this change which was adopted obviously to help spread the wealth among the competing nations.

There is no doubt that more countries now can send their gymnasts onto the floor for the finals. No country is really penalized when only their two top scorers (in head-to-head competition) are moved into the individual finals.

The honor roll of medalists at the gymnastics ran pretty much to form. A disclaimer could be entered following the rather unexpected victory of Yelena Davydova, 18, U.S.S.R. in the all-

around competition. There was never a doubt about her all-around abilities. Simply stated, however, it was expected that judges, by their very nature, might favor the better known and more established international stars.

When 36 gymnasts came out for a final fling to decide the all-around title, it was expected that Nadia, Nelli Kim, Natalia Shaposhikova and Max Gnauck would be battling for top honors. The four "biggest names" did exceptionally well. But Davydova started the adrenalin juices flowing for the judges with an innovative performance in the floor exercise.

But the final order of finish Davydova, Gnauck and Comaneci (tie), Shaposhnikova, and Kim certainly accurately reflects the relative abilities of the world's top gymnasts on that day among those who competed in Moscow.

The Japanese and the USA were absent from the men's competition. This set up a dual meet of the U.S.S.R. against the rest of the world. The Soviets won — earning 15 out of a possible 28 medals. In addition to six firsts for the U.S.S.R. men to two for the rest of the world (Hungary and Bulgaria), the host gymnasts notched seven seconds out of 7 (the 8th was in the team competition for which the U.S.S.R. was ineligible since they had already won gold in the same event), and one bronze. The rest of the world picked up the other seven bronze medals.

In the women's competition the result was somewhat closer. The "rest of the world" led with 13 medals and East Germany accounted for six, but the Soviets earned four firsts, one second, and two thirds to lead the parade.

One of the most tense battles ever for gold in the women's combined exercise all-around event centered around the four top gymnasts in Moscow. Nadia Comaneci was shooting for gold when she gracefully mounted the 4-inch-wide balance beam. Her favorite event of the four individual exercises, the balance beam, presented a golden opportunity for Nadia to win a second Olympic combined exercise all-around title. She was good, but not great. In spite of the thousands of words written about her, Nadia was scored at 9.85 which wasn't enough to win.

Davydova won the gold medal on the uneven parallel bars. She approached the apparatus with the aplomb and poise of a gymnast several years her senior. Every move Davydova made on the uneven parallel bars was the move of a champion, a queen of all gymnasts. The Soviet citizenry who failed to fill the stands for the finals were delighted. So were the judges whose sense of agreement caused a posting of 9.95 for the exercise. Victory was hers — perhaps the biggest moment she will ever experience in sports. Neil Amdur, writing in *The New York Times* observed, "until she scored a triumph in the Soviet Cup, the 4-foot-8-inch, 75-pounder, had never won a gold medal in a national or international competition."

The Soviet's men's coach dismissed the absence of the defending team champions from Japan. Leonid Arkayev, coach, claimed the outcome would have been no different since Japan only accounted for the team silver and one bronze in the individual events at the '79 world's. To underscore the Soviet superior performances in the team competition look at the final point score: The U.S.S.R. had 589.60 and East Germany 581.25. Four years ago, Japan nipped the U.S.S.R. gymnasts 576.85 to 576.45. East Germany and Hungary, two, three in '80, were three, four at Montreal.

The Soviets recast their men's team with only two holdovers from Montreal, Ditaitin and Andrianov. In the Montreal Games all-around champion Andrianov was trailed by Ditaitin in sixth place.

Sports remains one of the few places where "nostalgia" is both accepted and acceptable. The nostalgic note in women's gymnastics came when Nelli Kim, a tower of strength for the Soviets over the last five or six years, shared the floor exercise title with Nadia, still the world's favorite — outside of Moscow.

Alexandr Ditiatin

East Germany's Women and
Soviet Men Take Swimming Honors

The East German women's team dominated the Olympic swimming more than any other team in the past . . . and perhaps more so than other teams can dominate in the future. Because of the absence of the USA, the Soviet men for the first time eclipsed all other nations and won more gold and silver medals than the other five nations *combined*.

Why is it said that the East Germans dominated the women's swimming more than any other team will dominate in the future? As its quadrennial Congress held in Moscow, the International Amateur Swimming Federation (FINA) decreed that in the future a maximum of two entries would be permitted each nation. Up through 1980, nations were permitted a maximum of three in each event, except relays.

The East German mermaids, a mixture of experienced hands and *wunderkind,* won twice as many medals as the other medaling nations combined (26-13), won eleven out of 13 events, and in six events swept first, second and third. Australia and the U.S.S.R. ladies each won a single gold.

In the men's competition, the Soviets won seven gold, garnered seven silver and three bronze. Sweden won a pair of gold medals, including one by U.S.-trainer Par Arvidsson, (a student at the University of California, Berkeley), winner of the 100m butterfly.

The golden boy of swimming, without a question of a doubt, was Vladimir Salnikov, U.S.S.R., beneficiary of training a year ago in both Mission Viejo and Gainesville. Salnikov contributed to the meet the No. 1 individual feat of the Olympic Games . . . he swam 1,500 meters freestyle in 14:58.27, the first man to break

Vladimir Salnikov

the 15-minute barrier, which, until a few years ago, was considered beyond reach.

Salnikov had previously set an Olympic record of 3:51.31 in the 400m freestyle and earned yet another medal of gold by swimming the second leg on the victorious Soviet 4 x 200m freestyle relay.

A third USA-trained Olympic champion is Britain's Duncan Goodhew, who had spent three years at North Carolina State University. He has yet another semester to earn his degree. Duncan won the 100m breaststroke.

The person most in the swim at the conclusion of the swimming races had to be the chief Soviet coach and organizer, Sergei Vaitsekhovsky, whose blueprint for the five-year men's plan bore fruit in the Olympic Games. The 51-year-old coach/organizer is a former modern pentathlete whose daughter, Elena, was the ladies

Olympic platform champion at Montreal four years ago.

Vaitsekhovsky, who left Gainesville with Salnikov on Jan. 7, just after President Carter's call for USA non-participation, said "The Americans surprised us by not keeping any of their training secrets from us, which means there must still be some decent people left in the world. We're sorry they aren't here."

The ascendency of the Soviet Union in men's swimming became apparent early on in the Olympic Games. Sergei Fesenko became the first-ever Soviet men's swimming gold medalist when he won the 200m butterfly.

Although the Soviets won seven out of the 13 gold medals in the men's races, the USA had won 12 out of the 13 at Montreal and nine out of 15 in Munich in 1972.

Dr. Harold Henning, a leader in U.S. aquatic sports, and a past president of the FINA, praised the pool as one of the "fastest" he had ever seen. A "fast pool" plays an important role in record-smashing at important international competitions.

In the women's competition there were six world records and 11 Olympic records. The men recorded one world record and notched four Olympic standards. At Montreal the USA men accounted for 11 world and Olympic records.

Trivia buffs a decade from now will glowingly intone the names of the two young ladies who prevented the East Germans from making a clean sweep of the 13 swimming races: Michelle Ford, an 18-year-old Australian, who had trained in the USA until six months before the Olympic

Barbara Krause

Games, won the 800 meters in Olympic record time over a pair of East Germans, including Ines Diers, Olympic 400m freestyle victor. The other non-East German winner was the Soviet 200m breaststroker, Linda Kachushite.

If Salnikov was the "golden boy" among the swimmers, the "golden girl" award must be bestowed on Rica Reinisch, the 15-year-old schoolgirl from Dresden. Rica won three gold medals, played a role in hanging up four world records and was the cynosure of all eyes in the eight days of competition.

Reinisch made a shambles of both backstroke events (as successor to fellow East German, Ulrike Richter) winning the 100m backstroke by 1.21 seconds and the 200m event by almost two full seconds. Birgit Treiber, also East Germany, was second in both backstrokes at Montreal, At Moscow she placed third in the longer race, alone.

Freestyler Barbara Krause missed the '76 Olympic Games because of illness. She stayed around for the next trip on the carousel and proved an able successor to her former cross-town rival, Kornelia Ender. Why "able successor"? That's simple. Krause, in what may have been her international swan song, set Olympic marks in both the 100m and 200m freestyle with clockings of 54.79 seconds (also a world record) and 1:58.33 in erasing Ender's accomplishments at Montreal.

For years the USA set the pace among freestylers. At Moscow, the East Germans swept the women's 100m, 200m and 400m races and placed two, three in the 800m freestyle.

The hometowners had to pack together their cheering for Soviet young ladies into one event . . . the 200m breaststroke. As they did at Montreal, the Soviets repeated by sweeping the 200m with a new trio of swimmers since Montreal. The winner, Lina Kachushite, set an Olympic record of 2:29.54 by nosing out team-mate Svetlana Varganova by seven hundredths of a second.

The only closer race for ladies witnessed Ines Geissler, East Germany, nosing out teammate Sybille Schonrock by one hundredth of a second. The winning time of 2:10.44 was an Olympic record.

Salnikov, '79 winner of *Swimmer of the Year* sobriquet from the popular magazine *Swimming World,* may never achieve the notoriety of a Mark Spitz, or the post-Olympic popularity and recognition of a John Naber. Yet more words were written about Salnikov in the American press than any other swimmer at Moscow.

Anita Verschoth, *Sports Illustrated,* wrote, "Vladimir Salnikov has reduced competitive swimming to its essentials. 'I like

Duncan Goodhew

Michelle Ford

to swim fast. I like to go as fast as I can and then see whether it turns out to be a record or not. With that kind of an attitude, I am never disappointed.' "

Sports Illustrated also revealed that Salnikov's designated coach, Igor Koshin, works in concert with a psychiatrist. Further, S.I. quotes Salnikov on the subject of his sports psychiatrist, "Before every competition our coach and our psychiatrist pay special attention to us. Some swimmers need to read a book, others need to listen to music. Some need a conversation with (psychiatrist) Gorbunov whose voice has a calming effect."

In a final tribute to Salnikov, *S.I.* wrote, "His achievements are scarcely diminished by the absence of American swimmers in Moscow, although Salnikov believes he might have swum faster if they had been there. But he swam well enough without their help."

It just might be that the presence of the Americans would have given the swimming meet the shot in the arm it needed for "excitement." But with the results etched in the book by the East German women and the U.S.S.R. men, swimming preeminence at least for 1980, has shifted to the East.

•

OFF THE DIVING BOARD

The absence of the American and People's Republic of China divers affected the overall quality of the diving competition in Moscow. But diving at the Olympic Games wouldn't be diving unless there was one big controversy to divert the journalists from writing about the victors. Moscow was no exception.

Irina Kalinina, U.S.S.R., clearly outdistanced all foes to win the women's springboard title (succeeding Jennifer Chandler, USA) to become only the second non-American to win the event. Ingrid Kramer Engel, East Germany, won the title in both 1960 and 1964. Kalinina won by a whopping 27 points, the biggest margin in the four diving events.

The controversy was centered on the men's springboard competition. And a spirited controversy it was. Protests, formal and informal, were to no avail.

The basis of the controversy was the opportunity for the No. 1 Soviet diver, Alekandr Portnov, being given a "second chance" because of crowd noise. It is recognized that where a diver is "disturbed" or "distracted" before he dives the judges can award him a "free dive."

Irina Kalinina

This is what happened. Portnov really "hit" the second chance and amassed enough points to nose out Mexico's champion, Carlos Giron, by fewer than 13 points. Mexico City citizens, for the second time in the Games, demonstrated in front of the Soviet Embassy there when the protest was disallowed.

Falk Hoffmann, East Germany, was relegated to a fourth place, non-medal placing, on the basis of Portnov's second chance. Some of his chagrin was removed when he did well off the ten-meter platform. "Doing well' meant that Hoffmann (a non-medalist in two previous Olympic Games, but also fourth off the springboard in '76 and sixth off the platform) won gold.

Hoffmann humbled Soviet ace, Vladimir Aleinik, by 16 points and the other U.S.S.R. diver, David Ambarisumyan, (7th at Montreal) by two more points.

•

C. Robert Paul, Jr.

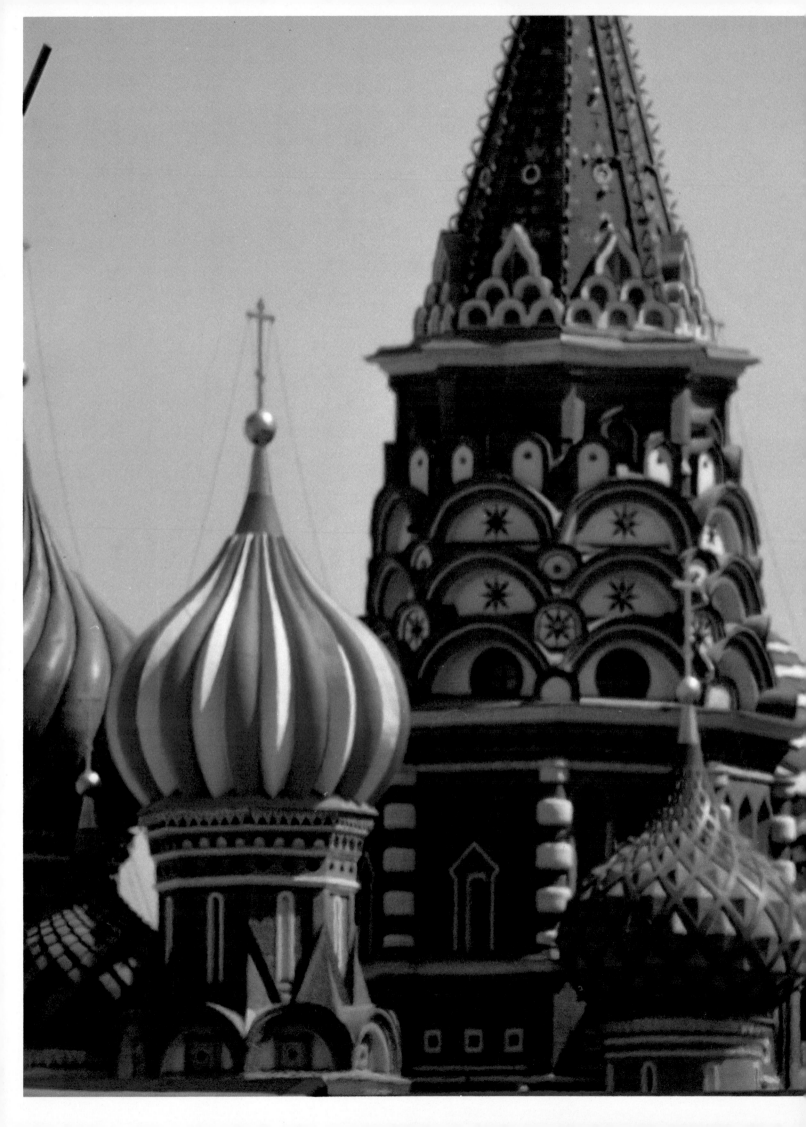

1980 RESULTS
OLYMPIC WINTER GAMES

There were 37 nations participating in the XIII Olympic Winter Games. In the official summaries of the 37 events, 22 nations are mentioned. The official abbreviations are used for each country.

AUT	Austria
BUL	Bulgaria
CAN	Canada
FIN	Finland
FRA	France
FRG	West Germany
GBR	Great Britain
GDR	East Germany
HOL	Netherlands
HUN	Hungary
ITA	Italy
JPN	Japan
LIE	Liechtenstein
NOR	Norway
POL	Poland
ROM	Romania
SUI	Switzerland
SWE	Sweden
TCH	Czechoslovakia
USSR	Soviet Union
USA	United States
YUG	Yugoslavia

Abbreviations for result tables

A	Date of competition
B	Place of competition
C	Number of competitors
H	Length of course
WR	World record
OR	Olympic record

SKIING

Ladies Alpine Events

Downhill

A: 2/17/80; B: Whiteface Mt.; C: 28; H: 2698 m

1. **Annemarie Moser**	**AUT**	**1:37.52**
2. **Hanni Wenzel**	**LIE**	**1:38.22**
3. **Marie-Theres Nadig**	**SUI**	**1:38.36**
4. Heidi Preuss	USA	1:39.51
5. Kathy Kreiner	CAN	1:39.53
6. Ingrid Eberle	AUT	1:39.63
7. Torill Fjeldstad	NOR	1:39.69
7. Cindy Nelson	USA	1:39.69

Slalom

A: 2/23/80; B: Whiteface Mt.; C: 47; H1: 461 m; H2: 465 m

1. **Hanni Wenzel**	**LIE**	**1:25.09**
2. **Christa Kinshofer**	**FRG**	**1:26.50**
3. **Erika Hess**	**SUI**	**1:27.89**
4. Mariarosa Quario	ITA	1:27.92
5. Claudia Giordani	ITA	1:29.12
6. Nadezhda Patrakeeva	USSR	1:29.20
7. Daniela Zini	ITA	1:29.22
8. Christin Cooper	USA	1:29.28

Giant Slalom

A: 2/20-21/80; B: Whiteface Mt.; C: 48; H1: 1231 m; H2: 1315 m

1. **Hanni Wenzel**	**LIE**	**2:41.66**
2. **Irene Epple**	**FRG**	**2:42.12**
3. **Perrine Pelen**	**FRA**	**2:42.41**
4. Fabienne Serrat	FRA	2:42.42
5. Christa Kinshofer	FRG	2:42.63
6. Annemarie Moser	AUT	2:43.15
7. Christin Cooper	USA	2:44.71
8. Maria Epple	FRG	2:45.56

Mens Alpine Events

Downhill

A: 2/14/80; B: Whiteface Mt.; C: 47; H: 3009 m

1. **Leonhard Stock**	**AUT**	**1:45.50**
2. **Peter Wirnsberger**	**AUT**	**1:46.12**
3. **Steve Podborski**	**CAN**	**1:46.62**
4. Peter Mueller	SUI	1:46.75
5. Pete Patterson	USA	1:47.04
6. Herbert Plank	ITA	1:47.13
7. Werner Grissmann	AUT	1:47.21
8. Valerie Tsyganov	USSR	1:47.34

Slalom

A: 2/22/80; B: Whiteface Mt.; C: 79; H1: 549 m; H2: 541 m

1. **Ingemar Stenmark**	**SWE**	**1:44.26**
2. **Phil Mahre**	**USA**	**1:44.76**
3. **Jacques Luethy**	**SUI**	**1:45.06**
4. Hans Enn	AUT	1:45.12
5. Christian Neureuther	FRG	1:45.14
6. Peter Popangelov	BUL	1:45.40
7. Anton Steiner	AUT	1:45.41
8. Gustav Thoeni	ITA	1:45.99

Giant Slalom

A: 2/19/80; B: Whiteface Mt.; C: 78; H1: 1354 m; H2: 1303 m

1. **Ingemar Stenmark**	**SWE**	**2:40.74**
2. **Andreas Wenzel**	**LIE**	**2:41.49**
3. **Hans Enn**	**AUT**	**2:42.51**
4. Bojan Krizaj	YUG	2:42.53
5. Jacques Luethy	SUI	2:42.75
6. Bruno Nockler	ITA	2:42.95
7. Joel Gaspoz	SUI	2:43.05
8. Boris Strel	YUG	2:43.24

Ladies Nordic Events

4 x 5 km Relay

A: 2/21/80; B: Mt. van Hoevenberg; C: 8

1. **GDR (Rostock, Anding, Hesse, Petzold)**	**1:02:11.10**
2. **USSR**	**1:03:18.30**
3. **NOR**	**1:04:13.50**
4. TCH	1:04:31.39
5. FIN	1:04:41.28
6. SWE	1:05:16.32
7. USA	1:06:55.41
8. CAN	1:07:45.75

5 km Cross-country

A: 2/15/80; B: Mt. van Hoevenberg; C: 38

1. **Raisa Smetanina**	**USSR**	**15:06.92**
2. **Hilkka Riihivuori**	**FIN**	**15:11.96**
3. **Kveta Jeriova**	**TCH**	**15:23.44**
4. Barbara Petzold	GDR	15:23.62
5. Nina Baldischeva	USSR	15:29.03
6. Galina Kulakova	USSR	15:29.58
7. Veronika Hesse	GDR	15:31.83
8. Helena Takalo	FIN	15:32.12

10 km Cross-country

A: 2/18/80; B: Mt. van Hoevenberg; C: 38

1. **Barbara Petzold**	**GDR**	**30:31.54**
2. **Hilkka Riihivuori**	**FIN**	**30:35.05**
3. **Helena Takalo**	**FIN**	**30:45.25**
4. Raisa Smetanina	USSR	30:54.48
5. Galina Kulakova	USSR	30:58.46
6. Nina Baldischeva	USSR	31:22.93
7. Marlies Rostock	GDR	31:28.79
8. Veronika Hesse	GDR	31:29.14

Mens Nordic Events

4 x 10 km Relay

A: 2/20/80; B: Mt. van Hoevenberg; C: 10

1. **USSR (Rochev, Bazhukov, Beliaev, Zimjatov)**	**1:57:03.46**
2. **NOR**	**1:58:45.77**
3. **FIN**	**2:00:00.18**
4. FRG	2:00:22.74
5. SWE	2:00:42.71
6. ITA	2:01:09.93
7. SUI	2:03:36.57
8. USA	2:04:12.17

15 km Cross-country

A: 2/17/80; B: Mt. van Hoevenberg; C: 63

1. **Thomas Wassberg**	**SWE**	**41:57.63**
2. **Juha Mieto**	**FIN**	**41:57.64**
3. **Ove Aunli**	**NOR**	**42:28.62**
4. Nikolai Zimjatov	USSR	42:33.96
5. Evgeny Beliaev	USSR	42:46.02
6. Josef Luszczek	POL	42:59.03
7. Alexandr Zavjov	USSR	43:00.81
8. Harri Kirvesniemi	FIN	43:02.01

30 km Cross-country

A: 2/14/80; B: Mt. van Hoevenberg; C: 57

1. **Nikolai Zimjatov**	**USSR**	**1:27:02.80**
2. **Rochev Vasili**	**USSR**	**1:27:34.22**
3. **Ivan Lebanov**	**BUL**	**1:28:03.87**
4. Thomas Wassberg	SWE	1:28:40.35
5. Jozef Luszczek	POL	1:29:03.64
6. Matti Pitkanen	FIN	1:29:35.03
7. Juha Mieto	FIN	1:29:45.08
8. Ove Aunli	NOR	1:29:54.02

50 km Cross-country

A: 2/23/80; B: Mt. van Hoevenberg; C: 43

1.	**Nikolai Zimjalov**	**USSR**	**2:27:24.60**
2.	**Juha Mieto**	**FIN**	**2:30:20.52**
3.	**Alexander Savjalov**	**USSR**	**2:30:51.52**
4.	Lars Erik Eriksen	NOR	2:30:53.03
5.	Sergei Saveliev	USSR	2:31:15.82
6.	Evgeny Beliaev	USSR	2:31:21.19
7.	Oddvar Braa	NOR	2:31:46.83
8.	Sven Ake Lundbåck	SWE	2:31:59.65

Nordic combined

A: 2/18-19/80; B: Intervale/Mt. van Hoevenberg; C: 31

1.	**Ulrich Wehling (227.2 jumping, 205 cross country)**	**GDR**	**432.200**
2.	**Jouko Karjalainen**	**FIN**	**429.500**
3.	**Konrad Winkler**	**GDR**	**425.320**
4.	Tom Sandberg	NOR	418.465
5.	Uwe Dotzauer	GDR	418.415
6.	Karl Lustenberger	SUI	412.210
7.	Alexander Maiorov	USSR	409.135
8.	Gunter Schmieder	GDR	404.075

Special Jump

Jump 70 m

A: 2/17/80; B: Intervale Ski Jump; C: 48

1.	**Anton Innauer (89 m, 90 m jumps)**	**AUT**	**266.3**
2.	**Manfred Deckert**	**GDR**	**249.2**
	Hirokazu Yagi	**JPN**	**249.2**
4.	Masahiro Akimoto	JPN	248.5
5.	Pentti Kokkonen	FIN	247.6
6.	Hubert Neuper	AUT	245.5
7.	Alfred Groyer	AUT	245.3
8.	Jouko Tormanen	FIN	243.5

Jump 90 m

A: 2/23/80; B: Intervale Ski Jump; C: 50

1.	**Jouko Tormanen (114.5 m, 133.5 m)**	**FIN**	**271.0**
2.	**Hubert Neuper**	**AUT**	**262.4**
3.	**Jari Puikkonen**	**FIN**	**248.5**
4.	Anton Innauer	AUT	245.7
5.	Armin Kogler	AUT	245.6
6.	Roger Ruud	NOR	243.0
7.	Hansjorg Sumi	SUI	242.7
8.	Jim Denney	USA	239.1

BIATHLON

Relay

A: 2/22/80; B: Mt. van Hoevenberg; C: 15

1.	**USSR (Alikin, Tichonov, Barnaschov, Aljabiev)**	**1:34:03.27**
2.	**GDR**	**1:34:56.99**
3.	**FRG**	**1:37:30.26**
4.	NOR	1:38:11.76
5.	FRA	1:38:23.60
6.	AUT	1:38:32.02
7.	FIN	1:38:50.84
8.	USA	1:39:24.29

10 km Individual Competition

A: 2/19/80; B: Mt. van Hoevenberg; C: 50

1.	**Frank Ullrich**	**GDR**	**32:10.69(2)**
2.	**Vladimir Alikin**	**USSR**	**32:53.10(0)**
3.	**Anatoli Aljabiev**	**USSR**	**33:09.16(1)**
4.	Klaus Siebert	GDR	33:32.76(2)
5.	Kjell Sobak	NOR	33:34.64(1)
6.	Peter Zelinka	TCH	33:45.20(1)
7.	Odd Lirhus	NOR	34:10.39(2)
8.	Peter Angerer	FRG	34:13.43(4)

20 km Individual Competition

A: 2/16/80; B: Mt. van Hoevenberg; C: 49

1.	**Anatoli Aljabiev**	**USSR**	**1:08:16.31(0)**
2.	**Frank Ullrich**	**GDR**	**1:08:27.79(3)**
3.	**Eberhard Roesch**	**GDR**	**1:11:11.73(2)**
4.	Svein Engen	NOR	1:11:30.25(3)
5.	Erkki Antila	FIN	1:11:32.32(4)
6.	Yvon Mougel	FRA	1:11:33.60(3)
7.	Vladimir Barnaschov	USSR	1:11:49.49(4)
8.	Vladimir Alikin	USSR	1:12:05.30(6)

Figures in Parentheses indicate missed targets

FIGURE SKATING

Ladies

A: 2/20-21-23/80; B: Fieldhouse Arena; C:22

			PLACE MARKS	TOTAL POINTS
1.	**Anett Poetzsch**	**GDR**	**11**	**189.00**
2.	**Linda Fratianne**	**USA**	**16**	**188.30**
3.	**Dagmar Lurz**	**FRG**	**28**	**183.04**
4.	Denise Biellman	SUI	43	180.06
5.	Lisa Marie Allen	USA	45	179.42
6.	Emi Watanabe	JPN	48	179.04
7.	Claudia Kristofics-Binder	AUT	60	176.88
8.	Susanna Driano	ITA	77	172.82

Men

A: 2/18-19-21/80; B: Fieldhouse Arena; C:17

			PLACE MARKS	TOTAL POINTS
1.	**Robin Cousins**	**GBR**	**13**	**189.48**
2.	**Jan Hoffmann**	**GDR**	**15**	**189.72**
3.	**Charles Tickner**	**USA**	**28**	**187.86**
4.	David Santee	USA	34	185.52
5.	Scott Hamilton	USA	45	181.78
6.	Igor Bobrin	USSR	55	177.40
7.	Jean-Christophe Simond	FRA	64	175.00
8.	Mitsuru Matsumura	JPN	75	172.28

Pair Skating

A: 2/15-17/80; B: Fieldhouse Arena; C: 12

			PLACE MARKS	TOTAL POINTS
1.	**Irina Rodnina/ Alexander Zaitsev**	**USSR**	**9**	**147.26**
2.	**Marina Cherkosova/ Sergei Shakrai**	**USSR**	**19**	**143.80**
3.	**Manuela Mager/ Uwe Bewersdorff**	**GDR***	**33***	**140.52**
4.	Marina Pestova/ Stanislav Leonovich	USSR*	31*	141.14
5.	Caitlin Carruthers/ Peter Carruthers	USA	46	137.38
6.	Sabine Baess/ Tassilo Thierbach	GDR	53	136.00
7.	Sheryl Franks/ Michael Botticelli	USA	64	133.84
8.	Christina Riegel/ Andreas Nischwitz	FRG	71	131.70

*Majority of better place marks

Ice Dancing

A: 2/15-17-19/80; B: Fieldhouse Arena; C: 12

			PLACE MARKS	TOTAL POINTS
1.	**Natalia Linichuk/ Gennadi Karponosov**	**USSR**	**13**	**205.48**
2.	**Krisztina Regoczy/ Andras Sallay**	**HUN**	**14**	**204.52**
3.	**Irina Moiseeva/ Andrej Minenkov**	**USSR**	**27**	**201.86**
4.	Liliana Rehakova/ Stanislav Drastich	TCH	39	198.02
5.	Jayne Torvill/ Christopher Dean	GBR	42	197.12
6.	Lorna Wighton/ John Dowding	CAN	54	193.80
7.	Judy Blumberg/ Michael Seibert	USA	66	190.30
8.	Natalia Bestemianova/ Andrei Bukin	USSR	75*	188.18

*Majority of better place marks

SPEED SKATING

500 m Ladies

A: 2/15/80; B: Sheffield Oval; C: 31

1.	**Karin Enke**	**GDR**	**41.78 OR**
2.	**Leah Mueller**	**USA**	**42.26**
3.	**Natalia Petruseva**	**USSR**	**42.42**
4.	Ann-Sofie Jarnstrom	SWE	42.47
5.	Makiko Nagaya	JPN	42.70
6.	Cornelia Jacob	GDR	42.98
7.	Beth Heiden	USA	43.18
8.	Tatiana Tarasova	USSR	43.26

1000 m Ladies

A: 2/17/80; B: Sheffield Oval; C: 37

1.	**Natalia Petruseva**	**USSR**	**1:24.10OR**
2.	**Leah Mueller**	**USA**	**1:25.41**
3.	**Sylvia Albrecht**	**GDR**	**1:26.46**
4.	Karin Enke	GDR	1:26.66
5.	Beth Heiden	USA	1:27.01
6.	Annie Borckink	HOL	1:27.24
7.	Sylvia Burka	CAN	1:27.50
8.	Ann-Sofie Jarnstrom	SWE	1:28.10

1500 m Ladies

A: 2/14/80; B: Sheffield Oval; C: 31

1.	**Annie Borckink**	**HOL**	**2:10.95OR**
2.	**Ria Visser**	**HOL**	**2:12.35**
3.	**Sabine Becker**	**GDR**	**2:12.38**
4.	Bjorg Eva Jensen	NOR	2:12.59
5.	Sylvia Filipsson	SWE	2:12.84
6.	Andrea Mitscherlich	GDR	2:13.05
7.	Beth Heiden	USA	2:13.10
8.	Natalia Petruseva	USSR	2:14.15

3000 m Ladies

A: 2/20/80; B: Sheffield Oval; C: 29

1.	**Bjorg Eva Jensen**	**NOR**	**4:32.13OR**
2.	**Sabine Becker**	**GDR**	**4:32.79**
3.	**Beth Heiden**	**USA**	**4:33.77**
4.	Andrea Mitscherlich	GDR	4:37.69
5.	Erwina Rys-Ferens	POL	4:37.89
6.	Mary Docter	USA	4:39.29
7.	Sylvia Filipsson	SWE	4:40.22
8.	Natalia Petruseva	USSR	4:42.59

500 m Men

A: 2/15/80; B: Sheffield Oval; C: 37

1. Eric Heiden	USA	38.03 OR
2. Evgeny Kulikov	USSR	38.37
3. Lieuwe de Boer	HOL	38.48
4. Frode Ronning	NOR	38.66
5. Daniel Immerfall	USA	38.69
6. Jarle Pedersen	NOR	38.83
7. Anatoli Medennikov	USSR	38.88
8. Gaetan Boucher	CAN	38.90

1000 m Men

A: 2/19/80; B: Sheffield Oval

1. Eric Heiden	USA	1:15.18OR
2. Gaeten Boucher	CAN	1:16.68
3. Frode Ronning	NOR	1:16.91
Vladimir Lobanov	USSR	1:16.91
5. Peter Mueller	USA	1:17.11
6. Bert de Jong	HOL	1:17.29
7. Andreas Dietel	GDR	1:17.71
8. Oloph Granath	SWE	1:17.74

1500 m Men

A: 2/21/80; B: Sheffield Oval; C: 36

1. Eric Heiden	USA	1:55.44OR
2. Kai Arne Stenshjemmet	NOR	1:56.81
3. Terje Andersen	NOR	1:56.92
4. Andreas Dietel	GDR	1:57.14
5. Juri Kondakov	USSR	1:57.36
6. Jan Egil Storholt	NOR	1:57.95
7. Tomas Gustafson	SWE	1:58.18
8. Vladimir Lobanov	USSR	1:59.38

5000 m Men

A: 2/16/80; B: Sheffield Oval; C: 29

1. Eric Heiden	USA	7:02.29OR
2. Kai Arne Stenshjemmet	NOR	7:03.28
3. Tom Erik Oxholm	NOR	7:05.59
4. Hilbert van der Duim	HOL	7:07.97
5. Oeyvind Tveter	NOR	7:08.36
6. Piet Kleine	HOL	7:08.96
7. Michael Woods	USA	7:10.39
8. Ulf Ekstrand	SWE	7:13.13

10,000 m Men

A: 2/23/80; B: Sheffield Oval; C: 25

1. Eric Heiden	USA	14:28.13 WR, OR
2. Piet Kleine	HOL	14:36.03
3. Tom Erik Oxholm	NOR	14:36.60
4. Michael Woods	USA	14:39.53
5. Oeyvind Tveter	NOR	14:43.53
6. Hilbert van der Duim	HOL	14:47.58
7. Viktor Leskin	USSR	14:51.72
8. Andreas Ehrig	GDR	14:51.94

ICE HOCKEY

Preliminary Round

Blue Group

	G	W	T	L	GF	GA
1. SWE	5	4	1	0	26	9
2. USA	5	4	1	0	25	10
3. TCH	5	3	0	2	34	16
4. ROM	5	1	1	3	13	29
5. FRG	5	1	0	4	21	30
6. NOR	5	0	1	4	9	36

Red Group

	G	W	T	L	GF	GA
1. USSR	5	5	0	0	51	11
2. FIN	5	3	0	2	26	18
3. CAN	5	3	0	2	28	12
4. POL	5	2	0	3	15	23
5. HOL	5	1	1	3	16	43
6. JPN	5	0	1	4	7	36

SCORES OF INDIVIDUAL GAMES

Blue Group

Sweden vs USA 2-2, vs Romania 8-0, vs.
W. Germany 5-2, vs. Norway 7-1, vs. Czecho 4-2.
USA vs. Czecho. 7-3, vs. Norway 5-1, vs.
Romania 7-2, vs. W. Germany 4-2.
Czechoslovakia vs. Norway 11-0, vs. Romania
7-2, vs. W. Germany 11-3.
Romania vs. W. Germany 6-4, vs. Norway 1-1.
West Germany vs. Norway 10-4.

Red Group

USSR vs. Japan 16-0, vs. Holland 17-4, vs. Poland
8-1, vs. Finland 4-2, vs. Canada 6-4.
Finland vs. Poland 4-5, vs. Japan 6-3, vs. Canada
4-3, vs. USSR 2-4, vs. Holland 10-4.
Canada vs. Holland 10-1, vs. Poland 5-1, vs.
Japan 6-0.
Poland vs. Finland 5-4, vs. Holland 3-5, vs. Japan
5-1.
Holland vs. Japan 3-3, vs. Poland 5-3.

Final Round

(1) USA vs. Sweden 2-2,* USSR 4-3, vs.
Finland 4-2.
(2) USSR vs. Finland 4-2*, vs. Sweden 9-2.
(3) Sweden vs. USA 2-2*, vs. Finland 3-3.
(4) Finland vs. USSR 2-4*

*Came forward from Preliminary Round.

Fifth place game: Czechoslavakia 6, Canada 1.

The Champions: USA

William Baker	Robert McClanahan
Neal Broten	John O'Callahan
David Christian	Mark Pavelich
Steven Christoff	Michael Ramsey
James Craig	William Schneider
Michael Eruzione, Capt.	David Silk
John Harrington	Eric Strobel
Steve Janaszak	Bob Suter
Mark Johnson	Philip Verchota
Kenneth Morrow	Mark Wells

LUGE

Single Seater Ladies

A: 2/13-16/80; B: Mt. van Hoevenberg; C: 26

1. Vera Zozulia (38.978, 39.167, 39.271 39.121)	URS	2:36.537
2. Melitta Sollmann	GDR	2:37.657
3. Ingrida Amantova	USSR	2:37.817
4. Elisabeth Demleitner	FRG	2:37.918
5. Ilona Brand	GDR	2:38.115
6. Margit Schumann	GDR	2:38.255
7. Angelika Schafferer	AUT	2:38.935
8. Astra Ribena	USSR	2:39.011

Single Seater Men

A: 2/13-16/80; B: Mt. van Hoevenberg; C: 30

1. Bernhard Glass (43.609, 43.780, 43.925, 43.482)	GDR	2:54.796
2. Paul Hildgartner	ITA	2:55.372
3. Anton Winkler	FRG	2:56.545
4. Dettlef Gunther	GDR	2:57.163
5. Gerhard Sandbichler	AUT	2:57.451
6. Franz Wilhelmer	AUT	2:57.483
7. Gerd Bohmer	FRG	2:57.769
8. Anton Wembacher	FRG	2:58.012

Two-Seater-Men

A: 2/19/80; B: Mt. van Hoevenberg; C: -;

1. GDR Hans Rinn/ Norbert Hahn (39.303, 40.028)		1:19.331
2. ITA		1:19.606
3. AUT		1:19.795
4. GDR		1:19.914
5. ITA		1:19.976
6. FRG		1:20.012
7. FRG		1:20.063
8. TCH		1:20.142

BOBSLED

Two-Man-Bob

A: 2/15-16/80; B: Mt. van Hoevenberg; C: 20

1. SUI II Erich Schaerer / Josef Benz (1:01.87, 1:02.76, 1:02.29, 1:02.44)	4:09.36
2. GDR II	4:10.93
3. GDR I	4:11.08
4. SUI I	4:11.32
5. USA II	4:11.73
6. USA I	4:12.12
7. AUT II	4:13.58
8. FRG 1	4:13.74

Four-Man-Bob

A: 2/23-24/80; B: Mt. van Hoevenberg; C: 17

1. GDR I Meinhard Nehmer/Bogdan Musiol, Bernhard Germeshausen/Hans Jurgen Gerhardt (59.86, 1:00.03, 59.73, 1:00.30)	3:59.92
2. SUI I	4:00.87
3. GDR II	4:00.97
4. AUT I	4:02.62
5. AUT II	4:02.95
6. SUI II	4:03.69
7. FRG I	4:04.40
8. ROM I	4:04.68

1980 RESULTS
OLYMPIC SUMMER GAMES

Countries whose NOC's are recognized by the IOC who participated in the Games of the XXII Olympiad

AFG	Afhghanistan
ALG	Algeria
AND	Andorra
ANG	Angola
AUS	Australia
AUT	Austria
BEL	Belgium
BEN	Benin
BIR	Burma
BOT	Botswana
BRA	Brazil
BUL	Bulgaria
CGO	People's Republic of Congo
CMR	Cameroun
COL	Colombia
CRC	Costa Rica
CUB	Cuba
CYP	Cyprus
DEN	Denmark
DOM	Dominican Republic
ECU	Ecuador
ESP	Spain
ETH	Ethiopia
FIN	Finland
FRA	France
GBR	Great Britain
GDR	German Democratic Republic
GRE	Greece
GUA	Guatemala
GUI	Guinea
GUY	Guyana
HOL	Netherlands
HUN	Hungary
IND	India
IRL	Ireland
IRQ	Iraq
ISL	Iceland
ITA	Italy
JAM	Jamaica
JOR	Jordan
KUW	Kuwait
LAO	Laos
LBA	Socialist People's Libyan Arab Jamahiriya
LES	Lesotho
LIB	Lebanon
LUX	Luxembourg
MAD	Madagascar
MEX	Mexico
MGL	Mongolia
MLI	Mali
MLT	Malta
MOZ	Mozambique
NCA	Nicaragua
NEP	Nepal
NGR	Nigeria
NZL	New Zealand
PER	Peru
POL	Poland
POR	Portugal
PRK	D.P.R. Korea
PUR	Puerto Rico
ROM	Romania
SEN	Senegal
SEY	Seychelles
SLE	Sierra Leone
SMR	San Marino
SRI	Sri Lanka
SUI	Switzerland
SWE	Sweden
SYR	Syria
TAN	Tanzania
TCH	Czechoslovakia
TRI	Trinidad and Tobago
UGA	Uganda
USSR	U.S.S.R.
VEN	Venezuela
VIE	Vietnam
YUG	Yugoslavia
ZAM	Zambia
ZIM	Zimbabwe

(*) denotes 1976 Olympic Champion

ARCHERY

Men (38 entries)

1.	Tomi Poikolainen	FIN	2455
2.	Boris Isachenko	USSR	2452
3.	Giancarlo Ferrari	ITA	2449
4.	Mark Blenkarne	GBR	2446**
5.	Bela Nagy	HUN	2446
6.	Vladimir Yesheyev	USSR	2432

(**) decided on most ''10s'' and ''9s''

Women (29 entries)

1.	Keto Losaberidze	USSR	2491
2.	Natalya Butuzova	USSA	2477
3.	Paivi Meriluoto	FIN	2449
4.	Zdenka Padevetova	TCH	2405
5.	Gwang Sun O	PRK	2401
6.	Catherina Floris	HOL	2382

ATHLETICS (Track and Field)

Men

100m (51 entries)

1.	Allan Wells	GBR	10.25
2.	Silvio Leonard	CUB	10.25
3.	Petar Petrov	BUL	10.39
4.	Aleksandr Aksinin	USSR	10.42
5.	Osvaldo Lara	CUB	10.43
6.	Vladimir Muravyov	USSR	10.44
7.	Marian Woronin	POL	10.46
8.	Hermann Panzo	FRA	10.49

200m (55 entries)

1.	Pietro Mennea	ITA	20.19
2.	Allan Wells	GBR	20.21
3.	*Donald Quarrie	JAM	20.29
4.	Silvio Leonard	CUB	20.30
5.	Bernhard Hoff	GDR	20.50
6.	Leszek Dunecki	POL	20.68
7.	Marian Woronin	POL	20.81
8.	Osvaldo Lara	CUB	21.19

400m (52 entries)

1.	Viktor Markin	USSR	44.60
2.	Richard Mitchell	AUS	44.84
3.	Frank Schaffer	GDR	44.87
4.	*Alberto Juantorena	CUB	45.09
5.	Alfons Brijdenbach	BEL	45.10
6.	Michael Solomon	TRI	45.55
7.	David Jenkins	GBR	45.56
8.	Joseph Coombs	TRI	46.33

800m (41 entries)

1.	Steven Ovett	GBR	1:45.4
2.	Sebastian Coe	GBR	1:45.9
3.	Nikolai Kirov	USSR	1:46.0
4.	Alberto Guimaraes	BRA	1:46.2
5.	Andreas Busse	GDR	1:46.9
6.	Detlef Wagenknecht	GDR	1:47.0
7.	Jose Marajo	FRA	1:47.3
8.	David Warren	GBR	1:49.3

1500m (40 entries)

1.	Sebastian Coe	GBR	3:38.4
2.	Jurgen Straub	GDR	3:38.8
3.	Steven Ovett	GBR	3:39.0
4.	Andreas Busse	GDR	3:40.2
5.	Vittorio Fontanella	ITA	3:40.4
6.	Jozef Plachy	TCH	3:40.7
7.	Jose Marajo	FRA	3:41.5
8.	Stephen Cram	GBR	3:42.0
9.	Dragan Zdravkovic	YUG	3:43.1

5,000m (35 entries)

1.	Miruts Yifter	ETH	13:21.0
2.	Suleiman Nyambui	TAN	13:21.6
3.	Kaarlo Maaninka	FIN	13:22.0
4.	Eamonn Coghlan	IRL	13:22.8
5.	Markus Ryffel	SUI	13:23.1
6.	Dietmar Millonig	AUT	13:23.3
7.	John Treacy	IRL	13:23.7
8.	Aleksandr Fedotkin	USSR	13:24.1

10,000m (40 entries)

1.	Miruts Yifter	ETH	27:42.7
2.	Kaarlo Maaninka	FIN	27:44.3
3.	Mohammed Kedir	ETH	27:44.7
4.	Tolossa Kotu	ETH	27:46.5
5.	*Lasse Viren	FIN	27:50.5
6.	Jorg Peter	GDR	28:05.6
7.	Werner Schildhauer	GDR	28:11.0
8.	Enn Sellik	USSR	28:13.8

110m hurdles (23 entries)

1.	**Thomas Munkelt**	**GDR**	**13.39**
2.	**Alejandro Casanas**	**CUB**	**13.40**
3.	**Aleksandr Puchkov**	**USSR**	**13.44**
4.	Andrei Prokofev	USSR	13.49
5.	Jan Pusty	POL	13.68
6.	Arto Bryggare	FIN	13.76
7.	Javier Moracho	ESP	13.78
8.	Yuri Chervanev	USSR	15.80

Marathon (74 entries, 53 finishers)

1.	***Waldemar Cierpinski**	**GDR**	**2:11:03**
2.	**Gerard Nijboer**	**HOL**	**2:11:20**
3.	**Setymkul Dzhumanazarov**	**USSR**	**2:11.35**
4.	Vladimir Kotov	USSR	2:12.05
5.	Leonid Moseyev	USSR	2:12.14
6.	Rodolfo Gomez	MEX	2:12.39
7.	Dereje Nedi	ETH	2:12.44
8.	Massimo Magnani	ITA	2:13.12

4 x 100m relay (16 entries)

1.	**USSR (Muravytov, Sidorov, Aksinin, Prokofev)**		**38.26**
2.	**POL (Zwolinski, Licznerski, Dunecki, Woronin)**		**38.33**
3.	**FRA (Richard, Pascal Barre, Patrick Barre, Panzo)**		**38.53**
4.	GBR		38.62
5.	GDR		38.73
6.	BUL		38.99
7.	NGR		39.12
8.	BRA		39.54

4 x 400m relay (24 entries)

1.	**USSR (Valiulis, Linge, Chernetsky, Markin)**		**3:01.1**
2.	**GDR (Thiele, Knebel, Schaffer, Beck)**		**3:01.3**
3.	**ITA (Malinverni, Zuliani, Tozzi, Mennea)**		**3:04.3**
4.	FRA		3:04.8
5.	BRA		3:05.9
6.	TRI		3:06.6
7.	TCH		3:07.0
8.	GBR		DNF

400m hurdles (22 entries)

1.	**Volker Beck**	**GDR**	**48.70**
2.	**Vasily Arkhipenko**	**USSR**	**48.86**
3.	**Gary Oakes**	**GBR**	**49.11**
4.	Nicolai Vassilev	USSR	49.34
5.	Rok Kopitar	YUG	49.67
6.	Horia Toboc	ROM	49.84
7.	Franz Meier	SUI	50.00
8.	Yanko Bratanov	BUL	56.35

3,000m steeplechase (31 entries)

1.	**Bronislaw Malinowski**	**POL**	**8:09.7**
2.	**Filbert Bayi**	**TAN**	**8:12.5**
3.	**Eshetu Tura**	**ETH**	**8:13.6**
4.	Domingo Ramon	ESP	8:15.8
5.	Francisco Sanchez	ESP	8:18.0
6.	Guiseppe Gerbi	ITA	8:18.5
7.	Boguslaw Maminski	POL	8:19.5
8.	Anatoly Dimov	USSR	8:19.0

20 km race walk (34 entries, 25 finishers)

1.	**Maurizio Damilano**	**ITA**	**1:23:35.5**
2.	**Pyotr Pochinchuk**	**USSR**	**1:24:45.4**
3.	**Roland Wieser**	**GDR**	**1:25:58.2**
4.	Yevgeny Yevsyukov	USSR	1:26:28.3
5.	Jose Marin	ESP	1:26:45.6
6.	Raul Gonzalez	MEX	1:27:48.6
7.	Bohdan Bulakowski	POL	1:28:36.3
8.	Karl-Heinz Stadtmuller	GDR	1:29:21.7

50 km race walk (27 entries, 15 finishers)

1.	**Hartwig Gauder**	**GDR**	**3:49:24.0**
2.	**Jorge Llopart**	**ESP**	**3:51:25.0**
3.	**Yevgeny Ivchenko**	**USSR**	**3:56:32.0**
4.	Bengt Simonsen	SWE	3:57:08.0
5.	Vyacheslav Fursov	USSR	3:58:32.0
6.	Jose Marin	ESP	4:03:08.0
7.	Stanislaw Rola	POL	4:07:07.0
8.	Willi Sawall	AUS	4:08:25.0

High Jump (30 entries)

			m.	ft. in.
1.	**Gerd Wessig**	**GDR**	**2.36**	**7' 9"** WR, OR
2.	***Jacek Wszola**	**POL**	**2.31**	**7' 7"**
3.	**Jorg Freimuth**	**GDR**	**2.31**	**7' 7"**
4.	Henry Lauterbach	GDR	2.29	7'6¼"
5.	Roland Dahlhauser	SUI	2.24	7'4¼"
6.	Vaso Komnenic	YUG	2.24	7'4¼"
7.	Adrian Proteasa	ROM	2.21	7' 3"
8.	Aleksandr Grigoriev	USSR	2.21	7' 3"

Long Jump (32 entries)

1.	**Lutz Dombrowski**	**GDR**	**8.54**	**28'0¼"**
2.	**Frank Paschek**	**GDR**	**8.21**	**26'11¼"**
3.	**Valery Podluzhnyi**	**USSR**	**8.18**	**26'10"**
4.	Laszlo Szalma	HUN	8.13	26'8"
5.	Stanislaw Jaskulka	POL	8.13	26'8"
6.	Viktor Belsky	USSR	8.10	26'7"
7.	Antonio Corgos	ESP	8.09	26'6½"
8.	Yordan Yanev	BUL	8.02	26'6¾"

Triple Jump (23 entries)

1.	**Jaak Uudmae**	**USSR**	**17.35**	**56'11"**
2.	**Viktor Saneev**	**USSR**	**17.24**	**56'6¾"**
3.	**Joao de Oliveira**	**BRA**	**17.22**	**56'6"**
4.	Keith Connor	GBR	16.87	55'4¼"
5.	Ian Campbell	AUS	16.72	54'10¼"
6.	Atanass Tchotchev	BUL	16.56	54'4"
7.	Bela Bakosi	HUN	16.47	54'0½"
8.	Kenneth Lorraway	AUS	16.44	53'11¼"

Pole Vault (19 entries)

1.	**Wladyslaw Kozakiewicz**	**POL**	**5.78**	**18'11½"** WR,OR
2.	**Konstantin Volkov**	**USSR**	**5.65**	**18'6½"**
2.	***Tadeusz Slusarski**	**POL**	**5.65**	**18'6½"**
4.	Philippe Houvion	FRA	5.65	18'6½"
5.	Jean-Michel Bellot	FRA	5.60	18'4½"
6.	Mariusz Klimczyk	POL	5.55	18'2½"
7.	Thierry Vigneron	FRA	5.45	17'10½"
8.	Sergei Kulibaba	USSR	5.45	17'10½"

Shot Put (16 entries)

1.	**Vladimir Kiselyov**	**USSR**	**21.35**	**70'0½"** OR
2.	**Aleksandr Baryshnikov**	**USSR**	**21.08**	**69'2"**
3.	***Udo Beyer**	**GDR**	**21.06**	**69'1¼"**
4.	Reijo Stahlberg	FIN	20.82	68'3¾"
5.	Geoffrey Capes	GBR	20.50	67'3"
6.	Hans-Jurgen Jacobi	GDR	20.32	66'8"
7.	Jaromir Vlk	TCH	20.24	66'5"
8.	Vladimir Milic	YUG	20.07	65'10¼"

Discus (17 entries)

1.	**Viktor Rasshchupkin**	**USSR**	**66.64**	**218'7"**
2.	**Imrich Bugar**	**TCH**	**66.38**	**217'9"**
3.	**Luis Delis**	**CUB**	**66.32**	**217'7"**
4.	Wolfgang Schmidt	GDR	65.64	215'4"
5.	Yuri Dumchev	USSR	65.58	215'2"
6.	Igor Douguinets	USSR	64.04	210'1"
7.	Emil Vladimirov	BUL	63.18	207'3"
8.	Velko Velev	BUL	63.04	206'10"

Hammer Throw (17 entries)

1.	**Yuri Sedykh**	**USSR**	**81.80**	**268'4"** WR,OR
2.	**Sergei Litvinov**	**USSR**	**80.64**	**264'6"**
3.	**Yuri Tamm**	**USSR**	**78.96**	**259'0"**
4.	Roland Steuk	GDR	77.54	254'5"
5.	Detlef Gerstenberg	GDR	74.60	244'9"
6.	Emanouil Dulgherov	BUL	74.04	242'11"
7.	Gianpaolo Urlando	ITA	73.90	242'5"
8.	Ireneusz Golda	POL	73.74	242'11"

Javelin Throw (18 entries)

1.	**Dainis Kula**	**USSR**	**91.20**	**299'2"**
2.	**Aleksandr Makarov**	**USSR**	**89.64**	**294'1"**
3.	**Wolfgang Hanisch**	**GDR**	**86.72**	**284'6"**
4.	Kheino Puuste	USSR	86.10	282'5"
5.	Antero Puranen	FIN	85.12	279'3"
6.	Pentti Sinersaari	FIN	84.34	276'8"
7.	Detlef Fuhrmann	GDR	83.50	273'11"
8.	*Miklos Nemeth	HUN	82.40	270'4"

Decathlon (21 entries, 16 finishers)

1.	**Daley Thompson**	**GBR**	**8,495** (10.62; 8.00m- 26'3"; 15.18m- 49' 9¾"; 2.08m- 6'10"; 48.01s; 14.47s; 42.2m- 138'7"; 4.70m- 15'5"; 64.16m- 210'6"; 4:39.9)
2.	**Yuri Kutsenko**	**USSR**	**8,331**
3.	**Sergei Zhelanov**	**USSR**	**8,135**
4.	Georg Werthner	AUT	8,050
5.	Josef Zeilbauer	AUT	8,007
6.	Dariusz Ludwig	POL	7,978
7.	Atanass Andonov	BUL	7,927
8.	Steffen Grummt	GDR	7,892

Women

100m (40 entries)

1.	**Ludmila Kondrateva**	**USSR**	**11.06**
2.	**Marlies Gohr**	**GDR**	**11.07**
3.	**Ingrid Auerswald**	**GDR**	**11.14**
4.	Linda Haglund	SWE	11.16
5.	Romy Muller	GDR	11.16
6.	Kathryn Smallwood	GBR	11.28
7.	Chantal Rega	FRA	11.32
8.	Heather Hunte	GBR	11.34

200m (30 entries)

1.	***Barbel Wockel**	**GDR**	**22.03 OR**
2.	**Natalya Bochina**	**USSR**	**22.19**
3.	**Merlene Ottey**	**JAM**	**22.20**
4.	Romy Muller	GDR	22.47
5.	Kathryn Smallwood	GBR	22.61
6.	Beverley Goddard	GBR	22.72
7.	Denise Boyd	AUS	22.76
8.	Sonia Lannaman	GBR	22.80

400m (entries)

1.	**Marita Koch**	**GDR**	**48.88 OR**
2.	**Jarmila Kratochvilova**	**TCH**	**49.46**
3.	**Christina Lathan**	**GDR**	**49.66**
4.	Irina Nazarova	USSR	50.07
5.	Nina Zyuskova	USSR	50.17
6.	Gabriele Lowe	GDR	51.33
7.	Pirjo Haggman	FIN	51.35
8.	Linsey MacDonald	GBR	52.40

800m (28 entries)

1.	**Nadezhda Olizarenko**	**USSR**	**1:53.5** WR,OR
2.	**Olga Mineyeva**	**USSR**	**1:54.9**
3.	**Tatyana Providokhina**	**USSR**	**1:55.5**
4.	Martina Kampfert	GDR	1:56.3
5.	Hildegard Ullrich	GDR	1:57.2
6.	Jolanta Januchta	POL	1:58.3
7.	Nikolina Chtereva	BUL	1:58.8
8.	Gabriella Dorio	ITA	1:59.2

1,500m (24 entries)

1.	*Tatyana Kazankina	USSR	3:56.6 OR
2.	Christiane Wartenberg	GDR	3:57.8
3.	Nadezhda Olizarenko	USSR	3:59.6
4.	Gabriella Dorio	ITA	4:00.3
5.	Ulrike Bruns	GDR	4:00.7
6.	Lubov Smolka	USSR	4:01.3
7.	Maricica Puika	ROM	4:01.3
8.	Ileana Silai	ROM	4:03.0

100m Hurdles (20 entries)

1.	Vera Komisova	USSR	12.56 OR
2.	Johanna Klier	GDR	12.63
3.	Lucyna Langer	POL	12.65
4.	Kerstin Claus	GDR	12.66
5.	Grzyna Rabsztyn	POL	12.74
6.	Irina Litovchenko	USSR	12.84
7.	Bettine Gartz	GDR	12.93
8.	Zofia Bielczyk	POL	13.08

4 x 100m Relay (7 entries, no heats)

1.	GDR (Muller, Wockel, Auerswald, Gohr)	41.60 WR, OR
2.	USSR (Komisova, Maslakova, Anisimova, Bochina)	42.10
3.	GBR (Hunte, Smallwood, Goddard, Lannaman)	42.43
4.	BUL	42.67
5.	FRA	42.84
6.	JAM	43.19
7.	POL	43.59

No eighth place

4 x 400m Relay (11 entries)

1.	USSR (Prorochenko, Goistchik, Zyuskova, Nazarova)	3:20.2
2.	GDR (Lowe, Krug, Lathan, Koch)	3:20.4
3.	GBR (MacDonald, Probert, Hoyte-Smith, MacGregor)	3:27.5
4.	ROM	3:27.7
5.	HUN	3:27.9
6.	POL	3:27.9
7.	BEL	3:31.6

No eighth place, Bulgaria withdrew after heats

High Jump (20 entries)

1.	Sara Simeoni	ITA	1.97m	6'5½" OR
2.	Urszula Kielan	POL	1.94	6'4½"
3.	Jutta Kirst	GDR	1.94	6'4½"
4.	*Rosemarie Ackermann	GDR	1.91	6'3¼"
5.	Marina Sysoeva	USSR	1.91	6'3¼"
6.	Christine Stanton	AUS	1.91	6'3¼"
6.	Andrea Reichstein	GDR	1.91	6'3¼"
8.	Cornelia Popa	ROM	1.88	6'2"

Long Jump (19 entries)

1.	Tatiana Kolpakova	USSR	7.06m	23'2" OR
2.	Brigitte Wujak	GDR	7.04	23'1¼"
3.	Tatiana Skachko	USSR	7.01	23'0"
4.	Anna Wlodarczyk	POL	6.95	22'9¾"
5.	Siegrun Siegl	GDR	6.87	22'6½"
6.	Jarmila Nygrynova	TCH	6.83	22'5"
7.	Siegrid Heimann	GDR	6.71	22'0¼"
8.	Lidiya Alfeyeva	USSR	6.71	22'0¼"

Discus (17 entries)

1.	*Evelin Jahl	GDR	69.96	229'6" OR
2.	Maria Petkova	BUL	67.90	222'9"
3.	Tatyana Lesovaya	USSR	67.40	221'1"
4.	Gisela Beyer	GDR	67.08	220'1"
5.	Margitta Pufe	GDR	66.12	216'11"
6.	Florenta Tacu	ROM	64.38	211'2"
7.	Galina Murashova	USSR	63.84	209'5"
8.	Svetla Bojkova	BUL	63.14	207'1"

Javelin (21 entries)

1.	Maria Colon	CUB	68.40	224'5" OR
2.	Saida Gunba	USSR	67.76	222'2"
3.	Ute Hommola	GDR	66.56	218'4"
4.	Ute Richter	GDR	66.54	218'4"
5.	Ivanka Vantcheva	BUL	66.38	217'9"
6.	Tatyana Biryulina	USSR	65.08	213'6"
7.	Zorgo Eva Raduly	ROM	64.08	210'3"
8.	*Ruth Fuchs	GDR	63.94	209'9"

Pentathlon (19 entries, 17 finished)

1.	Nadezhda Tkachenko	USSR	5,083 WR, OR

(13.29 100m hurdles, 16.84-55' 3" shotput, 1.84-6'0½" high jump, 6.73-22' 0½" long jump, 2:05.20 800m)

2.	Olga Rukavishnikova	USSR	4,937
3.	Olga Kuragina	USSR	4,875
4.	Ramona Neubert-Gohler	GDR	4,698
5.	Margit Papp	HUN	4,562
6.	Burglinde Pollak	GDR	4,553
7.	Valentina Dimitrova	BUL	4,458
8.	Emilia Kounova	BUL	4,431

Shotput (14 entries)

1.	Ilona Slupianek	GDR	22.41	73'6¼" WR, OR
2.	Svetlana Krachevskaya	USSR	21.42	70'3¼"
3.	Margitta Pufe	GDR	21.20	69'6¾"
4.	Nunu Abashidze	USSR	21.15	69'4¾"
5.	Verjinia Vesselinova	BUL	20.72	67'11¾"
6.	Elena Stoyanova	BUL	20.22	66'4"
7.	Nataliya Akhrimenko	USSR	19.74	64'9¼"
8.	Ines Reichenbach	GDR	19.66	64'6"

BASKETBALL

Men

Championship Game: YUG 86 ITA 77

Third-Place Game: USSR 117 ESP 94

In the top six teams in the semi-finals, BRA was awarded 5th, CUB 6th.

Championship Flight:

	USSR	YUG	ITA
USSR	—	91-101	85-87
YUG	101-91	—	102-81
ITA	87-85	81-102	—
CUB	90-109	84-112	72-79
ESP	102-119	91-95	89-95
BRA	88-101	95-96	90-77

	CUB	ESP	BRA
USSR	109-90	119-102	101-88
YUG	112-84	95-91	96-95
ITA	79-72	95-89	77-90
CUB	—	95-96	93-94
ESP	96-95	—	110-81
BRA	94-93	81-110	—

Placings 7-12

	POL	AUS	TCH
7. POL	+	101-74	88-84
8. AUS	74-101	—	91-86
9. TCH	84-88	86-91	—
10. SWE	70-67	55-64	61-83
11. SEN	64-84	66-95	72-88
12. IND	84-88	75-93	65-133

	SWE	SEN	IND
7. POL	67-70	84-64	113-67
8. AUS	64-55	95-64	93-75
9. TCH	83-61	88-72	133-65
10. SWE	—	70-64	119-63
11. SEN	64-70	—	81-59
12. IND	63-119	59-81	—

Preliminary Round

Group A 1. USSR 3-0, 2. BRA 2-1, 3. TCH 1-2, 4. IND 0-3.
Group B 1. YUG 3-0, 2. ESP 2-1, 3. POL 1-2, 4. SEN 0-3.
Group C 1. ITA 2-1, CUB 2-1, AUS 2-1, SWE 0-3.

The Scoring Leaders: 1. Ian Davies, AUS 205; 2. Drazen Dalipagic, YUG 195; 3. Dragan Kicanovic, YUG 189; 4. Stanislav Kropilak, TCH 184; 5. Candido-Antonio Sibilio, ESP 173; 6. Oscar Daniel Schmidt, BRA and Sergei Belov, USSR 169.

The Champions: YUG-Andro Knego, Dragan Kicanovic,* Rajko Zizic, *Mihovil Nakic, Zeljko Jerkov, *Branko Skroce, Zoran Slavnic, Kresimir Cosic, Ratko Radovanovic, *Duje Krstulovic, Drazen Dalipagic, Mirza Delibasic. (*) Did not play in the championship game.

Women

Championship Game: USSR 104 BUL 73

Third-Place Game: YUG 68 HUN 65

In the final standings CUB placed 5th and ITA 6th. Standings in Round Robin Tournament:

USSR 5-0, BUL 4-1, YUG 3-2, HUN 2-3, CUB 1-4, ITA 0-5.

Round-Robin Tournament Scores:

	BUL	CUB	HUN
BUL	—	84-64	90-75
CUB	64-84	—	66-76
HUN	75-90	76-66	—
ITA	65-102	63-79	70-83
USSR	122-83	95-56	120-62
YUG	79-81	85-81	61-48

	ITA	USSR	YUG
BUL	102-65	83-122	81-79
CUB	79-63	56-95	81-85
HUN	83-70	62-120	48-61
ITA	—	53-119	57-69
USSR	119-53	—	97-62
YUG	69-57	62-97	—

The Scoring Leaders: 1. Lenke Kiss, HUN 191, 2. Iuliana Semenova, USSR 131; 3. Sofija Pekic, YUG 121; 4. Evladia Slavtcheva, BUL 112; 5. Judit Megyesi, BUL 102; 6. Caridad Despaigne, CUB 93.

The Champions: USSR-Angele Rupshene, Lubov Sharmay, Vida Besselene, Olga Korosteleva, Tatiana Ovechkina, Nadezda Olkhova, Iuliana Semenova, Ludmila Rogozina, Nelly Feriabnikova, Olga Sukharnova, Tatiana Nadyrova, Tatiana Ivinskaya. All team members played in the championship game.

BOXING

NOTE: The first mentioned bronze medalist competed against the Olympic champions in the semi-finals.

Light Flyweight (48 kg/106 lbs.)

(22 entries) Result/Judges Voting

1. **Shamil Sabyrov**	**USSR**	**3-2 dec.**
2. **Hipolito Ramos**	**CUB**	
3. ***Byong Uk Li**	**PRK**	
3. ***Ismail Moustafov**	**BUL**	

(*) defeated semi-finalists

Flyweight (51 kg/112 lbs.)

(22 entries)

1. **Petar Lessov**	**BUL**	**RSC 2:08 2nd round**
2. **Viktor Miroshnickenko**	**USSR**	
3. ***Hugh Russell**	**IRL**	
3. ***Janos Varadi**	**HUN**	

Bantamweight (54 kg/119 lbs.)

(34 entries)

1. **Juan Hernandez**	**CUB**	**5-0 dec.**
2. **Bernardo Pinango**	**VEN**	
3. ***Michael Anthony**	**GUY**	
3. ***Dumitru Cipere**	**ROM**	

Featherweight (57 kg/126 lbs.)

(35 entries)

1. **Rudi Fink**	**GDR**	**4-1 dec.**
2. **Adolfo Horta**	**CUB**	
3. ***Viktor Rybakov**	**USSR**	
3.* **Krzysztof Kosedowski**	**POL**	

Lightweight (60 kg/132 lbs.)

(29 entries)

1. **Angel Herrera**	**CUB**	**RSC 13 sec. 3rd round**
2. **Viktor Demianenko**	**USSR**	
3. ***Kazimierz Adach**	**POL**	
3. ***Richard Nowakowski**	**GDR**	

Light Welterweight (63.5 kg/139 lbs.)

(30 entries)

1. **Patrizio Oliva**	**ITA**	**4-1 dec.**
2. **Serik Konakbaev**	**USSR**	
3. ***Anthony Willis**	**GBR**	
3. ***Jose Aguilar**	**CUB**	

Welterweight (67 kg/148 lbs½)

(29 entries)

1. **Andres Aldama**	**CUB**	**4-1 dec.**
2. **John Mugabi**	**UGA**	
3. ***Karl-Heinz Kruger**	**GDR**	
3. ***Kazimierz Szczerba**	**POL**	

Light Middleweight (71 kg/157 lbs.)

(23 entries)

1. **Armando Martinez**	**CUB**	**4-1 dec.**
2. **Aleksandr Koshkin**	**USSR**	
3. ***Jan Franek**	**TCH**	
3. ***Detlef Kastner**	**GDR**	

Middleweight (75 kg/165 lbs.)

(19 entries)

1. **Jose Gomez**	**CUB**	**4-1 dec.**
2. **Viktor Savchenko**	**USSR**	
3. ***Valentin Silaghi**	**ROM**	
3. ***Jerzy Rybicki**	**POL**	

Light Heavyweight (81 kg/179 lbs.)

(16 entries)

1. **Slobodan Kacar**	**YUG**	**4-1 dec.**
2. **Pawel Skrzecz**	**POL**	
3. ***Herbert Bauch**	**GDR**	
3. ***Ricardo Rojas**	**CUB**	

Heavyweight (over 179 lbs.)

(14 entries)

1. **Teofilo Stevenson**	**CUB**	**4-1 dec.**
2. **Pyotr Zaev**	**USSR**	
3. ***Istvan Levai**	**HUN**	
3. ***Jurgen Fanghanel**	**GDR**	

CANOEING

Women

Kayak — singles — 500m (11 entries)

1. **GDR (Birgit Fischer)**	**1:57.96**
2. **BUL (Vania Ghecheva)**	**1:59.48**
3. **USSR (Antonina Melnikova)**	**1:59.66**
4. ROM (Maria Stefan)	2:00.90
5. POL (Ewa Eichler)	2:01.23
6. SWE (Agneta Andersson)	2:01.33
7. HUN (Katalin Povazsan)	2:01.52
8. FRA (Beatrice Knopf)	2:02.91
9. GBR (Lucy Perret)	2:04.89

Kayak — doubles — 500m (12 entries)

1. **GDR (Genauss, Bischof)**	**1:43.88**
2. **USSR (Alexeyeva, Trofimova)**	**1:46.91**
3. **HUN (Rakusz, Zakarias)**	**1:47.95**
4. ROM	1:48.04
5. SWE	1:49.27
6. FRA	1:49.48
7. POL	1:51.31
8. GBR	1:52.76
9. BUL	1:53.12

Men

Kayak — singles — 500m (17 entries)

1. **USSR (Vladimir Parfenovich)**	**1:43.43**
2. **AUS (John Sumegi)**	**1:44.12**
3. **ROM (*Vasile Diba)**	**1:44.90**
4. YUG (Milan Janic)	1:45.63
5. GDR (Frank Peter Bischof)	1:45.97
6. SWE (Anders Andersson)	1:46.32
7. NZL (Ian Ferguson)	1:47.36
8. TCH (Felix Masar)	1:48.18
9. HUN (Zoltan Sztaniti)	1:48.34

Kayak — doubles — 500m (18 entries)

1. **USSR (Parfenovich, Chukhrai)**	**1:32.38**
2. **ESP (Menendez, Del Riego)**	**1:33.65**
3. **GDR (Helm, *Olbricht)**	**1:34.00**
4. FRA	1:36.22
5. AUS	1:36.45
6. ROM	1:36.96
7. POL	1:37.20
8. HUN	1:37.66
9. SWE	1:39.92

Kayak — singles — 1,000m (20 entries)

1. **GDR (*Rudiger Helm)**	**3:48.77**
2. **FRA (Alain Lebas)**	**3:50.20**
3. **ROM (Ion Birladeanu)**	**3:50.49**
4. AUS (John Sumegi)	3:50.63
5. ITA (Oreste Perri)	3:51.95
6. TCH (Felix Masar)	3:52.10
7. YUG (Milan Janic)	3:53.50
8. NZL (Ian Ferguson)	3:53.78
9. SWE (Anders Andersson)	3:54.54

Kayak — doubles — 1,000m (16 entries)

1. **USSR (Parfenovich, Chukharai)**	**3:26.72**
2. **HUN (Szabo, Joos)**	**3:28.49**
3. **ESP (Ramos-Misione, Menendez)**	**3:28.66**
4. ROM	3:28.94
5. GDR	3:31.02
6. CUB	3:31.12
7. HOL	3:33.18
8. NZL	3:33.83
9. ITA	3:52.32

Kayak — quadruple — 1,000m (12 entries)

1. **GDR (Helm, Olbricht, Marg, Duvigneau)**	**3:13.76**
2. **ROM (Zafiu, Diba, Geanta, Esanu)**	**3:15.35**
3. **BUL (Borissov, Milenkov, Khristov, Manev)**	**3:15.46**
4. POL	3:16.33
5. HUN	3:17.27
6. FRA	3:17.60
7. USSR	3:19.83
8. AUS	3:19.87
9. SWE	3:20.74

Canoe — singles — 500m (11 entries)

1. **USSR (Sergei Postrekhin)**	**1:53.37**
2. **BUL (Lubomir Lubenov)**	**1:53.49**
3. **GDR (Olaf Heukrodt)**	**1:54.38**
4. HUN (Tamas Wichmann)	1:54.58
5. POL (Marek Lbik)	1:55.90
6. FIN (Timo Gronlund)	1:55.94
7. ROM (Lipat Varabiev)	1:56.80
8. TCH (Raomir Blazik)	1:56.83
9. YUG (Matija Ljubek)	2:03.43

Canoe — doubles — 500m (10 entries)

1. **HUN (Foltan, Vaskuti)**	**1:43.39**
2. **ROM (Potzaichin, Capusta)**	**1:44.12**
3. **BUL (Ananiev, Ilkov)**	**1:44.83**
4. POL	1:45.10
5. TCH	1:46.48
6. USSR (*Petrenko, *Vinogradov)	1:46.95
7. ESP	1:48.18
8. SWE	1:48.69
9. FRA	1:50.33

Canoe — Singles — 1,000m (12 entries)

1. **BUL (Lubomir Lubenov)**	**4:12.38**
2. **USSR (Sergei Postrekhin)**	**4:13.53**
3. **GDR (Eckhard Leue)**	**4:15.02**
4. TCH (Libor Dvorak)	4:15.25
5. ROM (Lipat Varabiev)	4:16.68
6. FIN (Timo Gronlund)	4:17.37
7. SWE (Thomas Falk)	4:20.66
8. YUG (Matija Ljubek)	4:22.40
9. HUN (Tamas Wichmann)	4:45.30

Canoe — Doubles — 1,000m (11 entries)

1. **ROM (Potzaichin, Simionov)**	**3:47.65**
2. **GDR (Heukrodt, Madeja)**	**3:49.93**
3. **USSR (Yurchenko, Lobanov)**	**3:51.28**
4. YUG	3:51.30
5. TCH	3:52.50
6. POL	3:53.01
7. BUL	3:53.89
8. HUN	3:54.31
9. SWE	3:58.62

CYCLING

Individual Road Race (52 finished) (189 km/118 miles)

1.	Sergei Sukhoruchenkov	USSR	4:48:28.9
2.	Czeslaw Lang	POL	4:51.26.9
3.	Yuri Barinov	USSR	4:51.26.9
4.	Thomas Barth	GDR	4:56:12.9
5.	Tadeusz Wojtas	POL	4:56:12.9
6.	Anatoly Yarkin	USSR	4:56:54.9

100km (62.5 miles) Team Road Race (23 teams, all finished)

1.	USSR (Kashirin, Logvin, Shelpakov, Yarkin)	2:01:21.7
2.	GDR (Boden, Drogan, Ludwig, Hartnick)	2:02:53.2
3.	TCH (Klasa, Konecny, Kostadinov, Skoda)	2:02:53.9
4.	POL	2:04:13.8
5.	ITA	2:04:36.2
6.	BUL	2:05:55.2

Sprint (18 entries)

1.	Lutz Hesslich	GDR
2.	Yave Cahard	FRA
3.	Sergei Kopylov	USSR
4.	*Anton Tkac	TCH
5.	Henrik Salee	DEN
6.	Heinz Isler	SUI

(*) '76 Olympic champion

1,000m Time Trial (18 entries)

1.	Lothar Thoms	GDR	1:02.955 WR
2.	Alexandr Panfilov	USSR	1:04.845 WR
3.	David Weller	JAM	1:05.241 WR
4.	Guido Bontempi	ITA	1:05.478 WR
5.	Yave Cahard	FRA	1:05.584 WR
6.	Heinz Isler	SUI	1:06.273 WR
7.	Petr Kocek	TCH	1:06.368 WR

4,000m Individual Pursuit (14 entries)

1.	Robert Dill-Bundi	SUI	4:35.66
2.	Alain Bondue	FRA	4:42.96
3.	Hans-Hendrik Orsted	DEN	4:36.54
4.	Harald Wolf	GDR	4:37.38
5.	Vladimir Osokin	USSR	n.t.
6.	Sean Yates	GBR	n.t.

4,000m Team Pursuit (13 entries)

1.	USSR (Manakov, Movchan, Osokin, Petrakov)	4:15.70
2.	GDR (Mortag, Unterwalder, Wiegand, Winkler)	4:19.67
3.	TCH (Cerny, Penc, Pokorny, Slama)	n.t.
4.	ITA	n.t.
5.	FRA	
6.	AUS	n.t.

EQUESTRIAN SPORTS

Grand Prix Dressage, Individual

		Points	Horse
1.	Elizabeth Theurer AUT	1370.0	Mon Cherie
2.	Yuri Kovshov USSR	1300.0	Igrok
3.	Viktor Ugryumov USSR	1234.0	Shkval
4.	Vera Misevich USSR	1231.0	Plot
5.	Kyra Kyrklund FIN	1121.0	Piccolo
6.	Anghelache Donescu ROM	960.0	Dor

Grand Prix Dressage, Team (4 entries)

1.	USSR (Kovshov, Ugryumov, Misevich)	4383.0
2.	BUL (Mandajiev, Ivanov, Gadjev)	3580.0
3.	ROM (Donescu, Veliku, Rosca)	3346.0
4.	POL	2945.0

Three-Day Event, Individual (28 entries, 17 finished)

			Horse
1.	Frederico Euro Roman ITA	108.60	Rossinan
2.	Aleksandr Blinov USSR	120.80	Galzun
3.	Yuri Salnikov USSR	151.60	Pintset
4.	Valery Volkov USSR	184.60	Tskheti
5.	Tzvetan Dontchev BUL	185.50	Medisson
6.	Miroslaw Szlapka POL	241.80	Erywan

Three-Day Event, Team (7 team entries, 4 finished)

1.	USSR (Blinov, Salnikov, Volkov, Rogozhin)	457.0
2.	ITA (F. Roman, Casagrande, M. Roman, Sciocchetti)	656.20
3.	MEX (Mendivil, Barcena, Perez, Vazquez)	1172.85
4.	HUN	1603.40

Grand Prix Jumping, Individual (16 entries, 14 finished)

			Horse
1.	Jan Kowalczyk POL	8.00	Artemor
2.	Nikolai Korolkov USSR	9.50	Espadron
3.	Joaquin Perez Heras MEX	12.00**	Alymony
4.	Oswaldo Mendez Herbruger GUA	12.00	Pampa
5.	Viktor Poganovsky USSR	15.50	Topky
6.	Wieslaw Hartman POL	16.00	Norton

**Won jump off.

Grand Prix Jumping, Team (6 teams)

1.	USSR (Chukanov, Poganovsky, **Asmaev, Korolkov)	20.25
2.	POL (Kozicki, Kowalczyk, Hartman, **Bobik)	56.00
3.	MEX (Perez Heras, Gomez Portugal, Tazzer, **Valdes Lacarra)	59.75
4.	HUN	124.00
5.	ROM	150.50
6.	BUL	159.50

(**) Not counted in team score.

FENCING

Men's Foil (37 entries)

			TF	TA
1.	Vladimir Smirnov	USSR	24	16
2.	Paskal Jolyot	FRA	24	17
3.	Aleksandr Romankov	USSR	22	15
4.	Sabirzahn Ruziev	USSR	20	19
5.	Lech Koziejowski	POL	15	21
6.	Petru Kuki	ROM	8	25

TF-Touches for   TA-Touches against

Men's Foil Team (9 entries)

1.	FRA (Flament, Jolyot, Boscherie, Bonnin)
2.	USSR (Romankov, Smirnov, Ruziev, Karagyran)
3.	POL (Robak, Zych, Koziejowski, Sypniewski)
4.	GDR
5.	ROM
6.	HUN
7.	CUB
8.	GBR
9.	KUW

Results: FRA-USSR 8-8 decided on hits for and hits against, 68-60; POL-GDR 9-5, ROM-HUN 9-7

Ladies Foil (33 entries)

1.	Pascale Trinquet	FRA	21	16
2.	Magda Maros	HUN	23	17
3.	Barbara Wysoczanska	POL	19	18
4.	Ecaterina Stahl	ROM	19	21
5.	Brigitte Latri-Gaudin	FRA	20	22
6.	Dorina Vaccaroni	ITA	14	22

Ladies Foil Team (9 entries)

1.	FRA (Latri-Gaudin, Trinquet, Boeri-Bebard, Brouquier)
2.	USSR (Sidorova, Gilyazova, Belova, Ushakova)
3.	HUN (Schwarczenberger, Maros, Stefanek, Szocs)
4.	POL
5.	ITA
6.	CUB
7.	GBR
8.	GDR

Results: FRA-USSR 9-6; HUN-POL 9-7; ITA-CUB 9-6

Epee (41 entries)

1.	Johan Harmenberg	SWE	22	21
2.	Erno Kolczonay	HUN	23	19
3.	Philippe Riboud	FRA	20	17
4.	Rolf Edling	SWE	18	16
5.	Alexandr Mozhaev	USSR	18	22
6.	Loan Popa	ROM	18	24

Epee, Team (12 entries)

1.	FRA (Riboud, Picot, Gardas, Boisee)
2.	POL (Jablkowski, Lis, Swornowski, Chronowski)
3.	USSR (Karagyan, Lukomsky, Abushakhmetov, Mozhaev)
4.	ROM
5.	SWE
6.	TCH

Results: FRA-POL 8-4; USSR-ROM 9-5, SWE-TCH 9-2

Sabre (30 entries)

1. **Viktor Krovopuskov**	**USSR**	**24**	**17**
2. **Mikhail Burtsev**	**USSR**	**23**	**18**
3. **Imre Gedovari**	**HUN**	**23**	**21**
4. Vassil Etropolski	BUL	17	23
5. Khristo Etropolski	BUL	19	21
6. Michele Maffei	ITA	15	21

Sabre, Team (8 teams)

1. **USSR (Burtsev, Krovopuskov, Sidyak, Nazlymov)**
2. **ITA (Maffei, Montano, Romano, Meglio)**
3. **HUN (Gedovari, Nebald, Gerevich, Hammang)**
4. POL
5. ROM
6. GDR
7. CUB
8. BUL

Results: USSR-ITA 9-2, HUN-POL 9-6, ROM-GDR 9-6

FIELD HOCKEY

Men

Championship Game: IND 4 ESP 3

Third-Place Game: USSR 2 POL 1

Fifth-Place Game: CUB 4 TAN 1

Classification Tournament Placings (Won-Lost-Tied):

1. ESP 4-0-1, 2. IND 3-0-2, 3. USSR 3-2-0, 4. POL 2-2-1, 5. CUB 1-4-0, 6. TAN 0-5-0

Round Robin Tournament Scores

	CUB	ESP	IND	POL	TAN	USSR
CUB	—	0-11	0-13	1-7	4-0	2-11
ESP	11-0	—	2-2	6-0	12-0	2-1
IND	13-0	2-2	—	2-2	18-0	4-2
POL	7-1	0-6	2-2	—	9-1	1-5
TAN	0-4	0-12	0-18	1-9	—	2-11
USSR	11-2	1-2	2-4	5-1	11-2	—

The Scoring Leaders: (by Points, not goals):
1. Juan Amat, ESP 16; 2. Surinder Singh, IND 15; 3. Vyatcheslav Lampeev; USSR 9; 4. Deavinder Singh, IND 8; 5. Bernabe Izquierdo, CUB 7; 6. Juan Luis Coghen, ESP 6.

The Champions: IND-**Schofield Allan, Chettri Bir Bhadur, Dung Dung Sylvanus, **Rajinder Singh, Deavinder Singh, **Gurmail Singh, Ravinder Pal Singh, Baskaran Vasudevan, Somaya Maneypanda, Maharaj Krishon Kaushik, Charanjit Kumar, Mervyn Fernandis, **Amarjit Rana Singh, Shahid Mohamed, Zafar Iqbal, Surinder Singh
(**) did not play in championship game.

Women

Final standing of round robin, no playoffs for first three places.

	ZIM	TCH	USSR	IND	AUT	POL
ZIM	—	2-2	2-0	1-1	4-1	4-0
TCH	2-2	—	0-2	2-1	5-0	1-0
USSR	0-2	2-0	—	3-1	0-2	6-0
IND	1-1	1-2	1-3	—	2-0	4-0
AUT	1-4	0-5	2-0	0-2	—	3-0
POL	0-4	0-1	0-6	0-4	0-3	—

Round Robin Tournament: Won-Lost-Tied
1. ZIM 3-0-2; 2. TCH 3-1-1; 3. USSR 3-2-0; 4. IND 2-2-1; 5. AUT 2-3-0; 6. POL 0-5-0.

The Scoring Leaders (by points, not goals)
1. Patricia Jean McKillop, ZIM and Natella Krasnikova, USSR 6 each; 3. Natalya Buzunova, USSR 5; 4. Rup Kumari Saini, IND 4; 5. Jirina Cermakova, TCH and Elizabeth Muriel Chase, ZIM 3 each.

The Champions: Sarah English, Anne Mary Grant, Brenda Joan Phillips, Patricia Jean McKillop, Sonia Robertson, Patricia Joan Davies, Maureen Jean George, Linda Margaret Watson, Susan Huggett, Gillian Margaret Cowley, Elizabeth Murial Chase, Sandra Chick, Helen Volk, Christine Prinsloo, Arlene Nadine Boxhall, Anthea Doreen Stewart

GYMNASTICS

Men

Team (9 full teams)

		Points
1. **USSR (Andrianov, Azarian, Ditiatin, Makuts, Markelov, Tkachyov)**		**589.60**
2. **GDR (Hemmann, Hoffmann, Mack, Nikolay, Bronst, Bruckner)**		**581.15**
3. **HUN (Donath, Guczoghy, Kelemen, Kovacs, Magyar, Vamos)**		**575.00**
4. ROM		572.30
5. BUL		571.55
6. TCH		569.80
7. CUB		563.20
8. FRA		559.20
9. PRK		551.35

All-Around (36 entries)

1. **Alexandr Ditiatin**	**USSR**	**118.650**
2. ***Nikolai Andrianov**	**USSR**	**118.225**
3. **Stoyan Deltchev**	**BUL**	**118.000**
4. Alexandr Tkachyov	USSR	117.700
5. Roland Bruckner	GDR	117.300
6. Michael Nikolay	GDR	116.750

Note: Maximum of 3 entries permitted from each country in all-around.

Pommel Horse (6 entries)

1. ***Zoltan Magyar**	**HUN**	**19.925**
2. **Alexandr Ditiatin**	**USSR**	**19.800**
3. **Michael Nikolay**	**GDR**	**19.775**
4. Roland Bruckner	GDR	19.725
5. Alexandr Tkachyov	USSR	19.475
6. Ferenc Donath	HUN	19.400

Note: Maximum of 2 entries permitted from each country in all individual events.

Long Horse Vault (6 entries)

1. ***Nikolai Andrianov**	**USSR**	**19.825**
2. **Alexandr Ditiatin**	**USSR**	**19.800**
3. **Roland Bruckner**	**GDR**	**19.775**
4. Ralf-Peter Hemmann	GDR	19.750
5. Stoyan Deltchev	BUL	19.700
6. Jiri Tabak	TCH	19.525

Rings (6 entries)

1. **Alexandr Ditiatin**	**USSR**	**19.875**
2. **Alexandr Tkachyov**	**USSR**	**19.725**
3. **Jiri Tabak**	**TCH**	**19.600**
4. Roland Bruckner	GDR	19.575
5. Stoyan Deltchev	BUL	19.475
6. Danut Grecu	ROM	10.850

Parallel Bars (6 entries)

1. **Alexandr Tkachyov**	**USSR**	**19.775**
2. **Alexandr Ditiatin**	**USSR**	**19.750**
3. **Roland Bruckner**	**GDR**	**19.650**
4. Michael Nikolay	GDR	19.600
5. Stoyan Deltchev	BUL	19.575
6. Roberto Leon	CUB	19.500

Horizontal Bar (6 entries)

1. **Stoyan Deltchev**	**BUL**	**19.825**
2. **Alexandr Ditiatin**	**USSR**	**19.750**
3. **Nikolai Andrianov**	**USSR**	**19.675**
4. Ralf-Peter Hemmann	GDR	19.525
4. Michael Nikolay	GDR	19.525
6. Sergio Suarez	CUB	19.450

Floor Exercise (6 entries)

1. **Roland Bruckner**	**GDR**	**19.750**
2. ***Nikolai Andrianov**	**USSR**	**19.725**
3. **Alexandr Ditiatin**	**USSR**	**19.700**
4. Jiri Tabak	TCH	19.675
5. Peter Kovacs	HUN	19.425
6. Lutz Hoffmann	GDR	18.725

Women

Team (8 full teams)

		Points
1. **USSR (Davydova, Filatova, Kim, Naimoushina, Shaposhnikova, Zakharova)**		**394.90**
2. **ROM (Comaneci, Dunka, Eberle, Ruhn, Turner, Grigoras)**		**393.50**
3. **GDR (Gnauck, Hinderoff, Kraker, Rensch, Sube, Suss)**		**392.55**
4. TCH		388.80
5. HUN		384.30
6. BUL		382.10
7. POL		376.25
8. PRK		364.05

All-Around (36 entries, max. of 3 from each country)

1. **Yelena Davydova**	**USSR**	**79.150**
2. **Maxi Gnauck**	**GDR**	**79.075**
2. ***Nadia Comaneci**	**ROM**	**79.075**
4. Natalia Shaposhnikova	USSR	79.025
5. Nelli Kim	USSR	78.425
6. Emilia Eberle	ROM	78.400

Horse Vault (6 entries, max. of 2 from each country)

1. **Natalia Shaposhnikova**	**USSR**	**19.725**
2. **Steffi Kraker**	**GDR**	**19.675**
3. **Melita Ruhn**	**ROM**	**19.650**
4. Yelena Davydova	USSR	19.575
5. Nadia Comaneci	ROM	19.350
6. Maxi Gnauck	GDR	19.300

Uneven Parallel Bars (6 entries)

1. **Maxi Gnauck**	**GDR**	**19.875**
2. **Emilia Eberle**	**ROM**	**19.850**
3. **Steffi Kraker**	**GDR**	**19.775**
3. **Melita Ruhn**	**ROM**	**19.775**
3. **Maria Filatova**	**USSR**	**19.775**
6. Nelli Kim	USSR	19.725

Balance Beam (6 entries)

1.	*Nadia Comaneci	ROM	19.800
2.	Yelena Davydova	USSR	19.750
3.	Natalia Shaposhnikova	USSR	19.725
4.	Maxi Gnauck	GDR	19.700
5.	Radka Zemanova	TCH	19.650
6.	Emilia Eberle	ROM	19.400

Floor Exercise (6 entries)

1.	*Nelli Kim	USSR	19.875
1.	Nadia Comaneci	ROM	19.875
3.	Natalia Shaposhnikova	USSR	19.825
3.	Maxi Gnauck	GDR	19.825
5.	Emilia Eberle	ROM	19.750
6.	Jana Labakova	TCH	19.725

JUDO

Extra Lightweight (60kg/132 lbs.) (29 entries)

1.	Thierry Rey	FRA
2.	Jose Rodriguez	CUB
3.	Aramby Emizh	USSR
3.	Tibor Kincses	HUN

Half Lightweight (65kg/143 lbs.) (29 entries)

1.	Nikolay Solodukhin	USSR
2.	Tsendying Damdin	MGL
3.	Ilian Nedkov	BUL
3.	Janusz Pawlowski	POL

Lightweight (71kg/157 lbs.) (30 entries)

1.	Ezio Gamba	ITA
2.	Neil Adams	GBR
3.	Karl-Heinz Lehmann	GDR
3.	Ravdan Davaadalai	MGL

Half Middleweight (78kg/172 lbs.) (24 entries)

1.	Shota Khabareli	USSR
2.	Juan Ferrer	CUB
3.	Bernard Tchoullouyan	FRA
3.	Harald Heinke	GDR

Middleweight (86kg/190 lbs.) (27 entries)

1.	Juerg Roethlisberger	SUI
2.	Issac Azcuy	CUB
3.	Alexandr Iatskevich	USSR
3.	Detlef Ultsch	GDR

Half Heavyweight (95kg/209 lbs.) (23 entries)

1.	Robert Van De Walle	BEL
2.	Tengiz Khubuluri	USSR
3.	Dietmar Lorenz	GDR
3.	Henk Numan	HOL

Heavyweight (Over 95 kg/over 209 lbs.) (18 entries)

1.	Angelo Parisi	FRA
2.	Dimitar Zaprianov	BUL
3.	Vladimir Kocman	TCH
3.	Radomir Kovacevic	YUG

Open Class (No weight limit) (21 entries)

1.	Dietmar Lorenz	GDR
2.	Angelo Parisi	FRA
3.	Arthur Mapp	GBR
3.	Andras Ozsvar	HUN

Other 1976 Olympic Champion entered in Open Class—Robert Van De Walle, BEL, up to 209 lbs.

MODERN PENTATHLON

Individual (43 entries, all finished)

			Points
1.	Anatoly Starostin	USSR	5,568
2.	Tamas Szmobathelyi	HUN	5,502
3.	Pavel Lednev	USSR	5,382
4.	Svante Rasmuson	SWE	5,373
5.	Tibor Maracsko	HUN	5,279
6.	Janusz Pyciak-Peciak	POL	5,268

Note: Starostin points-1068 riding, 1000 fencing, 1110 shooting, 1216 swimming, 1174 running

Team (12 entries, all finished)

1.	USSR (Starostin, Lednev, Lipeev)	16,126
2.	HUN (Szmobathelyi, Maracsko, L. Horvath)	15,912
3.	SWE (Rasmuson, Pettersson, G. Horvath)	15,845
4.	POL	15,634
5.	FRA	15,345
6.	TCH	15,339

ROWING

Men (2,000m)

Single Sculls (14 entries)

1.	*FIN (Pertti Karppinen)	7:09.61
2.	USSR (Vasily Yakusha)	7:11.66
3.	GDR (Peter Kersten)	7:14.88
4.	TCH (Vladek Lacina)	7:17.57
5.	SWE (Hans Svensson)	7:19.38
6.	GBR (Hugh Matheson)	7:20.28

Double Skulls (9 entries)

1.	GDR (Dreipke, Kroppelien)	6:24.33
2.	YUG (Pancic, Stanulov)	6:26.34
3.	TCH (Pecka, Vochoska)	6:29.07
4.	GBR	6:31.13
5.	USSR	6:35.34
6.	POL	6:39.66

Quadruple Sculls (12 entries)

1.	GDR (Dundr, Bunk, Heppner, Winter)	5:49.81
2.	USSR (Shapochka, Barbakov, Kleshnev, Dovgan)	5:51.47
3.	BUL (Nikolov, Petrov, Roussev, Dobrev)	5:52.38
4.	FRA	5:53.45
5.	ESP	6:01.19
6.	YUG	6:10.76

Pairs Without Coxswain (15 entries)

1.	GDR (*B. Landvoigt, *J. Landvoigt)	6:48.01
2.	USSR (Y. Pimenov, N. Pimenov)	6:50.50
3.	GBR (Wiggin, Carmichael)	6:51.47
4.	ROM	6:53.49
5.	TCH	7:01.54
6.	SWE	7:02.52

Pairs With Coxswain (11 entries)

1.	GDR (*Jahrling, *Ulrich, *Spohr)	7:02.54
2.	USSR (Pereverzev, Kryuchkin, Lukyanov)	7:03.35
3.	YUG (Mrduljas, Celent, Reic)	7:04.92
4.	ROM	7:07.17
5.	BUL	7:09.21
6.	TCH	7:09.41

Fours Without Coxswain (11 entries)

1.	GDR (Thiele, *Decker, *Semmler, *Brietzke)	6:08.17
2.	USSR (Kamkin, Dolinin, Kulagin, Yeliseyev)	6:11.81
3.	GBR (Beattie, McNuff, Townsend, Cross)	6:16.58
4.	TCH	6:18.63
5.	ROM	6:19.45
6.	SUI	6:26.46

Fours With Coxswain (12 entries)

1.	GDR (Wendisch, U. Diessner, W. Diessner, Dohn, Gregor)	6:14.51
2.	USSR (Garonskis, Di. Krishianis, Dz. Krishianis, Tikmers, Berzynsh)	6:19.05
3.	POL (Stellak, Tomasiak, Nowak, Stadniuk, Kubiak)	6:22.52
4.	ESP	6:26.23
5.	BUL	6:28.13
6.	SUI	6:30.26

Eights With Coxswain (9 entries)

1.	GDR (Krauss, Koppe, Kons, Friedrich, Doberschutz, *Karantz, Duhring, Hoing, Ludwig)	5:49.05
2.	GBR (McDougall, Whitwell, Clay, Mahoney, Justice, Pritchard, McGowan, Stanhope, Moynihan)	5:51.92
3.	USSR (Kokoshin, Tishchenko, Tkachenko, Pintskus, Normantas, Lugin, Mantsevich, Maistrenko, Dmitrienko)	5:52.66
4.	TCH	5:53.73
5.	AUS	5:56.74
6.	BUL	6:04.05

Women (1,000m)

Single Sculls (11 entries)

1.	ROM (Sanda Toma)	3:40.69
2.	USSR (Antonina Makhina)	3:41.65
3.	GDR (Martina Schroter)	3:43.54
4.	BUL (Rossitza Spassova)	3:47.22
5.	GBR (Beryl Mitchell)	3:49.71
6.	POL (Beata Dziadura)	3:51.45

Double Sculls (7 entries)

1.	USSR (Khloptseva, Popova)	3:16.27
2.	GDR (Linse, Westphal)	3:17.63
3.	ROM (Homeghi, Rosca Racila)	3:18.91
4.	BUL	3:23.14
5.	POL	3:27.25
6.	HUN	3:35.70

Quadruple Sculls with Coxswain (7 entries)

1.	GDR (Reinhardt, Ploch, Lau, *Zobelt, Buhr)	3:15.32
2.	USSR (Pustovit, Matievskaya, Vasilchenko, Lubimova, Cheremisina)	3:15.73
3.	BUL (Serbezova, Bontcheva, Nakova, Bakova, Gheorghieva)	3:16.10
4.	ROM	3:16.82
5.	POL	3:20.95
6.	HOL	3:22.64

Pairs Without Coxswain (6 entries)

1. GDR (Steindorf, Klier)		**3:30.49**
2. POL (Dluzewska, Koscianska)		**3:30.95**
3. BUL (Barboulova, Kubatova)		**3:32.39**
4. ROM		3:35.14
5. USSR		4:12.53

No sixth starter selected.

Fours With Coxswain (6 entries)

1. GDR (Kapheim, Frohlich, Noack, Saalfeld, Wenzel)		**3:19.27**
2. BUL (Ghurova, Modeva, Todorova, Velinova, Filipova)		**3:20.75**
3. USSR (Fadeyeva, Sovetnikova, Studneva, Semyonova, Cheremisina)		**3:20.92**
4. ROM		3:22.08
5. AUS		3:26.37

No sixth starter selected.

Eights With Coxswain (6 entries)

1. GDR (Boesler, Niesser, Kopke, Schutz, Kuhn, *Richter, Sandig, Metze, *Wilke)		**3:03.32**
2. USSR (Pivovarova, Umanets, Prishchepa, Zhulina, Stetsenko, Tereshina, Preobraz-henskaya, Pazyun, Frolova)		**3:04.39**
3. ROM (Aposteanu, Zagoni, Frintu, Bucur, Puscatu, Iliuta, Constantinescu, Bondar, Dobritoiu)		**3:05.63**
4. BUL		3:10.03
5. GBR		3:13.85

No sixth starter selected.
(*) Members of winning crews 1976 Olympic Games.

SOCCER

Championship Game: TCH 1 GDR 0

Third-Place Game: USSR 2 YUG 0

Semi-Final Games: GDR 1 USSR 0; TCH 2 YUG 0

Eighth-Final Games: USSR 2 KUW 1, TCH 3 CUB 0, GDR 4 IRQ 0, YUG 3 ALG 0.

Classification Round:

Group A: 1. USSR 3-0, 2. CUB 2-1, 3. VEN 1-2, 4. ZAM 0-3

Group B: 1. TCH 1-0-2, 2. KUW 1-0-2, 3. COL 1-1-1, 4. NGR 0-2-1

Group C: 1. GDR 2-0-1, 2. ALG 1-1-1, 3. ESP 0-0-3, 4. SYR 0-2-1.

Group D: 1. YUG 2-0-1, 2. IRQ 1-0-2, 3. FIN 1-1-1, 4. CRC 0-3-3

Note: Above Won-Lost-Tied,. Or Won-Lost, only

The Scoring Leaders: 1. Sergei Andreev, USSR 5; 2. Wolf-Rudiger Netz, GDR, Ladislav Vizek, TCH, Fyodor Cherenkov 4 each; 5. Faisal Aldaakhil, KUW, Yuri Gavrilov, USSR, Frank Terletzki, GDR 3 each.

The Champions: TCH-Stanislav Seman, Ludek Macela, Josef Mazura, Libor Radimec, Zdenek Rygel, Petr Nemec, Ladislav Vizek, Jan Berger, Jindrich Svoboda, Lubos Pokluda, Werner Licka, **Rostislav Vaclavicek, **Jaroslav Netolicka, Oldrich Rott, Frantisek Stambacher, **Frantisek Kunzo.
(**) Did not play in championship game.
Note: The winning goal in the championship game was scored by Svoboda in the 77th minute of the game.

SHOOTING

Trap Shooting (34 entries)

1. Luciano Giovannetti	**ITA**	**198**
2. Rustan Yambulatov	**USSR**	**196***
3. Jorg Damme	**GDR**	**196****
4. Josef Hojny	TCH	196
5. Eladio Vallduvi	ESP	195
6. Alexandr Asanov	USSR	195
7. Silvano Basagni	ITA	194
8. Burchardt Hoppe	GDR	192

(*) won 2nd shoot off for 2nd place
(**) won 1st shoot off for 3rd place

Skeet Shooting (46 entries)

1. Hans Kjeld Rasmussen	**DEN**	**196***
2. Lars-Goran Carlsson	**SWE**	**196****
3. Roberto Castrillo	**CUB**	**196*****
4. Pavel Pulda	TCH	196
5. Celso Giardini	ITA	196
6. Guillermo Torres	CUB	195
7. Francisco Perez	ESP	195
8. Ari Westergard	FIN	195

(*) won 2nd shoot off after five tied.
(**) placed 2nd in 2nd shoot off.
(***) placed 3rd in 2nd shoot off.

Running Game Target (19 entries)

1. Igor Sokolov	**USSR**	**589 WR**
2. Thomas Pfeffer	**GDR**	**589 WR**
3. Alexandr Gazov	**USSR**	**587**
4. Andreas Doleschall	HUN	584
5. Tibor Bodnar	HUN	584
6. Jorma Lievonen	FIN	584
7. Giovanni Mezzani	ITA	582
8. Hans-Jurgen Helbig	GDR	579

Free Pistol (33 entries)

1. Aleksandr Melentev	**USSR**	**581 WR**
2. Harald Vollmar	**GDR**	**568**
3. Lubtcho Diakov	**BUL**	**565**
4. Gil San Soh	PRK	565
5. Seppo Saarenpaa	FIN	565
6. Serguey Pyzhianov	USSR	564
7. Ragnar Skanaker	SWE	563
8. Paavo Palokangas	FIN	561

Rapid Fire Pistol (40 entries)

1. Corneliu Ion	**ROM**	**596***
2. Jurgen Wiefel	**GDR**	**596****
3. Gerhard Petritsch	**AUT**	**596*****
4. Vladas Turla	USSR	595
5. Roberto Ferraris	ITA	595
6. Afanasy Kuzmin	USSR	595
7. Marin Stan	ROM	595
8. Rafael Rodriguez	CUB	594

(*) won in 3rd shoot off, 148-147
(**) lost in 3rd shoot off, 147-148
(**) lost out in first shoot off for 1st

Small Bore Rifle, Prone (56 entries)

1. Karoly Varga	**HUN**	**599*EWR**
2. Hellfried Heilfort	**GDR**	**599 EWR**
3. Petar Zaprianov	**BUL**	**598**
4. Krzysztof Stefaniak	POL	598
5. Timo Hagmaan	FIN	597
6. Alexandr Mastianin	USSR	597
7. Nonka Matova	BUL	597
8. Walter Frescura	ITA	597

(*) won on countback to 5th of six series of ten shots, 100 to 99.

Small Bore Rifle, 3-Position (39 entries)

1. Viktor Vlasov	**USSR**	**1173 WR**
2. Bernd Hartstein	**GDR**	**1166**
3. Sven Johansson	**SWE**	**1165**
4. Mauri Roppanen	FIN	1164
5. Alexandr Mitrofanov	USSR	1164
6. Nonka Matova	BUL	1163
7. Hellfried Heilfort	GDR	1162
8. Eugeniusz Pedzisz	POL	1156

SWIMMING

Men

100m freestyle (39 entries)

1. Jorg Woithe	**GDR**	**50.40**
2. Per Holmertz	**SWE**	**50.91**
3. Per Johansson	**SWE**	**51.29**
4. Sergei Kopliakov	USSR	51.34
5. Raffaele Franceschi	ITA	51.69
6. Sergei Krasyuk	USSR	51.80
7. Rene Ecuyer	FRA	52.01
8. Graeme Brewer	AUS	52.22

200m freestyle (42 entries)

1. Sergei Kopliakov	**USSR**	**1:49.81OR**
2. Andrei Krylov	**USSR**	**1:50.76**
3. Graeme Brewer	**AUS**	**1:51.60**
4. Jorg Woithe	GDR	1:51.86
5. Ron McKeon	AUS	1:52.60
6. Paolo Revelli	ITA	1:52.76
7. Thomas Lejdstrom	SWE	1:52.94
8. Fabrizio Rampazzo	ITA	1:53.25

400m freestyle (28 entries)

1. Vladimir Salnikov	**USSR**	**3:51.31OR**
2. Andrei Krylov	**USSR**	**3:53.24**
3. Ivar Stukolkin	**USSR**	**3:53.95**
4. Djan Madruga	BRA	3:54.15
5. Daniel Machek	TCH	3:55.66
6. Sandor Nagy	HUN	3:56.83
7. Max Metzker	AUS	3:56.87
8. Ron McKeon	AUS	3:57.60

1,500m freestyle (17 entries)

1. Vladimir Salnikov	**USSR**	**14:58.27 WR OR**
2. Alexandr Chaev	**USSR**	**15:14.30**
3. Max Metzker	**AUS**	**15:14.49**
4. Rainer Strohbach	GDR	15:15.29
5. Borut Petric	YUG	15:21.78
6. Rafael Escalas	ESP	15:21.88
7. Zoltan Wladar	HUN	15:26.70
8. Eduard Petrov	USSR	15:28.24

100m backstroke (33 entries)

1. Bengt Baron	**SWE**	**56.53**
2. Viktor Kuznetsov	**USSR**	**56.99**
3. Vladimir Dolgov	**USSR**	**57.63**
4. Miloslav Rolko	TCH	57.74
5. Sandor Wladar	HUN	57.84
6. Fred Eefting	HOL	57.95
7. Mark Tonelli	AUS	57.98
8. Gary Abraham	GBR	58.38

200m backstroke (25 entries)

1. Sandor Wladar	**HUN**	**2:01.93**
2. Zoltan Verraszto	**HUN**	**2:02.40**
3. Mark Kerry	**AUS**	**2:03.14**
4. Vladimir Shemetov	USSR	2:03.48
5. Fred Eefting	HOL	2:03.92
6. Michael Soderlund	SWE	2:04.10
7. Douglas Campbell	GBR	2:04.23
8. Paul Moorfoot	AUS	2:06.15

100m breaststroke (25 entries)

1. Duncan Goodhew	**GBR**	**1:03.34**
2. Arsen Miskarov	**USSR**	**1:03.82**
3. Peter Evans	**AUS**	**1:03.96**
4. Alexandr Fedorovsky	USSR	1:04.00
5. Janos Dzvonyar	HUN	1:04.67
6. Lindsay Spencer	AUS	1:05.04
7. Pablo Restrepo	COL	1:05.91
8. Alban Vermes	HUN	disq.

200m breaststroke (20 entries)

1.	**Robertas Zulpa**	**USSR**	**2:15.85**
2.	**Alban Vermes**	**HUN**	**2:16.93**
3.	**Arsen Miskarov**	**USSR**	**2:17.28**
4.	Gennady Utenkov	USSR	2:19.64
5.	Lindsay Spencer	AUS	2:19.68
6.	Duncan Goodhew	GBR	2:20.92
7.	Peter Berggren	SWE	2:21.65
8.	Jor Walter	GDR	2:22.39

100m butterfly (34 entries)

1.	**Par Arvidsson**	**SWE**	**54.92**
2.	**Roger Pyttel**	**GDR**	**54.94**
3.	**David Lopez**	**ESP**	**55.13**
4.	Kees Vervoorn	HOL	55.25
5.	Evgeny Seredin	USSR	55.35
6.	Gary Abraham	GBR	55.42
7.	Xavier Savim	FRA	55.66
8.	Alexei Markovsky	USSR	55.70

200m butterfly (25 entries)

1.	**Sergei Fesenko**	**USSR**	**1:59.76**
2.	**Philip Hubble**	**GBR**	**2:01.20**
3.	**Roger Pyttel**	**GDR**	**2:01.39**
4.	Peter Morris	GDR	2:02.27
5.	Mikhail Gorelik	USSR	2:02.44
6.	Kees Vervoorn	HOL	2:02.52
7.	Par Arvidsson	SWE	2:02.61
8.	Stephen Poulter	GBR	2:02.93

400m individual medley (24 entries)

1.	**Aleksandr Sidorenko**	**USSR**	**4:22.89OR**
2.	**Sergei Fesenko**	**USSR**	**4:23.43**
3.	**Zoltan Verraszto**	**HUN**	**4:24.24**
4.	Andras Hargitay	HUN	4:24.48
5.	Djan Madruga	BRA	4:26.81
6.	Miloslav Rolko	TCH	4:26.99
7.	Leszek Gorski	POL	4:28.89
8.	Daniel Machek	TCH	4:29.86

4 x 100m Medley Relay (13 entries)

1.	**AUS (Kerry, Evans, Tonelli, Brooks)**	**3:45.70**
2.	**USSR (Kuznetsov, Miskarov, Seredin, Kopliakov)**	**3:45.92**
3.	**GBR (Abraham, Goodhew, Lowe, Smith)**	**3:47.71**
4.	GDR	3:48.25
5.	FRA	3:49.19
6.	HUN	3:50.29
7.	HOL	3:51.81
8.	BRA	3:53.24

4 x 200m freestyle relay (13 entries)

1.	**USSR (Kopliakov, Salnikov, Stukolkin, Krylov)**	**7:23.50**
2.	**GDR (Pfutze, Woithe, Grabs, Strobach)**	**7:28.60**
3.	**BRA (Fernandes, Mattioli, Delgado, Madruga)**	**7:29.30**
4.	SWE	7:30.10
5.	ITA	7:30.37
6.	GBR	7:30.81
7.	AUS	7:30.82
8.	FRA	7:36.08

Springboard Diving (24 entries)

1.	**Aleksandr Portnov**	**USSR**	**905.025**
2.	**Carlos Giron**	**MEX**	**892.140**
3.	**Franco Cagnotto**	**ITA**	**871.500**
4.	Falk Hoffmann	GDR	858.510
5.	Aleksandr Kosenkov	USSR	855.120
6.	Christopher Snode	GBR	844.470
7.	Vyacheslav Troshin	USSR	820.050
8.	Ricardo Camacho	ESP	749.340

Platform Diving (23 entries)

1.	**Falk Hoffmann**	**GDR**	**835.650**
2.	**Vladimir Aleinik**	**USSR**	**819.705**
3.	**David Ambartsumyan**	**USSR**	**817.440**
4.	Carlos Giron	MEX	809.805
5.	Dieter Waskow	GDR	802.800
6.	Thomas Knuths	GDR	783.975
7.	Sergei Nemtsanov	USSR	775.860
8.	Niki Stajkovic	AUT	725.145

Women

100m freestyle (30 entries)

1.	**Barbara Krause**	**GDR**	**54.79 WR, OR**
2.	**Caren Metschuck**	**GDR**	**55.16**
3.	**Ines Diers**	**GDR**	**55.65**
4.	Olga Klevakina	USSR	57.40
5.	Conny Van Bentum	HOL	57.63
6.	Natalya Strunnikova	USSR	57.83
7.	Guylaine Berger	FRA	57.88
8.	Agneta Eriksson	SWE	57.90

200m freestyle (22 entries)

1.	**Barbara Krause**	**GDR**	**1:58.33OR**
2.	**Ines Diers**	**GDR**	**1:59.64**
3.	**Carmela Schmidt**	**GDR**	**2:01.44**
4.	Olga Klevakina	USSR	2:02.29
5.	Reggie De Jong	HOL	2:02.76
6.	June Croft	GBR	2:03.15
7.	Natalya Strunnikova	USSR	2:03.74
8.	Irina Aksyonova	USSR	2:04.00

400m freestyle (19 entries)

1.	**Ines Diers**	**GDR**	**4:08.76OR**
2.	**Petra Schneider**	**GDR**	**4:09.16**
3.	**Carmela Schmidt**	**GDR**	**4:10.86**
4.	Michelle Ford	AUS	4:11.65
5.	Irina Aksyonova	USSR	4:14.40
6.	Annelies Maas	HOL	4:15.79
7.	Reggie De Jong	HOL	4:15.95
8.	Olga Klevakina	USSR	4:19.18

800m freestyle (14 entries)

1.	**Michelle Ford**	**AUS**	**8:28.90OR**
2.	**Ines Diers**	**GDR**	**8:32.55**
3.	**Heike Dahne**	**GDR**	**8:33.48**
4.	Irina Aksyonova	USSR	8:38.05
5.	Oxana Komissarova	USSR	8:42.04
6.	Pascale Verbauwen	BEL	8:44.84
7.	Ines Geissler	GDR	8:45.28
8.	Yelena Ivanova	USSR	8:46.45

100m backstroke (26 entries)

1.	**Rica Reinisch**	**GDR**	**1:00.86 WR, OR**
2.	**Ina Kleber**	**GDR**	**1:02.07**
3.	**Petra Reidel**	**GDR**	**1:02.64**
4.	Carmen Bunaciu	ROM	1:03.81
5.	Carine Verbauwen	BEL	1:03.82
6.	Larisa Gorchakova	USSR	1:03.87
7.	Monique Bosga	HOL	1:04.47
8.	Manuela Carosi	ITA	1:05.10

200m backstroke (21 entries)

1.	**Rica Reinisch**	**GDR**	**2:11.77 WR, OR**
2.	**Cornelia Polit**	**GDR**	**2:13.75**
3.	**Birgit Treiber**	**GDR**	**2:14.14**
4.	Carmen Bunaciu	ROM	2:15.20
5.	Yolande Van der Straeten	BEL	2:15.58
6.	Carine Verbauwen	BEL	2:16.66
7.	Lisa Forrest	AUS	2:16.75
8.	Larisa Gorchakova	USSR	2:17.72

100m breaststroke (25 entries)

1.	**Ute Geweniger**	**GDR**	**1:10.22**
2.	**Elvira Vasilkova**	**USSR**	**1:10.41**
3.	**Susanne Nielsson**	**DEN**	**1:11.16**
4.	Margaret Kelly	GBR	1:11.48
5.	Eva-Marie Hakansson	SWE	1:11.72
6.	Susannah Brownsdon	GBR	1:12.11
7.	Lina Kachushite	USSR	1:12.21
8.	Monica Bonon	ITA	1:12.51

Note: Ute Geweniger, GDR, WR 1:10.11 in heats

200m breaststroke (25 entries)

1.	**Lina Kachushite**	**USSR**	**2:29.54OR**
2.	**Svetlana Varganova**	**USSR**	**2:29.61**
3.	**Yulia Bogdanova**	**USSR**	**2:32.39**
4.	Susanne Nielsson	DEN	2:32.75
5.	Irena Fleissnerova	TCH	2:33.23
6.	Ute Geweniger	GDR	2:34.34
7.	Bettina Lobel	GDR	2:34.51
8.	Sylvia Rinka	GDR	2:35.38

100m butterfly (24 entries)

1.	**Caren Metschuck**	**GDR**	**1:00.42**
2.	**Andrea Pollack**	**GDR**	**1:00.90**
3.	**Christiane Knacke**	**GDR**	**1:01.44**
4.	Ann Osgerby	GBR	1:02.21
5.	Lisa Curry	AUS	1:02.40
6.	Agneta Martensson	SWE	1:02.61
7.	Mariam Paris	CRC	1:02.89
8.	Janet Osgerby	GBR	1:02.90

200m butterfly (21 entries)

1.	**Ines Geissler**	**GDR**	**2:10.44OR**
2.	**Sybille Schonrock**	**GDR**	**2:10.45**
3.	**Michelle Ford**	**AUS**	**2:11.66**
4.	Andrea Pollack	GDR	2:12.13
5.	Dorota Brzozowska	POL	2:14.12
6.	Ann Osgerby	GBR	2:14.83
7.	Agneta Martensson	SWE	2:15.22
8.	Alla Grishchenkova	USSR	2:15.70

400m individual medley (16 entries)

1.	**Petra Schneider**	**GDR**	**4:36.29** WR, OR
2.	**Sharron Davies**	**GBR**	**4:46.83**
3.	**Agnieszka Czopek**	**POL**	**4:48.17**
4.	Grit Slaby	GDR	4:48.54
5.	Ulrike Tauber	GDR	4:49.18
6.	Stoyanka Dangalakova	USSR	4:49.25
7.	Olga Klevakina	USSR	4:50.91
8.	Magdalena Bialas	POL	4:53.30

4 x 100m freestyle relay (9 entries)

1.	**GDR (Krause, Metschuck, Diers, Hulsenbeck)**	**3:42.71** WR, OR
2.	**SWE (Ljungdahl, Gustafsson, Martensson, Eriksson)**	**3:48.93**
3.	**HOL (Van Bentum, Van Velsen, De Jong, Maas)**	**3:49.51**
4.	GBR	3:51.71
5.	AUS	3:54.16
6.	MEX	3:55.41
7.	BUL	3:56.34
8.	ESP	3:58.73

4 x 100m medley relay (10 entries)

1.	**GDR (Reinisch, Geweniger, Pollack, Metschuck)**	**4:06.67** WR, OR
2.	**GBR (Jameson, Kelly, A. Osgerby, Croft)**	**4:12.24**
3.	**USSR (Kruglova, Vasilkova, Grishchenkova, Strunnikova)**	**4:13.61**
4.	SWE	4:16.91
5.	ITA	4:19.05
6.	AUS	4:19.90
7.	ROM	4:21.27
8.	BUL	4:22.38

Springboard diving (29 entries)

1.	**Irina Kalinina**	**USSR**	**725.910**
2.	**Martina Proeber**	**GDR**	**698.895**
3.	**Karin Guthke**	**GDR**	**685.245**
3.	Zhanna Tsirulnikova	USSR	673.665
5.	Martina Jaschke	GDR	668.115
6.	Valerie McFarlane	AUS	651.045
7.	Irina Sidorova	USSR	650.265
8.	Lourdes Gonzalez	CUB	640.005

Platform diving (17 entries)

1.	**Martina Jaschke**	**GDR**	**596.250**
2.	**Servard Emirzyan**	**USSR**	**576.465**
3.	**Liana Tsotadze**	**USSR**	**575.925**
4.	Ramona Wenzel	GDR	542.070
5.	Yelena Matyushenko	USSR	540.180
6.	Elsa Tenorio	MEX	539.445
7.	Valerie McFarlane	AUS	499.785
8.	Ildiko Kelemen	HUN	476.535

TEAM HANDBALL

Men

Championship Game: GDR 23 USSR 22

Third-Place Game: ROM 20 HUN 18

Fifth-Place Game: ESP 24 YUG 23

Seventh-Place Game: POL 23 SUI 22

Ninth-Place Game: DEN 28 ALG 20

Eleventh-Place Game: CUB 32 KUW 24

Preliminary Pool (Won-Lost-Tied)

Group A: 1. GDR 4-0-1, 2. HUN 3-0-2, 3. ESP 2-2-1, 4. POL 2-2-1, 5. DEN 1-4-0, 6. CUB 0-4-1

Group B: 1. USSR 4-1-0, 2. ROM 4-1-0, 3. YUG 4-1-0, 4. SUI 2-3-0, 5. ALG 1-4-0, 6. KUW 0-5-0

Scores of Preliminary Pool Matches

Group A	HUN	GDR	DEN	ESP	CUB	POL
HUN	—	14-14	16-15	20-17	26-22	20-20
GDR	14-14	—	24-20	21-17	27-20	22-21
DEN	15-16	20-24	—	19-20	30-18	12-26
ESP	17-20	17-21	20-19	—	24-24	24-22
CUB	22-26	20-27	18-30	24-24	—	19-34
POL	20-20	21-22	26-12	22-24	34-19	—

Group B	ALG	KUW	ROM	USSR	YUG	SUI
ALG	—	30-17	18-26	10-33	18-22	18-26
KUW	17-30	—	12-32	11-38	10-44	14-32
ROM	26-18	32-12	—	22-19	21-23	18-16
USSR	33-10	38-11	19-22	—	22-17	22-15
YUG	22-18	44-10	23-21	17-22	—	26-21
SUI	26-18	32-14	16-18	15-22	21-26	—

The Scoring Leaders: 1. Jerzy Klempel, POL 44; 2. Ernst Zuellig, SUI 40; 3. Vasile Stinga, ROM 36; 4. Jesus Agramonte, CUB 34; 5. Pavle Jurina, YUG, Frank Wahl, GDR, and Ahcene Djeffal, ALG 33 each.

The Champions: GDR-Siegfried Voigt, Gunter Dreibrodt, Peter Rost, Klaus Gruner, Hans-Georg Beyer, Dietmar Schmidt, Hartmut Kruger, Lothar Doering, **Ernst Gerlach, Frank Wahl, Ingolf Wiegert, Wieland Schmidt, Rainer Hoft, **Georg Jaunich.

(**) Did not play in the championship match.

Women

Final Standings of Round Robin Tournament, no playoffs for first three places.

Final Standings (Won-Lost-Tied): **1. USSR 5-0-0; 2. YUG 3-1-1; 3. GDR 3-1-1;** 4. HUN 1-3-1; 5. TCH 1-3-1; 6. *CGO 0-5-0.

Scores of the Matches:

	GDR	USSR	HUN	TCH	YUG	CGO
GDR	—	13-18	19-9	16-10	15-15	28-6
USSR	18-13	—	16-12	17-7	18-9	30-11
HUN	9-19	12-16	—	10-10	10-11	39-10
TCH	10-16	7-17	10-10	—	15-25	23-10
YUG	15-15	9-18	19-10	25-15	—	39-9
CGO	6-28	11-30	10-39	10-23	9-39	—

The Scoring Leaders: 1. Biserka Visnjic, YUG 33; 2. Svetlana Kitic, YUG 29; 3. Tatiana Kochergina, USSR 28; 4. Marianna Nagy, HUN 26; 5. Jana Kutkova, TCH 22; 6. Olga Zubareva, USSR 21.

The Champions: USSR-Natalia Timoshkina, Larisa Karlova, Irina Palchikova, Tatiana Kochergina, Ludmila Poradnik, Larisa Savkina, **Aldona Nenenene, Yulia Safina, Olga Zubareva, Valentina Lutaeva, Lubov Odinokova, Sigita Strechen, **Natalia Lukianenko, Zinaida Turchina.

(**) Did not play in championship match.

VOLLEYBALL

Men

Championship Game: USSR 3, BUL 1 (15-7, 15-13, 14-16, 15-11)

Third-place Game: ROM 3, POL 1 (15-10, 9-15, 15-13, 15-9)

Fifth-Place Game: BRA 3, YUG 2 (14-16, 15-9, 8-15, 15-10, 15-8)

Seventh-Place Game: CUB 3 TCH 1 (14-16, 15-7, 15-10, 15-6)

Ninth-Place Game: ITA 3 LBA 0 (15-2, 15-1, 15-4)

Semi-Final Games: USSR 3 ROM 0; BUL 3 POL 0; YUG 3 CUB 2; BRA 3 TCH 0

Preliminary Pool:

Group A: 1. USSR 4-0, 2. BUL 3-1, 3. CUB 1-3, 4. TCH 1-3, 5. ITA 1-3.

Group B: 1. POL 3-1, 2. ROM 3-1, 3. BRA 2-2, 4. YUG 2-2, 5. LBA 0-4.

The Champions: Yuri Panchenko, Vyacheslav Zaitsev, Alexandr Savin, Pavel Selivanov, Vladimir Dorokhov, Alexandr Yermilov, Oleg Moliboga, Vladimir Kondra, Vladimir Chernyshev, Fyodor Lashchenov, Valery Krivov, Vilyar Loor

Women

Championship Game: USSR 3 GDR 1 (15-12, 11-15, 15-13, 15-7)

Third-Place Game: BUL 3 HUN 2 (15-5, 13-15, 6-15, 15-4, 15-8)

Fifth-Place Game: CUB 3 PER 1 (15-9, 15-7, 12-15, 15-5)

Seventh-Place Game: BRA 3 ROM 0 (15-8, 15-12, 15-12)

Semi-Final Games: USSR 3 HUN 0, GDR 3 BUL 2, CUB 3 BRA 0, PER 3 ROM 0.

Preliminary Pool:

Group A: 1. USSR 3-0, 2. GDR 2-1, 3. CUB 1-2, 4. PER 0-3.

Group B: 1. BUL 2-1, 2. HUN 2-1, 3. ROM 2-1, BRA 0-3.

The Champions: Nadezhda Radzevich, Nataliya Razumova, Olga Solovova, Yelena Akhaminova, Larisa Pavlova, Yelena Andreyuk, Irina Makagonova, Lubov Kozyreva, Svetlana Nikishina, Ludmila Chernysheva, Svetlana Badulina, Lidia Loginova.

WATER POLO

Championship Round

Team	G	W	L	Tie	Goals For	Agst	Pts.
1. USSR	5	5	0	0	34	21	10
2. YUG	5	3	1	1	34	32	7
3. HUN	5	3	2	0	32	30	6
4. ESP	5	2	3	0	28	31	4
5. CUB	5	0	3	2	31	38	2
6. HOL	5	0	4	1	26	33	1

Scores of the Games

	HUN	HOL	USSR	ESP	YUG	CUB
HUN	—	8-7	4-5	6-5	7-8	7-5
HOL	7-8	—	3-7	5-6	4-5	7-7
USSR	5-4	7-3	—	6-2	8-7	8-5
ESP	5-6	6-5	2-6	—	6-7	9-7
YUG	8-7	5-4	7-8	7-6	—	7-7
CUB	5-7	7-7	5-8	7-9	7-7	—

Placings 7-12

Team	G	W	L	Tie	For	Agst	Pts.
7. AUS	5	4	0	1	30	19	9
8. ITA	5	4	1	0	26	18	8
9. ROM	5	3	1	1	36	26	7
10. GRE	5	2	3	0	28	28	4
11. SWE	5	1	4	0	23	40	2
12. BUL	5	0	5	0	25	37	0

Leading Scorers: 1. Manuel Estiarte, ESP 21; 2. Gianni De Magistris, ITA and Jorge Rizo, CUB 20; 4. Charles Turner, AUS 17; 5. Sotirios Stathakis, GRE 16; 6. Zoran Gopcevic YUG, and Tamas Farago, HUN 14.

Classifiction Round:

Group A: 1. HUN, 2. HOL, 3. ROM, 3. GRE

Group B: 1. USSR, 2. ESP, 3. ITA, 4. SWE

Group C: 1. YUG, 2. CUB, 3. AUS, 4. BUL

The Champions: Evgeny Sharonov, Sergei Kotenko, Vladimir Akimov, Yevgeny Grishin, Mait Riysman, Aleksandr Kabanov, Aleksei Barkalov, Erkin Shagaev, Georgy Mshvenieradze, Mikhail Ivanov, Vyacheslav Sobchenko

WEIGHTLIFTING

Flyweight (up to 52 kg/115 lbs.)

	kg snatch	C&J	Total	pounds Total
1. Kanybek Osmanoliev* USSR	107.5	137.5	245 OR	540 OR
2. Bong Chol Ho PRK	10	135	245 OR	540 OR
3. Gyong Si Han PRK	110	135	245 OR	540 OR
4. Bela Olah HUN	110	135	245 OR	540 OR
5. Stefan Leletko POL	105	135	240	529
6. Ferenc Hornyak HUN	107.5	130	237.5	524

(*) Title decided on basis of bodyweight. Osmanoliev was the lightest of the four with the same total lifts.

Bantamweight (up to 56 kg/123 lbs.)

1. Daniel Nunez CUB	125	150	275 WR	606 WR
2. Yurik Sarkisian USSR	112.5	157.5	270.0 Jr.WR	595 Jr.WR
3. Tadeusz Dembonczyk POL	120	145	265	584
4. Andreas Letz GDR	115	150	265	584
5. Eui Yong Yang PRK	112.5	150	262.5	579
6. Imre Stefanovics HUN	115	145	260	573

Featherweight (up to 60 kg/132 lbs.)

1. Viktor Mazin USSR	130.0	160.0	290.0 OR	639 OR
2. Stefan Dimitrov BUL	127.5	160.0	287.5	634
3. Marek Seweryn POL	127.5	155.0	282.5	623
4. Antoni Pawlak POL	120.0	155.0	275.0	606
5. Julio Loscos CUB	125.0	150.0	275.0	606
6. Frantisek Nedved TCH	122.5	150.0	272.5	601

Lightweight (up to 67.5kg/148.5 lbs.)

1. Yanko Roussev USSR	147.5	195.0	342.5 WR	755 WR
2. Joachim Kunz GDR	145.0	190.0	335.0	739
3. Mintcho Pachov BUL	142.5	182.5	325.0	733
4. Daniel Senet FRA	147.5	175.0	322.5	711
5. Gunter Ambrass GDR	140.0	180.0	320.0	705
6. Zbigniew Kaczmarek POL	140.0	177.5	317.5	699

Middleweight (up to 75 kg/165 lbs.)

1. Assen Zlatev BUL	160.0	200.0	360.0 WR	794 WR
2. Alexandr Pervy USSR	157.5	200.0	357.5	788
3. Nedeltcho Kolev BUL	157.5	187.5	345.0	760
4. Julio Echenique CUB	145.0	182.5	327.5	722
5. Dragomir Ciorolan ROM	140.0	182.5	322.5	711
6. Tapio Kinnunen FIN	142.5	177.5	320.0	705

Light Heavyweight (up to 82.5 kg/181.5 lbs.)

1. Yurik Vardanyan USSR	177.5	222.5	400.0 WR	882 WR
2. Blagoi Blagoev BUL	175.0	197.5	372.5	821
3. Dusan Poliacik TCH	160.0	207.5	367.5	810
4. Jan Lisowski POL	150.0	205.0	355.0	783
5. Krassimir Drandarov BUL	155.0	200.0	355.0	783
6. Pawel Rabczewski POL	155.0	195.0	350.0	772

Middle Heavyweight (up to 90 kg/198 lbs.)

1. Peter Baczako USSR	170.0	207.5	377.5	832
2. Roumen Alexandrov BUL	170.0	205.0	375.0	827
3. Frank Mantek GDR	165.0	205.0	370.0	816
4. Dalibor Rehak TCH	165.0	200.0	365.0	805
5. Witold Walo POL	160.0	200.0	360.0	793
6. Lubomir Srsen TCH	160.0	197.5	357.5	787

First Heavyweight (up to 100 kg/220 lbs.)

1. Ota Zaremba TCH	180.0	215.0	395.0 OR	871 OR
2. Igor Nikitin USSR	177.5	215.0	392.5	864
3. Alberto Blanco CUB	172.5	212.5	385.0	848
4. Michael Hennig GDR	165.0	217.5	382.5	843
5. Janos Solyomvari HUN	175.0	205.0	380.0	838
6. Manfred Funke GDR	170.0	207.5	377.5	832

Second Heavyweight (up to 110 kg/242 lbs.)

1. Leonid Taranenko USSR	182.5	240.0	422.5 WR	931 WR
2. Valentin Christov BUL	185.0	220.0	405.0	891
3. Gyorgy Szlai HUN	172.5	217.5	390.0	860
4. Leif Nilsson SWE	167.5	212.5	380.0	838
5. Vinzenz Hortnagl AUT	170.0	202.5	372.5	821
6. Stefan Tasnadi ROM	165.0	195.0	360.0	794

Super Heavyweight (over 110 kg/over 242 lbs.)

1. Sultan Rakhmanov USSR	195.0	245.0	440.0 EOR	970 EOR
2. Jurgen Heuser GDR	182.5	227.5	410.0	904
3. Tadeusz Rutkowski POL	180.0	227.5	407.5	897
4. Rudolf Strejcek TCH	182.5	220.0	402.5	886
5. Bohuslav Braum TCH	180.0	217.5	397.5	876
6. Francisco Mendez CUB	175.0	220.0	395.0	870

Note: Vasily Alexeev failed to lift his opening weight in the snatch, 180 kg (396 lbs.)

Recapitulation: There were 39 Olympic records established; 14 world records, one Olympic record equaled, and one junior world record for total lift established. In the total lift category there were eight Olympic records made, of which five were also world total lift records.

WRESTLING

Free-Style

Paperweight (48 kg/105.5 lbs.)
1. **Claudio Pollio ITA**, 2. **Se Hong Jang PRK**, 3. **Sergei Kornilaev USSR**, 4. Jan Falandys POL, 5. Singh Mahabir IND, 6. Laszlo Biro HUN, 7. Roumen Yordanov BUL, 8. Gheorghe Rasovan ROM.

Flyweight (52 kg/115 lbs.)
1. **Anatoly Beloglazov USSR**, 2. **Wladyslaw Stecyk POL**, 3. **Nermedin Selimov BUL**, 4. Lajos Szabo HUN, 5. Dok Ryong Jang PRK, 6. Nanzadying Burgedaa MGL, 7. Koce Efremov YUG, 8. Hartmut Reich GDR.

Bantamweight (57 kg/126 lbs.)
1. **Sergei Beloglazov USSR**, 2. **Ho Pyong Li PRK**, 3. **Dugarsuren Quinbold MGL**, 4. Ivan Tzotchev BUL, 5. Aurel Neagu ROM, 6. Wieslaw Konczak POL, 7. Karim Salman Muhsin IRQ, 8. Sandor Nemeth HUN.

Featherweight (62 kg/137 lbs.)
1. **Magomedgasan Abushev USSR**, 2. **Mikho Doukov BUL**, 3. **Georges Hadjlioannidis GRE**, 4. Raul Cascaret CUB, 5. Aurel Suteu ROM, 6. Ulzibayar Nasanjargal MGL, 7. Brian Aspen GBR, 8. Zoltan Szalontai HUN.

Lightweight (68 kg/150 lbs.)
1. **Saipulla Absaidov USSR**, 2. **Ivan Yankov BUL**, 3. **Saban Sejdi YUG**, 4. Singh Jagmander 5. Eberhard Probst GDR, 6. Octavian Dusa ROM, 7. Ali Hussain Faris IRQ, 8. Pekka Rauhala FIN.

Welterweight (74kg/165 lbs.)
1. **Valentin Raitchev BUL**, 2. **Jamtsying Davaajav MGL**, 3. **Dan Karabin TCH**, 4. Pavel Pinigin USSR, 5. Ryszard Scigalski POL, 6. Singh Rajander IND, 7. Istvan Feher HUN, 8. Riccardo Niccolini ITA.

Middleweight (82 kg/180 lbs.)
1. **Ismail Abilov BUL**, 2. **Magomedhan Aratsilov USSR**; 3. **Istvan Kovacs HUN.**, 4. Henryk Mazur POL, 5. Abdula Memedi YUG, 6. Zevegying Duvchin MGL, 7. Gunter Busarello AUT, 8. Mohammad Eloulabi SYR.

Light Heavyweight (90 kg/198 lbs.)
1. **Sanasar Oganesyan USSR**, 2. **Uwe Neupert GDR**, 3. **Aleksander Cichon POL**, 4. Ivan Ghinov BUL, 5. Dashdorj Tserentogtokh, MGL, 6. Christophe Andanson FRA, 7. Ion Ivanov ROM, 8. Mick Pikos AUS.

Heavyweight (100kg/220 lbs.)
1. **Ilya Mate USSR**, 2. **Slavtcho Tchervenkov BUL**, 3. **Julius Strnisko TCH**, 4. Harald Buttner GDR, 5. Vasile Puscasu ROM, 6. Tomasz Busse POL, 7. Barbaro Morgan, CUB, 8. Khorloo Bayanmunk MGL.

Super Heavyweight (No limit, more than 100 kg/ 220 lbs.)
1. **Soslan Andiev USSR**, 2. **Jozsef Balla HUN**, 3. **Adam Sandruski POL**, 4. Roland Gehrke GDR, 5. Andrei Ianko ROM, 6. Mamadou Sakho SEN, 7. Petar Ivanov BUL, 8. Arturo Diaz CUB.

Greco-Roman Style

Paperweight (48 kg/105.5 lbs.)
1. **Zaksylik Ushkempirov USSR**, 2. **Constantin Alexandru ROM**, 3. **Ferenc Seres HUN**, 4. Pavel Khristov BUL, 5. Reijo Haaparanta FIN, 6. Alfredo Olvera MEX, 7. Vincenzo Maenza ITA, 8. Roman Kierpacz POL.

Flyweight (52 kg/115 lbs.)
1. **Vakhtang Blagidze USSR**, 2. **Lajos Racz HUN**, 3. **Mladen Mladenov BUL**, 4. Nicu Ginga ROM, 5. Antonin Jelinek TCH, 6. Stanislaw Wroblewski POL, 7. Taisto Halonen FIN, 8. Abdulnasser Eloulabi SYR.

Bantamweight (57 kg/126 lbs.)
1. **Shamil Serikov USSR**, 2. **Josef Lipien POL**, 3. **Benni Ljungbeck SWE**, 4. Mihai Botila ROM, 5. Antonino Caltabiano ITA, 6. Josef Krysta TCH, 7. Gyula Molnar HUN, 8. Gheorghi Donev BUL.

Featherweight (62 kg/137 lbs.)
1. **Stilianos Migiakis GRE**, 2. **Istvan Toth HUN**, 3. **Boris Kramorenko USSR**, 4. Ivan Frgic YUG, 5. Panayot Kirov BUL, 6. Kazimierz Lipien POL, 7. Radwan Karout SYR, 8. Michal Vejsada TCH.

Lightweight (68 kg/150 lbs.)
1. **Stefan Rusu ROM**, 2. **Andrzej Supron POL**, 3. **Lars-Erik Skiold SWE**, 4. Suren Nalbandyan USSR, 5. Buyandelger Bold MGL, 6. Ivan Atanassov BUL, 7. Reinhard Hartmann AUT, 8. Karoly Gaal HUN.

Welterweight (74 kg/165 lbs.)
1. **Ferenc Kocsis HUN**, 2. **Anatoly Bykov USSR**, 3. **Mikko Huntala FIN**, 4. Yanko Chopov BUL, 5. Lennart Lundell SWE, 6. Vitezslav Macha TCH, 7. Gheorghe Minea ROM, 8. Jacques Van Lancker BEL.

Middleweight (82 kg/180 lbs.)
1. **Gennady Korban USSR**, 2. **Jan Dolgowicz POL**, 3. **Pavel Pavlov BUL**, 4. Leif Andersson SWE, 5. Detlef Kuhn GDR, 6. Mihaly Toma HUN, 7. Mohammad Eloulabi SYR, 8. Miroslaw Janota TCH.

Light Heavyweight (90 kg/198 lbs.)
1. **Norbert Nottny HUN**, 2. **Igor Kanygin USSR**, 3. **Petre Dicu ROM**, 4. Frank Andersson SWE, 5. Thomas Horschel GDR, 6. Jose Poll CUB, 7. Christophe Andanson FRA, 8. Georges Pozidis GRE.

Heavyweight (100 kg/220 lbs.)
1. **Gheorgi Raikov BUL**, 2. **Roman Bierla POL**, 3. **Vasile Andrei ROM**, 4. Refik Memisevic YUG, 5. Georges Pikildis GRE, 6. Oldrich Dvorak TCH, 7. Nikolai Balboshin USSR, 8. Svend Erikson Studsgarrd DEN.

Super Heavyweight (no limit, over 100 kg/220 lbs.)
1. **Alexandr Kolchinky USSR**, 2. **Alexandre Tomov BUL**, 3. **Hassan Bchara LIB**, 4. Jozsef Farkas HUN, 5. Prvoslav Ilic YUG, 6. Arturo Diaz CUB, 7. Roman Codrean, ROM, 8. Marek Galinski POL.

YACHTING

Soling
1. **DEN (Jensen, Bandolowski, Hansen) (1-5-5-2-1-1)**	**23.00**
2. **USSR (B. Budnikov, A. Budnikov, Polyakov)**	**30.40**
3. **GRE (Boudouris, Gavrilis, Rapanakis)**	**31.10**
4. GDR	37.40
5. HOL	45.00
6. BRA	47.10

Flying Dutchman
1. **ESP (Abascal, Noguer) (4-1-2-4-1-1)**	**19.00**
2. **IRL (Wilkins, Wilkinson)**	**30.00**
3. **HUN (S. Detre, Z. Detre)**	**45.70**
4. GDR	51.40
5. USSR	51.70
6. DEN	54.50

Star
1. **USSR (Mankin, Muzychenko) (2-1-1-5-1-6)**	**24.70**
2. **AUT (Raudaschl, Ferstyl)**	**31.70**
3. **ITA (Gorla, Peraboni)**	**36.10**
4. SWE	44.70
5. DEN	45.70
6. HOL	49.40

Finn
1. **FINN (Ekso Rechardt) (4-1-4-3-1-9)**	**36.70**
2. **AUT (Wolfgang Mayrhofer)**	**46.70**
3. **USSR (Andrei Balashov)**	**47.40**
4. BRA (Claudio Biekarck)	53.00
5. GDR (Jochen Schumann)	54.50
6. SWE (Kent Carlson)	63.70

Toronado
1. **BRA (Welter, Lars Bjorkstrom) (3-1-3-1-1-5)**	**21.40**
2. **DEN (Due, Kjergard)**	**30.40**
3. **SWE (Marstrom, Ragnarsson)**	**33.70**
4. USSR	35.10
5. HOL	39.00
6. FIN	47.70

"470"
1. **BRA (Soares, Penido) (2-1-6-1-5-6)**	**36.40**
2. **GDR (Borowski, Swensson)**	**38.70**
3. **FIN (Lindgren, Tallberg)**	**39.70**
4. HOL	49.40
5. POL	53.00
6. ESP	54.10

(For the Gold Medalists-the best six finishes are shown)

VIII Pan American Games

San Juan, Puerto Rico

July 1-15, 1979

XIII Olympic Winter Games

Lake Placid, USA

February 13-24, 1980

The Games of the XXII Olympiad

Moscow, USSR

July 19-August 3, 1980

A REVIEW OF

THE UNITED STATES TEAMS

In tribute to
great American athletes who
participated in the
VIII Pan American Games
in San Juan, the
XIII Winter Games
in Lake Placid, and
who were selected as the
United States Team
for the
Summer Olympics.

Table of Contents

Robert J. Kane

OFFICERS AND ADMINISTRATIVE LEADERS UNITED STATES OLYMPIC COMMITTEE, 1977-1980

John B. Kelly, Jr.

E. Newbold Black IV

Joel Ferrell, Jr.

William E. Simon

Tenley E. Albright

Philip O. Krumm

Douglas F. Roby

Julian K. Roosevelt

Miguel de Capriles

Patrick H. Sullivan

Henry W. Buse, Jr.

F. Don Miller

Robert J. Kane
President

John B. Kelly, Jr.
First Vice President

E. Newbold Black IV
Second Vice President

Joel Ferrell, Jr.
Third Vice President

William E. Simon
Treasurer

Tenley E. Albright
Secretary

Philip O. Krumm
Immediate Past President

Douglas F. Roby
IOC Member for the U.S.

Julian K. Roosevelt
IOC Member for the U.S.

Miguel de Capriles
USOC delegate to PASO

Patrick H. Sullivan
Counselor

Lt. Gen. Henry W. Buse, Jr.
USMC (Ret), Assistant to the President

Col. F. Don Miller
USA (Ret), Executive Director

U.S.O.C. Executive Board

R. Abrahamson   J. Apodaca   L. Arnold   W. Baughman   H. Berg   I. Bernstein   D. Brown   P. Buehning   A. P. Clark

A. De Frantz   E. Dennis   R. Dermond   L. Drum   G. Edwards   M. Elliott   W. Fehring   J. Fell   H. Fitzhugh

C. Gibson   R. Giegengack   T. Gompf   J. Greer   J. Growney   A. Hart   R. Helmick   H. Henning   D. Heritage

G. Howie   R. Jones   G. Killian   W. Kem   W. Knecht   C. Knepp   F. Lay   J. Layton   D. Maggard

A. McGuire   H. Miller   L. Morrison   L. Mustin   S. Ochowicz   W. Peck   D. Porter   R. Purdy   H. Rathner

E. Seubert   D. Shavlik   B. Shaw   C. Shenk   R. Sheppard   R. Smith   R. Stearns   D. Steinman   J. Strahl

W. T. Tutt   L. Walker   M. Walker   E. Williams   G. Wilson   H. Zimman   E. Steitz   D. Bean

U.S.O.C. Executive Board

(*) Not members of Executive Board, August 31, 1980, but these persons had served during the quadrennium.

M. Cusack

E. Daniel

W. Davenport

C. Foster

F. Fullerton

A. Gerli

W. Hickey

M. Hogue

L. Hough

S. Malless

H. Marsh

W. McDonald

R. Sablo

J. Scalzo

R. Schwartz

J. D. Tooker

A. Toro

W. Tutt

Richard Abrahamson
Athletic Representative, Portland, Oregon

Jerry Apodaca
President's Representative, Santa Fe, New Mexico

Lloyd C. Arnold
National Council of YMCA's, New York, N.Y.

*Carl Battaglia
Luge, Utica, New York

Major Wayne Baughman, USAF
Athletic Representative, Colorado Springs, Colo.

Dawn Bean
Synchronized Swimming, Santa Ana, California

Harold E. Berg
Member at Large, Los Angeles, California

Irwin Bernstein
Fencing, Westfield, New Jersey

David W. Brown
State Olympic Organizations, Springfield, N.J.

Peter Buehning
Team Handball, Far Hills, New Jersey

Lt. Gen. A. P. Clark, USAF (ret)
Explorer Scouts, Monument, Colorado

Matthew Cusack
Catholic Youth Organization, Yongers, New York

Ellie Daniel
Athletic Representative, Los Angeles, California

Willie Davenport
Athletic Representative, Baton Rouge, Louisiana

Anita De Frantz
Athletic Representative, Philadelphia, Pa.

Dr. Evie Dennis
Track and Field, Denver, Colorado

Russell C. Dermond
Canoe & Kayak, Westwood, New Jersey

Loren Drum
Athletic Representative, San Antonio, Texas

Gene Edwards
Soccer, Milwaukee, Wisconsin

Michael Elliott
Athletic Representative, Durango, Colorado

*William P. (Dutch) Fehring
Baseball, Menlo Park, California

*John B. Fell
Bobsledding, Lake Placid, New York

Harry Fitzhugh
Gymnastics, La Jolla, California

*Charles U. Foster
Figure Skating, Duxbury, Massachussets

Frank Fullerton
Judo, El Paso, Texas

Anne Gerli
Figure Skating, New York, New York

Charles Gibson
Skiing, Fairfield, Connecticut

Robert F. Giegengack
Track & Field, Bethany, Connecticut

Thomas E. Gompf
Aquatics, Miami, Florida

John K. Greer
Men's Field Hockey, Cos Cob, Connecticut

James Growney
National Federation of State High School Associations
Robbinsville, New Jersey

Albert E. Hart, Jr.
Equestrian Sports, New York, New York

Robert H. Helmick
Amateur Athletic Union
Des Moines, Iowa

Harold W. Henning, DDS
Aquatics, Naperville, Illinois

Doris Heritage
Athletic Representative, Seattle, Washington

William Hickey
Bobsledding, Keeseville, New York

Major Micki Hogue, USAF
Athletic Representative, West Germany

Larry Hough
Athletic Representative, Washington, D.C.

George Howie
Speed Skating, Oconomowoc, Wisconsin

*Robert O. Jones
Secretary of State's
Representative, Washington, D.C.

George E. Killian
National Junior College Athletic
Association, Hutchinson, Kansas

*Wey Seng Kem
Judo, Raytown, Missouri

William J. Knecht
Rowing, Camden, New Jersey

Chris Knepp
Athletic Representative, Houston, Texas

*Floyd Lay
Basketball, Gainesville, Florida

John B. Layton
Shooting, Washington, D.C.

David I. Maggard
National Collegiate Athletic
Association, Berkeley, California

Stan Malless
Tennis, Indianapolis, Indiana

Henry Marsh
Athletic Representative, Salt Lake City, Utah

Vice Adm. Wesley McDonald, USN
Armed Forces, Washington, D.C.

Al McGuire
President's Representative,
Milwaukee, Wisconsin

Howard C. Miller
Member at Large, Chicago, Illinois

Dr. Leotus Morrison
Association for Intercollegiate Athletics
for Women, Harrisonburg, Virginia

*Adm. Lloyd Mustin, USN (ret)
Shooting, Washington, D.C.

Charles Neff
Luge, Painesville, Ohio

Sheila Young Ochowicz
Athletic Representative, Lake Placid, N.Y.

Wilbur Peck
Volleyball, Indianapolis, Indiana

Don S. Porter
Softball, Oklahoma City, Oklahoma

*Robert Purdy
Bobsledding, Keene, New York

Herbert Rathner
Secretary of State's Representative,
Washington, D.C.

Rudolph Sablo
Weightlifting, New York, New York

Joseph Scalzo
Wrestling, Toledo, Ohio

Roland Schwartz
Boxing, Cincinnati, Ohio

Ernest Seubert
Cycling, Cedar Grove, New Jersey

Donna Shavlik
Member at Large, Washington, D.C.

Burt Shaw
Aquatics, Long Beach, California

Clayton Shenk
Archery, Lancaster, Pennsylvania

Robert Sheppard
Member at Large, Chicago, Illinois

Robert Smith
Baseball, Greenville, Illinois

Richard Stearns
Yachting, Chicago, Illinois

Daniel Steinman
Modern Pentathlon, Hatboro, Pennsylvania

Edward Steitz
Basketball, Springfield, Massachusetts

Dr. John Strahl
National Association for Intercollegiate
Athletics Greenville, Illinois

Beatrice Toner
Women's Field Hockey, Hempstead, N.Y.

Joseph D. Tooker, Jr.
Member at Large, New York, N.Y.

Andras Toro
Athletic Representative, El Cerrito, Cal.

William Tutt
Member at Large, Colorado Springs, Colo.

W. Thayer Tutt
Ice Hockey, Colorado Springs, Colo.

Dr. LeRoy T. Walker
American Association for Health, Physical
Education, Recreation and Dance, Durham,
N.C.

Mrs. Marie Walker
Roller Skating, Groton, Connecticut

Edward Williams
Athletic Representative, Brooklyn Heights,
New York

George M. Wilson
Biathlon, Falls Church, Washington

Harold O. Zimman
Jewish Welfare Board, Marblehead, Mass.

U.S.O.C. Administrative Personnel Delegation at Olympic and Pan American Games

(Photographs are in alphabetical order, without regard to administrative designation, except USOC Officers and Executive Staff are included with photographs of USOC Executive Board.)

(Unless specifically designated as 1979 Pan American Games (A), 1980 Olympic Winter Games (B), or the Games of the XXII Olympiad (C), the following served in their respective capacities for all three Games.)

U.S.O.C. OFFICERS
Robert J. Kane, President, Ithaca, New York
John B. Kelly, Jr., First Vice President, Philadelphia, Pennsylvania
E. Newbold Black, IV, Second Vice President, Wellesley, Massachussetts
Joel Ferrell, Jr., Third Vice President, Washington, D.C.
Tenley Albright, M.D., Secretary, Brookline, Massachussetts
William E. Simon, Treasurer, Far Hills, N.J.
Douglas F. Roby, 10C Member, Ypsilanti, Michigan
Julian K. Roosevelt, 10C Member, Oyster Bay, New York
Miguel de Capriles, PASO Member, San Francisco, California (A)

EXECUTIVE STAFF
Lt. Gen. W. Henry Buse, Jr., USMC (ret.), Chairman, Games Preparation Committee, Severana Park, Maryland
Col. F. Don Miller, USA (Ret.), Secretary General, U.S.O.C., Colorado Springs, Colorado
Patrick H. Sullivan, Counsellor, New York, New York

CHIEFS OF MISSION
Captain Josiah Henson, USN (Ret.), Falls Church, Virginia (A)
George Howie, Oconomowoc, Wisconsin (B)
James R. Jack, Salt Lake City, Utah (C)

ATTACHE
Edwin H. Mosler, Jr., New York, New York (B)

TEAM SERVICES COMMITTEE CHAIRMEN
John B. Kelly, Jr., General Chairman, Philadelphia, Pennsylvania
Albert Buckingham, Sioux City, Iowa, Housing Chairman
Irving Dardik, M.D., Chairman, Medical & Training Services, Teaneck, New Jersey
T. Harold Forbes, Jr., Ticket Services Chairman, New York, New York
George E. Killian, Transportation Chairman, Hutchinson, Kansas
Hermann G. Rusch, Food Chairman, White Sulphur Springs, West Virginia
Ross H. Smith, Apparel, Supplies, and Equipment Chairman, Wayland, Mass.

OLYMPIC HOUSE STAFF PERSONNEL
William E. Bachert, Financial Assistant, Upper Montclair, New Jersey (A)
Rochelle Evans, Public Relations Secretary, Colorado Springs, Colorado (B)
Marilyn Crawford, Operations Dept. Secretary, Colorado Springs, Colorado (A)
Ernest Hinck, Assistant Treasurer, Colorado Springs, Colorado
Dennis Keegan, Director of Public Relations, Colorado Springs, Colorado (B)
Jerry Lace, Director of Operations, Colorado Springs, Colorado
Larry McCollum, Operations Dept., Colorado Springs, Colorado
Mary Patricia McSherry, Staff Secretary, Colorado Springs, Colorado (A)
R. Michael Moran, Communications Division, Colorado Springs, Colorado
C. Robert Paul, Jr., Director of Communications, Colorado Springs, Colorado
Louice Perry, Staff Secretary, Colorado Springs, Colorado

ATHLETES' REPRESENTATIVES
Kathy Kretschmer, San Francisco, California (A)
Frederick V. Newhouse, Baton Rouge, Louisiana (A)
Rick Colella, Seattle, Washington (B)
Suna Murray, Boston, Massachussetts (B)

S. Babagian   W. Bachert   R. Beeten   R. Bergman   D. Blanchard   P. Boltz

C. Bonci   C. Bradley   J. Brock   D. Bryant   A. Buckingham   B. Callahan

R. Colella   M. Crawford   A. Daly   I. Dardik   C. Demers   E. Dennis

R. Evans   G. Finerman   H. Forbes   G. Goodhart   S. Hatchell   J. Henson

E. Hinck   M. Hodges   G. Howie   C. Hubbell   J. Jack   D. Keegan

T. Kerin   A. Kiev   G. Killian   B. Kola   K. Krtetschmer   J. Lace

B. Lewis   M. Linkovich   L. McCollum   M. P. McSherry   W. Mieves   M. K. Mizelle

R. Moore

M. Moran

E. Mosler

F. Newhouse

A. Ortolani

J. Patmont

J. Pickering

C. Reber

N. Rhinehart

H. Rusch

T. Russo

R. Smith

F. Stabley

L. Standifer

R. Steadman

T. Taft

G. Weldon

T. Young

D. Yugo

J. Mott

S. Murray

G. Nagobads

R. Paul

L. Perry

N. Peterson

MEDICAL AND TRAINING SERVICES

Anthony Daly, M.D., Head Physician, Inglewood, California

Robert Beeten, Head Trainer, Colorado Springs, Colorado

Sherry Kosek Babagian, Stanford University, Stanford, California (A) (C)

Roy T. Bergman, M.D., Escanaba, Michigan (A) (C)

David Blanchard, Stanford University, Stanford, California (A) (C)

Christine Bonci, University of Pennsylvania, Philadelphia, Pennsylvania (C)

Carl O. Demers, Deerfield Academy, Deerfield, Massachussetts (C)

Gerald Finerman, M.D., U.C.L.A. Los Angeles, California (A)

George Goodheart, D.C., Detroit, Michigan (B)

Carol Hubbell, Minneapolis, Minnesota (A)

Tom Kerin, University of North Carolina, Chapel Hill, North Carolina (A) (C)

Ari Kiev, M.D., New York, New York (A)

Bruce Kola, Colorado College, Colorado Springs, Colorado (B)

Marsha King Mizelle, Gunter AFS, Alabama (B)

Mike Linkovich, Bowdoin College, Brunswick, Maine (C)

Bob Moore, San Diego State, San Diego, California (A) (C)

George Nagobads, University of Minnesota, Minneapolis, Minnesota (B)

Alfred Ortolani, Pittsburgh State, Pittsburg, Kansas (A) (C)

Jerome Patmont, M.D., University of California, Berkeley, California (A) (C)

John Pickering, University of Illinois, Champaign, Illinois (B)

Calvin Reber, M.D., Auburn University, Auburn, Alabama (B)

Nasby Rhinehart, Montana University, Billings, Montana (A)

Tony Russo, Glendora, California (A) (C)

Doug Shaw, M.D., Santa Barbara, California (C)

Larry Standifer, Eugene, Oregon (C)

Richard Steadman, M.D., South Lake Tahoe, California

Timothy Taft, M.D., University of North Carolina, Chapel Hill, North Carolina (A) (C)

Gail Weldon, U.C.L.A., Los Angeles, California (A) (C)

Troy Young, Arizona State, Tempe, Arizona (C)

Dave Yugo, University of Las Vegas-Nevada, Las Vegas, Nevada (A)

ARMED FORCES REPRESENTATIVES

Maj. Miles Hodges, USMC, Washington, D.C. (A)

Mr. Paul Boltz, U.S. Army Depot, Mechanicsburg, Pennsylvania (A)

Mr. Ben Lewis, Navy Department, Washington, D.C. (B)

WOMEN'S ADMINISTRATORS

Carol Bradley, Park City, Utah (B)

Dr. Evie Dennis, Denver, Colorado (A)

MEDIA AND PHOTOGRAPHIC SERVICES

R. Michael Moran, Chief, Colorado Springs, Colorado

James Brock, Dallas, Texas (A) (B)

Don Bryant, University of Nebraska, Lincoln, Nebraska (B)

William Callahan, University of Missouri, Columbia, Missouri (B)

Steve Hatchell, Big Eight Conference, Kansas City, Missouri (B)

Walter Meives, University of Wisconsin, Madison, Wisconsin

Edwin H. Mosler, Jr., New York City (A)

James Mott, University of Wisconsin, Madison, Wisconsin (B)

Nancy Peterson, Stanford California, Stanford, California (B)

Fred Stabley, Michigan State University, E. Lansing, Michigan (B)

VIII
Pan American
Games
San Juan
Puerto Rico

July 1-15, 1979

U.S.A. Gold Medal Winners

ARCHERY
Individual Men:
Rodney Baston
Individual Women:
Lynette Johnson
Team: Judi Adams, Rodney Baston, Richard Bednar, Lynette Johnson, Nancy Myrick, Richard McKinney, Darrell O. Pace, Carol Strausburg.

ATHLETICS (Track and field) MEN
Duncan Atwood, Javelin; Matt Centrowitz, 5000m; Bob Coffman, Decathlon; Tony Darden, 400m, 4 x 400m Relay; Herman Frazier, 4 x 400m Relay; Harvey Glance, 4 x 100m Relay; Franklin Jacobs, High Jump; David Laut, Shot Put; Henry Marsh, 3000m Steeplechase; Renaldo Nehemiah, 110m Hurdles; Maurice Peoples, 4 x 400m Relay; Donald Paige, 1500m; Steve Riddick, 4 x 100m Relay; Mike Roberson, 4 x 100m Relay; James Robinson, 800m; James Walker, 400m Hurdles, 4 x 400m Relay; Mac Wilkins, Discus; Clifford Wiley, 4 x 100m Relay.

ATHLETICS (Track and Field) WOMEN
Evelyn Ashford, 100m, 200m; Valerie Brisco, 4 x 100m Relay; Rosalyn Bryant, 4 x 400m Relay; Chandra Cheeseborough, 4 x 100m Relay; Sharon Dabney, 400m, 4 x 400m Relay; Mary Decker, 1500m; Karen Hawkins, 4 x 100m Relay; Patricia Jackson, 4 x 400m Relay; Essie Kelley, 800m, 4 x 400m Relay; Deby LaPlante, 100m Hurdles; Kathy McMillan, Long Jump; Janice Merrill, 3000m; Brenda Morehead, 4 x 100m Relay; Louise Ritter, High Jump.

BASKETBALL — MEN
Michael Brooks, Samuel Clancy, John Duren, Ronnie Lester, Kyle Macy, Kevin McHale, Michael O'Koren, Ralph Sampson, Isaiah Thomas, Ray Tolbert, Danny Vranes, Michael Woodson.

BOXING
Jackie Beard, Bantamweight;* Lemuel Steeples, Light Welterweight; Bernard Taylor, Featherweight; Tony Tucker, Light Heavyweight.

*Killed in plane crash, Warsaw, Poland, March 14, 1980.

CYCLING
100-Kilometer Time Trial Team:
Thomas Doughty, George Mount, Thomas Sain, Wayne Stetina.

DIVING
Greg Louganis, Men's Platform, Men's Springboard; Barbara Weinstein, Women's Platform; Denise Christensen, Women's Springboard.

EQUESTRIAN SPORTS
Hilda Gurney (Keen), Dressage; Michael Matz (Jet Run), Jumping, Individual and Team; William "Buddy" Brown (Sandsa-blaze), Jumping, Team; Norman Dello Joio (Allegro), Jumping, Team; Melanie Smith (Val de Loire), Jumping, Team.

FENCING
Scott Bozek, Paul Pesthy, Peter Schifrin, and Lee Shelley, Epee, Team.

GYMNASTICS — WOMEN
Jackie Cassello, Side Horse Vault; Jeannine Creek, Floor Exercise.

ROLLER SKATING
Fleurette Arsenault, Dancing; Robbie Coleman, Pairs Skating; Natalie Dunn, Women's Singles; Patrick Jones, Pairs Skating; Dan Littel, Dancing; Fred Morante, Men's Singles; Tom Peterson, 5,000, Pack-Style, 10,000m Pack-Style, 10,000m Relay, 20,000m Cross-Country; Chris Snyder, 10,000m Relay; Ken Sutton, 500m Against Clock.

ROWING
Eight Oars With Coxswain:
John Chatzky, Sean Colgan, Mike Hess, Bruce Ibbotson, Walter Lubsen, Philip Stekl, David Townsley, Kerry Turner, Tom Woodman.

SHOOTING — INDIVIDUAL
Robert Green, Trapshooting; Donald Nygord, Air Pistol; John Satterwhite, Skeet Shooting; Lt. Col. Lones Wigger, English Match, Small Bore Rifle, 3-Position.

SHOOTING — TEAM
Air Rifle:
Edward Etzel, Michael Gross, Wanda Jewell, Ernest Vande Zande
English Match:
Dennis Ghiselli, Boyd Goldsby, Ernest Vande Zande, Lones Wigger
Small Bore Rifle, 3-Position:
Edward Etzel, Rod Fitz-Randolph, Lones Wigger, Thomas Whitaker
Air Pistol:
Eric Buljung, Donald Hamilton, Charles McCowan, Donald Nygord
Trapshooting:
Charvin Dixon, Robert Green, Ernest Neel, Walter Zobell, Jr.
Skeet Shooting:
Joseph Clemmons, Matthew Dryke, Jeffrey Sizemore, John Satterwhite
Center Fire Pistol:
Samuel Baiocco, Jimmie Dorsey, Darius Young, Jerry Wilder.

SOFTBALL — WOMEN
Kathryn Arendsen, Gwen Berner, Susan Enquist, Suzie Gaw, Melannie Kyler, Shirley Mapes, Brenda Marshall, Paula Noel, Sylvia Ortiz, Marilyn Rau, Barbara Reinalda, Dorothy Richardson, Diane Schumacher, Linda Spagnolo, Kathleen Strahan, Paula Stufflebeam, Joan Van Ness, Julie Winklepleck.

SWIMMING — MEN
Jack Babashoff, 4 x 100m Freestyle Relay; Craig Beardsley, 200m Butterfly; Rowdy Gaines, 200m Freestyle, 4 x 100m Freestyle Relay, 4 x 200m Freestyle Relay; Brian Goodell, 400m Freestyle, 1500m Freestyle, 4 x 200m Freestyle Relay; Bob Jackson, 100m Backstroke, 4 x 100m Medley Relay; Kris Kirchner, 4 x 200m Freestyle Relay; Steve Lundquist, 100m Breaststroke, 200m Breaststroke, 4 x 100m Medley Relay; David McCagg, 100m Freestyle, 4 x 100m Freestyle Relay, 4 x 100m Medley Relay; Robert Placak, 100m Butterfly, 4 x 100m Medley Relay; Peter Rocca, 200m Backstroke; Jesse Vassallo, 200m Individual Medley, 400m Individual Medley.

SWIMMING — WOMEN
Tracy Caulkins, 200m Individual Medley, 400m Individual Medley, 4 x 100m Medley Relay, 4 x 100m Freestyle Relay; Stephanie Elkins, 4 x 100m Freestyle Relay; Linda Jezek, 100m Backstroke, 200m Backstroke, 4 x 100m Medley Relay; Kim Linehan, 800m Freestyle; Mary T. Meagher, 200m Butterfly; Tami Paumier, 100m Breaststroke; Jill Sterkel, 100m Butterfly, 4 x 100m Medley Relay, 4 x 100m Freestyle Relay; Sippy Woodhead, 100m Freestyle, 200m Freestyle, 400m Freestyle, 4 x 100m Medley Relay, 4 x 100m Freestyle Relay.

SYNCHRONIZED SWIMMING
Team:
Michelle Barone, Michele Beaulieu, Gerry Brandley, Suzanne Cameron, Laura Florio, Tracie Ruiz, Linda Shelley, Pam Tryon.

TENNIS
Susie Hagey, Women's Singles, Women's Doubles; Ann Henricksson, Women's Doubles; Andy Kohlberg, Men's Doubles; Mel Purcell, Men's Singles, Men's Doubles.

WATER POLO
Douglas Burke, Christopher Dorst, Gary Figueroa, Steve Hamann, Eric Lindroth, Andrew McDonald, Kevin Robertson, Peter Schnugg, Terry Schroeder, Jon Svendsen, Joseph Vargas.

WEIGHTLIFTING
Mark Cameron, 242 Pounds (Heavyweight), Total Lift, Snatch, Clean and Jerk Lift; Tom Stock, Over 242 Pounds (Superheavyweight), Total Lift, Snatch, Clean and Jerk Lift.

WRESTLING — FREE-STYLE
Roy Baker, 198 Pounds; Joseph Corso, 125 Pounds; Russell Hellickson, 220 Pounds; Jimmy Jackson, Heavyweight; Lee Kemp, 163 Pounds; Daniel Lewis, 180 Pounds; Andre Metzger, 136 Pounds; Gene Mills, 114 Pounds; Andrew Rein, 150 Pounds; William Rosado, 106.5 Pounds.

WRESTLING — GRECO-ROMAN
Daniel Chandler, 180 Pounds; John Matthews, 163 Pounds, Brad Rheingans, 220 Pounds; Bruce Thompson, 114 Pounds.

YACHTING
Steve Cucchiaro, "470" Class; David Curtis, Soling Class; Mark Reynolds, Snipe Class. Francis Edward Charles, "470" Class; David B. Barton, Soling Class; James McCleery, Soling Class; Robert Martin, Snipe Class.

Silver Medals

ARCHERY
Individual Men, Darrell Pace; Individual Women, Carol Strausburg.

ATHLETICS (Track and Field) MEN
Willie Banks, Triple Jump; Benn Fields, High Jump; Harvey Glance, 100m; Todd Harbour, 1500m; Herb Lindsay, 500m; William McCullough, 3000m Steeplechase; Neal Pyke, 20k Walk; Greg Woepse, Pole Vault.

ATHLETICS (Track and Field) WOMEN
Jodi Anderson, Pentathlon; Julie Brown, 800m, 1500m, 3000m; Lynn Cannon, Javelin; Brenda Morehead, 100m; Maren Seidler, Shot Put; Pam Spencer, High Jump.

BASKETBALL — WOMEN
Carol Blazejowski, Barbara Brown, Denise Curry, Tara Heiss, Kris Kirchner, Nancy Lieberman, Ann Meyers, Jill Rankin, Jackie Swaim, Jan Trombly, Rosie Walker, Holly Warlick.

BOXING
Richard Sandoval, Light Flyweight; James Shuler, Light Middleweight.

DIVING
Phil Boggs, Men's Springboard; Janet Ely Thorburn, Women's Platform and Springboard.

EQUESTRIAN SPORTS
Gwen Stockebrand (Bao), Individual Dressage

FENCING
Edward Donofrio, Team Foil; Stanley Lekach, Team Sabre; Michael Marx, Team Foil; Gregory Massialas, Team Foil; John Nonna, Team Foil; Edgar House, Team Sabre; Paul Pesthy, Individual Epee; Phillip Reilly, Team Sabre; Peter Westbrook, Team and Individual Sabre.

GYMNASTICS — MEN
Daniel Muenz, Parallel Bars

GYMNASTICS — WOMEN
Heidi Anderson, Floor Exercise; Jeannine Creek, All-Around.

JUDO
Jesse Goldstein, Over 209 Pounds; Edward Liddie, 132 Pounds.

ROLLER SKATING
Curtis Cook, 10,000m Relay, 3000m Pack-Style, Men's 500m Against the Clock; Suzanne Dooley, 5000m Relay, 5000m Pack-Style; Linda Dorso, Women's 500m; Mark Howard, Dancing; Alexander Kane IV, Men's Singles; Tina Kneisley, Pairs Skating; LinSue Peterson, 5000m Relay; Paul Price, Pairs Skating; Cindy Smith, Dancing; Chris Snyder, Men's 10,000m Pack-Style, 20,000m Cross Country; Kenneth Sutton, 10,000m Relay, Men's 500m Two at a Time; Jo Anne Young, Women's Singles.

ROWING
Chris Alsopp, Double Sculls; Richard Cashin, Pairs Without Coxswain; David Fellows, Pairs Without Coxswain; Jesse Franklin, Fours Without Coxswain; Tom Howes, Double Sculls; Mike Teti, Fours Without Coxswain; Darrell Vreugdenhil, Fours Without Coxswain; Jim Watenpaugh, Fours Without Coxswain.

SHOOTING
Individual:
Charvin Dixon, Trapshooting; Mathew Dryke, Skeet Shooting; Rod Fitz-Randolph, Small Bore Rifle, 3-Position; John McNally, Rapid Fire Pistol; Donald Nygord, Air Pistol; Ernest Vande Zande, Air Rifel; Jerry Wilder, Center Fire Pistol.

SHOOTING — TEAM
Rapid Fire Pistol:
Terence Anderson, William McMillan, John McNally, Darius Young.

SOFTBALL — MEN
Floyd Batt, James Bracken, Thomas Connor, Darryl Day, John Ege, Gene Green, Charles Grimes, Rickey Gruber, Ted Hicks, Al Lewis, Bruce Miller, William Pfeiffer, Robert A. Quinn, Robert H. Quinn, David Scott, Jeffrey Seip, Tyrone Stofflet, Angelo Veronesi.

SWIMMING — MEN
David Larson, 200m Freestyle; John Simons, 200m Breaststroke; Jesse Vassallo, 200m Backstroke,* Greg Winchell, 100m Breaststroke.
(*) deceased, 1979

SWIMMING — WOMEN
Lisa Buese, 100m Butterfly; Tracy Caulkins, 400m Freestyle, 100m Breaststroke; Jennifer Hooker, 800m Freestyle; Kim Linehan, 200m Freestyle; Karinne Miller, 200m Butterfly; Jill Sterkel, 100m Freestyle; Anne Tweedy, 400m Individual Medley.

SYNCHRONIZED SWIMMING
Michele Barone, Duet; Michele Beaulieu, Singles; Linda Shelley, Duet.

TENNIS
Fritz Buehning, Mixed Doubles; Ann Henricksson, Mixed Doubles; Trey Lewis, Women's Singles.

WEIGHTLIFTING
Guy Carlton, 220 Pounds (First Heavyweight), Total Lift, Clean and Jerk Lift; Tom Hirtz, 181 Pounds (Light Heavyweight), Total Lift, Snatch, Clean and Jerk Lift; David Jones, 149 Pounds (Lightweight), Total Lift, Clean and Jerk Lift; Phillip Sanderson, 132 Pounds (Featherweight), Total Lift, Snatch, Clean and Jerk Lift; Kurt Setterberg, 220 Pounds (First Heavyweight), Snatch.

WRESTLING — GRECO-ROMAN
Brian Gust, 125 Pounds; Pete Lee, Heavyweight; Gary Pelcl, 150 Pounds; Jerry Schmitz, 198 Pounds.

YACHTING
Jeffrey Lenhart, Snipe Class; Cameron Lewis, Laser Class; Skip Whyte, "470" Class; Randall Alan Smith, Snipe Class; Charles Millican, "470" Class.

Bronze Medals

ATHLETICS (Track and Field) MEN
James Butts, Triple Jump; Don Coleman, 200m; Marco Evoniuk, 50k Walk; Charles Foster, 110m Hurdles; Emitt King, 100m; Carl Lewis, Long Jump; Todd Scully, 20k Walk; Frank Shorter, 10,000m; Willie Smith, 400m.

ATHLETICS (Track and Field) WOMEN
Patricia Jackson, 400m; Cathy Sulinski, Javelin.

BOXING
Jerome Coffee, Flyweight; Rufus Hadley, Heavyweight.

DIVING
Phil Boggs, Men's Platform.

FENCING
Nikki Franke, Women's Foil, Team and Individual; John Nonna, Men's Foil; Ann Russell, Women's Team Foil; Vincent H. Senser, Women's Team Foil; Debra Waples, Women's Team Foil.

GYMNASTICS — MEN
Jeffrey LaFleur, Still Rings.

JUDO
Brett Barron, 172 Pounds; Miguel Tudela, 209 Pounds; Leo White, 189 Pounds.

ROLLER SKATING
Elaine Coley, Women's 500m, 5000m Relay; LinSue Peterson, Women's 3000m, Pack-Style, 5000m Relay; Chris Snyder, Men's 3000m, Pack-Style.

ROWING
Bruce Beall, Quadruple Sculls; Steve Christiansen, Fours with Coxswain; Fred Fox, Fours with Coxswain; John Hartigan, Fours with Coxswain; Mark Miller, Fours with Coxswain; Rick Paczewski, Fours with Coxswain; Alan Shealy, Quadruple Sculls; Gregg Stone, Quadruple Sculls; Christopher Wood, Quadruple Sculls.

SHOOTING
Samuel Biaocco, Center Fire Pistol - Individual.

SWIMMING — MEN
Bobby Hackett, 1500m Freestyle; John Newton, 100m Freestyle; Scott Spann, 200m Individual Medley.

SWIMMING — WOMEN
Libby Kinkead, 200m Backstroke; Patty Spees, 200m Breaststroke; Anne Tweedy, 200m Individual Medley.

WEIGHTLIFTING
Guy Carlton, 220 Pounds (First Heavyweight), Snatch; James Curry, 198 Pounds (Light Heavyweight), Snatch; David Jones, 149 Pounds (Lightweight), Snatch; Charles Nootens, 242 Pounds (Heavyweight), Total Lift, Clean and Jerk Lift.

WRESTLING — GRECO-ROMAN
John Hughes, 136 Pounds; Gregg Williams, 106.5 Pounds.

YACHTING
Stewart Neff, Laser Class; Bill Shore, Bonnie Lee Shore, and Bill Hartnett, Lightning Class.

U.S. Team Scores Its Greatest Success in VIII Games

The United States Team to the VIII Pan American Games scored the greatest success of any nation ever to participate in the Western Hemispheric Championships since the inaugural Games in Buenos Aires in 1951. The 515 athletes covered themselves with personal and team glory and showed the other 32 participating nations how seriously the USA considers this competition restricted to the Americas.

There may have been some question about the claimant to the first gold medal awarded in San Juan. Some claimed the first Pan American Champion of the VIII Games was Guy Lorton, Jr. of Canada in the air rifle in which the USA marksmen were awarded the "team" gold medals. Others supported the claim of Kenneth Sutton, USA, in the 500 meters roller skating, the first ever medal awarded in that sport in the Pan American Games.

There was no doubt about the winner of the 242nd and final Pan American gold medal awarded immediately prior to the start of the magnificent Closing Ceremony in Hiram Bithorn Park. *Jet Run*, a gelding owned by Fitz-Eugene Dixon of Whitemarsh, Pa., and ridden by Michael Matz, retained top laurels in the individual show jumping. Four years earlier *Jet Run*, owned and ridden by Alfredo Senderos of Mexico, had won the gold medal in the same event. Since the 1975 Pan American Games, Mr. Dixon had purchased the horse from Sr. Senderos.

More than 4,400 athletes from 33 Western Hemisphere nations stood at attention in rain-soaked Hiram Bithorn Park, under a blazing sun, as more than 5,000 Puerto Rican boys and girls performed native dances and presented artistic gymnastic routines to the thunderous applause of a jam-packed stadium.

Selected by the USA team captains, basketball's Ann Meyers carried the national ensign as the USA delegation paraded into the stadium nattily attired in strictly American dress designed by Levi Strauss and Company. For the Closing Ceremony the USA flagbearer was Kathy Arendsen, star pitcher for the gold medalist softball team.

Statistically speaking, the USA won more gold medals and accumulated the largest total number of medals of any nation ever to participate in the Pan American Games. The log showed 126 gold medals (six more than the previous high at Chicago in 1959). The total medal count for the USA forces was 263, 17 more than in Mexico four years earlier.

In the individual sports the USA earned gold medals in all except two. However, in the team sports the USA yielded first place to Cuba. The Islanders won the championships in women's basketball (succeeding the USA) while retaining its laurels in baseball, and winning both volleyball crowns. The Cubans also won silver medals in soccer and water polo.

The USA retained the men's basketball title (outscoring Puerto Rico in a tense contest played before a hostile and aroused crowd), regained the water polo title, won the first ever womens' softball diadem and

dropped the championship men's softball game to Canada.

As expected, the USA showed its greatest strength in athletics (track and field) and the aquatic sports (swimming, diving, synchronized swimming and water polo).

The success scored by the men's and women's track and field teams went almost unchallenged. The men won 14 Pan American titles, the women 11 (an all-time high). Performance-wise there was no question that the USA has widened the athletic disparity between its track and field athletes and the rest of the Western Hemisphere.

The swimmers won 28 of 29 titles (the women lost a breaststroke event), the divers placed 1-2 in three of the four events, 1-3 in the other, and the water polo team was unbeaten in regaining the title yielded four years earlier.

For sheer drama the boxing tournament was the best ever seen in the Americas — 114 boxers were entered in the 11 weight divisions. The USA advanced eight to the semifinal round and all but two of the eight made it into the championship round.

Although the USA boxers ousted four of six Cubans in the early rounds, the Cubans won five gold medals (only one from the USA in the final round).

Lemuel Steeples, light welterweight, USA was chosen the recipient of the Col. Don Hull Trophy as the outstanding boxer in the tournament.

The USA again proved to have the

strongest wrestling squads. In the Greco-Roman competition the USA won four titles and then came back in the free-style matches to win all ten titles. World champion Lee Kemp won his first Pan American title at 163 pounds and Russ Hellickson captured his third straight 220-pound crown.

The new sports on the Pan American calendar were men's and women's softball, men's and women's roller skating (speed, artistic and roller hockey) and archery. The addition of these sports added materially to the USA medals success.

It was gold in women's softball, silver in men's softball; 1-2 finishes in men's and women's individual contests, archery individual contests, and in roller skating ten gold, 13 silver and five bronze.

Not to be overlooked on the mythical honor roll was the success of the marksmen. Included among the 12 gold, eight silver and one bronze were four gold medals won by Lt. Col. Lones Wigger, USA, with a pair of individual gold medals in the English Match and small bore rifle, three position events along with two more golds in the synthetic "team" competitions in these two events.

Four years ago the USA swept all five tennis titles. At San Juan, the USA won four of the five, finishing runner-up in the mixed doubles. The tennis team was selected by the U.S. Tennis Association from the collegiate ranks.

For the first time each country was permitted to enter two boats in each of the

Tracy Caulkins, Jesse Vassallo and Sippy Woodhead won 11 Gold Medals

yachting classes. Again, a change worked to the advantage of the USA, which won three gold, three silver and a single bronze.

Cuba dominated the weightlifting and fencing competitions. In weightlifting, there were 30 gold medals up for grabs in the ten weight divisions (one medal for each of the two lifts and a third for the total lift). Mark Cameron and Tom Stock, both USA swept all three gold medals in the two heaviest weight classes and only Canada prevented Cuba from sweeping the other 24 gold medals by snagging a gold in the snatch lift of the middleweight class.

The USA yielded No. 1 placing in fencing to the Islanders as Cuba won six gold, two silver and two bronze to the USA with a 1-4-3 medals' performance.

Special mention must be made of the gymnastics team and the road cyclists.

The USA opted to compete only in the individual events with three men and women gymnasts because of special compulsory exercises designed for use in the Pan American Games. Even so, in the women's competition, before more than 10,000 frenetic enthusiasts in the Roberto Clemente Coliseum, Jackie Cassello, Silver Spring, Md., a 13-year-old fearless gymnast with unlimited potential, won a gold medal in the vault and silver on the balance beam; Jeannine Creek, 17, Great Falls, Montana, was the gold medalist in the floor exercises and Heidi Anderson, on the 17th anniversary of her birth, was runner-up to Miss Creek in the floor exercises.

The road cyclists won the first ever USA Pan American gold medal in the 100-kilometer team race by a margin of 3½ minutes over the Cubans.

The USA ''Mythical'' Honor Roll of Individual Champions, alphabetically, includes:

EVELYN ASHFORD, 100m and 200m, track and field.

JACKIE BEARD, bantamweight, boxing.

JACKIE CASSELLO, vaulting, gymnastics.

RUSSELL HELLICKSON, 220 pounds, free-style wrestling.

TOM PETERSON, four championships, speed roller skating.

JAMES ROBINSON, 800 meters, track and field.

LEMUEL STEEPLES, light welterweight, boxing.

TOM STOCK, super heavyweight, weightlifting.

JESSE VASSALLO, world record, 200m individual medley, swimming.

LT. COL. LONES WIGGER, USA four gold medals, shooting.

SIPPY WOODHEAD, five gold medals and one world record (200m freestyle) swimming.

GREG LOUGANIS, winner of both diving titles.

IN MEMORIAM. Gregory Winchell, 18, Fullerton, Cal., silver medalist in the 100m breaststroke, was fatally injured in a motorcycle accident several weeks after the completion of the Games.

Lemuel Steeples, 23, St. Louis, gold medalist in the light welterweight boxing division, met a tragic death in an airplane crash at Warsaw, Poland, May 14, en route to an international boxing match with other outstanding USA boxers.

OBSERVATION: If asked, ''Was this trip necessary?'' and honest answer would be a resounding, ''Yes . . . and it was a successful trip, too.''

TEAM SPORTS

	Gold	Silver	Bronze	USA Finish Place
Baseball	Cuba*	Dominican Republic	Puerto Rico	4th
Basketball, Men's	USA*	Puerto Rico	Brazil	1st
Basketball, Women's	Cuba	USA	Canada	2nd
Field Hockey	Argentina*	Canada	Mexico	6th
Roller Hockey	Argentina	Brazil	Chile	4th
Soccer	Brazil*	Cuba	Argentina	5th
Softball, Men's	Canada	USA	Puerto Rico	2nd
Softball, Women's	USA	Puerto Rico	Belize	1st
Volleyball, Men's	Cuba*	Brazil	Canada	4th
Volleyball, Women's	Cuba*	Peru	Brazil	4th
Water Polo	USA	Cuba	Canada	1st

Recapitulation: Cuba 4-2-0; USA 3-2-0; Argentina 2-0-1; Brazil 1-2-2; Canada 1-1-3; Puerto Rico 0-2-2; Dominican Republic 0-1-0; Peru 0-1-1; Belize 0-0-1; Chile 0-0-1

*Retained Championship

UNOFFICIAL MEDALS COUNT

Country	Gold	Silver	Bronze	Total
USA	126	94	46	266
Cuba	65	49	32	146
Canada	24	44	67	135
Mexico	3	4	28	37
Argentina	12	7	17	36
Brazil	9	13	14	36
Puerto Rico	2	9	11	22
Venezuela	1	4	7	12
Dominican Republic	0	5	7	12
Chile	1	4	6	11
Colombia	0	1	8	9
Panama	0	3	1	4
Jamaica	0	3	0	3
Guyana	0	2	1	3
Peru	0	1	2	3
Ecuador	0	0	2	2
Bahamas	0	1	0	1
Virgin Islands	0	0	1	1
Netherlands Antilles	0	0	1	1
El Salvador	0	0	1	1
Belize	0	0	1	1

TABLE OF MEDALS AND FINISH PLACES — USA

Sport	Gold	Silver	Bronze	Finish Place	Total Medals
Archery, M & W	4	2	0	1st	6
Athletics, M	14	8	9	1st	31
Athletics, W	11	8	2	1st	21
Baseball	—	—	—	4th	—
Basketball, M	1	—	—	1st	1
Basketball, W	—	1	—	2nd	1
Boxing	4	2	2	1st	8
Cycling	1	0	0	DNP	1
Diving, M & W	4	3	1	1st	8
Equestrians Sports	3	1	0	1st	4
Fencing, M & W	1	4	3	2nd	8
Field Hockey, M	—	—	—	6th	—
Gymnastics, M & W	2	4	1	3rd	7
Judo	0	2	3	4th	5
Roller Skating, M & W	10	13	5	1st	28
Roller Hockey	—	—	—	4th	—
Rowing	1	3	3	3rd	7
Shooting	12	8	1	1st	21
Soccer	—	—	—	5th	—
Softball, M	—	1	—	2nd	1
Softball, W	1	—	—	1st	1
Swimming, M	15	3	4	1st	22
Swimming, W	13	9	2	1st	24
Synchronized Swimming	1	2	0	2nd	3
Tennis, M & W	4	2	0	1st	6
Volleyball, M	—	—	—	4th	—
Volleyball, W	—	—	—	4th	—
Water Polo	1	—	—	1st	1
Weightlifting	6	11	6	2nd	23
Wrestling	14	4	2	1st	20
Yachting	3	3	2	1st	8

Archery

The results were as expected, the USA made a clean sweep of the medals. Only the names of the medalists were surprising. In fact, the USA did place 1-2-3 in both men's and ladies individual shooting but under the rules of the Pan American Games only two medals may be garnered by any one country in individual competitions.

Rodney Baston, a 23-year-old airman stationed at the Barksdale, Louisiana, Air Force Base earned the gold medal by out-shooting the Olympic champion, Darrell Pace, also a member of the U.S. Air Force, and the 1978 world champion, Richard McKinney.

McKinney led at the end of the first F.I.T.A. round of 144 arrows with 1,262 out of a possible 1,440 points. However, world champion McKinney slumped on the second F.I.T.A. round (possibly hampered by several rain squalls) with Baston and Pace surging on to capture the gold and silver medals. Baston's total was 2,521. Of course the USA ran away with team honors, out-pointing Canada 7,509 to 6,918.

There were only 12 archers in the in-augural women's archery event. Again, the USA swept to victory. In fact, the four archers placed 1, 2, 3, 4 in the matter of points, but were only able to take home a gold and silver.

Lynette Johnson, 22, then of Cypress, Cal., posted the top score in five of the eight rounds over four distances. She took over the lead after the 60-meter shoot on the first of four strenuous days of competition which was twice almost washed out by torrential rainstorms.

At the end of the first F.I.T.A. round Johnson led, followed by Carol Strausburg, USA and Canada's Linda Kazienko. On the second round Judi Adams, youngest mem-ber of USA team, stepped up the pace but still finished eight points behind silver medalist Strausburg whose final total was 2,290 with Johnson winning the gold with her 2,423 points.

Again, the team competition was "no contest," the USA winning by more than 400 points over Canada, 6,995 to 6,579.

TEAM PERSONNEL

J. Adams   R. Baston   R. Bednar

L. Johnson   R. McKinney   N. Myrick

D. Pace   C. Strausburg

C. Fowkes   K. Tate

TEAM PERSONNEL
Judi Adams, 19, Phoenix, Arizona
Rodney W. Baston, USAF, 23, Bossier City,
   Louisiana
Richard L. Bednar, 22, Suffield, Ohio
Lynette Rae Johnson, 22, Cypress, California
Nancy Elaine Myrick, 40, Foley, Alabama
Richard L. McKinney, 25, Muncie, Indiana
Darrell O. Pace, USAF, 22, Cincinnati, Ohio
Carol Strausburg, 34, Huntington Beach,
   California

Manager: Mrs. Katryn Tate, Austin, Texas
Coach: C. R. "Bud" Fowkes, Verona,
   Pennsylvania

OFFICIAL SUMMARIES
Women's Events
Individual - 1. LYNETTE JOHNSON, USA 2,423; 2. CAROL STRAUSBURG, USA 2,290; 3. JUDI ADAMS, USA 2,285*; 4. NANCY MYRICK, USA 2,250*; 5. Joan McDonald, Canada 2,205 (bronze medal); 6. Nancy Love, Canada 2,067.
Team — 1. USA 6,995; 2. Canada 6,579; 3. Brazil 5,991; 4. Puerto Rico 5,985; 5. Mexico 5,785; 6. Colombia 5,774.

Men's Events
Individual — 1. RODNEY BASTON, USAF, USA 2,521; 2. DARRELL PACE, USAF, USA 2,492; 3. RICHARD Mc-KINNEY, USA 2,492*; 4. RICHARD BEDNAR, USA 2,412*; 5. Stan Siatkowski, Canada 2,391 (bronze medal).
Team — 1. USA 7,509; 2. Canada 6,918; 3. Mexico 6,779; 4. Brazil 6,579; 5. Cuba 6,451; 6. Costa Rica 6,417.

(*) Under Pan American Games rules, only two entrants from a country can win medals in individual events.

Rodney Baston, Archery Gold Medalist

Athletics (Track & Field) Men

The USA men's track and field team assaulted the record books in the VIII Pan American Games, and came away with a basketful of records along with its multitude of gold medals. Two of the triumphs were especially sweet for the United States delegation.

In the 800 meters, 24-year old James Robinson of Oakland, California, burst out of a logjam down the stretch and overhauled Cuba's Olympic gold medal winner, Alberto Juantorena, to win in a fast 1:46.30, a new Pan Am record. Then, in the 400 meters, 21-year old Tony Darden of Norristown, Pennsylvania, added insult to injury by whipping the Cuban star in 45.11.

Cuba's Silvio Leonard swept the sprints, winning the 100 meters in a record 10.13 and the 200 meters in 20.37. Another double gold medal winner was Brazil's excellent jumper, Joao Carlos De Oliviera, who won the long jump (26-10) and the triple jump (56-8).

The USA's Renaldo Nehemiah swept past Cuba's Alejandro Casanas easily in winning the 110m hurdles in a clocking of 13.21, a Pan American Games record. Nehemiah had been ill and was confined to his room for almost three days after his arrival in San Juan, but still managed the gold medal.

Bob Coffman of Houston, Texas, continued a string of recent USA successes in the decathlon, winning the event with a Games record 8,078 points.

Only five nations — The USA, Cuba, Canada, Mexico and Brazil, shared in the gold medal harvest, with the United States winning 14 of the 24 events, Cuba winning three, and Mexico also garnering three gold medals.

A total of seven new Pan American Games records were set in the men's portion of the track and field competition at the Parque Sixto Escobar facility near the oceanfront in San Juan.

TEAM PERSONNEL

Duncan Atwood, 23, Seattle, Washington (Javelin)
Willie Banks, 23, Los Angeles, California (Triple Jump)
Andy Bessette, 26, Vernon, Connecticut (Hammer Throw)
James Butts, 29, Los Angeles, California (Triple Jump)
Matt Centrowitz, 24, Brooklyn, New York (5000m)
Robert Coffman, 28, Houston, Texas (Decathlon)
Donald Coleman, 28, Eugene, Oregon (200m)
John Crist, 24, Raleigh, North Carolina (Decathlon - did not compete)
Tony Darden, 21, Norristown, Pennsylvania (400m, 4 x 400m Relay)
Boris Djerassi, 27, Brooklyn, New York (Hammer Throw - did not compete)
Robert Doyle, 30, Central Falls, Rhode Island (Marathon)
Dwayne Evans, 20, Phoenix, Arizona (200m)

TEAM PERSONNEL

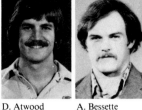

D. Atwood   A. Bessette   J. Butts

T. Fleming   C. Foster   H. Frazier

H. Lindsay   H. Marsh   V. O'Sullivan

F. Shorter   W. Smith   J. Walker

Marco Evoniuk, 21, Longmont, Colorado (50k Walk)
Rod Ewaliko, 25, Seattle, Washington (Javelin)
Allen Feuerbach, 31, Los Gatos, California (Shot Put)
Benn Fields, 24, Salisbury Mills, New York (High Jump)
Thomas Fleming, 28, Bloomfield, New Jersey (Marathon)
Charles Foster, 26, Durham, North Carolina (110m Hurdles)
Herman Frazier, 24, Tempe, Arizona (4 x 400m Relay)
Harvey Glance, 22, Phenix City, Alabama (100m, 4 x 100m Relay)
Bill Green, 18, Palo Alto, California (Did not compete)
Todd Harbour, 20, So. Tadre, Texas (1500m)
Franklin Jacobs, 21, Patterson, New Jersey (High Jump)
Emitt King, 20, Bessemer, Alabama (100m)
David Laut, 22, Oxnard, California (Shot Put)
Carl Lewis, 18, Willingboro, New Jersey (Long Jump)
Herbert Lindsay, 24, Boulder, Colorado (5000m)
Henry Marsh, 25, Eugene Oregon (3000m Steeplechase)

TEAM PERSONNEL

M. Centrowitz   R. Coffman   D. Coleman

H. Glance   B. Green   T. Harbour

M. Peoples   S. Riddick   M. Roberson

M. White   C. Wiley   J. Bush

William McCullough, 26, Santa Monica, California (3000m Steeplechase)
Renaldo Nehemiah, 20, Scotch Plains, New Jersey (110m Hurdles)
Vincent O'Sullivan, 22, Flushing, New York (50k Walk)
Billy Olson, 21, Abilene, Texas (Pole Vault) (Did not compete)
Donald Paige, 22, Marcy, New York (1500m)
Maurice Peoples, 28, Laurel, Maryland (4 x 400m Relay)
Neal Pyke, 30, Belmont, California (20k Walk)
Steve Riddick, 27, Philadelphia, Pennsylvania (4 x 100m Relay)
Michael Roberson, 23, Tallahassee, Florida (4 x 100m Relay)
James Robinson, 24, Oakland, California (800m)
Ricardo Rojas, 27, Boulder, Colorado (10,000m)
Todd Scully, 30, Blackburg, Virginia (20k Walk)
Frank Shorter, 31, Boulder, Colorado (10,000m)
Willie Smith, 23, Auburn, Alabama (400m)
James Walker, 21, Atlanta, Georgia (400m Hurdles, 4 x 400m Relay)
Michael White, 20, Richmond, California (800m)

TEAM PERSONNEL

B. Djerassi   D. Evans   A. Feuerbach

E. King   D. Laut   C. Lewis

J. Robinson   R. Rojas   T. Scully

L. Calhoun   T. Haydon   J. Newton III

M. Rosen   K. Shannon

Clifford Wiley, 24, Houston, Texas
   (4 x 100m Relay)
Mac Wilkins, 28, Soquel, California
   (Discus)
Greg Woepse, 22, Orange, California
   (Pole Vault)

Head Coach: James Bush, Marina Del Rey,
   California
Asst. Coach: Ken Shannon, Snohomish,
   Washington
Asst. Coach: Lee Calhoun, Macomb,
   Illinois
Head Manager: Ted Haydon, Chicago,
   Illinois
Asst. Manager: Mel Rosen, Auburn,
   Alabama
Asst. Manager: Joseph Newton III, Oak
   Brook, Illinois.

Athletics/Summaries

MEN

100 Meters:
1. Silvio Leonard, Cuba, 10.13 sec. (PAR)**;
2. HARVEY GLANCE, USA, 10.19; 3.
EMITT KING, USA, 10.30; 4. Nelson
Rocha dos Santos, Brazil, 10.33; 5. Roi da
Silva, Brazil, 10.41; 6. Osvaldo Lara, Cuba,
10.47.

200 Meters:
1. Silvio Leonard, Cuba, 20.37 sec.; 2. James
Gilkes, Guyana, 20.46; 3. DONALD COLE-
MAN, USA, 20.56; 4. Altevir Araujo,
Brazil, 20.60; 5. Floyd Brown, Jamaica,
20.74; 6. Desai Williams, Canada, 20.98.
DWAYNE EVANS, USA, did not finish.

400 Meters:
1. TONY DARDEN, USA, 45.11 sec.; 2.
Alberto Juantorena, Cuba, 45.24; 3.
WILLIE SMITH, USA, 45.30; 4. Bertland
Cameron, Jamaica, 45.97; 5. Brian Saunders,
Canada, 46.16; 6. Colin Bradford, Jamaica,
46.36.

800 Meters:
1. JAMES ROBINSON, USA, 1:46.30
(PAR); 2. Alberto Juantorena, Cuba,
1:46.40; 3. Agberto Conceicao, Brazil,
1:46.80; 4. Owen Hamilton, Jamaica,
1:47.30; 5. Emilio Ulloa, Chile, 1:49.40;
6. Leandro Civil, Cuba, 1:49.50.
(MICHAEL WHITE, USA, did not qualify.)

1500 Meters:
1. DONALD PAIGE, USA, 3:40.05 (PAR);
2. TODD HARBOUR, USA, 3:41.05; 3.
Agberto Conceicao, Brazil, 3:41.05; 4.
Eduardo Castro, Mexico, 3:42.01; 5. John
Craig, Canada, 3:42.06; 6. Peter Spir,
Canada, 3:46.00.

3000 Meter Steeplechase:
1. HENRY MARSH, USA, 8:43.60; 2.
WILLIAM McCULLOUGH, USA,
8:44.70; 3. Demetrio Cabanillas, Mexico,
8:52.40; 4. Jose Cobo, Cuba, 9:01.60; 5.
Greg Duhaime, Canada, 9:02.00; 6. Modesto
Compres, Dominican Republic, 9:07.90.

5000 Meters:
1. MATT CENTROWITZ, USA, 14:01.00;
2. HERB LINDSAY, USA, 14:04.10; 3.
Enrique Aquino, Mexico, 14:05.90; 4. Peter
Butler, Canada, 14:07.60; 5. Jaime Velez
Rosado, Puerto Rico, 14:17.20; 6. Victor
Mora Garcia, Colombia, 14:17.70.

10,000 Meters:
1. Rodolfo Gomez, Mexico, 29:02.40; 2.
Enrique Aquino, Mexico, 29:03.90; 3.
FRANK SHORTER, USA, 29:06.40; 4.
RICK ROJAS, USA, 29:09.80; 5. Peter
Butler, Canada, 29:20.40; 6. Victor Mora
Garcia, Colombia, 29:27.40.

110 Meter Hurdles:
1. RENALDO NEHEMIAH, USA, 13.20
sec. (PAR); 2. Alejandro Casanas, Cuba,
13.46; 3. CHARLES FOSTER, USA, 13.56;
4. Pat Fogarty, Canada, 14.13; 5. Rafael
Echavarria, Mexico, 14.15; 6. Dionicio Vera,
Cuba, 14.32.

400 Meter Hurdles:
1. JAMES WALKER, USA, 49.66 sec.; 2.
Antonio Diaz, Brazil, 50.85; 3. Frank Mon-
tieth, Cuba, 51.30; 4. Julio Ferrer Andino,
51.48; 5. Ian Newhouse, Canada, 51.52; 6.
Donizete Araujo, Brazil, 51.72. (USA had
only one entry.)

20-Kilometer Walk:
1. Daniel Bautista, Mexico, 1 hr. 28 min.
15.0 sec.**; 2. NEAL PYKE, USA,
1:30:17.0; 3. TODD SCULLY, USA,
1:32:30.0; 4. Santiago Fonseca, Honduras,
1:35:20.0; 5. Marcel Jobin, Canada,
1:38:42.0; 6. Domingo Colin, Mexico,
1:40:02.0.

50-Kilometer Walk:
1. Raul Gonzalez, Mexico, 4 hr. 5 min.
17.0 sec.; 2. Martin Bermudez, Mexico,
4:11:13.0; 3. MARCO EVONIUK, USA,
4:24:23.0; 4. Ernesto Alfaro Bermudez,
Colombia, 4:39:36.0; 5. VINCENT O'SUL-
LIVAN, USA, 4:44:20.0; 6. Nicolas Soto
Colo, Puerto Rico 4:51:40.0.

Marathon:
1. Radames Gonzalez, Cuba, 2 hr. 24 min.
9.0 sec.; 2. Luis Barbosa, Colombia,
2:24:44.0; 3. Richard Hughson, Canada,
2:25:34.0; 4. Hector Rodriguez Camacho,
Colombia, 2:25:51.0; 5. Emundo Warnke
Bravo, Chile, 2:26:14.0; 6. THOMAS
FLEMING, USA, 2:28:06.0. (ROBERT
DOYLE, USA, finished 20th.)

4 x 100 Meters Relay:
1. USA (MIKE ROBERSON, HARVEY
GLANCE, CLIFF WILEY, STEVE
RIDDICK) 38.85 sec.; 2. Cuba, 39.14;
3. Brazil, 39.44; 4. Jamaica, 39.83; 5.
Canada, 39.92; 6. Puerto Rico 40.28.

4 x 400 Meters Relay:
1. USA (JAMES WALKER, HERMAN
FRAZIER, MAURICE PEOPLES, TONY
DARDEN) 3:03.80; 2. Jamaica, 3:04.70;
3. Cuba, 3:06.30; 4. Canada, 3:09.20;
5. Brazil, 3:10.90; 6. Trinidad & Tobago,
3:11.60.

Long Jump:
1. Joao de Oliveira, Brazil, 8.18m (26-10)**
2. David Girat, Cuba, 8.15m (26-9); 3.
CARL LEWIS, USA, 8.13m (26-8); 4.
Altevir Araujo, Brazil, 7.73m (25-4¼); 5.
Ray Quinones, Puerto Rico, 7.52m (24-8);
6. Richard Rock, Canada, 7.31m (23-11
3/4). (USA had only one entry, LARRY
MYRICKS was injured and did not
compete.)

Shot Put:

1. DAVID LAUT, USA, 20.22m (66-4) (PAR); 2. Bishop Dolegiewicz, Canada, 19.67m (64-6½); 3. Bruno Pauletio, Canada, 19.61m (64-4); 4. AL FEUERBACH, USA, 18.85m (61-10¼); 5. Luis Delis, Cuba, 18.21m (59-9); 6. Nicolas Hernandez (Nicaragua) 16.37m (53-8½).

Discus Throw:

1. MAC WILKINS, USA, 63.30m (207-8) (PAR); 2. Bradley Cooper, Bahamas, 62.16m (203-11¼); 3. Luis Delis, Cuba, 61.60m (202-2); 4. Juan Martinez, Cuba, 60.80m (199-5½); 5. Borys Chambul, Canada, 59.42m (194-11½); 6. Rob Gray, Canada, 54.30m (178-1½). (USA had only one entrant.)

Javelin Throw:

1. DUNCAN ATWOOD, USA, 84.16m (276-1½) (PAR); 2. Antonio Gonzalez, Cuba, 84.12m (275-11½); 3. Raul Pupo, Cuba, 81.96m (268-10½); 4. Phil Olson, Canada, 76.28m (250-3); 5. Amado Morales, Puerto Rico, 76.00m (249-4); 6. ROD EWALIKO, USA, 75.78m (248-7½).

High Jump:

1. FRANKLIN JACOBS, USA, 2.26m (7-5) (PAR); 2. BENN FIELDS, USA, 2.19m (7-2¼); 3. Milt Ottey, Canada, 2.19m (7-2¼); 4. Juan Cennielles, Cuba, 2.17m (7-1½); 5. Dean Bauck, Canada, 2.15m (7-0 3/4); 6. Carlos Acosta, Peurto Rico, 2.15m (7-0 3/4).

Triple Jump:

1. Joao de Oliveira, Brazil, 17.27m (56-8)**; 2. WILLIE BANKS, USA, 16.88m (55-4½); 3. JAMES BUTTS, USA, 16.69m (54-9); 4. Alejandro Herrera, Cuba, 16.46m (54.0); 5. Carmelo Martinez, Cuba, 16.28m (53-5); 6. Francisco de Oliveira, Brazil, 15.93m (52-3¼).

Pole Vault:

1. Bruce Simpson, Canada, 5.15m (16-10 ¾); 2. GREG WOEPSE, USA, 5.05m (16-6 ¾); 3. Brian Morrisette, Virgin Islands, 4.85m (15-11); (No further placings; Billy Olson of USA did not compete because of injury).

Hammer Throw:

1. Scott Neilson, Canada, 69.64m (228-6) (PAR); 2. Cuillermo Orozco, Cuba, 68.48m (224-8); 3. Genovevo Morejon, Cuba, 67.66m (222-0); 4. ANDY BESSETTE, USA, 66.22m (217-3); 5. Jose Vallejos, Argentina, 59.50m (195-2½); 6. Daniel Gomez, Argentina, 58.58m (192.2). (BORIS DJERASSI, USA, did not compete.)

Decathlon:

1. BOB COFFMAN, USA, 8,078 pts. (PAR); 2. Tito Steiner, Argentina, 7,638; 3. Zenon Smiechowski, Canada, 7,210; 4. Roberto Steinmetz, Argentina, 7,021; 5. Roberto McFarlane, Costa Rica, 5,669; 6. Rigoberto Salazar, Cuba, 5,717. (USA had only one entry.)

(PAR) = Pan American Record
**Repeated as champion

Athletics (Track & Field) Women's

The USA women mirrored the success of their male counterparts at the Pan American Games, even bettering the men by winning 11 of the 15 possible gold medals at the Games and setting eight of the new Pan Am marks that were established.

Sprinter Evelyn Ashford of Los Angeles, now firmly established as the USA's best bet in the short races, was a double gold medal winner, taking the 100 meters in :11.07 (she set a Pan Am record of 11.02 in the heats) and the 200 meters in a record time of 22.24 seconds.

As a matter of fact, USA women won everything from 100 meters through the 3,000 meters, and tacked on gold medals in both relay races. All were record performances, too, except the 400 meters win by Essie Kelley, Prairie View A & M.

The powerful Cuban women's trio of Maria Sarria (shotput), Carmen Romero (discus), and Maria Colon (javelin) swept through those field events to break the USA stranglehold on the gold medals. The only other gold medal won by a nation other than the USA and Cuba came in the pentathlon, where Diane Jones Konihowski of Canada racked up 4,686 points to cop the top honors.

Cuba's Romero established herself in an "elite" category by winning her third consecutive Pan American Games gold medal in the discus. She also won in 1971 at Cali and in 1975 at Mexico City.

The USA's Julie Brown also had a rewarding Pan American Games, taking silver medals in the 800 meters, 1500 meters and 3,000 meters, pushing the winning entries to meet records in each case.

TEAM PERSONNEL

Jodi Anderson, 21, Van Nuys, California (Pentathlon)
Evelyn Ashford, 22, Los Angeles, California (100m, 200m)
Valerie Brisco, 19, Los Angeles, California (200m, 4 x 100m Relay)
Julie Brown, 24, San Diego, California (800m, 1500m, 3000m)
Rosalyn Bryant, 23, Los Angeles, California (4 x 400m Relay)
Lynn Cannon, 28, Chico, California (Javelin)
Chandra Cheeseborough, 20, Jacksonville, Florida (4 x 100m Relay)
Sharon Dabney, 21, Philadelphia, Pennsylvania (400m, 4 x 400m Relay)
Mary Decker, 20, Eugene, Oregon (1500m)
Jane Frederick, 27, Orinda, California (Long Jump, Pentathlon)
Lorna Griffin, 23, Seattle, Washington (Discus)
Karen Hawkins, 20, Houston, Texas (4 x 100m Relay)
Patricia Jackson, 21, Prairie View, Texas (400m, 4 x 400m Relay)

TEAM PERSONNEL

E. Ashford   J. Brown   R. Bryant

J. Frederick   L. Griffin   K. Hawkins

K. McMillan   J. Merrill   B. Morehead

C. Sulinski   A. Turbyne   L. Winbigler

B. Lyle   P. Scanlan

Essie Kelley, 22, Prairie View, Texas (800m, 4 x 400m Relay)
Deby LaPlante, 26, LaMesa, California (100m Hurdles)
Kathy McMillan, 21, Raeford, North Carolina (Long Jump)
Janice Merrill, 23, New London, Connecticut (3000m)
Brenda Morehead, 21, Toledo, Ohio (100m, 4 x 100m Relay)
Louise Ritter, 21, Denton, Texas (High Jump)
Maren Seidler, 28, Los Gatos, California (Shot Put)
Pamela Spencer, 21, Northridge, California (High Jump)

TEAM PERSONNEL

L. Cannon

C. Cheeseborough

S. Dabney

P. Jackson

E. Kelley

D. LaPlante

L. Ritter

M. Seidler

P. Spencer

E. Goodnight

B. Jacket

L. Knudson

Cathy Sulinski, 21, South San Francisco, California (Javelin)

Ann Turbyne, 22, Winslow, Maine (Shot Put)

Lynne Winbigler, 26, Eugene, Oregon (Discus)

Candy Young, 17, Beaver Falls, Pennsylvania (100m Hurdles)

Head Coach: Lyle Knudson, Logan, Utah
Asst. Coach: Bert Lyle, Denton, Texas
Asst. Coach: Barbara Jacket, Prairie View, Texas
Head Manager: Eileen Goodnight, Fairview Park, Ohio
Asst. Manager: Philip Scanlan, Long Beach, California

Athletics / Summaries

WOMEN

100 Meters:
1. EVELYN ASHFORD, USA, 11.07 sec. (Note: Ashford set PAR of 11.02 in semi-finals); 2. BRENDA MOREHEAD, USA, 11.11; 3. Angela Taylor, Canada, 11.36; 4. Silvia Chivas, Cuba, 11.48; 5. Leleith Hodges, Jamaica, 11.49; 6. Rose Allwood, Jamaica, 11.69.

200 Meters:
1. EVELYN ASHFORD, USA, 22.24 sec. (PAR); 2. Angela Taylor, Canada, 22.74; 3. Merlene Ottey, Jamaica, 22.79; 4. VALERIE BRISCO, USA, 22.84; 5. Jacqueline Pusey, Jamaica, 23.08; 6. Candy Ford, Bermuda, 23.70.

100 Meter Hurdles:
1. DEBY LaPLANTE, USA, 12.90 sec. (PAR); 2. Sharon Lane, Canada, 13.56; 3. Grisel Machado, Cuba, 13.60; 4. CANDY YOUNG, USA, 13.67; 5. Cecilia Branch, Canada, 14.03; 6. Beatriz Capoiosto, Argentina, 14.18.

400 Meters:
1. SHARON DABNEY, USA, 51.81; 2. June Griffith, Guyana, 51.81; 3. PATRICIA JACKSON, USA, 52.32; 4. Aurelia Penton, Cuba, 52.71; 5. Micheline Racette, Canada, 53.30; 6. Helen Blake, Jamaica, 53.41.

800 METERS:
1. ESSIE KELLEY, USA, 2:01.20 (PAR); 2. JULIE BROWN, USA, 2:01.20; 3. Aurelia Penton, Cuba, 2:02.10; 4. Anne Morelli, Canada, 2:03.00; 5. Nery McQueen, Cuba, 2:05.40; 6. Alejandra Ramos, Chile, 2:06.20.

1500 Meters:
1. MARY DECKER, USA, 4:05.70 (PAR); 2. JULIE BROWN, USA, 4:06.40; 3. Penny Werthner Bales, Canada, 4:14.80; 4. Francine Gendron, Canada, 4:15.00; 5. Alejandra Ramos, Chile, 4:24.80; 6. Ileana Hockings, Puerto Rico, 4:27.30.

3000 Meters:
1. JANICE MERRILL, USA, 8:53.06 (PAR 1st time run); 2. JULIE BROWN, USA, 8:59.90; 3. Geri Fitch, Canada, 9:35.07; 4. Carmen Garduno, Mexico, 9:49.50; 5. Carmen Montanez, Puerto Rico, 10:14.08; 6. Angelita Lind Soliveras, Puerto Rico, 10:30.08.

4 x 100 Meters Relay:
1. USA (VALERIE BRISCO, KAREN HAWKINS, CHANDRA CHEESE-BOROUGH, BRENDA MOREHEAD) 43.30 sec.; 2. Jamaica, 44.18; 3. Cuba, 46.26; 4. Brazil, 46.98; 5. Dominican Republic, 47.25. (Puerto Rico disqualified.)

4 x 400 Meters Relay:
1. USA (SHARON DABNEY, PATRICIA JACKSON, ROSALYN BRYANT, ESSIE KELLEY) 3:29.40 (PAR); 2. Cuba, 3:36.30; 3. Canada, 3:37.60; 4. Brazil, 3:45.70; 5. Puerto Rico, 3:49.40. (No sixth)

Long Jump:
1. KATHY McMILLAN, USA, 6.46m (21-2¼); 2. Ana Alexander, Cuba, 6.31m (20-8¼); 3. Eldina Echevarria, Cuba, 6.27m (20-7); 4. Diane Jones Konihowski, Canada, 6.10m (20-0¼); 5. JANE FREDERICK, USA, 6.10m (20-0¼); 6. Shonel Ferguson, Bahamas, 6.07m (19-11).

Shot Put:
1. Maria Sarria, Cuba, 18.81m (61-8½) (PAR)**; 2. MAREN SEIDLER, USA, 18.57m (60-11¼); 3. Carmen Ionesco, Canada, 16.50m (54-1½); 4. ANN TUR-BYNE, USA, 16.45m (53-11½); 5. Hilda Ramirez, Cuba, 15.96m (52-4); 6. Lucette Moreau, Canada, 14.90m (48-11).

Discus Throw:
1. Carmen Romero, Cuba, 60.58m (198-9) (PAR)**; 2. Maria Betancourt, Cuba, 60.44m (198-3½); 3. Carmen Ionesco, Canada, 57.14m (187-5½); 4. LORNA GRIFFIN, USA, 54.08m (177-5); 5. Lucette Moreau, Canada, 52.52m (172-3½); 6. LYNN WINBIGLER, USA, 51.66m (169-6).

Javelin Throw:
1. Maria Colon, Cuba, 62.30m (204-5) (PAR); 2. LYNN CANNON, USA, 56.48m (185-3½); 3. CATHY SULINSKI, USA, 56.44m (185-2); 4. Laurie Kern, Canada, 55.70m (182-9); 5. Marli Dos Santos, Brazil, 52.66m (172-9); 6. Ana Nunez, Cuba, 48.84m (160-3).

High Jump:
1. LOUISE RITTER, USA, 1.93m (6-4) (PAR); 2. PAM SPENCER, USA, 1.87m (6-1 ¾); 3. Debbie Brill, Canada, 1.85m (6-0 ¾); 4. Julie White, Canada, 1.85m (6-0 ¾); 5. Maria Domingues, Brazil, 1.83m (6.0); 6. Angela Carbonell, Cuba, 1.81m (5.11¼).

Pentathlon:
Diane Jones Konihowski, Canada, 4,605 pts.; 2. JODI ANDERSON, USA, 4,434; 3. Jill Ross, Canada, 4,108; 4. Olga Maria Verissimo, Brazil, 3,865; 5. Nancyesper Vallecilla, Ecuador, 3,818; 6. Ivonne Nedderman, Argentina, 3,815. (JANE FREDERICK, USA, was 10th.)

**Retained Championship

Baseball

It was a case of not enough hitting for the United States at the Pan American Games, and the team finished 5-3, good for fourth place. Coach Jerry Kindall of the University of Arizona put together a fine pitching staff, headed by righthander Tim Leary of UCLA, but the Yankee bats never responded in the key games.

The USA opened with three straight wins over mediocre opposition. Kindall's club thrashed the Bahamas, 12-2, as lefty Brian Snyder of Clemson threw a two-hitter and fanned nine opposing batters.

Mexico was drubbed, 18-0, as Leary, the first-round draft choice of the New York Mets a month earlier, threw a three-hitter. Terry Francona (Arizona), the son of former major leaguer Tito Francona, had four hits and drove in three runs to pace a 14-hit USA attack.

Canada was next to fall to the U.S., this time by 10-0 as lefty Craig Lefferts of the University of Arizona went the distance and allowed just four hits. Centerfielder Greg Baker of Indiana State hit his second homer of the Games, a seventh inning grandslam, to pace the triumph.

But in the next game, a crucial tilt with the Dominican Republic, the luck ran out. Leary and D.R. ace Johnny Tavarez battled tooth and nail for nine innings in a scoreless duel. But in the bottom of the ninth, Leary walked one batter before Enrique Cruz homered to end the game and hand the USA its first loss.

The U.S. handled Venezuela, 7-2, but then lost consecutive games to gold medal-winning Cuba, 7-1, and to Puerto Rico, 4-2, to take itself out of gold medal contention fast.

Second baseman Mike Gallego, a UCLA frosh, batted .423 to finish fifth in overall hitting in the Games, while Francona hit .419, good for sixth among all batters. First baseman Mark Strucher of Georgia Southern drove in nine runs to rank fourth. Lefty Peter Sinopoli of Maryland recorded a perfect 0.00 ERA over 11⅓ innings of relief pitching to lead the Games in that category.

TEAM PERSONNEL
Gregory Baker, 21, Kokomo, Indiana (Outfield)
Jose Fernandez, 21, Miami, Florida (Outfield)
Terry Francona, 20, New Brighton, Pennsylvania (Outfield)
Michael Gallego, 18, Pico Rivera, California (Second Base)
Francis Galloway, 21, Sumter, South Carolina (Pitcher)
Scott Gardner, 21, Lubbock, Texas (Pitcher)
Daniel Hanggie, 20, Brea, California (Third Base)
Douglas Latrenta, 21, Smithtown, New York (Outfield)
Timothy Leary, 20, Santa Monica, California (Pitcher)
Craig Lefferts, 21, Tucson, Arizona (Pitcher)
Michael Madden, 21, Colorado Springs, Colorado (Pitcher)

TEAM PERSONNEL

G. Baker   J. Fernandez   T. Francona

D. Hanggie   D. Latrenta   T. Leary

D. Pagel   R. Reynolds   J. Semerad

R. Witt   P. Zuvella

Michael Mullikin, 20, Easton, Maryland (Shortstop)
David Pagel, 20, Blissfield, Michigan (Shortstop)
Ron Reynolds, 20, Wichita, Kansas (Catcher)
John Semerad, 22, Staten Island, New York (Catcher)
Peter Sinopoli, 22, Silver Spring, Maryland (Pitcher)
Brian Snyder, 21, Centerville, Virginia (Pitcher)
Mark Strucher, 21, Merritt Island, Florida (First Base)
Richard Witt, 21, Spokane, Washington (Catcher)
Paul Zuvella, 20, Milpitas, California (Shortstop)

TEAM PERSONNEL

M. Gallego   F. Galloway   S. Gardner

C. Lefferts   M. Madden   M. Mullikin

P. Sinopoli   B. Snyder   M. Strucher

R. Groch   G. Kindall   J. Stallings

Head Coach: Jerry Kindall, Tucson, Arizona
Asst. Coach: Richard Groch, Marysville, Michigan
Manager: Jack Stallings, Register, Georgia

BASEBALL SUMMARIES

FINAL STANDINGS
Country	W	L	Pct.
Cuba	8	0	1.000
Dominican Republic	7	1	.875
Puerto Rico	6	2	.750
United States	5	3	.625
Bahamas	3	5	.375
Venezuela	3	5	.375
Colombia	2	6	.250
Canada	1	7	.125
Mexico	1	7	.125

Scores of All Games
	Cuba	Dom. R.	P.R.	USA	Bah.	Ven.	Colo.	Can.	Mex.
Cuba	—	9-0	11-3	7-1	12-0	8-7	12-1	9-8	9-6
Dominican Republic	0-9	—	5-3	2-0	4-0	5-3	4-2	6-0	8-0
Puerto Rico	3-11	3-5	—	4-2	10-2	9-5	3-0	7-3	8-6
United States	1-7	0-2	2-4	—	12-2	7-2	5-4	10-0	18-0
Bahamas	0-12	0-4	2-10	2-12	—	6-5	12-1	4-1	3-4
Venezuela	7-8	3-5	5-9	2-7	5-6	—	4-0	7-2	7-2
Colombia	1-12	2-4	0-3	4-5	1-12	0-4	—	11-6	9-3
Canada	8-9	0-6	3-7	0-10	1-4	2-7	6-11	—	7-2
Mexico	6-9	0-8	6-8	0-18	4-3	2-7	3-9	2-7	—

Basketball — Men

Perhaps the most satisfying gold medal of all went to the USA men's basketball team at the Pan American Games. This solid group of players, none of them exceptionally flashy, overcame adversity of all kinds and a hostile home crowd in a packed arena in the title game to win all the marbles.

The 113-94 whipping of previously unbeaten Puerto Rico, before over 12,000 fans packed into Roberto Clemente Coliseum and whipped into a frenzy over their team's early heady success, was a team effort that mirrored the coaching of Indiana's Bobby Knight perfectly.

Up by 54-39 at the half and seemingly headed for a rout of Puerto Rico in the gold medal game, the USA let its margin slip to just three points, 73-70, with less than eight minutes left.

Knight called time out and inserted quick Isiah Thomas, a high schooler from Chicago, into the lineup. Thomas made three steals and a block in two minutes as the U.S. roared away to a 12-point lead and took total command of the game, never to be challenged again.

LaSalle strongman Michael Brooks, a bullish 6-7 forward, led the USA in scoring with 27 points (and added 13 rebounds), while Indiana's Mike Woodson chipped in with 23 points, and Thomas added 21 for the winners.

The U.S. had landed in the title game opposite Puerto Rico by virtue of triumphs over Canada (97-76), Argentina (99-73), Cuba (101-83), and Brazil (106-88) in the championship round. The team was undefeated in the preliminary round, but had squeakers with Brazil (82-78) and Panama (88-83) in the process.

It was the seventh gold medal in eight sets of Pan American Games for the United States men, who have not been victorious only once, in 1971 at Cali, when Cuba and Brazil ousted them in a preliminary round.

Five players averaged in double figures for the U.S. — Woodson (18.3), Brooks (17.4), Kyle Macy of Kentucky (12.1 before being sidelined with a broken jaw after seven games), Mike O'Koren of North Carolina (11.6) and Ronnie Lester of Iowa (10.7).

Macy was struck with an unprovoked blow from Cuba's Tomas Hererra during a 101-83 final round USA win and had to be flown back to the University of Kentucky Medical Center for immediate surgery on a broken left mandible. After the Games, Coach Knight went to Lexington to award Macy his gold medal personally in a hospital mini-ceremony.

TEAM PERSONNEL

M. Brooks   S. Clancy   J. Duren

M. O'Koren   R. Sampson   I. Thomas

R. Knight   M. Krzyzewski   F. Taylor

TEAM PERSONNEL

Michael Brooks, 20, Philadelphia, Pennsylvania
Samuel Clancy, 21, Pittsburgh, Pennsylvania
John Duren, 20, Washington, D.C.
Ronnie Lester, 20, Chicago, Illinois
Kyle Macy, 22, Peru, Indiana
Kevin McHale, 21, Hibbing, Minnesota
Michael O'Koren, 21, Jersey City, New Jersey
Ralph Sampson, 19, Harrisonburg, Virginia
Isiah Thomas, 18, Chicago, Illinois
Ray Tolbert, 20, Anderson, Indiana
Danny Vranes, 20, Salt Lake City, Utah
Michael Woodson, 21, Indianapolis, Indiana

Head Coach: Robert Knight, Bloomington, Indiana
Asst. Coach: Michael Krzyzewski, West Point, New York
Manager: Frederick Taylor, Columbus, Ohio

TEAM PERSONNEL

R. Lester   K. Macy   K. McHale

R. Tolbert   D. Vranes   M. Woodson

GOLD MEDAL GAME BOX SCORE
UNITED STATES (113)

	FG	FT-FTA	PTS.
Tolbert	1	0-0	2
O'Koren	4	2-4	10
Clancy	0	0-0	0
Sampson	0	0-0	0
Vranes	1	1-1	3
McHale	6	0-1	12
Thomas	9	3-4	21
Brooks	8	11-16	27
Lester	5	5-8	15
Woodson	10	3-3	23
TOTALS	44	25-37	113

PUERTO RICO (94)

	FG	FT-FTA	PTS.
Torres	8	3-7	19
Vicens	0	0-0	0
Cruz	2	3-5	7
Bermudez	2	0-0	4
Rodriguez	10	0-0	20
Quinones	2	2-2	6
Fantauzzi	2	0-0	4
Santiago	1	0-0	2
Morales	0	0-0	0
Cora	6	1-1	13
Dalmau	8	3-5	19
Valderas	0	0-0	0
TOTALS	41	12-20	94

Scoring by Halves:

USA	54	59---	113
Puerto Rico	39	55---	94

Attendance - 12,000 (Est.)

MEN'S BASKETBALL SUMMARIES

QUALIFYING ROUND GROUP A	W	L	QUALIFYING ROUND GROUP B	W	L	FINAL ROUND (Championship Round)	W	L
USA	4	0	Puerto Rico	4	0	USA	5	0
Cuba	2	2	Argentina	3	1	Puerto Rico	4	1
Brazil	2	2	Canada	2	2	Brazil	2	3
Panama	1	3	Mexico	1	3	Canada	2	3
Virgin Islands	1	3	Dominican Republic	0	4	Cuba	2	3
						Argentina	0	5

FINAL ROUND SCORES	USA	Puerto Rico	Brazil	Canada	Cuba	Argentina
USA	—	113-94	106-88	97-76	101-83	99-73
Puerto Rico	94-113	—	109-107	89-75	90-76	109-75
Brazil	88-106	107-109	—	77-79	85-77	106-101
Canada	76-97	75-89	79-77	—	56-67	93-78
Cuba	83-101	76-90	77-85	67-56	—	91-81
Argentina	73-99	75-109	101-106	78-93	81-91	—

Basketball — Women

A USA women's basketball team that had breezed by five earlier foes by an average of 37 points a game fell victim to a rash of mistakes and turnovers in the gold medal game and lost a heartbreaking 91-86 decision to Cuba in a major upset. This was the same USA team that had captured the FIBA World Championship earlier in the year at Seoul, Korea, though without competition from the Socialist nations, which boycotted the championships.

Horrible free throw shooting in the gold medal game killed whatever chances the USA had to defeat the charged-up Cubans. Coach Pat Head's charges managed to connect on only 10 of 22 chances at the free throw line, though outshooting the Cubans from the field, 38-35. Center Rosie Walker hit on only 5 of 16 free throws, but still kept the U.S. in the game with her game-high 27 points, many of them down the stretch.

The USA led by one, 46-45, at halftime, but had committed 16 turnovers to destroy leads that ranged from 7-12 points at various stages. The second half was a little better, but not good enough.

Behind the shooting of Ann Meyers and Walker, the USA built up an eight-point lead midway in the second half. But Cuba, behind the deadly shooting of Denise Despaigne, narrowed the lead to three with a little under four minutes to go. A pair of three-point plays put the Cubans ahead to stay seconds later.

A brief inability to cope with a suddenly-alive Cuban fast break, plus lapses on defense and failure to come up with key rebounds, spelled defeat for the USA gals.

The U.S. had roared past Puerto Rico, 124-69, in the opening game, then routed four more foes, including a 99-89 win over Canada that was a rematch of the World Championship finale at Seoul, enroute to the title game against likewise unbeaten Cuba.

It was a sad ending to an otherwise bountiful year for the U.S. women, and Cuba stamped itself as a team to watch in future international competition in women's cage circles.

TEAM PERSONNEL

Carol Blazejowski, 22, Fairview, New Jersey
Barbara Brown, 20, Dallas, Texas
Denise Curry, 19, Davis, California
Tara Heiss, 22, Bethesda, Maryland
Kris Kirchner, 19, New Providence, New
   Jersey
Nancy Lieberman, 21, Far Rockaway,
   New York
Ann Meyers, 24, La Habra, California
Jill Rankin, 21, Phillips, Texas
Jackie Swaim, 21, Jacksonville, Texas
Jan Trombly, 22, Chazy, New York
Rosie Walker, 22, Emerson, Arkansas
Holly Warlick, 21, Knoxville, Tennessee

Head Coach: Patricia Head, Knoxville,
   Tennessee
Asst. Coach: Betty Jo Crumm, Weather-
   ford, Texas
Manager: Lea Plarski, Alton, Illinois

TEAM PERSONNEL

C. Blazejowski   B. Brown   D. Curry

T. Heiss   K. Kirchner   N. Lieberman

A. Meyers   J. Rankin   J. Swaim

J. Trombly   F. Warlick

B. J. Crumm   P. Head   L. Plarski

WOMEN'S BASKETBALL SUMMARIES
FINAL ROUND-ROBIN STANDINGS:

	W	L	PCT.
Cuba	6	0	1.000
United States	5	1	.833
Canada	4	2	.667
Brazil	3	3	.500
Mexico	2	4	.333
Puerto Rico	1	5	.167
Bolivia	0	6	.000

GOLD MEDAL GAME BOX SCORE
UNITED STATES (86)

	FG	FT-FTA	PTS.
Walker	11	5-16	27
Blazejowski	0	0-0	0
Curry	2	0-0	4
Heiss	2	0-0	4
Lieberman	6	1-1	13
Warlick	1	0-0	2
Trombly	2	0-0	4
Swaim	0	1-3	1
Rankin	7	0-0	14
Brown	0	2-2	2
Kirchner	1	0-0	2
Meyers	6	1-1	13
TOTALS	38	10-22	86

CUBA (91)

	FG	FT-FTA	PTS.
Delepaz	1	0-0	2
Aties	5	6-6	16
Reinoso	2	0-0	4
Despaigne	9	5-7	23
Corvea	1	0-2	2
Salmon	3	2-6	8
Borrell	3	0-0	6
Charro	2	0-0	4
Skeet	6	8-11	20
Bequer	3	0-1	6
TOTALS	35	21-33	91

USA	46	40---	86
Cuba	45	46---	91

Total Fouls - USA 27, Cuba 21
Fouled Out - None
Attendance - 9,600

Scores of All Games:

	Cuba	USA	Canada	Mexico	Bolivia	Puerto Rico	Brazil
Cuba	—	91-86	90-81	87-62	112-65	91-53	74- 70
United States	86-91	—	99-89	92-58	85-35	124-69	111-73
Canada	81-90	89-99	—	77-66	94-47	93-61	102-83
Mexico	62-87	58-92	66-77	—	84-68	78-76	91-112
Bolivia	65-112	35-85	47-94	68-84	—	60-93	71-108
Puerto Rico	53-91	69-124	61-93	76-78	93-60	—	81-85
Brazil	70-74	73-111	83-102	112-91	108-71	85-81	—

Boxing

Boxing in the amateur ranks has enjoyed a resurgence since the USA won five Olympic championships in Montreal. The 114 boxers entered in the Pan American Games tournament were assessed the strongest field ever to participate in the Western Hemisphere Championships.

Although there is no team title, the "point system" devised by the International Amateur Boxing Association gave top honors to the USA by one point over Cuba with Puerto Rico a close third. The Col. Don Hull, Trophy, in honor of the U.S. Army (ret.) past president of the Americas boxing confederation, was awarded to Lemuel Steeples, USA, winner of the light welterweight title.

In the matter of gold medals the Cubans won five and the USA four. The other two were gained by the host boxing team from Puerto Rico.

Bernard Taylor, a silver medalist in Mexico, moved up to the featherweight class and copped top honors by scoring a solid victory over Venezuela's Naudi Pinero in the final round to boost his overall ring log to 402-8.

The "luck" of the blind draw pitted six USA boxers against Cubans in the first round. The most notable success in the first round matches was Tony Tucker's resounding triumph over the veteran Cuban Sixto Soria, '76 Olympic Games runner-up. Although Tucker suffered a gash over his eye in this battle, he boxed masterfully yet cautiously to win the light heavyweight title.

One of the most impressive boxers in the tournament was 17-year-old Jackie Beard, bantamweight. Beard showed ring guile well beyond his years as he outboxed Hector Lazaro, Cuba, in the semi-final and won handily over Puerto Rico's Luis Pizzaro in the final before a full house of 10,000 in the Roberto Clemente Coliseum.

Lemuel Steeples won four straight unanimous decisions on his way to the light welterweight crown. In the semi-final he had too many punches and too much class in outpointing Cuba's Jose Aguilar and later thoroughly trounced Argentina's Hugo Hernandez for the gold medal.

One of the best prospects uncovered in the Pan American Games was light heavyweight Tony Tucker, 21, National AAU Champion. After whipping the Cuban veteran Sixto Soria, he decisively whipped Pat Fennel, Canada, when the referee stopped the contest in the semi-final and had an easy time with Puerto Rico's Dennis Jackson in the championship bout.

Cuba came up with three outstanding champions, headed by Teofilo Stevenson who added his second Pan American title to his two Olympic and one world amateur heavyweight title. In the semi-final Stevenson floored Bubba Hadley (USA) and the referee stepped in to stop the contest. The Cuban was equally awesome in taking out Puerto Rico's Narciso Maldonado, also in the first round. Two victories in 3 minutes and 44 seconds elapsed time.

Apparently the referee was the only person in the Roberto Coliseum who failed to see Jose Molina, Puerto Rico, butt Jim Shuler,

TEAM PERSONNEL

D. Armstrong   J. Beard   J. Coffee

E. Green   R. Hadley   R. Sandoval

J. Shuler   L. Steeples   B. Taylor

T. Tucker   J. B. Williamson

J. McCarron   P. Nappi   R. Pettigrew

USA in the championship contest in the middleweight division. The butt opened up an old cut over Shuler's eye and the attending physician caused the fight to be stopped.

TEAM PERSONNEL
Davey Lee Armstrong, 23, Santa Monica, California (Lightweight)
*Jackie Beard, 17, Jackson, Tennessee (Bantamweight)
Jerome Coffee, 21, Nashville, Tennessee (Flyweight)
Edward Green, U.S. Army, 25, Fort Bragg, North Carolina (Welterweight)
Rufus "Bubba" Hadley, U.S. Marine Corps, 18, Camp LeJeune (Heavyweight)
Richard Sandoval, 18, Pomona, California (Light Flyweight)
James Shuler, 20, Philadelphia, Pennsylvania (Light Middleweight)
*Lemuel Steeples, 23, St. Louis, Missouri (Light Welterweight)

*Bernard Taylor, 22, Charlotte, North Carolina (Featherweight)
*Tony Tucker, 21, Grand Rapids, Michigan (Light Heavyweight)
J. B. Williamson, 22, Indianapolis, Indiana (Middleweight)

Head Manager: James McCarron, Lexington, Massachusetts
Head Coach: Pat Nappi, Syracuse, New York
Asst. Coach: Richard Pettigrew, Norfolk, Virginia

(*) Pan American Games champions

OFFICIAL SUMMARIES
Light Flyweight:
1. Hector Ramirez, Cuba; 2. RICHARD SANDOVAL, USA; 3. Gilberto Sosa, Mexico and Edurado Burgos, Chile.

Flyweight:
1. Alberto Mercado, Puerto Rico; 2. Pedro Nolasco, Dominican Republic; 3. JEROME COFFEE, USA and Ian Clyde, Canada.

Bantamweight:
1. JACKIE BEARD, USA; 2. Luis Pizarro, Puerto Rico; 3. Santiago Caballero, Venezuela and Hector Lazaro, Cuba.

Featherweight:
1. BERNARD TAYLOR, USA; 2. Naudi Pinero, Venezuela; 3. Felipe Orosco, Colombia and Ramon Sosa, Argentina.

Lightweight:
1. Adolofo Horta, Cuba; 2. Roberto Andino, Puerto Rico; 3. Guillermo Fernandez, Venezuela and Rafael Rodriguez, Dominican Republic. (DAVEY ARMSTRONG, USA eliminated in second round by Adolofo Horta, Cuba.)

Light Welterweight:
1. LEMUEL STEEPLES, USA; 2. Hugo Hernandez, Argentina; 3. Pedro Cruz, Puerto Rico and Jose Aguilar, Cuba.

Welterweight:
1. Andres Aldama, Cuba; 2. Mike McCallum, Jamaica; 3. Javier Colin, Mexico and Jose Baret, Dominican Republic. (EDWARD GREEN, USA eliminated by Mike McCallum, Jamaica, quarter-final round.)

Light Middleweight:
1. Jose Molina, Puerto Rico; 2. JAMES SHULER, USA; 3. Jorge Amparo, Dominican Republic and Francisco Jesus, Brazil.

Middleweight:
1. Jose Gomez, Cuba; 2. Carlos Fonseca, Brazil; 3. Alfred Thomas, Guyana and Oscar Florentin, Argentina. (J. B. WILLIAMSON, USA, eliminated in first round by Jose Gomez, Cuba.)

Light Heavyweight:
1. TONY TUCKER, USA; 2. Dennis Jackson, Puerto Rico; 3. Clemente Ortiz, Dominican Republic and Pat Fennel, Canada.

Heavyweight:
1. Teofilo Stevenson, Cuba; 2. Narcisco Maldonado, Puerto Rico; 3. RUFUS "BUBBA" HADLEY, USA and Luis Castillo, Ecuador.

Cycling

The results of the cycling track events were disappointing. Especially so after the cycling program opened with the USA scoring its first-ever triumph in the 100-kilometer team road race. The margin of victory over the favored Cuban cyclists was more than three-and-one-half minutes.

The cycling quartet bringing gold to the USA for the first time was composed of Wayne Stetina, a Phi Beta Kappa graduate of the University of Indiana and a two-time Olympian, along with Andrew Weaver, a Florida University student, Thomas Sain and Tom Doughty, another '76 Olympian.

The USA, also, was in the thick of the struggle for honors in the individual 170-kilometer road race, ten times around a 17-kilometer course. The winner, Carlos Cardet of Cuba who is a 22-year-old physical education instructor, averaged nearly 24 miles an hour for the 106.25 miles over an extremely hilly course. The brothers Stetina, Wayne and Dale, were nosed out by the length of a gnat's eyelash for the bronze medal.

In the track events the USA cyclists placed fifth and sixth, not entirely what was expected when the cyclists left for the cycling events in Cuomo.

Hero of the cycling events was Canada's Gordon Singleton, 23, right across the border from Niagara Falls, Ontario. He was the Pan American Games champion in both the match sprint series and the 1,000-meter time trial series. Singleton was a double gold medalist at the 1978 British Commonwealth Games in Edmonton, Alberta.

The Canadians also won the 4,000-meter individual pursuit race when Claude Langlois sped by Chile's Fernando Vera to earn the gold. The announced times were 4:44.71 to 4:45.91.

Eight countries shared in the medals, four winning gold. Canada won three gold and one bronze, but the Cubans won a medal in each of the events, winding up with one gold (individual road race), three silver and two bronze.

TEAM PERSONNEL
Track Team:
Scott Andrews, 22, Northbrook, Illinois
Jerry Ash, 32, Burbank, California
Les Barczewski, 22, Milwaukee, Wisconsin
Leigh Barczewski, 23, Milwaukee, Wisconsin
Mark Brian Gorski, 19, Itasca, Illinois
David Grylls, 20, Grosse Pointe, Michigan
Kurtis Allan Miller, 20, San Jose, California
Leonard Nitz, 22, Sacramento, California
Gustare Graham Pipenhagen, 23, Chicago, Illinois
Danny Van Haute, 22, Chicago, Illinois
Roger Jay Young, 26, Detroit, Michigan

Road Team:
Robert Cook, 21, Englewood, Colorado
Thomas Doughty, 26, Hobart, Indiana
John Howard, 31, Austin, Texas
Ian Jones, 19, Stamford, Connecticut
George Mount, 23, Berkeley, California
Marc Pringle, 22, Seattle, Washington
Thomas Sain, 22, Bisbee, Arizona
Thomas Schuler, 22, Birmingham, Michigan
Dale Stetina, 22, Indianapolis, Indiana

TEAM PERSONNEL

 J. Ash
 Les Barczewski
 Lei Barczewski
 G. Mount
 L. Nitz
 G. Pipenhagen
 D. Van Haute
 A. Weaver
 S. Wood
 S. Aldridge E. Borysewicz E. Burke

Wayne Stetina, 25, Indianapolis, Indiana
Andrew Weaver, 20, Gainesville, Florida
Steven Wood, 18, Albuquerque, New Mexico

Manager: Edward Burke
Head Coach: Edward Borysewicz, Newark, New Jersey
Road Coach: Oliver Martin, Larchmont, New York
Assistant Road Coach: Mike Neel, Etna, California
Track Coach: Carl Leusenkamp, Aloha, Oregon
Mechanic: Steve Aldridge, Ridgefield Park, New Jersey

OFFICIAL SUMMARIES
100-Kilometer Time Trial:
1. USA (DOUGHTY, MOUNT, SAIN, W. STETINA) 2 hr. 15 min. 42.25 sec.; 2. Cuba 2:19:26.14; 3. Canada 2:23:14.54; 4. Mexico 2:25:10.30; 5. Colombia 2:26:01-42 6. Brazil 2:27:16.01.

170-Kilometer Road Race:
1. Carlos Cardet, Cuba 4 hr. 30 min. 39.35 sec.; 2. Bernardo Colex, Mexico 4:30:40.97; 3. Gonzalo Marin, Colombia 4:35:51.30; 4. WAYNE STETINA, USA; 5. DALE STETINA, USA; 6. Juan Morales, Colombia.

TEAM PERSONNEL

 T. Doughty
 D. Grylls
 I. Jones
 T. Sain
 D. Stetina
 W. Stetina
 R. Young
 C. Leusenkamp M. Neel

Match Sprints:
1. Gordon Singleton, Canada; 2. Jorge Perez, Cuba; 3. Dagoberto Pino, Cuba; 4. David Weller, Jamaica; 5. LEIGH BARCZEWSKI, USA; 6. Jose Ruschansky, Argentina. JERRY ASH, USA eliminated in repechage final by L. Rawlins, Trinidad and Tobago. (25 entries)

1,000-Meter Time Trial:
1. Gordon Singleton, Canada 1 min. 7.30 sec.; 2. David Weller, Jamaica 1:08.67; 3. Richard Tormen, Chile 1:08.83; 4. Antonio Madera, Cuba 1:09.64; 5. Jose Ruschansky, Argentina 1:09.79; 6. JERRY ASH, USA 1:09.86. (16 entries)

4,000-Meter Individual Pursuit:
1. Claude Langlois, Canada; 2. Fernando Vera, Chile; 3. Juan Rivera, Cuba; 4. Balbino Jaramillo, Colombia; 5. DAVID GRYLLS, USA; 6. Pedro Caino, Argentina. (12 entries)

4,000-Meter Team Pursuit:
1. Chile (Tormen, Vera, Aliste, Munoz); 2. Cuba; 3. Argentina; 4. Brazil.

Note: The USA team of NITZ, PIPENHAGEN, YOUNG and GRYLLS had the third fastest time in the qualification round and then was eliminated in the quarter-final round by Brazil, the eventual fourth place finisher.

Equestrian

"Jet Run Was Star in Equestrian Competition," shouted the headline in the San Juan *Star*. This was the same *Jet Run* which won the gold medal in the show jumping competition four years earlier. The difference was not inconsequential. In '75 *Jet Run* was owned and ridden by Alfred Senderos of Mexico. In '79 *Jet Run's* new owner was Philadelphia sportsman F. Eugene Dixon, ridden by Michael Matz and the horse is on loan to the U.S. Equestrian Team. Among the *afficionados* stationed around the ring it was the consensus that the 11-year-old gelding is just entering his prime jumping years.

For the first time the team show jumping competition preceded the individual competition. The team jumping competition and the dressage individual competition were conducted at the new $11,000,000 National Equestrian Center which had been constructed under the watchful eye and direction of German Rieckehoff, No. 1 sportsman on the Island, President of the Puerto Rico Olympic Committee, and International Olympic Committee member for Puerto Rico.

The individual show jumping finals (with carryover scores from the team jumping) preceded the Closing Ceremony in Hiram Bithorn Stadium. *Jet Run* stood fourth or fifth after the team jumping and Michael Matz guided the horse through two rounds with nary a fault on the two final rounds. *Butch Cassidy* ridden by Gerardo Tazzer, Mexico, was second, a scant two points behind after six rounds of competition over jumping courses designed by many-time USA equestrian team rider, Frank Chapot.

Hilda Gurney and *Keen*, USA have been partners in a number of dressage competitions. At the end of the first day of the testing Gurney and *Keen* were somewhat in the ruck. But on the second day the Los Angeles school teacher of gifted children forged ahead and won the gold medal, succeeding Canada's '75 winning entry of *Jungheirr II* and Christilot Boylen.

In the team show jumping competition the winning USA horses were *Sandsablaze, Allegro, Jet Run,* and *Val de Loire.* The "low score" for the winning USA team was accorded Melanie Smith of Memphis and Stonnington, Connecticut, astride *Val de Loire,* wearing "lucky number" 111. Melanie was in contention for the gold medal in the individual jumping until she came a cropper on one of the jumps late in the competition. She wound up fifth.

TEAM PERSONNEL

W. Brown   N. Dello Joio   H. Gurney

M. Matz   M. Smith   G. Stockebrand

L. Zang   W. Ardito   J. Burton

B. de Nemethy   F. McCashin   M. Van Bruggen

TEAM PERSONNEL

Dressage:
Linda Frances Zang (Fellow Traveller), 19, Birmingham, Michigan
Hilda Gurney (Keen), 35, Woodland Hills, California
Gwen Stockebrand (Bao), 24, Cotati, California

Show Jumping:
William (Buddy) Brown (Sandsablaze), 23, Kirkwood, Pennsylvania
Norman Dello Joio (Allegro), 23, South Salem, New York
Michael Matz (Jet Run), 28, Plymouth Meeting, Pennsylvania
Melanie Smith (Val de Loire), 29, Stonington, Connecticut

Team Leader: Maj. Gen. Jonathan Burton, USA (ret), South Hamilton, Massachusetts
Coaches: Bertalan De Nemethy, Gladstone, New Jersey
Veterinarians: William Ardito, D.V.M., Dix Hills, New York
Fred McCashin, D.V.M., Southern Pines, North Carolina

OFFICIAL SUMMARIES
Dressage, Individual:
1. HILDA GURNEY (Keen), USA 1,357; 2. GWEN STOCKEBRAND (Bao), USA 1,231; 3. Carmen deMier (Gondolero), Colombia 1,180; 4. Gerson Borges (Urapuru ExZimbo), Brazil 1,097; 5. Ingrid Troyko (Nuage), Brazil 953. (5 entries)

Dressage, Team:
Note: Since there were only two teams entered, the competition was considered "unofficial." The USA finished ahead of Brazil 4,616 to 3,939.

Show Jumping, Team:
1. USA (SANDSABLAZE, ALLEGRO, JET RUN, VAL DE LOIRE) 39.545 faults; 2. Canada 66.045; 3. Mexico 100.245; 4. Venezuela 147.315; 5. Puerto Rico 244.245; 6. Colombia 276.850.

Show Jumping, Individual:
1. Jet Run (MICHAEL MATZ) USA 13.265 faults; 2. Butch Cassidy (Gerardo Tazzer), Mexico 15.330; 3. Brother Sam (Ian Miller), Canada 21.005; 4. Mr. O.D. (Alvaro Tejada), Guatemala 27.425; 5. Val de Loire (MELANIE SMITH), USA 29.530; 6. Crimson Tide (Michael Vaillancourt), Canada 30.790. (16 entries)

Fencing

The USA solidified its position as the No. 2 nation in Hemispheric fencing at the Pan American Championships. But the No. 2 position is *not* to be accepted lightly since previously the USA had enjoyed No. 1. The new fencing power in the Western Hemisphere is Cuba with six out of a possible eight gold medals.

The other two gold medals went to the USA epee team which defeated Cuba and Argentina and Mario De Brelaz, Argentina the new epee champion. De Brelaz earned top honors by outfencing Paul Pesthy, veteran USA fencer/modern pentathlete, 5-3 in the final.

In addition to Pesthy's silver medal, Peter Westbrook, 27, a veteran of Olympic competition, finished runner-up to Cuba's Manuel Ortiz in the sabre. Peter was third four years earlier.

The heartening aspect of the fencing competition was that the USA medaled in each of the four individual and four team competitions.

In women's fencing the new foil champion is Cuba's Maria del Risco who dethroned two-time champion Margarita Rodriguez, also Cuba. In the final del Risco won 5-3 over the 32-year-old former champion.

TEAM PERSONNEL

Women's Foil:
Gay Kristine D'Asaro, 24, San Jose, California
Nikki Franke, 28, Philadelphia, Pennsylvania
Ann Patricia Russell, 32, Bayonne, New Jersey
Vincent Hurley Senser, 24, San Jose, California
Debra Lynn Waples, 26, Lake Oswego, Oregon

Men's Foil:
Edward Donofrio, 27, Baltimore, Maryland
Michael Marx, 20, Tigard, Oregon
Gregory Massialas, 23, San Jose, California
John Nonna, 30, Pleasantville, N.Y.

Men's Epee
E. Scott Bozek, 28, Herndon, Virginia
Paul K. Pesthy, 41, San Antonio, Texas
Peter Schifrin, 21, San Jose, California
C. Lee Shelley, 23, Cliffside Park, New Jersey

Men's Sabre:
Stanley Lekach, 32, Upton, New York
Edgar House, 26, New York City, New York
Alex Orban, 39, Hackensack, New Jersey
Philip Reilly, 27, North Bellmore, New York
Peter Westbrook, 27, New York City

Team Captain: Anthony J. Keane, East Brunswick, New Jersey
Manager: Marius Valsamis, M.D., Brooklyn, New York
Armorer: Joseph Byrnes, Elizabeth, New Jersey
Coach: Michael A. D'Asaro, San Jose, California
Coach: Csaba Elthes, New York City, New York

TEAM PERSONNEL

E. Bozek   G. D'Asaro   E. Donofrio

M. Marx   G. Massialas   J. Nonna

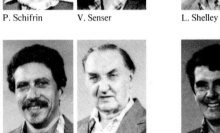

A. Russell   P. Schifrin   V. Senser

J. Byrnes   M. D'Asaro   C. Elthes

TEAM PERSONNEL

N. Franke   E. House   S. Lekach

A. Orban   P. Pesthy   P. Reilly

L. Shelley   D. Waples   P. Westbrook

A. Keane   M. Valsamis

OFFICIAL SUMMARIES
Women's Foil:

Women's Foil, Individual:
1. Maria del Risco, Cuba; 2. Margarita Rodriguez, Cuba; 3. NIKKI FRANKE, USA

Women's Foil, Team:
1. Cuba (del Risco, Rodriguez, Garcia, Alfonso); 2. Canada; 3. USA (WAPLES, SENSER, D'ASARO, RUSSELL, FRANKE).

Men's Foil, Individual:
1. Heriberto Gonzalez, Cuba; 2. Fernando Lopez, Argentina; 3. JOHN NONNA, USA.

Men's Foil, Team:
1. Cuba (Favier, Gonzalez, Jones, Hernandez); 2. USA (MARX, MASSIALAS, DONOFRIO, SCHIFRIN, NONNA); 3. Argentina.

Sabre, Individual:
1. Manuel Ortiz, Cuba; 2. PETER WESTBROOK, USA; 3. Jose Laverdeza, Cuba.

Sabre, Team:
1. Cuba (Ortiz, Hernandez, Laverdeza, Salazar); 2. USA (WESTBROOK, REILLY, LEKACH, ORBAN, HOUSE); 3. Argentina.

Epee, Individual:
1. Mario de Brelaz, Argentina; 2. PAUL PESTHY, USA; 3. Luis Quiroga, Cuba.

Epee, Team:
1. USA (SCHIFRIN, MASSIALAS, PESTHY, BOZEK, SHELLEY); 2. Cuba; 3. Argentina.

Field Hockey

Powerful Argentina continued to rule the field hockey competition at the Pan American Games, winning the gold medal for the fourth straight time since the sport was added to the program in 1967.

Following a sixth-place finish (out of six) four years ago, the "new" United States team built over the last four years climbed to sixth, this time in a nine-team field at San Juan.

The USA opened with a 2-1 triumph over Jamaica by taking a 2-0 advantage before a torrential rain hit the playing field and changed the complexion of the game. Mike Newton and Moogie Maruquin scored the goals for the U.S.

The USA later defeated Trinidad and Tobago, 1-0, to set up a crucial game with Cuba. And, after playing Cuba to a deadlock, the game had to be replayed.

In the longest game in Pan American Games history, the USA lost to the Cubans after five overtime periods on the second series of penalty shots in the marathon encounter.

In the championship game, Argentina defeated Canada to retain its laurels. The U.S. defeated Barbados, 3-2, to take sixth place.

TEAM PERSONNEL
Keith Cox, 23, Brooklyn, New York
Lance Eichert, 24, Ventura, California
Robert Gregg, 25, Allentown, Pennsylvania
Albert Holder, 39, Baltimore, Maryland
Manzar Iqbal, 20, Livermore, California
Hewlett Johnson, 29, Yonkers, New York
Charles King, 28, Long Beach, California
Euclid Mahon, 31, Brooklyn, New York
Marvin Maruquin, 30, Ventura, California
Gary Newton, 21, Ventura, California
Michael Newton, 27, Ventura, California
Bikram Randhawa, 26, Hercules, California
Alva Serrette, 27, Brooklyn, New York
John Stockdill, 27, Ventura, California
Carlos Valencia, 25, Oxnard, California
Gregory Vlastelica, 23, San Jose, California

Head Coach: Neville Berman, Johannesburg, So. Africa
Asst. Coach: Frank Noodt, Howell, New Jersey
Manager: Verle Harris, Moorpark, California

TEAM PERSONNEL

 K. Cox
 L. Eichert
 S. Gregg
 C. King
 E. Mahon
 M. Maruquin
 A. Serrette
 J. Stockdill
 C. Valencia
 N. Berman
 V. Harris
 F. Noodt

TEAM PERSONNEL

 A. Holder
 M. Iqbal
 H. Johnson
 G. Newton
 M. Newton
B. Randhawa
 G. Vlastelica

FIELD HOCKEY SUMMARIES
FINAL TEAM STANDINGS

	W	L	T
Argentina	6	0	0
Canada	5	1	0
Mexico	4	2	0
Chile	3	2	1
USA	3	2	2
Cuba	2	3	2
Barbados	2	3	1
Trinidad & Tobago	1	3	1
Jamaica	0	5	1
Puerto Rico	0	5	0

SCORES OF THE ROUND-ROBIN TOURNAMENT
Argentina (6-0-0): vs. USA (5-2), vs. Trinidad & Tobago (7-0), vs. Cuba (9-0), vs. Jamaica (5-1), vs. Mexico (6-1), vs. Canada (3-0).
Canada (5-1-0): vs. Chile (4-1), vs. Barbados (5-2), vs. Puerto Rico (8-0), vs. Mexico (7-0), vs. Cuba (9-1), vs. Argentina (0-3).
Mexico (4-2-0): vs. Barbados (2-1), vs. Puerto Rico (10-0), vs. Chile (3-2), vs. Canada (0-7), vs. Argentina (1-6), vs. Cuba (5-3).
Chile (3-2-1): vs. Canada (1-4), vs. Barbados (1-1), vs. Puerto Rico (3-0), vs. Mexico (2-3), vs. Jamaica (1-0), vs. USA (3-2).
USA (3-2-2): vs. Jamaica (2-1), vs. Argentina (2-5), vs. Trinidad & Tobago (1-0), vs. Cuba (3-3), vs. Cuba (2-2*), vs. Barbados (3-2), vs. Chile (2-3).
*Awarded to Cuba as advancement game.
Cuba (2-3-2): vs. Trinidad & Tobago (2-0), vs. Jamaica (1-0), vs. Argentina (0-9), vs. USA (3-3), vs. USA (2-2*), vs. Canada (1-9), vs. Mexico (3-5).
*Awarded as win over USA as advancement game.
Barbados (2-3-1): vs. Mexico (1-2), vs. Chile (1-1), vs. Canada (2-5), vs. Puerto Rico (4-1), vs. USA (2-3), vs. Jamaica (3-2).
Trinidad & Tobago (1-3-1): vs. Cuba (0-2), vs. Jamaica (1-1), vs. Argentina (0-7), vs. USA (0-1), vs. Puerto Rico (3-2).
Jamaica (0-5-1): vs. USA (1-2), vs. Cuba (0-1), vs. Argentina (1-5), vs. Chile (0-1), vs. Trinidad & Tobago (1-1), vs. Barbados (2-3).
Puerto Rico (0-5-0): vs. Mexico (0-10), vs. Chile (0-3), vs. Canada (0-8), vs. Barbados (1-4), vs. Trinidad & Tobago (2-3).

Gymnastics

It wasn't supposed to be a successful competition for USA gymnasts. The best gymnasts were at home preparing for world and international competitions, passing up the Pan American Games where the Organizing Committee had accepted a set of specially designed exercises which would never again be used.

The "specially designed" exercises were handed to the young ladies one day before the competition. They were late in arriving at San Juan because they had been participating in the trials for the world team. The three young U.S. ladies were tremendously successful, the men a bit less successful.

The women's division presented an exciting and thrilling final evening in the Roberto Clemente Coliseum. The crowd was captivated by Jackie Cassello of Silver Spring, Maryland. Jackie stands 4'9" and weighs in the low 70's. But in the vaulting she proved best and earned a nifty 9.80 in the final to annex the gold. Jackie finished second on the balance beam.

Jeannine Creek had placed second in the all-around competition in spite of unfamiliarity with the compulsory routines.

The individual floor exercise final was a head-to-head confrontation between Miss Creek and Heidi Anderson who on that particular day was celebrating her 17th birthday. There was little to choose between Jeannine and Heidi, but the judges separated them by .07 points with Creek, from Great Falls, Montana, winning the gold.

Again quoting from *The San Juan Star,* "As expected, the Cuban men were indomitable, winning everything in sight. Sergio Suarez was that country's *numero uno,* scooping up three golds. Roberto Richard and Jorge Roche (also Cuba) were double winners." The team standings for men read Cuba, Canada, Brazil.

It should be noted that the patrons jamming the Coliseum resorted to frequent hooting the officials whom they felt were unusually lenient in scoring the Cubans.

The USA three-person contingent did win two medals in the men's competition. Dan Muenz, a student at Southern Illinois University, finished runner-up to Cuba's Roberto Richard on the parallel bars.

Jeff LaFleur, 25, a gymnastics coach at the University of Minnesota, copped a bronze medal on the still rings, behind a pair of Cubans.

None of the USA men gymnasts placed among the top six in the combined exercises.

TEAM PERSONNEL
Men's Team:
Carl A. Antoniolla, 20, New Haven, Connecticut
Bob Desiderio, 23, State College, Pennsylvania
Jeffrey La Fleur, 25, Minneapolis, Minnesota
Daniel J. Muenz, 21, Carbondale, Illinois

Head Manager: William T. Meade, Carbondale, Illinois
Head Coach: Armando Vega, L.S.U., Baton Rouge, Louisiana

TEAM PERSONNEL

C. Antoniolla   R. Desiderio   J. LaFleur

D. Muenz   W. Meade   A. Vega

Women's Team:
Heidi Ann Anderson, 17, Furlong, Pennsylvania
Jackie Cassello, 13, Silver Spring, Maryland
Jeannine Creek, 17, Great Falls, Montana
Linda Marie Kardos, 17, Bethel Park, Pennsylvania

Head Manager: Mrs. Ernestine Weaver, Gainesville, Florida
Head Coach: Don Peters, Long Beach California

OFFICIAL SUMMARIES
MEN'S EVENTS
Team:
1. Cuba 666.80; 2. Canada 654.30; 3. Brazil 611.65; Venezuela 600.45; 5. Mexico 588.90; 6. Puerto Rico 502.20.

Floor Exercise:
1. Sergio Sanchez, Cuba 19.20; 2. Warren Long, Canada 19.00; 3. Jorge Roche, Cuba 18.55; 4. Marc Epprecht, Canada 18.30; 5. JEFFREY LaFLEUR, USA 18.15; 6. DANIEL MUENZ, USA 17.83.

All-Around:
1. Sergio Suarez, Cuba 112.95; 2. Jorge Roche, Cuba 112.40; 3. Enrique Bravo, Cuba 111.40; 4. Warren Long, Canada 111.35; 5. Roberto Richard, Cuba 111.40; 6. Adolfo Fernandez, Cuba 110.80.

Parallel Bars:
1. Roberto Richard, Cuba 19.18; 2. DANIEL MUENZ, USA 18.75; 3. Enrique Bravo, Cuba 18.53; 4. Jean Choquette, Canada 18.20; 5. JEFFREY LaFLEUR, USA 18.10; 6. Joao Luiz Ribeiro, Brazil 16.85.

Horizontal Bars:
1. Jorge Roche, Cuba 19.45; 2. Roberto Richard, Cuba 19.25; 3. Warren Long, Canada 19.10; 4. DANIEL MUENZ, USA 18.93; 5. JEFFREY LaFLEUR, USA 18.73; 6. Jean Choquette, Canada 18.53.

Still Rings:
1. Jorge Roche, Cuba 19.23; 2. Mario Castro, Cuba 18.88; 3. JEFFREY LaFLEUR, USA 18.60; 4. Pierre Clavel, Canada 18.55; 5. DANIEL MUENZ, USA 18.40; 6. Nigel Rothwell, Canada 18.23.

TEAM PERSONNEL

H. Anderson   J. Cassello   J. Creek

M. Kardos   D. Peters   E. Weaver

Long Horse Vault:
1. Sergio Suarez, Cuba 19.48; 2. Warren Long, Canada 19.33; 3. Richard Mazabel Lazo, Peru 18.90; 4. Andre Vallerand, Canada and JEFFREY LaFLEUR, USA 18.88; 6. Herbert Hoeger Zibauer, Venezuela 18.75.

Pommeled Horse:
1. Roberto Richard, Cuba 19.30; 2. Enrique Bravo, Cuba 18.82; 3. Jean Choquette, Canada 18.50; 4. Marc Epprecht, Canada 17.95; 5. DANIEL MUENZ, USA 17.70; 6. Joao Luiz Ribeiro, Brazil 17.00.

WOMEN'S EVENTS
Team:
1. Canada 449.20; 2. Cuba 439.35; 3. Brazil 430.50; 4. Puerto Rico 401.05; 5. Mexico 386.05; 6. Venezuela 371.40.

Floor Exercise:
1. JEANNINE CREEK, USA 19.35; 2. HEIDI ANDERSON, USA 19.28; 3. Monica Goermann, Canada 19.28; 4. Sherry Hawco, Canada 19.13; 5. Lillian Moreira Carrascoza, Brazil 18.53; 6. Vicenia Cruzata, Cuba 18.43.

Side Horse Vault:
1. JACKIE CASSELLO, USA 19.48; 2. Elfi Schlegel, Canada 19.33; 3. Elsa Chivas and Tania Gonzalez, Cuba 19.13 (tie); 5. HEIDI ANDERSON, USA 19.00; 6. Lillian Moreira Carrascoza, Brazil and Monica Goermann, Canada 18.90.

Uneven Parallel Bars:
1. Monica Goermann, Canada 19.08; 2. Tania Gonzalez, Cuba and Elfi Schlegel, Canada 18.98 (tie); 4. JEANNINE CREEK, USA 18.93; 5. Elsa Chivas, Cuba 18.88; 6. JACKIE CASSELLO, USA 18.83.

Balance Beam:
1. Sherry Hawco, Canada 18.90; 2. JACKIE CASSELLO, USA 18.68; 3. Elsa Chivas, Cuba and Monica Goermann, Canada 18.38 (tie); 4. JEANNINE CREEK, USA 18.25; 6. Michelle Popoff, Mexico 18.18.

All-Around:
1. Monico Goermann, Canada 76.30; 2. JEANNINE CREEK, USA 75.15; 3. Elfi Schlegel, Canada 75.10; 4. Sherry Hawco 75.05; 5. Diana Carnegie, Canada 74.80; 6. JACKIE CASSELLO, USA 74.65; 13. HEIDI ANDERSON, USA 73.00.

Judo

Brazil supplanted Canada as the No. 1 judo power in the Western Hemisphere. Cuba has moved into a contending position and the USA, shutout in a quest for gold, must content itself with fourth place.

Suffice to say the Big Four in Hemispheric Judo competition swept all eight gold and earned 23 of the 32 medals available. In each of the eight weight classes one gold, one silver, and two bronze medals to the defeated semi-finalists are awarded.

The biggest surprise came in the light middleweight class (up to 143 pounds). Three years ago in Montreal, Cuba's Hector Rodriguez was an Olympic champion. At San Juan he was a bronze medalist. The winner of the gold was Canada's Brad Farron.

Osvaldo Simoes, Brazil, at 350 pounds was the biggest of all entries. In the heavyweight class Simoes was one of two defeated semi-finalists, placing behind champion Jose Ibanez, Cuba and Jesse Goldstein, USA.

The final evening of competition was the open class. Puerto Rico was counting on its best, Hector Estevez, a fourth degree black belt. Ibanez was seeking to add the "open" title as a companion piece for his heavyweight laurels and Simoes clearly had some revenge motives. Ibanez had won the heavyweight title and had finished runner-up in the open class four years earlier.

Ibanez fell in the semi-finals of the open class competition. The final brought together Simoes and the Island hero, Estevez.

Spectators will long heatedly discuss whether Estevez yelled "uncle" or didn't yell "uncle" when Simoes applied an arm lock. The arbiter handling the match, from neutral Great Britain, ruled that Simoes applied a hold which could have resulted in a broken arm or a dislocated shoulder. Thus, the cry of "uncle" was considered moot. Simoes was awarded the gold medal and a measure of revenge since he had eliminated Ibanez in the semi-final round.

USA silver medals came about after Brazil's Luis Shinohara had narrowly defeated Ed Liddie who had been born in France and is now a New York City resident and a student at Cumberland College in Kentucky.

On the opening night of competition, Jesse Goldstein, 1979 National AAU runner-up, finished second in the heavyweight class. He yielded to the great Cuban Ibanez in the final.

TEAM PERSONNEL

B. Barron   S. Gibbons   J. Goldstein

E. Liddie   J. Martin   T. Masterson

M. Tudela   L. White

T. Kitaura   P. Maruyama

TEAM PERSONNEL

Brett Barron, 19, San Francisco, California (78 kg)

Shawn Gibbons, 20, St. Petersburg, Florida (Open Class)

Jesse Goldstein, 24, Toms River, New Jersey (Over 95 kg)

Edward Liddie, 19, New York, New York (60 kg)

James Martin, 25, Wheeling, Illinois (65 kg)

Thomas Masterson, 29, St. Petersburg, Florida (71 kg)

Miguel Tudela, 24, Los Angeles, California (95 kg)

Leo White, Jr., 21, Seaside, California (86 kg)

Manager: Tamo Kitaura, Redwood City, California

Coach: Major Paul K. Maruyama, U.S. Air Force Academy, Colorado

OFFICIAL SUMMARIES
(Number of players in each class shown in parentheses)

Open Class:
1. Oswaldo Simoes, Brazil; 2. Hector Estevez, Puerto Rico; 3. Jose Ibanez, Cuba and Joe Meli, Canada. (SHAWN GIBBONS, USA, did not place.) (9)

Over 95 Kilograms (over 209 pounds):
1. Jose Ibanez, Cuba; 2. JESSE GOLDSTEIN, USA; 3. Oswaldo Simoes, Brazil and Jaime Felipa, Dutch Antilles. (7)

Up to 95 Kilograms (209 pounds):
1. Carlos Pacheco, Brazil; 2. Venancio Gomez, Cuba; 3. MIGUEL TUDELA, USA and Sergio Kormornickie, Argentina. (6)

Up to 86 Kilograms (189 pounds):
1. Louis Jani, Canada; 2. Alexis Mundo, Venezuela; 3. LEO WHITE, USA and Eduardo Novoa, Chile. (13)

Up to 78 Kilograms (172 pounds):
1. Carlos Cunha, Brazil; 2. Radames Lora, Dominican Republic; 3. BRETT BARRON, USA and Juan Ferrer, Cuba. (14)

Up to 71 Kilograms (156 pounds):
1. Guillermo D'Nelson, Cuba; 2. Kevin Doherty, Canada; 3. Roberto Machusso, Brazil and Andres Puentes, Mexico. (THOMAS DENNIS MASTERSON, USA did not place.) (12)

Up to 65 Kilograms (143 pounds):
1. Brad Farron, Canada; 2. Luis Omnura, Brazil; 3. Gerrardo Padilla, Mexico and Hector Rodriguez, Cuba. (JAMES ALLEN MARTIN, USA, did not place.) (12)

Up to 60 Kilograms (132 pounds):
1. Luis Shinohara, Brazil; 2. EDWARD J. LIDDIE, USA; 3. Phil Takahashi, Canada and Rafael Gonzalez, Mexico. (12)

Roller Skating

Roller skating's three separate disciplines: speed, artistic and roller hockey were added to the program for the Pan American Games as a result of an active campaign engendered by the U.S. Amateur Confederation of Roller Skating.

USA athletes won ten out of 16 gold medals available for the speed skating and artistic skating events. The roller hockey team finished fourth out of five, one notch in front of the hosts from Puerto Rico.

In the speed skating events the No. 1 attraction was a Tacoma, Washington skate salesman, Tom Peterson. Tom had put on skates for the first time at his grandparents skate center at the age of 13 or 14 *months*.

Peterson won four gold medals, but none was more satisfying than the winner's award for the 20,000-meter cross-country race conducted on a straight patch of roadway along the coast—covering the 12½-mile distance at a rate of almost 25 miles an hour.

Teammate Ken Sutton had opened the speed skating events by capturing the 500m "against the clock."

Among the ladies, Argentina's Nora Vega blanketed the field with two individual awards and another for the relay.

The USA *not* unexpectedly swept all titles in the artistic events. Three-time world champion Natalie Dunn of Bakersfield, California, made what was announced her final competitive appearance and won the artistic singles crown.

Fred Morante, USA led a 1-2 sweep in the men's artistic singles with a superb performance to score a .4-point victory over teammate Lex Kane, 57.7 to 57.3.

The USA also placed 1-2 in the dancing and the pairs competitions. Fleurette Arsenault and Danny Littel were the favorites in the dancing and scored over teammates Cindy Smith and Mark Howard. The pairs gold medal was a triumph for Robbie Coleman and Patrick Jones, the Tennessee duo, placing ahead of Tina Kneisley and Paul Price, ages 16 and 17 respectively, compared to 17 and 21 for the champions.

Despite being held to a 2-2 deadlock by Brazil, Argentina claimed the roller hockey by outscoring Brazil in the other games. Does it seem fair that Argentina's 46-0 shutout over Puerto Rico should be the deciding factor when Brazil could only outscore the Islanders 27-0? But that's the way deadlocks are broken when two teams have identical won-and-lost records in international competition, after playing to a deadlock, head to head.

TEAM PERSONNEL

F. Arsenault

R. Coleman

E. Coley

L. Dorso
S. Dotterer

N. Dunn

J. Gustafson

S. Hoffecker

M. Howard

D. Littel

F. Morante

L. Peterson

C. Smith

C. Snyder

K. Sutton

J. Butera
O. Dunn
B. Sisson

TEAM PERSONNEL

C. Cook
D. DeSoto
S. Dooley

J. Ferguson
R. Ferguson
W. Gerhart

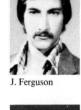
P. Jones

A. Kane

T. Kneisley

T. Peterson

M. Pounds

P. Price

D. Willauer

J. Young

C. Wahlig

TEAM PERSONNEL

Speed Roller Skating:

Elaine Carol Coley, 20, Ft. Lauderdale, Florida
Suzanne Dooley, 30, Livonia, Michigan
Linda Marie Dorso, 21, Cincinnati, Ohio
LinSue Peterson, 19, Tacoma, Washington
Curtis Cook, 21, Greenacres, Washington
Thomas Peterson, 20, Tacoma, Washington
Christopher Snyder, 23, Euless, Texas
Kenneth Sutton, 18, Muskegon, Michigan

Artistic Roller Skating:

Fleuerette Arsenault, 21, Cambridge, Massachusetts (dancing)
Robbie Melinda Coleman, 17, Memphis, Tennessee (pairs)
Natalie Dunn, 22, Bakersfield, California (singles)
Tina Patricia Kneisley, 16, Marion, Ohio (pairs)
Cindy Denise Smith, 18, Petersburg, Virginia (dancing)
Jo Anne Young, 19, Norfolk, Virginia (singles)
Mark Edward Howard, 19, Richmond, Virginia (dancing)
Patrick Thomas Jones, 21, Memphis, Tennessee (pairs)
Danny Littel, 27, Farmingdale, New York (dancing)
Fred Morante, 19, Plainview, New York (singles)
Paul James Price, 17, Howell, Michigan (pairs)
Alexander Kane IV, 23, Pontiac, Michigan (singles)

Roller Hockey:

David DeSoto, 23, Cumberland, Maryland
Samuel Dotterer, 21, Gilbertsville, Pennsylvania
James Ferguson, 24, Cumberland, Maryland
Ralph Ferguson II, 20, Cumberland, Maryland
William Gerhart, 26, Sassamansville, Pennsylvania
Scott Hoffecker, 24, Pottstown, Pennsylvania
Michael Pounds, 21, Lubbock, Texas
Douglas Willauer, 24, Boyertown, Pennsylvania

Artistic Coach: Jane Ann Puracchio Butera, Euclid, Ohio
Speed Coach: Charles Wahlig, Wilmington, Delaware
Roller Hockey Coach: Billy Lloyd Sisson, Lubbock, Texas
Technician: Omar Dunn, Bakersfield, California

OFFICIAL SUMMARIES
SPEED ROLLER SKATING:
MEN'S EVENTS

500 Meters Against Clock:
1. KEN SUTTON, USA 51.01 sec.;
2. CURTIS COOK, USA 51.82;
3. Reynaldo Vega, Argentina 52.37.

500 Meters, Two-at-a-Time:
1. Raul Subiledt, Argentina 51.71 sec.;
2. KEN SUTTON, USA 51.95; 3. Reynaldo Vega, Argentina 52.22.

3,000 Meters Pack Style:
1. Raul Subiledt, Argentina 5 min. 34.43 sec.;
2. CURTIS COOK, USA 5:35.10; 3. CHRIS SNYDER, USA 5:35.43.

5,000 Meters Pack Style:
1. TOM PETERSON, USA 9 min. 48.20 sec.; 2. Carlos Lugea, Argentina 9:49.06;
3. Humberto Triana, Colombia 9:54.30.

10,000 Meters Pack Style:
1. TOM PETERSON, USA 21 min. 52.71 sec.; 2. CHRIS SNYDER, USA 21:57.47;
3. Agustin Ramirez, Colombia 22:00.54.

10,000 Meters Relay:
1. USA (PETERSON, SNYDER) 17 min. 42.87 sec.; 2. USA (COOK, SUTTON) 17:49.02; 3. Argentina (Subiledt, Lugea) 17:52.61.

20,000 Meters Cross-Country:
1. TOM PETERSON, USA 36 min. 37:00 sec.; 2. CHRIS SNYDER, USA 36:45.00;
3. Raul Subiledt, Argentina 37:43.02.

WOMEN'S EVENTS

500 Meters Against Clock:
1. Nora Vega, Argentina 55.29 sec.;
2. LINDA DORSO, USA 56.45; 3. ELAINE COLEY, USA 1:00.83.

3,000 Meters, Pack Style:
1. Nora Vega, Argentina 5 min. 50.76 sec.;
2. Claudia Rodriguez, Argentina 6:08.86;
3. LINSUE PETERSON, USA 6:08.88;
4. SUZANNE DOOLEY, USA 6:13.31.

5,000 Meters, Pack Style:
1. Claudia Rodriguez, Argentina 11 min. 42.02 sec.; 2. SUZANNE DOOLEY, USA 11:43.28; 3. Sonia Fregeiredo, Argentian 11:46.26; 4. LINSUE PETERSON, USA 11:56.26.

500 Meters, Two-at-a-Time:
1. Nora Vega, Argentina 56.72 sec.; 2. ELAINE COLEY, USA 57.58; 3. LINDA DORSO, USA 1:00.68.

5,000 Meters Relay:
1. Argentina (Vega, Rodriguez) 9 min. 29.71 sec.; 2. USA (PETERSON, DOOLEY) 9:32.14; 3. USA (DORSO, COLEY) 10:51.43.

ARTISTIC SKATING:
Men's Singles:
1. FRED MORANTE, USA 57.7 points;
2. ALEXANDER KANE IV, USA 57.3;
3. Guy Aubin, Canada 55.4.

Women's Singles:
1. NATALIE DUNN, USA 58.40 points;
2. JOANNE YOUNG, USA 57.90; 3. Sylvia Gingras, Canada 56.70.

Pairs:
1. USA (ROBBIE COLEMAN AND PATRICK JONES) 57.2 points; 2. USA (TINA KNEISLEY AND PAUL PRICE) 57.1; 3. Canada (Guy Aubin and Sylvia Gingras) 55.6.

Dancing:
1. USA (FLEURETTE ARSENAULT AND DAN LITTEL) 231.8; 2. USA (CINDY SMITH AND MARK HOWARD) 231.9; 3. Canada (Lori Beal and Robert Dalgleish) 222.3.

ROLLER HOCKEY:
Final Team Standing:
1. Argentina (3-0-1); 2. Brazil (2-1-1); 3. Chile (2-2-0); 4. USA (2-2-0); 5. Puerto Rico (0-4-0).

Scores of the Games:
Argentina vs. Chile 5-2; vs. Brazil 2-2 (tie); vs. Puerto Rico 46-0; vs. USA 6-1.
Brazil vs. Puerto Rico 27-0; vs. Chile 2-0.
Chile vs. Puerto Rico 29-0; vs. USA 4-1.
USA vs. Puerto Rico 25-0; vs. Brazil 1-5.

Rowing

"Cuba is now Striking Gold in Crew Competition" was the frightening headline in one San Juan newspaper the day after the rowing finals where the Cubans won three gold and three bronze medals in the eight final events of men's rowing competition. Second place was accorded to Canada with two championships and a trio of bronze medals.

Most disquieting was the performance of the USA flotilla, victory only in the eights with coxswain, three silver medals and three bronze. It was a bitter experience in the Hemispheric competitions.

The eight with coxswain, coached by Ted Nash and composed of sweepswingers from Pennsylvania, Washington, Cornell, St. Joseph's and stroked by Bruce Ibbotson of California State at Fullerton was awesome in victory. The "varsity eight" was almost two lengths ahead of Canada and the highly-regarded Cubans finished another three lengths astern.

The biggest disappointment was single sculler Jim Dietz. In the preliminary heat Dietz, rowing for the New York A.C., scored a notable triumph over defending champion Ricardo Ibarra of Argentina. It looked like a Dietz-Ibarra race in the final. But fate decreed otherwise. Shortly after the start, Dietz' oar struck a buoy and ruined the rhythm of the USA sculler. In fact, even with a fine sprint in the final 500m, Dietz could not catch Canada's Philip Monckton who was making his debut in a single. Ibarra retained his title.

The USA lost one gold medal in a photo finish. The picture showed that the Canadian double sculls entry outrowed the USA duo of Chris Alsopp and Tom Howes on the final stroke. It was a crushing defeat for the USA duo which had led the race at each checkpoint, 500m, 1,000m, and 1,500m.

Mark down Cuba as a rowing power to be reckoned with in the future races in this hemisphere. Just down the road, the Cubans might challenge in other international competitions. Four years ago the log of the Cubans read one gold, two silver and one bronze. In 1975 at Mexico City the USA flotilla posted an overall mark of 3-3-1 in the seven-race regatta.

TEAM PERSONNEL

 C. Alsopp

 B. Beall

  C. Boit

 S. Colgan

 R. Curtis

 J. Dietz

 J. Hartigan

 M. Hess

 T. Howes

 T. Kiefer

 D. Krmpotich

 W. Lubsen

 P. Stekl

 G. Stone

 M. Teti

 D. Vreugdenhil

 T. Watenpaugh

 C. Wood

 L. Gluckman

 T. Nash

 J. O'Hara

TEAM PERSONNEL

 R. Cashin

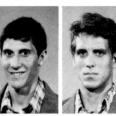 J. Chatzky

S. Christensen

 D. Fellows

 F. Fox

J. Franklin

 J. Huss

 B. Ibbotson

R. Johnson

 M. Miller

 R. Paczewski

A. Shealy

 J. Townsend

 D. Townsley

K. Turner

  T. Woodman

 D. Rose

 J. Wolf

TEAM PERSONNEL

Single Sculls:
James W. Dietz, 30, New Rochelle, New
York

Double Sculls:
Christopher Alsopp, 24, Seattle, Washington
Thomas Andrews Howes, 27, Arlington,
Massachusetts

Quadruple Sculls:
Bruce Beall, 27, Boston, Massachusetts
Alan Shealy, 25, Cambridge, Massachusetts
Gregg Stone, 26, Cambridge, Massachusetts
Christopher Wood, 26, Belmont,
Massachusetts

Paris Without Coxswain:
Richard Cashin, 26, Belmont, Massachusetts
David Fellows, 26, Cambridge,
Massachusetts

Pairs With Coxswain:
Christopher Boit, coxswain, 22, Woods
Hole, Massachusetts
Thomas N. Keifer, 21, Salisbury,
Connecticut
Ridgely Johnson, 21, New York City,
New York

Fours Without Coxswain:
Jesse Franklin, 24, Littleton, Colorado
Michael Teti, 22, Upper Darby, Pennsylvania
Darrell Vreugdenhil, 30, Philadelphia,
Pennsylvania
Jim Watenpaugh, 24, King of Prussia,
Pennsylvania

Fours With Coxswain:
Steven Christensen, 22, Dayton, Ohio
Frederick Fox, 24, Seattle, Washington
John D. Hartigan, 39, coxswain, Medord
Lakes, New Jersey
Mark Miller, 22, Brewster, Washington
Richard Paczewski, 24, Philadelphia,
Pennsylvania

Eights With Coxswain:
John A. Chatzky, coxswain, 22,
Philadelphia, Pennsylvania
Sean Colgan, 23, Philadelphia, Pennsylvania
Michael J. Hess, 23, Delta, B.C., Canada
Bruce Ibbetson, 26, Tustin, California
Walter H. Lubsen, Jr., 22m Alexandria,
Virginia
Philip W. Stekl, 23, Middletown,
Connecticut
David S. Townsley, 22, Mammoth,
Wyoming
Kerry J. Turner, 22, Alhambra, California
Thomas H. Woodman, 23, Newtown,
Square, Pennsylvania

Spare Oarsmen:
Richard I. Curtis, 32, Greenport, New York
Kenneth B. Foote, 27, Oslo, Norway
John B. Huss, 22, Longmont, Colorado
David M. Krmpotich, 24, Philadelphia,
Pennsylvania
Joseph L. Townsend, 34, Greenport,
New York

Coaches: Lawrence Gluckman, Cambridge,
Massachusetts
Ted Nash, King of Prussia, Pennsylvania
Dietrich Rose, Philadelphia, Pennsylvania
Manager: Julian Wolf, Los Angeles,
California
Boatman: James O'Hara, New York City,
New York

OFFICIAL SUMMARIES

Single Sculls:
1. Ricardo Ibarra, Argentina 6:39.52;
2. Philip Monckton, Canada 6:42.01;
3. JIM DIETZ, USA 6:43.49.

Double Sculls:
1. Canada (Patrick Walters, Bruce Ford)
6:03.35; 2. USA (CHRIS ALSOPP, TOM
HOWES) 6:03.37; 3. Cuba 6:11.43.

Pairs Without Coxswain:
1. Canada (Brian Dick, Tim Storm) 6:32.33;
2. USA (DAVID FELLOWS, RICHARD
CASHIN) 6:36.77; 3. Cuba 6:51.43.

Pairs With Coxswain:
1. Brazil (Wandir Kuntze, Laidlo Ribeiro,
Manoel Therezo, cox.) 6:53.23; 2. Argentina
6:57.82; 3. Cuba 6:58.87.

Petit Final:
1. USA (RIDGELY JOHNSON, TOM
KIEFER, CHRIS BOIT, COX.) 7:16.69;
2. Puerto Rico 7:47.49.

Quadruple Sculls:
1. Cuba (Cedar Herrera, Nelson Simon,
Roberto Quintero, Miguel Castro) 5:39.64;
2. Brazil 5:41.87; 3. USA (CHRISTOPHER
WOOD, BRUCE BEALL, GREGG
STONE, ALAN SHEALY) 5:45.60.

Fours Without Coxswain:
1. Cuba (Wenceslao Borroto, Emeregildo
Palacios, Ismael Same, Manuel Blanco)
5:50.41; 2. USA (JIM WATENPAUGH,
JESSE FRANKLIN, DERRELL VREUG-
DENHIL, MIKE TETI) 5:53.76; 3. Brazil
6:07.05.

Fours With Coxswain:
1. Cuba (Antonio Riano, Juan Alfonso,
Alfredo Villardares, FRancisco Mora, En-
rique Carrillo, coxswain) 6:43.41; 2. Canada
6:46.79; 3. USA (FRED FOX, RICK
PACZEWSKI, MARK MILLER, STEVE
CHRISTIANSEN, JOHN HARTIGAN,
COXSWAIN) 7:35.47.

Eights With Coxswain:
1. USA (KERRY TURNER, DAVID
TOWNSLEY, PHILIP STEKL, TOM
WOODMAN, WALTER LUBSEN, MIKE
HESS, SEAN COLGAN, BRUCE IBBOT-
SON, JOHN CHATZKY, COXSWAIN)
5:24.39; 2. Canada 5:31.00; 3. Cuba 5:43.09.

Don Paige on his way to winning the 1500m Gold Medal at San Juan.

Shooting

The USA continued to reign supreme in the hemispheric shooting competitions. It was a glorious field day for the shotgunners, riflemen and pistol shooters. The log showed 12 gold, eight silver and one bronze. Underscoring the supremacy of the USA marksmen was a record of winning a medal in eight of the nine events on the program.

Lt. Col. Lones Wigger, U.S. Army, continued to gain new honors atop old. The best rifleman in the world won the English match, the small bore rifle, three position, and was a member of the winning USA synthetic teams in both events.

Mark this one down for history. In the English match Wigger missed his first shot and then hit 599 in a row to tie the world record. He edged out a brilliant newcomer to international competition in the small bore rifle, three-position event, Rod Fitz-Randolph of Tennessee Tech, 1,162 to 1,154.

The only woman to win a medal in the Pan American shooting competition was Lt. Wanda Jewell, a member of the winning air rifle "team."

In the four pistol events, the USA garnered but a single gold medal. Donald Nygord outshot teammate Donald Hamilton, 385 to 380 (out of a possible 400) in the air pistol.

The USA shotgunners had a perfect record—1, 2 sweeps in the individual and gold medal in the "team" for the trapshooting and clay pigeon events.

John Satterwhite, an Olympian, won the individual skeet title which competition wound up on July 4. Satterwhite broke two more targets than teammate Matthew Dryke, 196 to 194.

In the clay pigeon event, Staff Sergeant Robert Green, U.S. Army, broke two more birds than teammate Charvin Dixon, 191 to 189. Although both Dixon and teammate Ernest Neel hit 189 birds, the silver medal went to Dixon by outshooting Neel 49 to 47 in the final 50 birds.

TEAM PERSONNEL
Rifle:
David I. Cramer, 36, Aliquippa, Pennsylvania (Air Rifle)
Edward F. Etzel, Jr., 26, Morgantown, West Virginia (Air Rifle)
Roderick M. Fitz-Randolph, Jr., 20, Palm Bay, Florida (Smallbore Rifle, 3-position)
Dennis E. Ghiselli, USMC, 23, Quantico, Virginia (English Match)
Boyd D. Goldsby, USAR, 32, Little Rock, Arkansas (English Match)
Michael W. Gross, 22, Menomonee Falls, Wisconsin (Air Rifle)
Lt. Wanda Rae Jewell, USA, 25, Ft. Benning, Georgia (Air Rifle)
David W. Kimes, 38, Monterey Park, California (Rifle)
Ernest John Vande Zande, USA, 31, Columbus, Georgia (Air Rifle, English Match)
Thomas J. Whitaker, USAR, 32, Belmont, California (Rifle)
Lt. Col. Lones Wigger, Jr., USA, 41, Ft. Benning, Georgia

TEAM PERSONNEL

T. Anderson

W. Atkinson

S. Baiocco

D. Cramer

C. Dixon

J. Dorsey

D. Ghiselli

B. Goldsby

R. Green

W. Jewell

D. Kimes

C. McCowan

J. Satterwhite

Jeff Sizemore

E. VandeZande

D. Young

W. Zobell

TEAM PERSONNEL

J. Brundin

E. Buljung

J. Clemmons

M. Dryke

E. Etzel

R. Fitz-Randolph

M. Gross

D. Hamilton

E. Hilden

W. McMillan

J. McNally

E. Neel

T. Whitaker

L. Wigger

J. Wilder

J. Berry

D. Boyd

H. Pearson

Jas. Sizemore

H. Skalsky

Shot Gun:
Joseph W. Clemmons, USA, 25, Columbus, Georgia (Skeet)
Charvin H. Dixon, 24, Seattle, Washington (Trap)
Matthew A. Dryke, USA, 20, Ft. Benning, Georgia (Skeet)
Robert P. Green, 28, Clinton, Utah (Trap)
Ernest W. Neel, USA, 33, Ft. Benning, Georgia (Trap)
John C. Satterwhite, 35, Redmond, Washington (Skeet)
Jeffrey D. Sizemore, 17, Corpus Christi, Texas (Skeet)
Walter W. Zobell, Jr., 29, Jackosn, Montana (Trap)

Pistol:
Terence M. Anderson, 34, New Orleans, Louisiana (Rapid Fire)
Samuel A. Baiocco, 43, Poway, California (Center Fire)
Jan R. Brundin, 41, Quakertown, Pennsylvania (Free)
Erich Buljung, USA, 35, Ft. Benning, Georgia (Free)
Donald L. Hamilton, 49, Kingston, Massachusetts (Free)
Charles E. McCowan, USA, 35, Columbus, Georgia (Free)
William W. McMillan, USMC (ret.), 50, Del Mar, California (Rapid Fire)
John T. McNally, 22, Columbus, Georgia (Rapid Fire)
Donald C. Nygord, 43, LaCrescenta, California (Air Pistol)
Jerry L. Wilder, 34, Remington, Indiana (Center Fire)
Darius R. Young, 41, Winterburn, Alberta, Canada (Rapid Fire)

Manager: Joseph B. Berry, USA (ret.), Lorton, Virginia
Assistant Manager: Homer Grogan Pearson, USNG, Nashville, Tennessee
Coach, Rifle Team: David I. Boyd, USMC, Triangle, Virginia
Coach, Pistol Team: Elmer W. Hilden, Yuma, Arizona
Coach: Harry L. Skalsky, Richmond, Virginia
Gunsmith: William T. Atkinson, Prescott, Arizona
Gunsmith: James B. Sizemore, USA, Phenix City, Alabama

OFFICIAL SUMMARIES
Air Rifle, Individual:
1. Guy Lorton, Jr., Canada 384; 2. ERNEST VANDE ZANDE, USA 379; 3. Mitchell Kurt, Canada 379; 4. EDWARD ETZEL, USA 379; 5. Adelso Pena 378; 6. MIKE GROSS, USA 376. Also, 10. WANDA JEWELL, USA 373. (29 entries)

Air Rifle, Team:
1. USA (E. VANDE ZANDE, E. ETZEL, M. GROSS, W. JEWELL) 1,507; 2. Cuba 1,494; 3. Argentina 1,478; 4. Canada 1,477; 5. Mexico 1,449; 6. Brazil 1,428.

English Match, Individual:
1. LT. COL. LONES WIGGER, USA 599 (equals world record); 2. Adelso Pena, Cuba 594; 3. Alfonso Mayer, Canada 592; 4. BOYD GOLDSBY, USA 592; 5. Jose Alvarez, Mexico 592; 6. DENNIS GHISELLI, USA 591. Also, 7. ERNEST VANDE ZANDE, USA 591. (33 entries)

English Match, Team:
1. USA (L. WIGGER, B. GOLDSBY, D. GHISELLI, E. VANDE ZANDE) 2,373; 2. Cuba 2,350; 3. Brazil 2,345; 4. Canada 2,343; 5. Mexico 2,340; 6. Puerto Rico 2,330.

Small Bore Rifle, 3-Position, Individual:
1. LT. COL. LONES WIGGER, USA 1,162; 2. ROD FITZ-RANDOLPH, USA 1,154; 3. EDWARD ETZEL, USA 1,148*; 4. Guy Lorton, Jr., Canada 1,146; 5. Jose Cruz, Cuba 1,140; 6. Arne Sorensen, Canada 1,138. Also, 15. THOMAS WHITAKER, USA 1,108. (30 entries)

Small Bore Rifle, 3-Position, Team:
1. USA (L. WIGGER, R. FITZ-RANDOLPH, E. ETZEL, T. WHITAKER) 4,572; 2. Canada 4,531; 3. Cuba 4,502; 4. Mexico 4,433; 5. Argentina 4,425; 6. Puerto Rico 4,272.

Free Pistol, Individual:
1. Walter Bauza, Argentina 555; 2. Luis Baquero, Cuba 547; 3. Thomas Guinn, Canada 547; 4. Pedro Bermudez, Cuba 542; 5. Wilfredo Audelo, Mexico 541; 6. Silvio Souza, Brazil 540. Also, 17. ERIC BUL-JUNG, USA 527; 20. DONALD HAMILTON, USA 525; 12. CHARLES McCOWAN, USA 534; 29. JAN BRANDIN, USA 506. (30 entries)

Free Pistol, Team:
1. Canada (E. Jans, T. Guinn, M. Wolo-chow, A. Tomsett) 2,138; 2. Cuba 2,134; 3. Puerto Rico 2,127; 4. Mexico 2,124; 5. Brazil 2,123; 6. USA (E. BULJUNG, J. BRANDIN, C. McCOWAN, D. HAMIL-TON) 2,092.

Air Pistol, Individual:
1. DONALD NYGORD, USA 385; 2. DONALD HAMILTON, USA 380; 3. Rafael Garden, Puerto Rico 380; 4. Leopoldo Martinez, Mexico 380; 5. Silvio Souza, Brazil 379; 6. CHARLES McCOWAN, USA 377. Also, 8. ERIC BULJUNG, USA 376. (38 entries)

Air Pistol, Team:
1. USA (D. NYGORD, D. HAMILTON, C. McCOWAN, E. BULJUNG) 1,518; 2. Brazil 1,488; 3. Puerto Rico 1,486; 4. Mexico 1,482; 5. Cuba 1,482; 6. Canada 1,474.

Rapid Fire Pistol, Individual:
1. Juan Hernandez, Cuba 590 (PAR); 2. JOHN McNALLY, USA 588; 3. Bernardo Tobar 587; 4. TERRENCE ANDERSON, USA 586; 5. WILLIAM McMILLAN, USA 586; 6. Rafael Rodriguez, Cuba 586. Also, 30. DARIUS YOUNG, USA 571. (38 entries)

Rapid Fire Pistol, Team:
1. Cuba (G. Ryes Bello, E. Acuna, J. Hernandez, R. Rodriguez) 2,339; 2. USA (W. McMILLAN, J. McNALLY, T. ANDERSON, D. YOUNG) 2,331; 3. Colombia 2,315; 4. Mexico 2,308; 5. Brazil 2,305; 6. Argentina 2,301.

Trapshooting, Individual:
1. ROBERT GREEN , USA 191; 2. CHARVIN DIXON, USA 189; 3. ERNEST NEEL, USA 189*; 4. George Leary, Canada 187; 5. WALTER ZOBELL, USA 186; 6. Fernando Walls, Mexico 183. (20 entries)

Trapshooting, Team:
1. USA (E. NEEL, C. DIXON, R. GREEN, W. ZOBELL) 563; 2. Brazil 533; 3. Canada 502; 4. Mexico 493; 5. Puerto Rico 461. No sixth place.

Skeet Shooting, Individual:
1. JOHN SATTERWHITE, USA 196; 2. MATHEW DRYKE, USA 194; 3. Firmo Roberti, Argentina 189; 4. Miguel Zerene, Chile; 5. Roberto Castrillo, Cuba 187; 6. Antonio Yazigi, Chile 184. Also, 14. JEFFREY SIZEMORE, USA 178; 23. JOSEPH CLEMMONS, USA 178. (37 entries)

Skeet Shooting, Team:
1. USA (J. SATTERWHITE, M. DRYKE, J. SIZEMORE, J. CLEMMONS) 566; 2. Chile 548; 3. Cuba 547; 4. Canada 541; 5. Brazil 533; 6. Puerto Rico 530.

Center Fire Pistol, Individual:
1. Oscar Yuston, Argentina 584; 2. JERRY WILDER, USA 583; 3. SAMUEL BAIOCCO, USA 580; 4. Juan Hernandez, Cuba 577; 5. Jain Ritchie, Brazil 577; 6. Jules Sobrian, Canada 575. Also, 8. DARIUS YOUNG, USA 574; 16. JIMMIE DORSEY, USA 568. (35 entries)

Center Fire Pistol, Team:
1. USA (J. WILDER, S. BAIOCCO, D. YOUNG, J. DORSEY) 2,305; 2. Canada 2,281; 3. Argentina 2,280; 4. Brazil 2,278; 5. Cuba 2,276; 6. Mexico 2,239.

(*) Under the Pan American Games rules, a country may not win more than two medals in any inndividual event. In shooting four entries are made by each nation because of the team prizes.

Soccer

Knocked out in the preliminary round at Mexico City four years earlier, the USA soccer team fared much better at San Juan, advancing to the semifinal round with a pair of triumphs over the Dominican Republic (6-0) and Puerto Rico (3-1). But that's where the success ended.

Operating without a number of key players who apparently were withheld by pressure from the North American Soccer League (the professional NASL), which had them under amateur contracts, the U.S. team lost semifinal round games to Argentina (4-0) and to Cuba (5-0). The USA was awarded fifth place in the final standings by virtue of its earlier victory over Puerto Rico.

Brazil, which had shared the gold medal with Mexico in 1975, this time took the top honors all alone by whipping Cuba, 3-0, in the final round. The bronze medal went to Argentina, which defeated Costa Rica, 2-0, in the final round after playing a tie with the Cubans.

The Brazilians actually scored two victories over Cuba, defeating the Islanders by 1-0 in the preliminary round on a goal at 68:00 by Cristavao Borges Dos Santos. In the championship game, a goal by Luiz Da Silva with nine minutes played started Brazil on its way to a 3-0 win that wrapped up the gold medal.

TEAM PERSONNEL
John Bowen, 19, Trenton, New Jersey
Robert Bozada, 20, Florissant, Missouri
Ken Clark, 20, St. Louis, Missouri
Tony Crudo, 20, Tampa, Florida
Don Ebert, 20, Florissant, Missouri
John Hayes, 18, Florissant, Missouri
Sandje Ivanchukov, 19, Tampa, Florida
Bernie James, 20, Bellevue, Washington
Curtis Leeper, 23, Ft. Lauderdale, Florida
David McWilliams, 22, Philadelphia, Pennsylvania
Joseph Morrone, 20, Storrs, Connecticut
Mark Peterson, 19, Federal Way, Washington
Roland Sikinger, 20, Houston, Texas
Demetrius Stamatis, 21, Bethlehem, Pennsylvania
Jeffrey Stock, 18, Federal Way, Washington
Steven Sullivan, 20, Florissant, Missouri
James Tietjens, 19, St. Louis, Missouri
Perry Van Der Beck, 20, Tampa, Florida

Head Coach: Walyer Chyzowych, Philadelphia, Pennsylvania
Assistant Coach: Robert Gansler, Glendale, Wisconsin
Assistant Coach: Steve Gay, Los Angeles, California

TEAM PERSONNEL

J. Bowen   R. Bozada   T. Clark

S. Ivanchukov   B. James   C. Leeper

R. Sikinger   D. Stamatis   J. Stock

W. Chyzowych

TEAM PERSONNEL

T. Crudo   D. Ebert   J. Hayes

D. McWilliams   J. Marrone   M. Peterson

S. Sullivan   J. Tietjens   P. Van Der Bech

G. Edwards   S. Gay   R. Gansler

SOCCER SUMMARIES

SOCCER STANDINGS
QUALIFYING ROUND:

Group A	W	L	T	GF	GA
United States	2	0	0	9	1
Puerto Rico	1	1	0	2	3
Dominican Republic	0	2	0	0	7
GROUP B					
Brazil	2	0	0	3	0
Cuba	0	1	1	2	3
Guatemala	0	1	1	2	4
GROUP C					
Argentina	2	0	0	3	0
Costa Rica	1	1	0	3	2
Bermuda	0	2	0	1	5

SEMIFINAL ROUND

GROUP A	W	L	T	GF	GA
Cuba	1	0	1	5	0
Argentina	1	0	1	4	0
United States	0	2	0	0	9
GROUP B					
Brazil	2	0	0	8	1
Costa Rica	1	1	0	5	3
Puerto Rico	0	2	0	0	9

Medal Games:
Gold Medal — Brazil 3, Cuba 0
Bronze Medal — Argentina 2, Costa Rica 0

USA SOCCER SCOREBOARD
Qualifying Round:
USA 6, Dominican Republic 0
USA 3, Puerto Rico 1

Semifinal Round:
Argentina 4, USA 0
Cuba 5, USA 0

Softball — Men's

Though sweeping through the round-robin unbeaten in eight games, and having beaten Canada twice in that span, the USA men's softball team found itself matched against the Canadians again, this time for the gold medal.

The USA went with its best pitcher, 38-year-old Ty Stofflet of Coplay, Pennsylvania, the best in the game, against Canada, and the fireballing pitcher deserves a better fate than what he got.

Stofflet struck out 18 batters in 13⅓ innings, but Canada's Rob Guenter was equally effective, fanning 18 batters himself. But with the gold medal on the line, Canada got a run in the bottom of the fourteenth inning to win a 1-0 game and cop top honors.

The top four teams from the eight-game round robin advanced to a final round of four, and the USA, Canada, Puerto Rico and Panama advanced. The USA beat Canada by 3-0 twice in earlier games before the superb title game.

The excellent USA pitching was the main reason why it went unbeaten through the round robin and into the final game. Stofflet and Gene Green both had no-hitters early in the tournament, but the USA bats were unusually quiet. The lack of batting punch eventually proved to be the downfall in the gold medal showdown with the adept Canadians.

Puerto Rico took the bronze medal by virtue of its 2-1 win over Panama in the final round.

TEAM PERSONNEL

Harold Batt, 40, Seattle, Washington (Catcher)
James Brackin, 30, Waldorf, Maryland (Infield)
Thomas Connor, 29, San Antonia, Texas (Infield)
Darryl Day, 32, Mt. Zion, Illinois (First Base)
John Ege, 30, Clear Lake, Iowa (Utility)
Gene Green, 31, Temple Hills, Maryland (Pitcher)
Charles Grimes, 29, Lakeland, Florida (Outfield)
Rickey Gruber, 29, Slatington, Pennsylvania (Utility)
Ted Hicks, 26, Midland, Michigan (Outfield)
Al Lewis, 34, Milford, Connecticut (Pitcher)
Bruce Miller, 30, Lansing, Michigan (Outfield)
William Pfeiffer, 32, Aurora, Illinois (Outfield)
Robert A. Quinn, 29, Aurora, Illinois (Catcher)
Robert H. Quinn, 32, Newton, New Jersey (Infield)
David Scott, 22, San Antonio, Texas (Pitcher)
Jeffrey Seip, 24, Gilbertsville, Pennsylvania (First Base)
Tyrone Stofflet, 38, Coplay, Pennsylvania (Pitcher)
Angelo Veronesi, 36, Poughkeepsie, New York (Infield)

TEAM PERSONNEL

F. Batt   J. Brackin   T. Connor

C. Grimes   R. Gruber   T. Hicks

R. A. Quinn   R. H. Quinn   D. Scott

A. Pendergast   R. Santilli   C. Smith

Head Coach: Clifford Smith, Aurora, Illinois
Assistant Coach: Rocco Santilli, Leesport, Pennsylvania
Manager: Andrew Pendergast, Bremerton, Washington

MEN'S SOFTBALL SUMMARIES

REGULAR ROUND-ROBIN RESULTS (8 Games)

	W	L	PCT.
United States	8	0	1.000
Canada	6	2	.750
Puerto Rico	6	2	.750
Panama	4	4	.500
Colombia	3	5	.375
Dutch Antilles	1	7	.142
Virgin Islands	1	7	.142
Venezuela	1	7	.142

TEAM PERSONNEL

D. Day   J. Ege   G. Green

A. Lewis   B. Miller   W. Pfeiffer

J. Seip   T. Stofflet   A. Veronesi

RESULTS OF ALL GAMES PLAYED
(Of teams in final round)

Canada (7-2): vs. Panama (2-0), vs. USA (0-3), vs. Puerto Rico (6-0), vs. Venezuela (1-0), vs. Virgin Islands (8-0), vs. Dutch Antilles (10-0), vs. Colombia (3-0), vs. USA (0-3), vs. USA (1-0)*

USA (8-1): vs. Virgin Islands (7-2), vs. Canada (3-0), vs. Dutch Antilles (14-0), vs. Colombia (4-0), vs. Panama (6-0), vs. Venezuela (1-0), vs. Puerto Rico (5-3), vs. Canada (3-0), vs. Canada (0-1)*

Puerto Rico (6-3): vs. Venezuela (1-0), vs. Colombia (2-1), vs. Canada (0-6), vs. Panama (5-0), vs. Dutch Antilles (3-0), vs. Virgin Islands (2-1), vs. USA (3-5), vs. Panama (2-1), vs. Canada (0-2)**

Panama (4-5): vs. Canada (0-2), vs. Virgin Islands (1-0), vs. Puerto Rico (0-5), vs. USA (0-6), vs. Colombia (5-1), vs. Dutch Antilles (4-1), vs. Puerto Rico (1-2) vs. Venezuela (3-1).

*Championship game
**Bronze medal game

Softball — Women's

A powerful USA women's softball team breezed to a gold medal in the first softball competition in Pan American Games history. The team, coached by Ralph Raymond, had only one loss, an early 2-1 game with tiny Belize, but was an easy winner thereafter.

Raymond's main problem was deciding which of his talented pitching staff to use each day when the USA played. In the deciding game, a 2-0 win over Puerto Rico, it was righthander Barbara Reinalda of Chino, California, who pitched a one-hitter to give the USA the gold medal.

Raymond also had the superb Kathy Arendsen, a righthander from Zeeland, Michigan, who compiled a 4-0 record, threw two no-hitters (including a perfect game), and struck out 62 batters in the four games. Arendsen struck out 17 of the 21 batters she faced in the perfect game, a 12-0 triumph over the Dominican Republis.

The USA also had top pitchers in Melannie Kyler of Mesa, Arizona (who threw a no-hitter) and Paula Noel of Phoenix, Arixona who also was a winner.

The USA finished with a 12-1 record in the double round-robin, losing only to Belize. Puerto Rico took the silver medal, and Belize copped the bronze medal with its 9-3 record overall.

TEAM PERSONNEL

Kathryn Arendsen, 20, Zeeland, Michigan (Pitcher)

Gwen Berner, 17, North Tonawanda, New York (Infield)

Susan Enquist, 21, San Clemente, California (Outfield)

Suzie Gaw, 19, Scottsdale, Arizona (Utility)

Melannie Kyler, 23, Mesa, Arizona (Pitcher)

Shirley Mapes, 21, Troy, Michigan (Infield)

Brenda Marshall, 23, Corpus Christi, Texas (Outfield)

Paula Noel, 28, Phoenix, Arizona (Pitcher)

Sylvia Ortiz, 24, Houston, Texas (Outfield)

Marilyn Rau, 28, Phoenix, Arizona (Catcher)

Barbara Reinalda, 22, Chino, California (Pitcher)

Dorothy Richardson, 17, Orlando, Florida (Utility)

Diane Schumacher, 25, Brooklyn, New York (First Base)

Linda Spagnolo, 20, East Hazelcrest, Illinois (First Base)

Kathleen Strahan, 23, Lansing, Michigan (Utility)

Paula Stufflebeam, 20, Tempe, Arizona (Outfield)

Joan Van Ness, 21, Waterford, Connecticut (Infield)

Julie Winklepleck, 22, Tucson, Arizona (Catcher)

Head Coach: Ralph Raymond, Worcester, Massachusetts
Assistant Coach: Lorene Ramsey, Pekin, Illinois
Manager: Constance Claussen, Omaha, Nebraska

TEAM PERSONNEL

K. Arendsen | G. Berner | S. Enquist

B. Marshall | P. Noel | S. Ortiz

D. Schumacher | L. Spagnolo | K. Strahan

C. Claussen | L. Ramsey | R. Raymond

WOMEN'S SOFTBALL SUMMARIES

FINAL ROUND-ROBIN STANDINGS (12-Game Set)

	W	L	PCT.
United States	11	1	.917
Belize	9	3	.750
Canada	9	3	.750
Puerto Rico	6	6	.500
El Salvador	3	9	.250
Bermuda	3	9	.250
Dominican Republic	1	11	.083

RESULTS OF ALL GAMES PLAYED:

(Of top four teams advancing to final round)

USA (12-1): vs. Canada (1-0), vs. El Salvador (10-0), vs. Dominican Republic (5-0), vs. Belize (1-2), vs. Dominican Republic (12-0), vs. Puerto Rico (1-0), vs. Bermuda (10-0), vs. Belize (2-0), vs. Bermuda (9-0), vs. El Salvador (9-0), vs. Canada (5-0), vs. Puerto Rico (1-0), vs. Puerto Rico (2-0)*

Belize (9-4): vs. Puerto Rico (1-0), vs. Bermuda (11-1), vs. Canada (0-9), vs. El Salvador (3-0), vs. USA (2-1), vs. El Salvador (3-0), vs. Canada (1-2), vs. Dominican Republis (7-0), vs. USA (0-2), vs. Puerto Rico (4-1), vs. Dominican Republic (7-0), vs. Bermuda (6-2), vs. Puerto Rico (3-6)**

TEAM PERSONNEL

S. Gaw | M. Kyler | S. Mapes

M. Rau | B. Reinalda | D. Richardson

P. Stufflebeam | J. Van Ness | J. Winklepleck

Canada (9-4): vs. USA (0-1), vs. Belize (9-10), vs. Bermuda (4-3), vs. Puerto Rico (1-0), vs. Dominican Republic (2-1), vs. Bermuda (6-0), vs. Belize (2-1), vs. Dominican Republic (7-0), vs. El Salvador (3-1), vs. USA (0-5), vs. El Salvador (3-0), vs. Puerto Rico (3-5), vs. Puerto Rico(1-5)***
***Elimination Game - final round.

Puerto Rico (8-7): vs. Belize (0-1), vs. El Salvador (4-1), vs. Dominican Republic (7-3), vs. El Salvador (9-4), vs. Canada (0-1), vs. USA (0-1), vs. Dominican Republic (4-2), vs. Belize (1-4), vs. Bermuda (3-2), vs. Bermuda (2-5), vs. Canada (5-3), vs. Canada (5-1), vs. USA (0-1), vs. Belize (6-3), vs. USA (0-2)*
*Gold Medal Game

(NOTE: 12-game round-robin determined the final four teams which played a final round for the Pan American Games championship.)

*Gold Medal Game

**Takes Bronze medal for third place.

MEDAL GAMES RESULTS:

Gold — USA 2, Puerto Rico 0
Bronze — Puerto Rico 6, Belize 3**

**Belize eliminated, takes third.

Swimming — Men

The United States men swept through their competition in record fashion at the Pan American Games, winning the gold medal in all 15 events, along with setting new Games' records in every one of them. The USA men finished 1-2 in just four of the individual events however.

The crowd favorite was easy to pick. It was Puerto Rican-born Jesus (Jesse) Vassallo, a 17-year old out of Mission Viejo, California, who set a new world record in winning the 200 meter individual medley (2:03.29), and also won the gold medal in the 400 meter individual medley in 4:21.63. Nicknamed "Cheyenne" by his mates, Vassallo also garnered a silver medal behind winner Peter Rocca in the 200 meter backstroke.

Olympian Brian Goodell of Mission Viejo and 18-year old Georgia highschooler Steve Lundquist joined Vassallo as double gold medalists in the individual events. Goodell won the 400m and 1500m freestyle races, while Lundquist, who is now a frosh at Auburn, won the 100m and 200m breaststroke events. Both added a third gold medal as members of winning USA relay teams.

The beautiful Escambron Pool facility was packed to the roof each night with cheering and appreciative swimming fans, many of them there to cheer on Vassallo and his brother, who swims for Puerto Rico. At one point, more than 2,000 Vassallo T-shirts dotted the crowd, courtesy of Jesse's uncle on the island.

There was not a single repeat individual champion from 1975 among the USA's individual winners, further testimony to the great strides that the nation's swimming program has made in the last four years.

USA coach Frank Keefe was surprised at the times, and stated that it was still "a little early in the summer" to record such fine clockings. Keefe, however, was far from displeased by the results on the victory stand each night in San Juan.

TEAM PERSONNEL
Jack Babashoff, 24, Tuscaloosa, Alabama (4 x 100m Freestyle Relay)
Craig Beardsley, 18, Harrington Park, New Jersey (200m Butterfly)
J. Clay Britt, 18, Rockville, Maryland (100m Backstroke)
Ambrose Gaines, 20, Winter Haven, Florida (200m Freestyle, 4 x 100m FS Relay, 4 x 200m FS Relay)
Brian Goodell, 20, Los Angeles, California (400m Freestyle, 1500m Freestyle, 4 x 200m FS Relay)
Robert Hackett, 19, Arlington, Massachusetts (1500m Freestyle)
Robert Jackson, 22, San Jose, California (100m Backstroke, 4 x 100m Medley Relay)
Kris Kirchner, 20, Austin, Texas (4 x 200m FS Relay)
David Larson, 20, Jesup, Georgia (200m Freestyle, 400m Freestyle, 4 x 200m FS Relay)
Steve Lundquist, 18, Jonesboro, Georgia (100m Breaststroke, 200m Breaststroke, 4 x 100m Medley Relay)

TEAM PERSONNEL

J. Babashoff   C. Beardsley   C. Britt

R. Jackson   K. Kirchner   D. Larson

G. Perry   R. Placak   D. Pursley

S. Spann   J. Vassallo   G. Winchell

R. Hannula   R. Jutkins   F. Keefe

David McCagg, 21, Fort Meyers, Florida (100m Freestyle, 100m Butterfly, 4 x 100m FS Relay, 4 x 100m Medley Relay)
John Newton, 22, Knoxville, Tennessee (100m Freestyle, 4 x 100m FS Relay)
Glynn Perry, 19, Gainsville, Florida (200m Butterfly, 400m Individual Medley)
Robert Placak, 20, Los Angeles, California (100m Butterfly, 4 x 100m Medley Relay)
Peter Rocca, 22, Berkeley, California (200m Backstroke)
John Simons, 18, Scottsdale, Arizona (200m Breaststroke)
Scott Spann, 21, Austin, Texas (200m Individual Medley)
Jesse Vassallo, 17, Mission Viejo, California (200m Backstroke, 200m Individual Medley, 400m Individual Medley)
Greg Winchell, 18, Fullerton, California (100m Breaststroke)

TEAM PERSONNEL

A. Gaines   B. Goodell   R. Hackett

S. Lundquist   D. McCagg   J. Newton

R. Quick   P. Rocca   J. Simons

R. Ballatore   R. Bussard

R. Reese

Head Coach: Frank Keefe, Drexel Hill, Pennsylvania
Assistant Coach: Ray Bussard, Knoxville, Tennessee
Assistant Coach: Ronald Ballatore, South Pasadena, California
Head Manager: Richard Hannula, Tacoma, Washington

SWIMMING SUMMARIES — MEN
100m Freestyle:
1. DAVID McCAGG, USA, 50.77 sec. (PAR); 2. Fernando Canales, Puerto Rico, 51.25; 3. JOHN NEWTON, USA, 51.45; 4. Bill Sawchuck, Canada, 52.93; 5. Ernesto Domenack, Peru, 53.26; 6. Jorge Fernandes, Brazil, 53.28.

200m Freestyle:
1. ROWDY GAINES, USA, 1:51.22 (PAR);
2. DAVID LARSON, USA, 1:52.24;
3. Djan Madruga, Brazil, 1:52.34; 4. Peter Szmidt, Canada, 1:53.57; 5. Fernando Canales, Puerto Rico, 1:53.57; 6. Bill Sawchuck, Canada, 1:53-86.

400m Freestyle:
1. BRIAN GOODELL, USA, 3:53.01 (PAR); 2. Djan Madruga, Brazil, 3:57.46; 3. Peter Szmidt, Canada, 3:58.34; 4. Robert Baylis, Canada, 3:59.21; 5. DAVID LARSON, USA, 4:00.07; 6. Diego Quiroga, Ecuador, 4:02.86.

1500m Freestyle:
1. BRIAN GOODELL, USA, 15:24.36 (PAR); 2. Djan Madruga, Brazil, 15:41.74; 3. BOBBY HACKETT, USA, 15:46.83; 4. Peter Szmidt, Canada, 15:56.91; 5. Diego Quiroga, Ecuador, 16:02.34; 6. Alejandro Lecot, Argentina, 16:04.63.

100m Butterfly:
1. ROBERT PLACAK, USA, 55.54 sec. (PAR); 2. Dan Thompson, Canada, 55.56; 3. Clay Evans, Canada, 56.63; 4. DAVID McCAGG, USA, 56.90; 5. Jorge Jaramillo, Colombia, 57.79; 6. Caio Filardi, Brazil, 57.85.

200m Butterfly:
1. CRAIG BEARDSLEY, USA, 2:00.49 (PAR); 2. George Nagy, Canada, 2:02.15; 3. Bill Sawchuck, Canada, 2:02.93; 4. GLYNN PERRY, USA, 2:03.84; 5. Filiberto Colon, Puerto Rico, 2:06.45; 6. Carlos Fontoura, Brazil, 2:06.50.

100m Breaststroke:
1. STEVE LUNDQUIST, USA, 1:03.82 (PAR); 2. GREG WINCHELL, USA, 1:04.76; 3. Graham Smith, Canada, 1:05.66; 4. Pablo Restrepo, Colombia, 1:06.00; 5. Greg Wurzbach, Canada, 1:06.64; 6. Miguel Santiesteban, Mexico, 1:06.72.

200m Breaststroke:
1. STEVE LUNDQUIST, USA, 2:21.97 (PAR); 2. JOHN SIMONS, USA, 2:22.45; 3. Pablo Restrepo, Colombia, 2:23.13; 4. Graham Smith, Canada, 2:23.26; 5. Greg Wurzbach, Canada, 2:25.07; 6. Helmuth Levy, Colombia, 2:27.02.

100m Backstroke:
1. BOB JACKSON, USA, 56.66 sec. (PAR); 2. Romulo Arantes, Jr., Brazil, 57.20; 3. Steve Pickell, Canada, 57.89; 4. CLAY BRITT, USA, 57.98; 5. Carlos Berrocal, Puerto Rico, 57.99; 6. Wade Flemons, Canada, 59.52.

200m Backstroke:
1. PETER ROCCA, USA, 2:00.98 (PAR); 2. JESSE VASSALLO, USA, 2:02.07; 3. Djan Madruga, Brazil, 2:04.74; 4. Romulo Arantes, Jr., Brazil, 2:04.99; 5. Conrado Porta, Argentina, 2:05.33; 6. Wade Flemons, Canada, 2:07.90.

200m Individual Medley:
1. JESSE VASSALLO, USA, 2:03.29 (PAR & World Record); 2. Graham Smith, Canada, 2:05.86; 3. SCOTT SPANN, USA, 2:06.29; 4. Bill Sawchuck, Canada, 2:07.51; 5. Helmuth Levy, Colombia, 2:08.73; 6. Jorge Varela, Mexico, 2:09.63.

Diving

TEAM PERSONNEL

P. Boggs   D. Christensen   G. Louganis

J. Thorburn   B. Weinstein

S. McFarland   B. Robbins

The USA, which won only two of the four gold medals in the 1975 Pan American Games at Mexico City, swept all four at San Juan in convincing fashion.

400m Individual Medley:
1. JESSE VASSALLO, USA, 4:21.63 (PAR); 2. Bill Sawchuck, Canada, 4:30.21; 3. Alex Bauman, Canada, 4:32.42; 4. GLYNN PERRY, USA, 4:32.53; 5. Jorge Varela, Mexico, 4:39.11; 6. Andrey Aguilar, Costa Rica, 4:39.44.

4 x 100m Freestyle Relay:
1. USA (ROWDY GAINES, JACK BABASHOFF, JOHN NEWTON, DAVID McCAGG) 3:23.71 (PAR)**; 2. Canada, 3:29.64; 3. Brazil, 3:30.86; 4. Puerto Rico, 3:32.75; 5. Mexico, 3:37.34; 6. Venezuela, 3:42.33.

4 x 100m Medley Relay:
1. USA (BOB JACKSON, STEVE LUNDQUIST, ROBERT PLACAK, DAVID McCAGG) 3:47.20 (PAR)**; 2. Canada, 3:50.02; 3. Puerto Rico, 3:54.53; 4. Brazil, 3:54.91; 5. Mexico, 3:59.17; 6. Argentina, 4:07.81.

4 x 200m Freestyle Relay:
1. USA (BRIAN GOODELL, DAVID LARSON, KRIS KIRCHNER, ROWDY GAINES) 7:31.28 (PAR)**; 2. Brazil, 7:38.92; 3. Canada, 7:39.27; 4. Puerto Rico, 7:38.92; 5. Mexico, 7:55.63; 6. Venezuela, 8:07.25.

(PAR) = Pan American Record
**Repeated as champion.

19-year-old Greg Louganis of El Cajon, California, a University of Miami sophomore, was tremendously impressive in winning both gold medals in the men's competition. The USA youngster unseated defending champion Carlos Giron of Mexico in the platform competition, then edged teammate Phil Boggs, the 1976 Olympic gold medalist, in the springboard event. Neither of Louganis' gold medals was severely challenged by the rest of the field.

Boggs, who was a United States Air Force Lieutenant during the Olympic Games in 1976, took the bronze medal in the platform, finishing well back of Louganis and Giron.

In the women's events, the USA scored a pair of 1-2 finishes, with 19-year-old Denise Christensen of Tucson, Arizona, taking the springboard gold medal. She's a student at the University of Texas at Austin. Miss Christensen nosed out the veteran Janet Ely Thorburn of Dallas, Texas, for the top honors. Mrs. Thorburn won the silver medal in the platform in 1975 at Mexico City.

In the women's platform competition, it was the talented 21-year old Barbara Weinstein of Cincinatti, Ohio, who took the gold medal, winning by a narrow margin over Mrs. Thorburn, who copped her second silver medal of the Pan American Games. Miss Weinstein is a top diver for the University of Michigan.

TEAM PERSONNEL
Philip Boggs, 29, Miami, Florida
Denise Christensen, 19, Tucson, Arizona
Gregory Louganis, 19, El Cajon, California
Janet Ely Thorburn, 25, Dallas, Texas
Barbara Weinstein, 21, Cincinnati, Ohio

Head Manager: Bryan Robbins, Dallas, Texas
Head Coach: Stephen McFarland, Miami, Florida

DIVING SUMMARIES
MEN
Platform:
1. GREG LOUGANIS, USA, 592.71; 2. Carlos Giron, Mexico, 552.60; 3. PHIL BOGGS, USA, 551.58; 4. Ken Armstrong, Canada, 505.65; 5. Raul Rueda, Mexico, 486.69; 6. Adolfo Jimenez, Dominican Republic, 453.45.

Springboard:
1. GREG LOUGANIS, USA, 627.84; 2. PHIL BOGGS, USA, 592.80; 3. Carlos Giron, Mexico, 580.35; 4. Carlos Ruiz, Cuba, 568.23; 5. Alex Becerril, Mexico, 507.99; 6. Donald Cranham, Canada, 504.30.

WOMEN
Platform:
1. BARBARA WEINSTEIN, USA, 402.21; 2. JANET ELY THORBURN, USA, 400.86; 3. Linda Cuthbert, Canada, 386.46; 4. Elizabeth Mackay, Canada, 365.55; 5. Regina Lowry, Cuba, 346.80.

Springboard:
1. DENISE CHRISTENSEN, USA, 477.96; 2. JANET ELY THORBURN, USA, 473.61; 3. Janet Nutter, Canada, 412.17; 4. Linda Cuthbert, Canada, 401.31; 5. Milargos Gonzalez, Cuba, 393.69.

Swimming — Women

The USA women were again totally dominant in the swimming competition at the Pan American Games, duplicating their 1975 feat of winning 13 of the 14 individual and relay races. In addition, USA women finished 1-2 in eight of the 12 individual races and set Pan American records in eleven individual races and both of the relays.

The individual star was 15-year old Cynthia "Sippy" Woodhead, a Riverside, California high schooler who was clearly the outstanding athlete in terms of medals, at the Games, winning five gold medals. The California teenager won the 100-meter, 200-meter, and 400-meter freestyle races, then added gold medals by anchoring the winning USA relay teams.

Woodhead and another youngster, 14-year old Mary T. Meagher of Louisville, Kentucky, also established world records. Woodhead set hers by winning the 200 meter freestyle in 1:58.43, and Meagher set hers by winning the 200 meter butterfly in a nifty clocking of 2:09.77.

16-year old Tracy Caulkins of Nashville, Tennessee, was another USA individual standout, winning gold medals in the 200 meter individual medley, 400 meter individual medley, and for her leg on the two victorious USA relay teams, giving her four golds in all.

19-year old Stanford University star Linda Jezek also was a big winner, capturing gold medals in the 100 meter and 200 meter backstroke events, as well as winning a gold medal on the USA 4 x 100m medley relay quartet.

The only race that a USA swimmer lost was the 200 meter breaststroke, where Canada's Anne Gagnon and Joanne Bedard went 1-2, with Patty Spees of the USA taking home the bronze medal for third place.

Not one of the winning USA swimmers was more than 19-years old (Jezek) and most were under 17 years. The amazing showing by perhaps the best women's swimming team ever put together by the United States was not unforseen, but the times were very good for the time of the year.

TEAM PERSONNEL

Lisa Buese, 16, Louisville, Kentucky
(100m Butterfly)
Kimberly Carlisle, 18, Cincinnati, Ohio
(100m Backstroke)
Tracy Caulkins, 16, Nashville, Tennessee
(400m Freestyle, 100m Breaststroke,
200m Individual Medley, 400m Individual
Medley, 4 x 100m Medley Relay)
Andrea Cross, 16, Nashville, Tennessee
(4 x 100m Freestyle Relay)
Stephanie Elkins, 15, Gainesville, Florida
(4 x 100m Freestyle Relay)
Jennifer Hooker, 18, Mission Viejo,
California (800m Freestyle)
Linda Jezek, 19, Stanford, California
(100m Backstroke, 200m Backstroke,
4 x 100m Medley Relay)
Libby Kinkead, 14, Wayne, Pennsylvania
(200m Backstroke)
Renee Laravie, 20, Gainesville, Florida
(200m Breaststroke)

TEAM PERSONNEL

L. Buese   K. Carlisle   T. Caulkins

L. Jezek   L. Kinkead   R. Laravie

T. Paumier   P. Spees   J. Sterkel

C. Graham   M. Plummer

Kimberly Linehan, 14, Sarasota, Florida
(800m Freestyle, 200m Freestyle)
Mary T. Meagher, 14, Louisville, Kentucky
(200m Butterfly)
Karinne Miller, 17, Hendersonville, Texas
(200m Butterfly)
Tami Paumier, 16, Columbia, Maryland
(100m Breaststroke)
Patricia Spees, 18, Oakland, California
(200m Breaststroke)
Jill Sterkel, 18, Hacienda Heights, California
(100m Butterfly, 100m Freestyle, 4 x 100m
FS Relay, 4 x 100m Medley Relay)
Anne Tweedy, 16, Santa Barbara, California
(200m Individual Medley, 400m Individual
Medley)
Cynthia Woodhead, 15, Riverside, California
(100m Freestyle, 200m Freestyle, 400m
Freestyle, 4 x 100m FS Relay, 4 x 100m
Medley Relay)

Head Manager: Mona Plummer, Phoenix,
Arizona
Assistant Manager: Ray Jutkins, Los
Angeles, California
Assistant Coach: Colleen Graham, Tarzana,
California
Assistant Coach: Randolph Reese, Gaines-
ville, Florida
Assistant Coach: Dennis Pursley, Louisville,
Kentucky

TEAM PERSONNEL

A. Cross   S. Elkins   J. Hooker

K. Linehan   M. Meagher   K. Miller

A. Tweedy   C. Woodhead

SWIMMING SUMMARIES — WOMEN

100m Freestyle:
1. SIPPY WOODHEAD, USA, 56.22 sec.
(PAR); 2. JILL STERKEL, USA, 56.24;
3. Gail Amundrud, Canada, 57.79; 4. Anne
Jardin, Canada, 58.06; 5. Shelley Cramer,
Virgin Islands, 59.68; 6. Maria Paris, Costa
Rica, 59.82.

200m Freestyle:
1. SIPPY WOODHEAD, USA, 1:58.43
(PAR & WORLD RECORD); 2. KIM
LINEHAN, USA, 2:01.92; 3. Gail
Amundrud, Canada, 2:03.38; 4. Anne
Jardin, Canada, 2:04.37; 5. Shelley Cramer,
Virgin Islands, 2:07.38; 6. Maria Guimaraes,
Brazil, 2:10.49.

400m Freestyle:
1. SIPPY WOODHEAD, USA, 4:10.56
(PAR); 2. TRACY CAULKINS, USA,
4:16.13; 3. Wendy Quirk, Canada, 4:17.34;
4. Anne Jardin, Canada, 4:25.45; 5. Andrea
Neumayer, Argentina, 4:29.39; 6. Maria
Perez, Colombia, 4:36.86.

800m Freestyle:
1. KIM LINEHAN, USA, 8:39.82 (PAR);
2. JENNIFER HOOKER, USA, 8:50.71;
3. Barb Shockey, Canada, 8:54.82; 4. Leslie
Brafield, Canada, 9:10.14; 5. Maria Perez,
Colombia, 9:13.59; 6. Andrea Neumayer,
Argentina, 9:13.93.

100m Butterfly:
1. JILL STERKEL, USA, 1:00.53 (PAR);
2. LISA BUESE, USA, 1:00.59; 3. Nancy
Garapick, Canada, 1:02.96; 4. Shelley
Cramer, Virgin Islands, 1:03.51; 5. Susan
Sloan, Canada, 1:03.52; 6. Maria Paris,
Costa Rica, 1:03.58.

200m Butterfly:
1. MARY MEAGHER, USA, 2:09.77 (PAR & WORLD RECORD); 2. Karinne Miller, USA, 2:15.05; 3. Nancy Garapick, Canada, 2:16.40; 4. Kelly Albright, Canada, 2:16.77; 5. Shelley Cramer, Virgin Islands, 2:17.88; 6. Rosana Juncos, Argentina, 2:24.51.

100m Breaststroke:
1. TAMI PAUMIER, USA, 1:12.20 (PAR); 2. TRACY CAULKINS, USA, 1:12.52; 3. Anne Gagnon, Canada, 1:14.38; 4. Robin Corsiglia, Canada, 1:14.64; 5. Elke Holtz, Mexico, 1:15.45; 6. Maria Matta, Brazil, 1:17.76.

200m Breaststroke:
1. Anne Gagnon, Canada, 2:35.75 (PAR); 2. Joanne Bedard, Canada, 2:40.22; 3. PATTY SPEES, USA, 2:40.79; 4. RENEE LARAVIE, USA, 2:41.84; 5. Alicia Boscatto, Argentina, 2:42.32; 6. Elko Holtz, Mexico, 2:44.50.

100m Backstroke:
1. LINDA JEZEK, USA, 1:03.33 (PAR); 2. Cheryl Gibson, Canada, 1:05.17; 3. Teresa Rivera, Mexico, 1:06.86; 4. Melinda Copp, Canada, 1:07.81; 5. Hilda Huerta, Mexico, 1:09.45; 6. Rosamaria Prado, Brazil, 1:09.57.

200m Backstroke:
1. LINDA JEZEK, USA, 2:16.07 (PAR); 2. Cheryl Gibson, Canada, 2:17.58; 3. LIBBY KINKEAD, USA, 2:20.19; 4. Suzanne Kwasny, Canada, 2:23.79; 5 5. Teresa Rivera, Mexico, 2:24.42; 6. Rosamaria Prado, Brazil, 2:28.03.

200m Individual Medley:
1. TRACY CAULKINS, USA, 2:16.11 (PAR); 2. Nancy Garapick, Canada, 2:19.36; 3. ANNE TWEEDY, USA, 2:20.33; 4. Joann Baker, Canada, 2:20.71; 5. Elke Holtz, Mexico, 2:26.13; 6. Maria Paris, Costa Rica, 2:26.54.

400m Individual Medley:
1. TRACY CAULKINS, USA, 4:46.05 (PAR); 2. ANNE TWEEDY, USA, 4:47.19; 3. Nancy Garapick, Canada, 4:53.37; 4. Cheryl Gibson, Canada, 4:59.54; 5. Elke Holtz, Mexico, 5:08.78; 6. Rosamaria Prado, Brazil, 5:10.81.

4 x 100m Medley Relay:
1. USA (LINDA JEZEK, TRACY CAULKINS, JILL STERKEL, SIPPY WOODHEAD) 4:13.24 (PAR)**; 2. Canada, 4:20.16; 3. Mexico, 4:30.59; 5. Argentina, 4:34.31; 5. Brazil, 4:35.27; 6. Puerto Rico, 4:43.86.

4 x 100m Freestyle Relay:
1. USA (STEPHANIE ELKINS, TRACY CAULKINS, JILL STERKEL, SIPPY WOODHEAD) 3:45.82 (PAR)**; 2. Canada, 3:50.18; 3. Mexico, 4:02.05; 4. Puerto Rico, 4:07.55; 5. Brazil, 4:08.97; 6. Argentina, 4:10.99.

(PAR) = Pan American Record
**Repeated as champion.

Synchronized Swimming

Canada, which showed that it was a force to be reckoned with in the 1975 Pan American Games, proved that it has made the strides necessary to win by copping almost all the top honors at San Juan.

Helen Vanderburg of Canada was the outstanding performer in the synchronized swimming competition, taking the gold medal in the solo, then teaming with Kelly Kryczka to win the duet competition.

The USA's Michele Beaulieu, Millbrae, California, took the silver medal behind Miss Vanderburg in the solo field. The USA combination of Michele Barone, San Jose, California, and Linda Shelley of Santa Clara, California, took the silver medal in the duet behind the triumphant Canadians.

The USA did repeat its gold medal performance of 1975 by winning the team competition over the three days at the Escambron aquatic facility near the oceanfront in San Juan.

It was a disquieting note for the United States, which up to 1978 had dominated the sport since its inception.

TEAM PERSONNEL
Michele Barone, 21, San Jose, California
Michele Beaulieu, 20, Millbrae, California
Gerri Brandly, 21, Santa Clara, California
Karen Callaghan, 18, Danville, California
Suzanne Cameron, 19, Danville, California
Tara Cameron, 20, San Mateo, California
Laura Florio Luzzi, 22, Hamden, Connecticut
Tracie Ruiz, 16, Bothell, Washington
Linda Shelley, 22, Santa Clara, California
Pamela Tryon, 21, Millbrae, California
Marie White, 20, San Jose, California

Head Coach: Gail Johnson, Santa Clara, California
Assistant Coach: Gail Emery, Lafayette, California
Manager: Janet Paulus, Trinidad, California

SYNCHRONIZED SWIMMING SUMMARIES
Singles:
1. Helen Vanderburg, Canada, 197.300; 2. MICHELE BEAULIEU, USA, 196.990; 3. Lourd de La Guardia, Cuba, 172.880; 4. Mireya Andrade, Mexico, 172.270; 5. Martha Aristazabal, Colombia, 162.360; 6. Victoria Lasala, Puerto Rico, 150.590.

Duet:
1. Canada (Helen Vanderburg & Kelly Kryczka) 196.370; 2. USA (MICHELE BARONE & LINDA SHELLEY) 194.860; 3. Mexico (Mireya Andrade and Gabriella Terroba) 179.230; 4. Cuba (Silvia Espinosa and Lourd de La Guardia) 174.150; 5. Colombia (Martha Aristazabal and Dinor Arias) 159.560; 6. Puerto Rico (Michele Hernandez Figueroa and Cody Robin) 154.180.

TEAM PERSONNEL

M. Barone   M. Beaulieu   G. Brandly

K. Callaghan   S. Cameron   T. Cameron

L. Florio-Luzzi   T. Ruiz   L. Shelley

P. Tryon   M. White

G. Emery   G. Johnson   J. Paulus

Team:
1. USA (MICHELE BARONE, LINDA SHELLEY, MICHELE BEAULIEU, GERRY BRANDLEY, SUZANNE CAMERON, LAURA LUZZI, TRACIE RUIZ, PAM TRYON) 196.57; 2. Canada, 193.52; 3. Mexico, 174.86; 4. Cuba, 173.59; 5. Colombia, 157.85; 6. Puerto Rico, 154.97.

Volleyball, Men's and Women's

The results of the men's and women's volleyball tournaments were disquieting. The USA women were rated all-even with Cuba going into the tournament. The Pre-Pan American tournament exhibition series for the USA women's team was perhaps the most successful for any USA team in any sport.

In the preliminary round of round-robin play the USA ladies won three straight matches without the loss of a single game. During the three-day layoff between the preliminary and final rounds, captain Patty Dowdell suffered a recurrence of a chronic back injury which has plagued her during her entire international career.

The loss of Miss Dowdell was devastating. In fact, the USA fell before Peru, the team they had knocked over in three straight games earlier. They also lost to Brazil and the defending champions from Cuba in the grand finale.

Against Cuba the only solace for the USA women's team was the winning of the first game, before dropping three straight. Thus, the up-and-at-'em USA team was relegated to fourth place, behind, in order, Cuba, Peru and Brazil.

The men's team, beefed up with the addition of a number of college players immediately before the Pan American tournament, may have been victimized by a tough "draw." The first two games were played against Cuba and Brazil.

Coming back from those three straight losses, the USA clipped off three straight to finish 4-3 and in fourth place among the seven-team field.

TEAM PERSONNEL — MEN'S

Joseph Battalia, 23, Arcadia, California
Douglas Beal, 32, Dayton, Ohio
Aldis Berzins, 22, Kennett Square, Pennsylvania
Richard Duwelius, 24, Dayton, Ohio
Tim Hovland, 20, Los Angeles, California
Michael McLean, 27, Arcadia, California
David Olbright, 26, Riverside, California
Pat Powers, 21, Los Angeles, California
Steve Salmons, 21, Los Angeles, California
Chris Smith, 22, Los Angeles, California
Paul Sunderland, 27, Malibu, California
Marc Waldie, 23, Wichita, Kansas

Head Coach: James Coleman, Dayton, Ohio
Assistant Coach: Kerry Klostermann, Dayton, Ohio
Manager: Gary Moy, Dayton, Ohio

OFFICIAL SUMMARIES — MEN'S
Final Standings:
1. Cuba 7-0; 2. Brazil 5-2; 3. Canada 5-2; 4. USA 4-3; 5. Mexico 4-3; 6. Puerto Rico 2-5; 7. Venezuela 0-7.

Scores of Round Robin:
Cuba vs. USA 15-13, 15-10, 16-14; vs. Puerto Rico 15-5, 15-6, 11-15, 17-15; vs. Canada 15-9, 15-4, 15-5; vs. Venezuela 15-1, 15-4, 15-2; vs. Mexico 15-13, 15-9, 15-13; vs. Brazil 15-4, 11-15, 13-15, 15-11, 15-11; vs. Dominican Republic 15-1, 15-7, 15-10.
USA: vs. Cuba 13-15, 10-15, 14-16; vs.

TEAM PERSONNEL

J. Battalia

D. Beal

A. Berzins

R. Duwelius

T. Hovland

M. McLean

D. Olbright

P. Powers

S. Salmons

C. Smith

P. Sunderland

M. Waldie

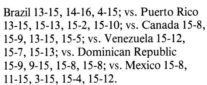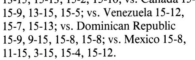
J. Coleman

K. Klostermann

G. Moy

Brazil 13-15, 14-16, 4-15; vs. Puerto Rico 13-15, 15-13, 15-2, 15-10; vs. Canada 15-8, 15-9, 13-15, 15-5; vs. Venezuela 15-12, 15-7, 15-13; vs. Dominican Republic 15-9, 9-15, 15-8, 15-8; vs. Mexico 15-8, 11-15, 3-15, 15-4, 15-12.

TEAM PERSONNEL — WOMEN'S
Janet Baier, 24, Washington, Missouri
Carolyn Marie Becker, 20, Norwalk, California
Laurel Brassey, 25, San Diego, California
Rita Crockett, 21, Houston, Texas
Patty Dowdell, 25, Houston, Texas
Laurie Flachmeier, 22, Garland, Texas
Debbie Green, 21, Westminster, California
Flora Hyman, 24, Inglewood, California
Debra Landreth, 22, El Segundo, California
Diane McCormick, 28, Charleroi, Pennsylvania
Terry Place, 21, Redondo Beach, California
Susan Woodstra, 22, Sacramento, California

TEAM PERSONNEL

J. Baier

C. Becker

L. Brassey

R. Crockett

P. Dowdell

L. Flachmeier

D. Green

F. Hyman

D. Landreth

D. McCormick

T. Place

S. Woodstra

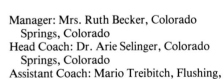
R. Becker

A. Selinger

M. Trebitch

Manager: Mrs. Ruth Becker, Colorado Springs, Colorado
Head Coach: Dr. Arie Selinger, Colorado Springs, Colorado
Assistant Coach: Mario Treibitch, Flushing, New York

OFFICIAL SUMMARIES — WOMEN'S
Final Round Placing: 1. Cuba (3-0); 2. Peru (2-1); 3. Brazil (1-2); 4. USA (0-3).

Final Round Scores:
Cuba vs. Brazil 16-14, 15-4, 15-7; vs. Peru 15-12, 15-12, 15-5; vs. USA 15-10; 7-15, 15-8, 15-12.
Brazil vs. USA 15-8, 7-15, 15-11, 7-15, 15-11.

Preliminary Round:
USA vs. Peru 15-8, 15-12, 15-13; vs. Puerto Rico 15-2, 15-2, 15-3; vs. Canada 15-6, 15-3, 15-4. USA had a 3-0 record in advancing to the final round of four teams.

Weightlifting

For the second straight time the weight-lifting competition was essentially a dual meet between Cuba and the USA. There are three medals in each of the two lifts and also for the total lift "poundage." Thus with ten weight classes, there are 90 medals available in the competition.

Recapitulation: The Cubans won eight out of the ten classes, medaled in each class, and produced a grand total of 24 gold, three silver, and one bronze. The USA swept gold medals in the two top weight classes thus accounting for a total of six gold, eleven silver and six bronze.

But the final score read Cuba 28 medals, USA 23.

Tom Stock, 27, a 302-pound Anheuser Busch salesman, dominated the super heavyweight class. Not only did Stock sweep all three gold medals, but he also established a new Pan American Games total lift record of 847 pounds, 11 pounds above the winning total lift of Cuba's Fernandez in 1975.

The veteran Mark Cameron gained some measure of revenge in the heavyweight class (up to 242 pounds). He was silver medalist in '75. Cameron, a recent recipient of a master's degree in biomechanics at the University of Maryland, had a great day and established another Pan American total lift mark with his grand total of 825 pounds (22 pounds higher than the '75 winner, Canada's Prior).

Thus, Stock and Cameron accounted for all six USA gold medals.

Among those who retained Pan American titles were Francisco Casamayor, Cuba (52 kilograms) and Robert Urrutia, Cuba (75 kg, he had won at 67.5 kg in '75).

TEAM PERSONNEL

Mark Cameron, 26, North Bergen, New Jersey (110 kg)
Guy Carlton, 25, LaPlace, Illinois (100 kg)
James Curry, Jr., 26, Berkeley, California (90 kg)
Robert Giordano, 28, Belleville, New Jersey (100 kg)
Thomas Hirtz, 32, San Francisco, California (82.5 kg)
David Russell Jones, 31, Eastman, Georgia (67.5 kg)
Lou Mucardo, 22, Woodbridge, New Jersey (90 kg)
Charles Edward Nootens, 38, Chicago, Illinois (110 kg)
Paul Salisbury, 31, Altamont, New York (90 kg)
Philip E. Sanderson, 32, Billings, Montana (60 kg)
Kurt Setterberg, 26, Masury, Ohio (100 kg)
Thomas D. Stock, 27, Belleville, Illinois (Over 110 kg)

Manager: Richard C. Smith, York, Pennsylvania
Coach: James Schmitz, San Francisco, California

TEAM PERSONNEL

M. Cameron G. Carlton J. Curry

T. Hirtz D. Jones L. Murcado

C. Nootens P. Sanderson K. Setterberg

T. Stock J. Schmitz R. Smith

OFFICIAL SUMMARIES

Flyweight (52 kg, 114 lbs.):

Total:
1. Francisco Casamayor, Cuba 233.5 kg (514 lbs.) (PAR); 2. Jose Diaz, Panama 212.5 kg; 3. Alexander Vasquez, Venezuela 205.0 kg. (No USA entry.)

Snatch:
1. Casamayor 103.5 kg (228 lbs.) (PAR); 2. Vazquez 95.0 kg; 3. Jose Diaz, Panama 90 kg.

Clean & Jerk:
1. Casamayor 130 kg (286 lbs.) (PAR); 2. Jose Diaz, Panama 122.5 kg; 3. Rafael Ortega, Dominican Republic 115.0 kg.

BANTAMWEIGHT (56 kg, 123 lbs.)
Total:
1. Daniel Nunez, Cuba 262.5 kg (578 lbs.) (PAR); 2. Laza De La Cruz, Dominican Republic 215.0 kg; 3. Francisco Benitez, Mexico 215.0 kg. (No USA entry.)

Snatch:
1. Nunez 117.5 kg (259 lbs.); 2. Cruz 95.0 kg; 3. Benitez 95.0 kg.

Clean & Jerk:
1. Nunez 145.0 kg (319 lbs.) (PAR); 2. Alberto Ruiz, Puerto Rico 122.5 kg; 3. Cruz 120 kg.

FEATHERWEIGHT (60 kg, 132 lbs.)
Total:
1. Victor Perez, Cuba 257.5 kg (567 lbs.) (PAR); 2. PHILIP SANDERSON, USA 250.0 kg (550 lbs.); 3. Angel Feliz Garcia, Dominican Republic 237.5 kg.

Snatch:
1. Perez 112.5 kg (248 lbs.) (PAR); 2. SANDERSON 107.5 kg, 237 lbs.); 3. Michelle Mercier, Canada 105.0 kg.

Clean & Jerk:
1. Perez 145.0 kg (319 lbs.) (PAR); 2. SANDERSON 142.5 kg (314 lbs.); 3. Garcia 135.0 kg.

LIGHTWEIGHT (67.5 kg, 149 lbs.)
Total:
1. Mario Ricardo, Cuba 300.0 kg (660 lbs.); 2. DAVID JONES, USA 267.5 kg (589 lbs.); 3. Rafael Falcon, Venezuela 260 kg.

Snatch:
1. Ricardo 135.0 kg (297 lbs.) (PAR); 2. Jacques Giasson, Canada 122.5 kg.; 3. JONES, USA 120 kg (264 lbs.).

Clean & Jerk:
1. Ricardo 165 kg. (363 lbs.); 2. JONES, USA 145 kg (319 lbs.); 3. Gary Bratty, Canada 142.5 kg.

MIDDLEWEIGHT (75 kg, 165 lbs.)
Total:
1. Roberto Urrutia, Cuba 340.0 kg (748 lbs.) (PAR); 2. Eric Rogers, Canada 277.5 kg; 3. Rogelio Weatherbee, Mexico 275.0 kg. (USA had no entry.)

Snatch:
1. Urrutia 150.0 kg (330 lbs.) (PAR); 2. Weatherbee, 120 kg; 3. Rogers 117.5 kg.

Clean & Jerk:
1. Urrutia 190 kg. (418 lbs.) (PAR); 2. Rogers 160 kg; 3. Weatherbee 155.0 kg.

LIGHT HEAVYWEIGHT (90 kg, 198 lbs.)
Total:
1. Daniel Zayas, Cuba 327.5 kg (715 lbs.); 2. Terry Hadlow, Canada 325.0 kg; 3. Nelson Carvalho, Brazil 280 kg.

Snatch:
1. Hadlow 145.0 kg (319 lbs.); 2. Zayas, Cuba 142.5 kg; 3. JAMES CURRY, USA 135.0 kg (297 lbs.).

Clean & Jerk:
1. Zayas, 185 kg (407 lbs.); 2. Larry Burke, Canada 182.0 kg; 3. Hadlow 180 kg.

MIDDLE HEAVYWEIGHT (82.5 kg, 181 181 lbs.)
Total:
1. Julio Echenique, Cuba 322.5 kg (710 lbs.) (PAR); 2. TOM HIRTZ, USA 310.0 kg (682 lbs.); 3. Jose Sequerra, Venezuela 282.5 kg.

Snatch:
1. Echenique, 147.5 kg (324 lbs.); 2. HIRTZ 147.5 kg (324 lbs.); 3. Jorge Cordero, Dominican Republic 127.5 kg.

Clean & Jerk:
1. Echenique 175.0 kg (385 lbs.) (PAR); 2. HIRTZ 162.5 kg (358 lbs.); 3. Sequerra 282.5 kg.

FIRST HEAVYWEIGHT (100 kg, 220 lbs.)
Total:
1. Alberto Blanco, Cuba 362.5 kg (798 lbs.) (PAR); 2. GUY CARLTON, USA 335 kg (737 lbs.); 3. Jose Guzman, Dominican Republic 277.5 kg.

Snatch:
1. Blanco 160 kg (352 lbs.) (PAR); 2. KURT SETTERBERG, USA 152.5 kg (336 lbs.); 3. CARLTON, USA 147.5 kg (323 lbs.).
NOTE: Mr. Setterberg suffered an arm injury and had to withdraw from the competition during the clean and jerk.

Clean & Jerk:
1. Blanco 197.5 kg (435 lbs.) (PAR); 2. CARLTON, USA 187.5 kg (413 lbs.); 3. Jacques Olger, Chile 155.0 kg.

HEAVYWEIGHT (110 kg, 242 lbs.)
Total:
1. MARK CAMERON, USA 375 kg (825 lbs.) (PAR); 2. Gabriel Gonzlez, Cuba 367.5 kg; 3. CHARLES NOOTENS, USA 342.5 kg (754 lbs.).

Snatch:
1. CAMERON 162.5 kg (358 lbs.) (PAR); 2. Gonzalez 160.0 kg; 3. NOOTENS 155 kg.

Clean & Jerk:
1. CAMERON 212.5 kg (478 lbs.) (PAR); 2. Gonzalez 207.5 kg; 3. NOOTENS 187.5 kg (413 lbs.).

SUPER HEAVYWEIGHT (Over 110 kg, 242 lbs.)
Total:
1. TOM STOCK, USA 385.0 kg (847 lbs.) (PAR); 2. Mark Cardinal, Canada 380.0 kg; 3. Jorge Gadala, El Salvador 300.0 kg.

Snatch:
1. STOCK, USA 170.0 kg (374 lbs.); 2. Cardinal 167.5 kg; 3. Adolfo Ortega, Mexico 130.0 kg.

Clean & Jerk:
1. STOCK 215.0 kg (473 lbs.); 2. Cardinal 212.5 kg; 3. Francisco Mercier, Cuba 210.0 kg.

Tennis

The USA settled for half a loaf rather than the whole loaf in the tennis tournaments at the Pan-American Games. The team was recruited from college players and won four gold and two silver medals.

At the outset there was unnecessary confusion while the tournament committee argued over how many entries each nation could have in each of the five divisions.

The USA did win both singles tournaments. In fact, the women's singles was an all-USA final with Susie Hagey, Stanford '79, upsetting the No. 1 seededplayer, Trey Lewis, University of Southern California '82 in three sets.

Mel Purcell, University of Tennessee '80, was carried to three sets in the semi-final before defeating Ecuador's Andres Gomez and also had to battle three sets to win the gold medal from Chile's Ricardo Acuna.

Purcell paired with his Tennessee teammate, Andy Kohlberg for a straight set triumph over the Chilean combination of Acuna and Hector Perez. Miss Hagey and her partner Ann Henriksson had smooth sailing to the doubles diadem, winning every match with consummate ease.

Each of the six members of the team won at least one medal and the double gold winners were Miss Hagey and Purcell.

TEAM PERSONNEL
Fritz Buehning, 19, Short Hills, New Jersey (Singles, mixed doubles)
Susie Hagey, 21, La Jolla, California (Singles, women's doubles)
Ann Henriksson, 19, Mahtomedi, Minnesota (Women's doubles, singles, mixed doubles)
Andy Kohlberg, 19, Larchmont, New York (Singles, men's doubles)
Trey Lewis, 19, San Pedro, California (Singles)
Mel Purcell, 19, Murray, Kentucky (Singles, men's doubles)

Manager: Gale Godwin, U.C.L.A.
Coach: William Glaves, Vanderbilt University

OFFICIAL SUMMARIES
Men's Singles:
Semi-final Round: Ricardo Acuna, Chile defeated FRITZ BUEHNING, USA 6-1, 2-6, 6-4; MEL PURCELL, USA defeated Andres Gomez, Ecuador 6-7, 6-2, 7-5.
First Place Match: PURCELL defeated Acuna 6-1, 2-6, 6-4.
Third Place Match: Gomez defeated BUEHNING 6-3, 7-6.
(20 entries)

Women's Singles:
Semi-final Round: TREY LEWIS, USA defeated Marlin Noriega, Venezuela 6-2, 3-6, 6-2; SUSIE HAGEY, USA defeated Maria Llamas, Mexico 6-4, 6-7, 6-2.
First Place Match: HAGEY defeated LEWIS 3-6, 6-0, 6-2.
Third Place Match: Llamas defeated Noriega 6-2, 6-1.
(14 entries)

TEAM PERSONNEL

F. Buehning

S. Hagey

A. Henricksson

A. Kohlberg

T. Lewis

M. Purcell

G. Godwin

Men's Doubles:
Semi-final Round: KOHLBERG-PURCELL, USA defeated Diaz-Fernandez, Puerto Rico 7-6, 6-4; Acuna-Perez, Chile defeated Ordaz-Haro, Mexico 6-3, 7-6.
First Place Match: KOHLBERG-PURCELL defeated Acuna-Perez 6-3, 6-2.
Third Place Match: Diaz-Fernandez defeated Ordaz-Haro 7-6, 4-6, 7-5.
(14 doubles teams)

Women's Doubles:
Semi-final Round: HENRICKSSON-HAGEY, USA defeated Gonzalez-Fernandez 6-1, 6-2; Marois-Pelletier, Canada defeated Noreiga-Boveda, Venezuela 6-4, 5-7, 6-3.
First Place Match: HENRICKSSON-HAGEY defeated Marois-Pelletier 6-0, 6-2.
Third Place Match: Gonzalez-Fernandez, Puerto Rico defeated Noreiga-Boveda, Venezuela 6-0, 6-4.
(10 doubles teams)

Mixed Doubles:
Semi-final Round: HENRICKSSON-BUEHNING, USA defeated Vallejo-Ordaz, Mexico 6-2, 6-1; Noriega-Boveda, Venezuela defeated Barlow-Brabenec, Canada 7-5, 4-6, 7-5.
First Place Match: Noriega-Boveda defeated HENRICKSSON-BUEHNING 6-4, 4-6, 6-3.
Third Place Match: Vallejo-Ordaz defeated Barlow-Brabenec 7-5, 6-4.
(11 doubles teams)

Water Polo

In a stirring finish, the USA water polo forces recaptured the gold medal they had lost to Mexico in 1975. The U.S. team battled a rash of serious injuries to cop the gold medal and reward the hard work of coach Monte Nitzkowski and his aides.

It was the USA's fourth gold medal in Pan American Games competition, and it came the hard way in a tense struggle with Cuba in the title game at the Escambron Pool.

The two unbeaten teams met head-on in the title game, and the USA prevailed by a score of 8-6. Cuba led by 3-2 after the first period, but the first of five goals by Gary Figueroa of Newport Beach, California, knotted the score at halftime.

Figueroa's tally off a penalty shot early in the third period gave the United States a 4-3 lead. He followed up with another, then Drew McDonald of Orinda, California, added another and it was 6-4 entering the fourth and final quarter.

Figueroa's two final period tallies were enough, and the USA went on to take the 8-6 triumph and mount the victory stand to accept their gold medals. Nitzkowski lauded the play of goalie Steve Hamann along with the rest of the squad.

The USA defense was so intense that the Cubans' leading scorer, Jorge Rizo, was held to a single goal. It was a rugged and very physical game, with both sides sustaining many minor cuts and bruises in the long contest.

Figueroa, whose father is a Puerto Rican native, led the Games in scoring with eleven goals.

TEAM PERSONNEL

D. Burke   C. Dorst   G. Figueroa

S. Hamann   E. Lindroth   A. McDonald

K. Robertson   P. Schnugg   T. Schroeder

J. Svendsen   J. Vargas

K. Lindgren   K. Nitzkowski   T. Sayring

TEAM PERSONNEL

Douglas Burke, 22, Modesto, California
Christopher Dorst, 23, Atherton, California
Gary Figueroa, 22, Newport Beach, California
Steve Hamann, 29, San Jose, California
Eric Lindroth, 27, Costa Mesa, California
Andrew McDonald, 23, Menlo Park, California
Kevin Robertson, 20, Berkeley, California
Peter Schnugg, 28, Palo Alto, California
Terry Schroeder, 20, Santa Barbara, California
Jon Svendsen, 25, Oakland, California
Joseph Vargas, 23, Hacienda Heights, California

Coach: Kenneth Nitzkowski, Huntington Beach, California
Assistant Coach: Kenneth Lindgren, Huntington Beach, California
Manager: Terry Sayring, Manhattan Beach, California

WATER POLO SUMMARIES

FINAL STANDINGS

	W	L	T	TP	GF	GA
United States	5	0	0	10	35	20
Cuba	4	1	0	8	41	25
Canada	2	2	1	5	29	31
Puerto Rico	1	2	2	4	28	36
Mexico	1	3	1	3	26	27
Brazil	0	5	0	0	20	42

Scores From The Round-Robin:

USA (5-0): vs. Mexico (7-5), vs. Puerto Rico (6-2), vs. Brazil (10-3), vs. Canada (6-4), vs. Cuba (8-6).

Cuba (4-1): vs. Mexico (5-4), vs. Puerto Rico (12-6), vs. Brazil (12-4), vs. Canada (6-3), vs. USA (6-8).

Canada (2-2-1): vs. USA (4-6), vs. Cuba (3-6), vs. Mexico (7-6), vs. Puerto Rico (8-8), vs. Brazil (7-5).

Puerto Rico (1-2-2): vs. USA (2-6), vs. Cuba (6-12), vs. Mexico (5-5), vs. Brazil (7-5), vs. Canada (8-8).

Mexico (1-3-1): vs. USA (5-7), vs. Cuba (4-5), vs. Puerto Rico (5-5), vs. Brazil (6-3), vs. Canada (6-7).

Brazil (0-5): vs. USA (3-10), vs. Cuba (4-12), vs. Mexico (3-6), vs. Puerto Rico (5-7), vs. Canada (5-7).

Tracy Caulkins won four Gold Medals at the Pan American Games.

Wrestling

(Free-Style and Greco-Roman)

The USA enjoyed great success in the free-style and Greco-Roman wrestling tournaments. In the Greco-Roman bouts which opened Pan American "grappling" USA and Cuba each won four gold, four bronze and two silver medals.

In the free-style tournament the USA garnered every one of the ten gold medals, Cuba's wrestlers accounted for all ten silver medals. Such results are not conducive to good competition.

The USA team had trained in the hot, humid Tennessee mountains under climatic conditions which approached the tough-to-encounter humidity of San Juan in July. The conditioning in Tennessee prepared the USA team for the worst and they were ready.

Among the free-style champions crowned, two deserve special mention. The veteran Russell Hellickson, 220 pounds, won his third straight Pan American title. He is a wrestling coach at the University of Wisconsin. Lee Kemp, '78 world champion who was to repeat later in '79, captured the Pan American title at 163 pounds.

Statistically speaking, in the free-style grappling the USA wrestlers pinned 27 opponents. Gene Mills, the NCAA bantam-weight champion from Syracuse, scored four straight victories by pinning his opponents. In his final bout, Mills won the 114.5-pound class by dispatching Cuba's Luis Ocuna in 4:01.

In the Greco-Roman tournament the USA grapplers won 21 matches by pinning their opponents' shoulders to the mat. Brad Rheingans, 220 pounds, retained his title by pinning three opponents. He culminated his march to the title by disposing of Cuba's Barbaro Morgan in 45 seconds.

Bruce Thompson, 27, retained top laurels in the 114.5-pound class, by pinning three straight opponents in a total of 9 minutes 27 seconds. Likewise, Dan Chandler was again returned winner in 180.5-pound class by pinning his three opponents, including Erasmo Estrada of Cuba in the quarter-final round.

Through this competition in Puerto Rico the USA demonstrated that its free-style wrestlers rank among the top two or three countries in the world, while much work still must be done in Greco-Roman before we are included among the elite nations of the world.

TEAM PERSONNEL

R. Baker   J. Corso   R. Hellickson

J. Jackson   L. Kemp   D. Lewis

A. Metzger   G. Mills   A. Rein

W. Rosado   G. Davis   B. Smith

TEAM PERSONNEL
Free-Style:

Roy Baker, 27, Plainview, New York (90 kg)
Joseph Corso, 27, Minneapolis, Minnesota (57 kg)
Russell Hellickson, 31, Oregon, Wisconsin (100 kg)
Jimmy Jackson, 22, Grand Rapids, Michigan (Heavyweight)
Lee Kemp, 22, Madison, Wisconsin (74 kg)
Daniel Lewis, 25, Anaheim, California (82 kg)
Andre Metzger, 19, Cedar Springs, Michigan (62 kg)
Gene Mills, 20, Syracuse, New York (52 kg)
Andrew Rein, 21, Stoughton, Wisconsin (68 kg)
William Rosado, 23, Tucson, Arizona (42 kg)

Manager: William Smith
Coach: Gene Davis, Lakewood, California

TEAM PERSONNEL

D. Chandler   B. Gust   J. Hughes

W. Lee   J. Matthews   G. Pelcl

B. Rheingans   J. Schmitz   B. Thompson

G. Williams   W. Baughman   J. Peckham

OFFICIAL SUMMARIES
48 Kilograms (106.5 lbs.)
1. WILLIAM ROSADO, USA; 2. Miguel Alonso, Cuba; 3. Alfredo Olivera, Mexico.

52 Kilograms (114 lbs.)
1. GENE MILLS, USA; 2. Luis Ocana, Cuba; 3. Jorge Olivera, Mexico.

57 Kilograms (125 lbs.)
1. JOE CORSO, USA; 2. Juan Rodriguez, Cuba; 3. Jose Felix Pinto, Panama.

62 Kilograms (136 lbs.)
1. ANDRE METZGER, USA; 2. Raul Cascaret, Cuba; 3. John Park, Canada.

68 Kilograms (150 lbs.)
1. ANDY REIN, USA; 2. Jose Ramos, Cuba; 3. Egon Beiler, Canada.

74 Kilograms (163 lbs.)
1. LEROY KEMP, USA; 2. Daniel Pozo, Cuba; 3. Mark Mongeon, Canada.

82 Kilograms (180 lbs.)
1. DANIEL LEWIS, USA; 2. Clark Davis, Canada; 3. Jose Carbajal, Cuba.

90 Kilograms (198 lbs.)
1. ROY BAKER, USA; 2. Jose Poll, Cuba; 3. Richard Deschatelefs, Canada.

100 Kilograms (220 lbs.)
1. RUSSELL HELLICKSON, USA; 2. Barbaro Morgan, Cuba; 3. Michael Kappel, Canada.

Heavyweight:
1. JIMMY JACKSON, USA; 2. Arturo Diaz, Cuba; 3. Wyatt Wishart, Canada.

NOTE: USA-Cuba-Canada won 28 out of 30 available medals in free-style wrestling.

TEAM PERSONNEL
Greco-Roman:
Daniel Chandler, 27, Anoka, Minnesota (82 kg)

Brian Gust, 30, Lakesville, Minnesota (57 kg)

John Hughes, 25, Meis, Minnesota (62 kg)

William "Pete" Lee, 28, Muncie, Indiana (Heavyweight)

John Matthews, 27, Flint, Michigan (74 kg)

Gary Pelcl, 30, Minneapolis, Minnesota (68 kg)

Brad Rheingans, 25, Appleton, Wisconsin (100 kg)

Jerome Schmitz, 24, St. Cloud, Minnesota (90 kg)

Bruce Thompson, 27, Rosemont, Minnesota (52 kg)

Gregg Williams, 21, Grand Junction, Colorado (42 kg)

Manager: Major Wayne Baughman, USAF, Colorado Springs, Colorado

Coach: James Peckham, Boston, Massachusetts

OFFICIAL SUMMARIES
48 Kilograms (106.5 lbs.)
1. Jorge Martinez, Cuba; 2. Alfredo Olivera, Mexico; 3. GREGG WILLIAMS, USA

52 Kilograms (114 lbs.)
1. BRUCE THOMPSON, USA; 2. Zollo Montano, Cuba; 3. Jorge Munoz, Mexico.

57 Kilograms (125 lbs.)
1. Leonel Perez, Cuba; 2. BRIAN GUST, USA; 3. Henry de Mola, Puerto Rico.

62 Kilograms (136 lbs.)
1. Douglas Yeats, Canada; 2. Rene Rodriguez, Cuba; 3. JOHN HUGHES, USA.

68 Kilograms (150 lbs.)
1. Howard Stupp, Canada; 2. GARY PELCL, USA; 3. Eduardo Garcia, Cuba.

74 Kilograms (163 lbs.):
1. JOHN MATTHEWS, USA; 2. Idalberto Barban, Cuba; 3. Brian Renker, Canada.

82 Kilograms (180 lbs.):
1. DANIEL CHANDLER, USA; 2. Erasmo Estrada, Cuba; 3. Louis Santerre, Canada.

90 Kilograms (198 lbs.):
1. Jose Poll, Cuba; 2. JERRY SCHMITZ, USA; 3. Steve Danier, Canada.

100 Kilograms (220 lbs.):
1. BRAD RHEINGANS, USA; 2. Barbaro Morgan, Cuba; 3. Raul Garcia, Mexico.

Heavyweight:
1. Arturo Diaz, Cuba; 2. PETE LEE, USA; 3. Miguel Zambrano, Peru.

NOTE: The following were double medalists:

Alfredo Olivera, Mexico (48 kg 3rd free-style; 2nd Greco-Roman)

Jose Poll, Cuba (90 kg 2nd free-style; 1st Greco-Roman)

Barbaro Morgan, Cuba (100 kg 2nd free-style; 2nd Greco-Roman)

Arturo Diaz, Cuba (Heavyweight, 2nd free-style, 1st Greco-Roman)

Bill Rosado, on his way to winning the 48k Free-style Gold Medal

Yachting

It was the most successful Pan American Games regatta, yet. Perhaps, it was a rule revision permitting the USA to enter two boats in each of the five classes. In re-capitulation the USA fleet earned three Pan American championships, placed second in three classes and also garnered a single bronze.

The best competition was among the 470 Class boats (on the program for the first time). In the seven-race regatta a skipper's six best place finishes count in determining the final placing. Four different skippers brought their boats across the finish line first during the 470 class regatta. The USA placed 1, 2 on the basis of Skip Whyte winning the final two races, while Steve Cucchiaro earned the silver on the basis of a second and third in those two final races.

Perhaps the most impressive sailing for the USA came in the Snipe Class. The defending champion, skipper Jeff Lenhart, had five seconds and one third. But Lenhart was only good enough for second place. Mark Reynolds, 23, swept the first six races and sat out the final one because his first place was assured.

David Curtis, 33, a sailmaker from Marblehead, Massachusetts, proved to be the class of the Soling helmsmen. Again, Curtis had first place clinched after the first six races — five firsts and a fourth.

It was a most satisfying regatta for the USA fleet: winning medals in all five classes and having only one of the ten boats winding up lower than fourth in the final standings.

TEAM PERSONNEL

Laser Class:
Cameron C. Lewis, 22, Sherborn, Massachusetts
Stewart P. Neff, 21, Oyster Bay, New York

Lightning Class:
Thomas G. Allen, III, 48, Buffalo, New York (Helmsman)
Thomas G. Allen, IV, 17, Buffalo, New York (Crew)
Anne S. Allen, 47, Buffalo, New York (Crew)
William A. Shore, 37, Newport, Rhode Island (Helmsman)
Bonnie Lee Shore, 36, Newport, Rhode Island (Crew)
Bill Hartnett, 26, Newport, Rhode Island (Crew)

Snipe Class:
Jeffrey Lenhart, 36, Costa Mesa, California (Helmsman)
Randall Smith, 18, La Jolla, California (Crew)
Mark Reynolds, 23, Miami, Florida (Helmsman)
Robert Martin, 22, San Diego, California (Crew)

TEAM PERSONNEL

A. Allen

T. Allen IV

D. Barton

J. Campbell

F. Charles

S. Cucchiaro

D. Curtis

B. Empey

W. Hartnett

J. Lenhart

R. Martin

J. McCleery

C. Millican

N. Nielsen

R. Smith

S. Walker

R. Whyte

H. Arnold

C. Eichenlaub

N. Freeman

C. Kober

Soling Class:
Stuart Walker, M.D., 56, Annapolis, Maryland (Helmsman)
Bruce Empey, 23, Anapolis, Maryland (Crew)
Ned Nielsen, 32, Fredericksburg, Virginia (Crew)
David A. Curtis, 33, Marblehead, Massachusetts (Helmsman)
David B. Barton, 22, Rye, New York (Crew)
James McCleery, 22, Larchmont, New York (Crew)

"470" Class:
Stephen J. Cucchiaro, 26, Beverly, Massachusetts (Helmsman)
Rollin "Skip" Whyte, Jr., 29, Watertown, Massachusetts (Helmsman)
Francis Edward Charles, 21, Cohasset, Massachusetts (Crew)
Charles Millican, 33, Sunapee, New Hampshire (Crew)

Spares:
James Joseph Campbell, 20, Pewaukee, Wisconsin
John Mueller, Jr., 35, Bay Village, Ohio
Ed Baird, 21, St. Petersburg, Florida

Team Leader: Charles Kober, San Diego, California
Shipwright: Carl M. Eichenlaub, San Diego, California
Team Physician: Dr. Homer Arnold, Austin, Texas
Assistant Manager: Norman Freeman, Sr., Ithaca, New York

OFFICIAL SUMMARIES

Snipe Class:
1. USA (MARK REYNOLDS) 0.00; 2. USA (JEFFREY LENHART) 20.70; 3. Brazil (Boris Oster Gren) 33.80; 4. Brazil (Michael Fedor) 35.40; 5. Argentina (Julio Labandeir) 60.70; 6. Argentina (Pedro Sisti) 70.40.

Soling Class:
1. USA (DAVID CURTIS) 24.00; 2. Brazil (Eduardo Sousa) 36.40; 3. Canada (Jim Beatty) 58.40; 4. Canada (Sid Dakin) 58.70; 5. Brazil (Augusto Campos) 70.80; 6. Puerto Rico (Eric Tulla) 73.00.

"470" Class:
1. USA (STEVE CUCCHIARO) 30.40; 2. USA (SKIP WHYTE) 34.70; 3. Canada (Jerry Rouss) 35.40; 4. Canada (Tam Matthews) 58.00; 5. Brazil (Marco Paradeda) 58.10; 6. Brazil (Marco Pinto Riz) 79.40.

Laser Class:
1. Canada (Terry Neilson) 17.00; 2. USA (CAMERON LEWIS) 26.00; 3. USA (STEWART NEFF) 33.10; 4. Canada (Eddy Martin) 43.10; 5. Brazil (Gasiao Davila) 44.10; 6. Brazil (John Spear) 50.40.

Lightning Class:
1. Brazil (Mario Buck Up) 39.70; 2. Canada (Gil Mercier) 52.10; 3. USA (BILL SHORE) 62.70; 4. USA (TOM ALLEN) 63.00; 5. Canada (Larry MacDonald) 74.70; 6. Chile (Manuel Gonzalez) 74.70.

U.S. Hockey Team--- 20 Unlikely Heroes

By Mike Moran,
Assistant Director of Communications,
USOC

For the first time since America put a man on the Moon, national pride burst from the seams of the land, and a feeling of giddiness prevailed. All of this because of the efforts of 20 young men, only two of them older than 23 years old, who made up the United States Olympic Hockey Team. What they did lifted this nation up by the boot-straps for a period of time that will never be forgotten.

This collection of unlikely heroes, collegians and a couple of ex-minor league knockarounds, whipped the Soviet Union on February 22, 4-3, then knocked off Finland two days later by 4-2 to win the gold medal at Lake Placid and send the nation into celebration.

The feat actually overshadowed perhaps the greatest individual effort in the history of the Olympic Games, that of winning five gold medals. The trick was turned in by Eric Heiden of Madison, Wis., the amazing speedskating great who totally dominated the field in winning all five events at Lake Placid, becoming also the first man ever to even enter all five. The 21-year-old stallion figuratively chewed up and spit out his competition, from 500 meters through 10,000 meters, ending his amazing effort by setting a world record in the 10,000, an event he was supposed to lack the endurance to win.

Heiden's heroics were the talk of the Games aside from the American hockey team. The popular youngster handled himself with unusual ease at daily press conferences and under constant pressure from the media and the American fans. His face adorned several magazine covers ahead of the Games, but there was little doubt that this special kind of athlete was equal to his challenge, and then some. His five gold medals at Lake Placid will live on in the hearts of sports historians, and the achievement may just be the greatest individual feat in modern sports history, because he went against the best in the world in each race, each day, and whipped them soundly.

There was little else for the American fans and athletes to cheer about, though the fabled success of the hockey team and Heiden's heroics tended to mask the overall lack of success by USA athletes.

One of the gutsiest sports stories of the year belongs to Alpine skier Phil Mahre of Yakima, Wash., who broke his ankle and seriously injured his leg a year before on the same slope in a World Cup race. The ankle was pieced together with pins and surgery, but his future, and his availability for the 1980 Olympic Winter Games was much in doubt.

Mahre not only showed up at Lake Placid, but his rehabilitation story was soon to become legend. Mahre, skiing against the great Ingemar Stenmark of Sweden, led after the first run of the men's slalom at White-face Mountain. But Stenmark, true to form under pressure, skied an amazing second run to edge Mahre for the gold medal and send Phil away with a silver. It was the only medal won by an American in skiing, and the first medal won by an American male skier since 1964 at Innsbruck.

Two silver medals went to speedskater Leah Poulos Mueller of Dousman, Wisconsin. She placed second in the 500 meters and the 1000 meters to Karin Enke of East Germany and Natalie Petruseva of the USSR, but her silver medals are a tribute to her determination and her ability to come back when she had retired from the sport, almost.

Another silver medal, and this one extremely controversial, went to figure skater Linda Fratianne of Los Angeles. It was accompanied by charges of unfair judging by her coach and others, and surrounded by a shadow of negativism. Fratianne skated beautifully in the finals, in fact better than winner Anett Potzsch of East Germany, but Fratianne's poor marks in the hated compulsory figures eventually killed her chance to win the gold medal.

And, perhaps, the biggest American story outside of hockey and Heiden concerned a pair of athletes who didn't compete at all.

Figure skating pair Tai Babilonia and Randy Gardner of Los Angeles were the pre-Games favorites to win the Pairs skating, despite the fact that the Soviet greats, Rodnina and Zaitsev, had returned after missing a year to become the parents of their first child. Babilonia and Gardner had broken a chain of 14 straight world Pairs titles by Soviet skaters at the World Championships a year before at Vienna, and they were not only the on-the-ice favorites, but the obvious sentimental favorites of the pro-USA throngs of over 10,000 that jammed the Olympic Ice Center to see the couple do their stuff. It was not to be.

Just a few days ahead of reporting to Lake Placid, Gardner suffered a pulled groin muscle in Los Angeles during a normal workout. After walking almost four miles on foot after the Opening Ceremonies on February 13 back to the city, he aggravated the injury in another workout.

The night of the competition, Gardner, to the horror of the onlookers, fell four times in the warmups and almost dropped Babilonia on her head during a lift. He had been injected with a pain-killer by a team physician, but it didn't help him.

Just before the couple was to perform, Nicks pulled them from the competition, ending a life-long dream of Olympic glory for the youngsters. A shocked crowd heard the announcement and saw Babilonia weep with grief as a stunned Gardner seemed as if he were in a daze. It was all over, and the Russians pair, skating beautifully, won the gold medal.

Charlie Tickner, suffering through a miserable short program, rebounded with a fine final program in the free skating to cop a bronze medal in the men's competition, though he, too, had been a pre-Games favorite along with Fratianne and Babilonia-Gardner. When the smoke cleared, all the U.S. Figure Skating team had to show was two silver medals and a tragic story.

The only other medal won by an American athlete was earned by 20-year-old speed skater Beth Heiden, the sister of the U.S. hero. Beth had been, perhaps unfairly, tagged as a favorite going into the Games in as many as three or four events. She also was suffering from a bad ankle and was below par physically. Pressure on her was tremendous. She did not skate well until the 3,000 meters, where she finally took third, and went home after a stormy final press briefing in which she broke down and cried, accusing the media of pressuring her into unsatisfactory performances at Lake Placid and unfair expectations.

But the success of the United States Hockey Team overshadowed everything else at the Games, even the skiing of Stenmark, the heroics of Heiden, the skiing of little Hanni Wenzel of Liechtenstein, the skating of the East Germans and the Russians, and the jumping of the Austrians.

Game by game as the Americans kept on winning, the following increased. Flags appeared everywhere, and chants of "U-S-A, U-S-A!" rocked the Olympic Ice Arena night after night as the kids gunned down opponent after opponent. Thousands stood by outside the arena on February 22 when the U.S. upset the Soviets, later spilling into the streets of Lake Placid, and joined by the 10,000 inside, lurched onto the frozen surface of Mirror Lake for an all-night celebration. The scene was repeated all over America in movie theaters, sporting events, music halls and saloons as the results came in. It shook America up, and it made America feel good about itself.

Not lost in the frenzy was the fact that the Americans still had to beat the Finns two days later for the gold medal. That game took place at the unearthly hour of 11:00 a.m. (just breakfast or brunch time elsewhere in the country) and the crowd was strangely detached for two periods. So were the hockey players, who trailed in the third period by 2-1 until a goal by Phil Verchota tied it at 2-2 with less than three minutes played in the final period.

The ending was swift and dramatic as Rob McClanahan and Mark Johnson tallied goals in the final ten minutes to ice the win and send America on its way to yet another bout with hysteria. The players, like goalie Jim Craig, captain Mike Eruzione, and the smallish Johnson, quickly became house-hold names, and their faces were to appear on countless television shows and magazine covers after the Games.

The United States team was flown by Air Force aircraft to Washington immediately after the Games to have lunch at the invitation of President Jimmy Carter and his wife at the White House, capping what was a magical two weeks in the little Adirondack Mountain town.

As ABC Sports hockey announcer Al Michaels asked millions of viewers as the clocked ticked off the final seconds in the dramatic and emotional triumph over the Soviets, "Do you believe in miracles?"

America, indeed, did believe.

Alpine Skiing

The United States had counted heavily on an intensive four-year program by the U.S. Ski Team to reap a record harvest of medals at Lake Placid, but fate and fortune did not smile on this group.

However, the fact that Phil Mahre of Yakima, Washington, became the first American man since 1964 to win an Olympic Ski medal was a highlight to build on for the next four years. In fact, Mahre came very close to becoming the first American man to win an Olympic gold medal in the Slalom. Only a tremendous second run by the Swedish legend, Ingemar Stenmark, on the slalom course kept the gallant Mahre from his gold medallion.

The silver medal for Phil was especially significant, because it was less than a year earlier when Mahre tore up his ankle on the same slope at Whiteface Mountain in World Cup competition. Many predicted that the severity of the injury would sideline Mahre for the rest of his career. But a great surgical job by Dr. Richard Steadman and a gutty rehabilitation effort by Mahre put him back on the slopes at Lake Placid and in position to win his Olympic medal.

That wasn't all, either. Mahre later received a gold medal from FIS for the alpine combined championship from Marc Hodler, the president of the international governing body which counts the Games as a world championship event.

That was to be the highlight of the entire competition for the Americans, who were not destined to win another medal at Lake Placid.

It was hoped that the veteran Cindy Nelson, a bronze medalist at Innsbruck in the 1976 Games in the Downhill, would be in position at Lake Placid to do even better — perhaps even win the gold medal. But it was not to be for the Lutsen, Minn., native who might have competed for the third and last time in the Olympic Winter Games at Lake Placid. She finished seventh behind the magnificent winner, Annemarie Moser of Austria, then took 13th in the Giant Slalom behind perhaps the Games' outstanding woman athlete, Hanni Wenzel of tiny Liechtenstein. Nelson was also in 11th place behind the fabulous Wenzel after the running of the Slalom. However, Cindy did win the silver medal from the FIS for her performance in the combined three women's events.

America was not without its usual surprises, however, as 18-year-old Heidi Preuss blazed to a fourth-place finish in the Downhill behind Moser, Wenzel and Marie-Theres Nadig of Switzerland to stamp herself as a Yankee to watch in the next four years of preparation for the Winter Games at Sarajevo, Yugoslavia.

TEAM PERSONNEL

C. Adgate   K. Anderson   C. Cooper

P. Mahre   S. Mahre   T. McKinney

H. Preuss   B. Taylor

J. Barrows   H. Goellner   B. Marolt

TEAM PERSONNEL

A. Fisher   H. Flanders   V. Fleckenstein

A. Mill   C. Nelson   P. Patterson

M. Rudigoz   H. Schoenhaar

Valentine's Day turned out to be all hearts and flowers for the most unlikely gold medalist of them all — Austria's Leonhard Stock. He had been brought along as part of the Austrian team as a last-minute addition. Stock had suffered torn knee ligaments in a fall in December, and his presence in Lake Placid thus bordered on the miraculous from the start. In addition, there was friction over his selection over 1979 World Cup winner Sepp Walcher.

At the end of the two runs, it was Stock with the gold medal and teammate Peter Wirnsberger with the silver medal. Canada's Steve Podborski, one of the famed "Kami-kaze Korps" earned the bronze for third.

Perhaps the biggest feat of them all, though, was the harvest of medals by the Wenzel family of little Liechtenstein, with Hanni Wenzel copping two golds and a silver medal, and brother Andreas grabbing a silver in the men's Giant Slalom behind Stenmark.

American men besides Mahre who did fare well included the veteran Pete Patterson, Sun Valley, Idaho, who had his finest Downhill ever in Olympic competition and took home a diploma for fifth place.

Phil Mahre, in addition to his silver medal in the Slalom, collected a 14th-place finish in the Downhill and a 10th in the Giant Slalom. His brother, Steve, was 15th in the Giant Slalom.

Women from the United States with high finishes included, besides Nelson and Preuss, an 7th-place finish by Christin Cooper of Sun Valley in the Giant Slalom and Cooper's 8th-place in the Slalom, also marking her as a future hopeful at Sarajevo.

ALPINE TEAM PERSONNEL

Cary Adgate, Boyne City, Mich.
  Men's Giant Slalom, DNF
Karl Anderson, Greene, Me.
  Men's Downhill, DNF
Christin Cooper, Sun Valley, Idaho
  7th, Women's Giant Slalom
  8th, Women's Slalom
Abbi Fisher, Center Conway, N.H.
  Women's Slalom, DNF
Holly Flanders, Deerfield, N.H.
  14th, Women's Downhill
Viki Fleckenstein, Syracuse, N.Y.
  Did Not Compete
*Phil Mahre, Yakima, Wash.
  14th, Men's Downhill
  10th, Men's Giant Slalom
  2nd, Men's Slalom
Steve Mahre, Yakima, Wash.
  15th, Men's Giant Slalom
  Men's Slalom, DNF
Andy Mill, Boulder, Colo.
  16th, Men's Downhill
Tamara McKinney, Lexington, Ky.
  Women's Slalom, DNF
  Women's Giant Slalom, DNF
**Cindy Nelson, Lutsen, Minn.
  7th, Women's Downhill
  13th, Women's Giant Slalom
  11th, Women's Slalom
Pete Patterson, Sun Valley, Idaho
  5th, Men's Downhill
  Men's Slalom, DNF
  Men's Giant Slalom, DNF
Heidi Preuss, Laconia, N.H.
  4th, Women's Downhill
  17th, Women's Giant Slalom
Billy Taylor, Orchard Park, N.Y.
  Men's Slalom, DNF

ALPINE STAFF

Bill Marolt, Team Leader, Park City, Utah
Harald Schoenhaar, Men's Coach, Park City, Utah
Jim Barrows, Men's Downhill Coach, Steamboat Springs, Colo.
Hermann Goellner, Women's Coach, Park City, Utah
Michel Rudigoz, Women's Downhill Coach, Park City, Utah

*—FIS gold medal, combined events, men
**—FIS silver medal, combined events, women

Biathlon

For the first time since Biathlon was added to the program of the Olympic Winter Games in 1960, the Scandinavian nations failed to win a medal in one of the biggest surprises of the Games. The East Germans and the Russians each copped four medals, and the remaining medal went to the West Germans. It was a strange position for the Scandinavian countries, where the sport was originated.

The surprise winner in the 20-kilometer event was young Anatoli Aljabiev of the Soviet Union, beating the pre-Games favorite, Frank Ullrich of East Germany, by eleven seconds over the roughly 12½-mile-course of cross-country skiing and rifle marksmanship expertise. Coupled with the shooting, and penalty loops for missing targets, Aljabiev's final margin was 3:11.0.

Ullrich gained revenge, to a degree, in the 10-kilometer sprint event, defeating Vladimir Alikin of the USSR and Aljabiev in the shorter event. Ullrich's margin of victory in the 10-kilometer event was almost one minute in the final tabulation.

The United States, which had been hoping for better things this time from its scholarly and promising team, did not fare well overall. Team leader Lyle Nelson, Olympic Valley, Cal., got a nifty 19th-place finish in the 10-kilometer spring despite an illness which curtailed his efforts in this race and later, in the 20-kilometer event as well. Teammates Don Nielsen (44th) and Peter Hoag (45th) competed as well in the shorter sprint.

In the brand-new 10-kilo event, Nelson almost did not compete at all because of a severe respiratory infection, but appeared to rally and eventually joined the field just before the race. He did not miss a single target in this event, but his lagging strength hurt his skiing, and he finished 19th, still a very encouraging effort for Americans. He was scratched from the 20-kilometer race because of the illness, however.

In the 20-kilometer event, American finishes included Martin Hagen (36th), Glen Jobe (38th) and Johnny Ruger (45th) in the deep and talented field of international athletes in this demanding sport.

The Americans pulled things together to finish a very respectable 8th in a field of fifteen teams in the 4 x 7.5K relay event. The foursome of Hagen, Nelson, Nielsen and Hoag was timed in 1:39.24.29 for the distance. The gold medal went to the powerful Soviet foursome, with East Germany second and West Germany third. However, the U.S. team and the Soviets each scored perfect marks in the shooting portion of the relay, with average skiing costing the Americans their long-sought first Olympic medal in Biathlon.

Despite the finishes, interest in the sport in America seemed to be growing, and the promise for 1984 is bright, perhaps even for that first, elusive Olympic medal.

TEAM PERSONNEL

M. Hagen   P. Hoag   G. Jobe

L. Nelson   D. Nielsen   J. Ruger

P. Lahdenpera   B. Spencer   A. Stegen

BIATHLON TEAM PERSONNEL

Martin Hagen, Jackson, Wyo.
  36th, 20-Kilometer Event
  Relay Event, first leg, 8th
Peter Hoag, Minneapolis, Minn.
  45th, 10-Kilometer Event
  Relay Event, fourth leg, 8th
Glen Jobe, Alturas, Cal.
  38th, 20-Kilometer Event
Lyle Nelson, Olympic Valley, Cal.
  19th, 10-Kilometer Event
  Relay Event, second leg, 8th
Don Nielsen, So. Strafford, Vt.
  44th, 10-Kilometer Event
  Relay Event, third leg, 8th
Johnny Ruger, Eldorado Springs, Colo.
  45th, 20-Kilometer Event

BIATHLON STAFF

Peter Lahdenpera, Team Leader, Ft. Collins, Colo.
Bill Spencer, Rifle Coach, Woodsville, N.H.
Art Stegen, Skiing Coach, New Paltz, N.Y.

Bobsled

The newest, and perhaps the finest, bobsled run in the world was the scene for the competition at Lake Placid for the XIII Olympic Winter Games. Rebuilt on the site of the old run, which was constructed in 1932 for the Games, the new run proved to be the fastest in history, dangerous, exciting, and just what the designers wanted it to be for all concerned.

East Germany's Meinhard Nehmer closed out his career in a blaze of glory, piloting the East Germany I sled to victory in the 4-man competition with riders Bosdan Musiol and Bernhard Germeshausen, and braker Hans Jurgen Gerhardt aboard. Coupled with his two gold medals at Innsbruck in 1976 as the driver of both East German sleds, it made a tidy haul for the farm machinery technician/army officer from the Baltic Sea isle of Boblin.

Nehmer's sled completed no less than two sub-one minute runs down the sleek refrigerated course at Lake Placid's Mt. Van Hoevenberg. His runs were :59.86 and :59.83 together with two other runs for a combined winning time of 3:59.92, almost a full second faster than the Swiss I sled driven by the great Erich Schaerer.

Schaerer and braker Josef Benz, however, came back to win the 2-man competition, whizzing around the oval in a combined four-run time of 4:09.36 to outdistance the East German combination of Germeshausen and Gerhardt aboard the East German II sled.

It was good news, and bad news for the hopeful USA sleds, which were expected to benefit from the fact that they had lots of practice on the new run ahead of the Games, despite some heavy delays due to damage and construction problems.

The good news was the performance of the 2-man sleds. USA II, driven by Brushton, N.Y., insurance agent Howard Siler and braked by Dick Nalley of Indianapolis, finished a respectable 5th. USA I, piloted by the veteran Brent Rushlaw of Saranac Lake, New York, and braked by Joe Tyler, finished right behind in 6th place, the best finishes in 24 years of bleak results in the sport by the Americans.

However, the 4-man competition was marred by friction, not only among the members of one of the U.S. entries and the head coach, but between the runners and the surface of the run.

First, driver Bob Hickey of the USA I sled defied proposed changes in that lineup by coach Gary Sheffield, insisting that the original team of himself, Jeff Jordan, Willie Davenport and braker Jeff Gadley remain intact. Sheffield had wanted to re-test two of the riders on that sled before the competition. The friction brought the news media into the fray and cast a pall over the USA hopes in the final runs.

TEAM PERSONNEL

A. Ashton   W. Davenport   J. Gadley

D. Lavigne   D. Nalley   B. Renton

R. Nelson   G. Sheffield

Second, following the final trials runs, it was decided to switch equipment, opting for the new Italian-made Podar sleds which were considered superior to what the Americans had been using. Trouble was, they forgot to get the right runners, and the warmer temperatures and unsuitable runners added up to slower times for the USA sleds.

The controversial USA I sled, driven by Hickey, finished a distant 12th, with the number two sled, composed of driver Howard Siler, riders Joe Tyler and Jeff Jost, and braker Dick Nalley, finishing an unlucky 13th. It relegated the Americans, once again, to also-ran status in a sport that the USA was once dominant in early Olympic Winter Games history. The USA has not won a medal in Bobsled since the 1952 Games at Oslo, Norway.

Hope comes for the future from the presence of the new run at Lake Placid, which will give American bobsledders much more practice and many more meets, plus an infusion of young talent. Sheffield points out that, compared to just 80 bobsledders in the country two years ago, there now are upwards of 160 hopefuls in the sport who will get the advantages of the new run and a beefed-up national program over the next four years.

TEAM PERSONNEL

 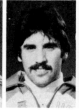 
B. Hickey   J. Jordan   J. Jost

B. Rushlaw   H. Siler   J. Tyler

BOBSLED TEAM PERSONNEL
Al Ashton, Norfolk, Virginia
   Did Not Compete
Willie Davenport, Baton Rouge, La.
   Rider, USA I, four-man, 12th
Jeff Gadley, Plattsburgh, N.Y.
   Braker, USA I, four-man, 12th
Bob Hickey, Keene, N.Y.
   Driver, USA I, four-man, 12th
Jeff Jordan, Athol, New York
   Rider, USA I, four-man, 12th
Jeff Jost, Burke, New York
   Rider, USA II, four-man, 13th
Dick Lavigne, Malone, New York
   Did Not Compete
Dick Nalley, Indianapolis, Indiana
   Braker, USA II, two-man, 5th
   Braker, USA II, four-man, 13th
Bill Renton, Virginia Beach, Virginia
   Did Not Compete
Brent Rushlaw, Saranac Lake, New York
   Driver, USA I, two-man, 6th
Howard Siler, Brushton, New York
   Driver, USA II, two-man, 5th
   Driver, USA II, four-man, 13th
Joe Tyler, Saranac Lake, New York
   Braker, USA I, two-man, 6th
   Rider, USA II, four-man, 13th

BOBSLED STAFF
Gary Sheffield, Head Coach, Lake Placid, New York
Robert Nelson, Manager, Troy, New York

Figure Skating

It was a bittersweet experience for the United States figure skating team at Lake Placid, remembered more for what didn't happen than what did. Hopes were sky-high at the beginning of the Games, but in the end it was frustration, tragedy and bitter memories for some.

The number one story of the competition was the injury to the USA's Randy Gardner that knocked him out of the competition in the Pairs along with his talented partner, Tai Babilonia.

Gardner suffered a pulled groin muscle in a pre-Games workout in Los Angeles, then aggrevated it at Lake Placid two days ahead of competition. When it came to the night of the Pairs competition, Gardner simply could not go. He had fallen repeatedly in the warmups, and Coach John Nicks was forced to pull the couple out of the Games, writing a sad ending to an eight-year dream for the California youngsters who were the favorites at Lake Placid.

Rodnina and Zaitsev, skating magnificently, went on to capture the gold medal, and it seemed to mold the shape of things to come for the American skaters. One by one their dreams turned sour on the final evening of competition.

First, it was the disaster in the short program for Charlie Tickner of Denver, another American given a nod as a gold medal favorite. His disastrous marks in the short program could not be overcome in the long program, and England's Robin Cousins swept past early leader Jan Hoffman of East Germany to the gold medal, with Tickner taking home the bronze. Teammates David Santee of Park Ridge, Illinois, and Scott Hamilton of Rosemont, Pennsylvania, finished fourth and fifth, respectively, to cap a solid American performance in the men's skating.

The script was somewhat different for little Linda Fratianne of Northridge, Cal., in the ladies singles. She came into the Games as the reigning world champion and the odds-on favorite to take home the gold.

In Fratianne's case, it was her mediocre scores in the compulsory figures, worth thirty percent of her score, that doomed her to failure. The 97-pound California skater responded with a magnificent effort in the short and long programs to try and turn the tide against East Germany's talented Anett Potzsch, but it was a case of time running out.

Fratianne captivated the crowd and most of the judges on the final night, bouncing around the ice to pieces from "Carmen" and sending the capacity throng into shouting, stamping, flag-waving ecstasy. Potzsch, on the other hand, could not afford any mistakes, and she didn't make one. Skating to Barbra Streisand's hit, "Don't Rain On My Parade" and "Funny Girl," the classy German skated a clean routine that, if not special in any way, was indeed solid. In the end, it was simply enough to win.

TEAM PERSONNEL

L. Allen   T. Babilonia   J. Blumberg

S. Franks   L. Fratianne   R. Gardner

M. Seibert   S. Smith   J. Summers

C. Ferguson   P. George

A tearful Fratianne contented herself with a silver medal and a lucrative professional contract back home. Teammates Lisa-Marie Allen of Colorado Springs and Sandy Lenz of Rockford, Illinois, both skated admirably and wound up fifth and ninth, respectively, in the talented field of skaters.

The Ice Dancing competition also ended on a controversial note, with catcalls and booing greeting the announcement that the gold medal had been awarded to the Soviet pair of Natalia Linichuk and Gennadi Karponosov.

The crowd had fallen in love with the Hungarians, Krisztina Rogoczy and Andras Salley, and with good reason. The duo skated magnificently in the early programs and was in great position to win it all.

Americans Judy Blumberg and Michael Seibert of Colorado Springs were seventh, and Stacey Smith and John Summers of Wilmington, Delaware, were ninth in the final tabulations.

It was a crazy outcome at Lake Placid, and because of the personal tragedy of the popular Gardner and Babilonia, may well be longer remembered for who didn't win rather than who did.

TEAM PERSONNEL

M. Botticelli   C. Carruthers   P. Carruthers

S. Hamilton   S. Lenz   D. Santee

TEAM PERSONNEL

Lisa-Marie Allen, Colorado Springs, Colo.
  5th, Ladies Singles
Tai Babilonia, Mission Hills, California
  Pairs, with Randy Gardner, Did Not
  Compete
Judy Blumberg, Colorado Springs, Colorado
  7th, Ice Dancing, with Michael Seibert
Michael Botticelli, Weston, Massachusetts
  7th, Pairs, with Sheryl Franks
Caitlin Carruthers, Wilmington, Delaware
  5th, Pairs, with Peter Carruthers (brother)
Peter Carruthers, Wilmington, Delaware
  5th, Pairs, with Caitlin Carruthers (sister)
Sheryl Franks, Lexington, Massachusetts
  7th, Pairs, with Michael Botticelli
Linda Fratianne, Northridge, California
  2nd, Ladies Singles
Randy Gardner, Marina del Rey, California
  Pairs, with Tai Babilonia, Did Not
  Compete because of injury.
Scott Hamilton, Haverford, Pennsylvania
  5th, Men's Singles
Sandy Lenz, Rockford, Illinois
  9th, Ladies Singles
David Santee, Park Ridge, Illinois
  4th, Men's Singles
Michael Seibert, Colorado Springs, Colo.
  7th, Ice Dancing, with Judy Blumberg
Stacey Smith, Wilmington, Delaware
  9th, Ice Dancing, with John Summers
John Summers, Wilmington, Delaware
  9th, Ice Dancing, with Stacey Smith
Charles Tickner, Littleton, Colorado
  3rd, Men's Singles

FIGURE SKATING STAFF

Claire Ferguson, Jamestown, Rhode Island
  Team Leader
Paul George, Wellesley, Massachusetts
  Team Leader

Ice Hockey

There has been, perhaps, no greater moment in American sport. And that includes the whole smorgasboard of sports in this nation, including Super Bowls, World Series, and national collegiate championships.

A United States hockey team seeded seventh in the field of twelve not only won the gold medal and beat the powerful USSR (which had manhandled the NHL's finest just a year before), but it rallied the American people and their sagging spirits at a time that they needed a lift. It made America HAPPY for a week or two, and this unlikely collection of collegians, ex-minor league players, and would-be Walter Mittys won the heart of a nation. Time stood still at Lake Placid for them, and history opened its pages to them. America's Team seized the opportunity to rewrite sports legends.

However, four days prior to the first game against Sweden, the U.S. team was subjected to a 10-3 humiliation by the Soviets in an afternoon exhibition contest in New York City in Medison Square Garden. The Americans were simply in awe of the Russians, so much so, in fact, the observers noticed some of the USA players applauding the Soviet stars in the introductions.

But a lot took place in the next week. The Americans needed a goal from Bill Baker of Minnesota with 0:27 left in the game to tie the Swedes, 2-2, in the opening game. It may have been the most important goal of the Games, because it was to ultimately mean the gold medal for the Americans at Lake Placid. A loss would have ruined it all in the eventual tie-breaker system if the USSR and USA finished dead-locked in won-loss marks in the medal round.

Next up on February 14, Valentine's Day, was powerful Czechoslovakia, the team generally given the best chance of unseating the Russians for the gold medal and the constant tormentor in European and World Championships of the intimidating Soviets. This time, with the first of the soon-to-be legendary chants of "U-S-A, U-S-A!" ringing from the throats of some 8,000 fans, the Yankees destroyed their opponents and sent the throng into a stomping, flag-waving frenzy that was to become the trademark of the Games.

The first period begin — typically — with the Czechs scoring first on a rebound shot by Jaroslav Pouzar at the 4:19 mark. But the USA quickly went ahead by 2-1 on goals by 25-year-old Mike Eruzione, a former minor leaguer and South Boston house painter who was to become the inspirational leader of this crew, and baby-faced Mark Pavelich, a veteran college star from Minnesota-Duluth. The period, however, ended at 2-2 when the Czechs scored at the 12:07 mark on a slap-shot by veteran Marian Statsny, one of three brothers in the lineup at the time.

TEAM PERSONNEL

B. Baker   N. Broten   D. Christian

J. Harrington   S. Janaszak   M. Johnson

M. Pavelich   M. Ramsey   B. Schneider

P. Verchota   M. Wells

TEAM PERSONNEL

S. Christoff   J. Craig   M. Eruzione

R. McClanahan   K. Morrow   J. O'Callahan

D. Silk   E. Strobel   B. Suter

R. Jasinski   C. Patrick   H. Brooks

Brooks told his charges between periods that they might as well realize that they could play against the best — and if they sucked it up, could probably even win.

The results of Brooks' talk were very quickly evident. The hard-checking Americans bounced Czechs off the boards and played a smothering defense that had the Europeans scuttling for their lives all period long. In between, Buzz Schneider and Wisconsin All-American Mark Johnson, whose father had been the Olympic coach in '76, lit the red light in back of the Czech goal to give the U.S. a 4-2 lead after two periods and a resounding 7-3 win over the second-best team in the field.

The Czech triumph was followed by lackluster triumphs over Norway on February 16 by 5-1, and then a February 18 victory over Romania by 7-2 in the antiquated Olympic Arena, the site of the 1932 competition, before a "full house" of just under 1,700 fans who sported just about as many flags.

Maybe it was that fact weighing heavily on the minds of the Americans on February 20 when they took the ice against the West Germans. For some reason, the West Germans have been historically rough on the United States in hockey, whether it was the World Championships or the Olympic Games. It was the West Germans who had knocked the USA out of the bronze medal at Innsbruck four years earlier with a bitter 4-1 triumph that left the Americans without a medal of any color.

West Germany jumped to a 2-0 lead after the first period over the listless U.S. team. But the pall lifted in the second period when a pair of Brooks' products at Minnesota scored back-to-back goals in less than two minutes to knot the score at 2-2. Rob McClanahan and Neal Broten were the ex-Gophers igniting the slumbering American team into the second period fireworks which extended into the third and final stanza in which McClanahan and Verchota scored early to give the USA a 4-2 triumph and set up the showdown with the Soviets.

It's doubtful that anybody, including Brooks, really thought that the Americans stood a chance against the Soviets on February 22 at Lake Placid. It's very probable that, until one particular play, that the American team would have settled for a good, hard-fought effort, like maybe a 4-3 or 5-3 loss to the Soviets.

The particular play came off the stick of Mark Johnson, pound-for-pound the best player in the Games, and the epitome of the "money" player.

With less than ten seconds left in the first period and the USA trailing by 2-1, Baker took a 55-foot slapshot from beyond the blue line. Soviet goalie Vladislav Tretjak, perhaps looking at the fading seconds on the scoreboard, casually kicked away the shot directly in front of the goal, where two defensemen were on patrol. It was a fatal mistake by Tretjak and turned around the outcome of the game.

The 5-9, 165-pound Johnson barrelled in from the blue line, dove in front of the flat-footed Russian defensemen, and slapped the puck past the startled Tretjak into the Soviet net as the horn sounded.

The second period resembled some sort of fencing match, with each team checking, checking, checking and playing rugged defense. The Soviet great, Alexandre Maltsev, got the only goal of the stanza, beating American goalie Jim Craig at the 2:18 mark on a slapshot from about 16 feet out on the right side. The USSR took that narrow 3-2 lead to the lockers, but America knew the best was yet to come . . . and it was.

The explosion heard 'round the world came suddenly, swiftly, like a Fourth of July firecracker. First it was Johnson (who else?) with an assist from slick Dave Silk, scoring at 8:39 on a rebound against new goalie Vladimir Myshkin, who replaced the embattled Tretjak in the second period. With the score tied at 3-3 and the arena in a frenzied chaos, it was less than two minutes later when Eruzione, the house painter and well-traveled minor leaguer, drilled in a screamer from close range to give the Americans a 4-3 lead. That left ten minutes to complete history. Ten minutes of defense against what would be a savage Russian attack.

But Craig, the former Boston University star, was equal to the challenge. He made no less than eight of his 39 saves in the next four minutes, three of them bordering on miracles, as the Soviets attacked the American net relentlessly.

With less than two minutes left, it suddenly appeared that the Soviets quit. The Americans began to move again on offense, and when they weren't taking the puck into the USSR zone, they poked it away from the frustrated Soviet forwards back down the ice. Suddenly everybody in the arena knew that the Americans were going to win, and there has never been a sweeter and more electric final minute in an American sporting event, bar none.

The next morning, Brooks brought all 20 players to a wild and wooly press conference before some 500 writers in the press center at the high school. But the euphoria was tempered with the sobering fact that the Americans still needed to beat the Finns a day later to win the gold. A loss or a tie could give the title to the Finns, the Russians, or even the Swedes, who had that 2-2 tie with the USA in the first game going for them.

The title game against Finland was played at 11:00 a.m., and for the first two periods, the emotion from the crowd of over 10,000 was just not there. Maybe it was too early on a Sunday morning, and maybe the Russian game had taken too much out of the players, but the slick-skating Finns took a 2-1 lead into the third period, and they had the partisan crowd squirming with agony as they blunted drive after drive by the sometimes listless American forwards. Craig had allowed two sloppy goals to boot. Something had to happen, and it did.

It was the rugged Verchota who finally got things going, knotting the game at 2-2 at the 2:25 mark into the third period on a rebound. It brought the crowd alive, finally, and the chants of "U-S-A, U-S-A" bounced off the ice and into the hearts of the American players.

It took another four minutes before McClanahan poked in the go-ahead goal with an assist from Dave Christian, a second-generation Olympic hockey player whose dad and uncle led the U.S. to a gold medal in 1960 at Squaw Valley. The 3-2 lead went to 4-2 at the 16:25 mark when Johnson, with an assist from Steve Christoff, jabbed in a deflection by Finnish goalie Jorma Valtonen to up the tally to 4-2 and ice the outcome. The final three minutes were a joy to behold, and the crowd went berserk with their heroes at the buzzer, with another fifteen minutes of unbridled joy on ice following the final horn. America's Kids had their gold and the U.S. team, "Best thing on ice since Scotch," according to one sign. etched itself forever into the hearts of a nation that needed a lift as the tumultuous 1980s began.

THE U.S. HOCKEY TEAM

Bill Baker, Grand Rapids, Minnesota
Neal Broten, Roseau, Minnesota
David Christian, Warroad, Minnesota
Steve Christoff, Richfield, Minnesota
Jim Craig, North Easton, Massachusetts
Mike Eruzione, Winthrop, Massachusetts
John Harrington, Burnsville, Minnesota
Steve Janaszak, White Bear Lake, Minnesota
Mark Johnson, Madison, Wisconsin
Ken Morrow, Davison, Michigan
Rob McClanahan, North Oaks, Minnesota
John O'Callahan, Charlestown, Mass.
Mark Pavelich, Eveleth, Minnesota
Mike Ramsey, Minneapolis, Minnesota
Buzz Schneider, Babbitt, Minnesota
David Silk, Burnsville, Minnesota
Eric Strobel, Rochester, Minnesota
Bob Suter, Madison, Wisconsin
Phil Verchota, Duluth, Minnesota
Mark Wells, St. Clair Shores, Michigan

HOCKEY STAFF

Herb Brooks, Shoreview, Minnesota
  Head Coach
Craig Patrick, Edina, Minnesota
  Assistant Coach
Ralph Jasinski, New Brighton, Minnesota
  Manager

PRE-MEDAL ROUND

(1st three teams in each division advance to medal round)

RED DIVISION

Team	W	L	T	GF/GA	Pts.
USSR	5	0	0	51/11	10
Finland	3	2	0	26/18	6
Canada	3	2	0	28/12	6
Poland	2	3	0	15/23	6
Holland	1	3	1	16/43	3
Japan	0	4	1	7/36	1

BLUE DIVISION

Team	W	L	T	GF/GA	Pts.
Sweden	4	0	1	26/7	9
United States	4	0	1	25/10	9
Czecho-slovakia	3	2	0	34/16	6
Romania	1	3	1	13/29	3
West Germany	1	4	0	21/30	2
Norway	0	4	1	9/36	1

MEDAL ROUND SCOREBOARD

Czechoslovakia 6, Canada 1 (5th Place)
UNITED STATES 4, Soviet Union 3
Finland 3, Sweden 3
Soviet Union 9, Sweden 2
UNITED STATES 4, Finland 2

FINAL STANDINGS

Team	W	L	T	Pts.
UNITED STATES	2	0	1	5
USSR	2	1	0	4
Sweden	0	1	2	2
Finland	0	2	1	1

USA Overall Scoreboard (6-0-1)

2	Sweden	2
7	Czechoslovakia	3
7	Romania	3
4	West Germany	2
5	Norway	1
4	Soviet Union	3
4	Finland	2
	(6-0-1)	

Nordic Skiing

The eighth-place finish by Jim Denney, the highest finish ever in jumping by a U.S. athlete off the 90-meter hill, was the lone bright spot for the U.S. Nordic Ski Team at Lake Placid, though optimism had run high for medals ahead of the Games in many quarters.

Team leaders were quoted as saying that there had been too little international competition in the month ahead of the Games and that the team may have raced and trained too hard in the same period, that they were perhaps burned out by the time the competition opened at Lake Placid.

Whatever the reason, there was disappointment for the cross-country skiers when Bill Koch, who had won a silver medal at Innsbruck in 1976, failed to win another this time. The veteran athlete from Putney, Vermont, dropped out of the 30-kilometer race early, the very event that he won the silver in during the '76 Games. Koch came back with a 16th-place finish in the 15k event, a 13th-place finish in the 50k, and then led off on the USA Relay team that took a good 8th place over 40 kilometers in the final event.

Twenty-three-year-old Walter Malmquist, Post Mills, Vermont, had a decent showing himself, finishing 12th in the Nordic Combined event. Malmquist was a strong second in the 70-meter jumping portion of the event to the gold medalist, Ulrich Wehling of East Germany, but slipped to 27th in the 15-kilometer cross country race event that completes the competition in that event.

The best the USA could do was the eighth by Denney in the 90-meter jumping and the eighth by the quartet of Koch, Tim Caldwell, Jim Galanes and Stan Dunklee in the 4 x 10k Relay Event that was won by the Russians.

The U.S. women fared no better. A seventh-place finish by the foursome of Alison Owen Spencer, Beth Paxson, Leslie Bancroft and Margaret Spencer in the 4 x 5k Relay Event was the highest finish among the American women.

Owen Spencer added 22nd place finished in the 5-kilo and 10-kilo cross country events to become the highest-ranking American woman competitor in the Games. Nobody else in the group finished better than 25th.

The oddity for the Americans came in the 70-meter special jumping where unheralded Jeff Davis of Steamboat Springs, Colo., uncorked a whopping 91-meter jump that was probably the greatest single jump ever by an American. It was subsequently disallowed by officials, who ruled out the jump and caused the entire competition to be re-started even though Davis was the 9th jumper off the hill at the time. Chalk that up to the strange twists of fate and judging in the sport.

Barbara Petzold of East Germany won a pair of gold medals, winning the women's individual 10k cross country event, then anchoring her team to a triumph in the 4 x 5k cross country relay event.

The jumping gold medalists were Anton Innauer of Austria in the 70-meter and Jouko Tormanen of Finland in the 90-meter special.

TEAM PERSONNEL

L. Bancroft   J. Broman   T. Caldwell

M. Devecka   S. Dunklee   J. Galanes

B. Koch   K. Lynch   J. Maki

A. Owen-Spencer   D. Peterson   E. Paxson

C. Ward   R. Zuehlke

J. Bower   B. Fisher   R. Kiesel

TEAM PERSONNEL

G. Crawford   J. Davis   J. Denney

J. Grahek   B. Haines   T. Kempainen

W. Malmquist   C. McNeill   D. Michael

J. Rabinowitz   D. Simoneau   M. Spencer

G. Kotlarek   J. Page

NORDIC TEAM PERSONNEL

Leslie Bancroft, Paris, Maine
   33rd, women's 5k event
   28th, women's 10k event
   7th, relay event, third leg
John Broman, Duluth, Minnesota
   Did Not Compete
Tim Caldwell, Putney, Vermont
   25th, men's 15k event
   8th, relay event, second leg
Gary Crawford, Steamboat Springs, Colo.
   28th, Nordic Combined event

Jeff Davis, Steamboat Springs, Colorado
   17th, 70-meter special jumping
   44th, 90-meter special jumping
Jim Denney, Duluth, Minnesota
   36th, 70-meter special jumping
   8th, 90-meter special jumping
Mike Devecka, Bend, Oregon
   Nordic Combined event, DNF

Stan Dunklee, Dover-Foxcroft, Maine
  22nd, men's 15k event
  30th, men's 30k event
  33rd, men's 50k event
  8th, relay event, fourth leg
Jim Galanes, Newfane, Vermont
  33rd, men's 15k event
  41st, men's 30k event
  8th, relay event, second leg
Jim Grahek, Ely, Minnesota
  Did Not Compete
Betsy Haines, Anchorage, Alaska
  37th, women's 5k event
Todd Kempainen, Minnetonka, Minnesota
  Did Not Compete
Bill Koch, Putney, Vermont
  16th, men's 15k event
  DNF, men's 30k event
  13th, men's 50k event
  8th, relay event, first leg
Kerry Lynch, Granby, Colorado
  18th, Nordic Combined event
Jim Maki, Coleraine, Minnesota
  26th, 70-meter special jumping
Walter Malmquist, Post Mills, Vermont
  12th, Nordic Combined event
  27th, 90-meter special jumping
David Michael, Anchorage, Alaska
  Did Not Compete
Chris McNeill, Polaris, Montana
  23rd, 70-meter special jumping
Alison Owen Spencer, Park City, Utah
  22nd, women's 5k event
  22nd, women's 10k event
  7th, relay event, second leg
Doug Peterson, Hanover, New Hampshire
  45th, men's 30k event
  DNF, men's 50k event
Judy Rabinowitz, Fairbanks, Alaska
  Did Not Compete
Daniel Simoneau, Livermore Falls, Maine
  Did Not Compete
Margaret Spencer, New Lane, Vermont
  31st, women's 10k event
  7th, relay event, fourth leg
Craig Ward, Lake Placid, New York
  Did Not Compete
Reed Zuehlke, Eau Claire, Wisconsin
  45th, 90-meter special jumping

NORDIC STAFF
John Bower, Team Leader, Park City, Utah
James Page, Nordic Combined Coach,
  Park City, Utah
Rob Kiesel, Cross Country Coach,
  Ketchum, Idaho
Bud Fisher, Assistant Coach, Williamstown,
  Massachussetts
Glenn Kotlarek, Jumping Coach, Duluth,
  Minnesota

Luge

The Luge competition at the XIII Olympic Winter Games proved to be a disaster for medal-winners from the '76 Games at Innsbruck. Not a single medal-winner repeated at Lake Placid, and spills, crashes and ruined hopes were the order of the week for these daring athletes on their speeding sleds.

The lumpy 1,000-meter men's course claimed the '76 gold medalist, East German Detlef Guenther, and early leader Ernst Haspinger of Italy, who crashed on the next-to-last curve on his final run, crossing the finish line ahead of his sled.

The men's winner turned out to be gutty Bernhard Glass, the only remaining East German in contention in the race, and a 22-year-old Army Sergeant. Italy's Paul Hildgartner took the silver medal and Anton Winkler of West Germany the bronze in the men's singleseater competition.

Twenty-four-year-old Vera Zozulia of the USSR earned the first Luge medal in Olympic history for her country by capturing the women's singleseater event in a tough field. It was the fitting end to an eight-year "crash" course by the USSR in the sport, even including the reported construction of a luge run exactly like the one at Lake Placid deep inside the Soviet Union someplace. Two-time world champion Melitta Sollman of East Germany was second, and surprising Insroda Amantova of the USSR was third for the bronze medal to continue the shocking Soviet success in a sport they had been on the outside of in previous Games.

Form held true in the doubles competition by the men, with pre-Games favorites Hans Rinn and Norbert Hahn of East Germany outdistancing the field to win the coveted gold medal. Right behind in second place were Paul Oschnitzer and Karl Brunner of Italy, with third going to George Fluckinger and Karl Schrott of Austria in a close race all the way down the run.

The United States lugers recorded their best efforts ever in Olympic competition in this crazy sport, with national champion Jeff Tucker of Westport, Connecticut, taking 12th in the men's singleseater, fisherman John Fee of Dutch Harbor, Alaska, taking 14th and bearded Rich Stithem of Sterling, Colorado, taking 20th in the field of 23 male lugers.

In the women's singles, national champion Debby Genovese of Rockford, Illinois, nursing a bruised shoulder finished a strong 15th, Lake Placid artist Donna Burke took 22nd. Three others were eliminated by spills on the icy course.

In the men's doubles, Ty Danco of Cleveland and Richard Healey, a garage owner from Annandale, New Jersey, combined for a U.S.-best-ever 11th place finish among the 19 entries. Ray Bateman and Frank Masley finished in 18th place after a mishap on their first run.

The new run at Lake Placid, however, promises bigger and better things in the future for Americans who will tackle this challenging and exciting sport that the Europeans have long dominated.

TEAM PERSONNEL

R. Bateman   D. Burke   S. Charlesworth

W. Danco   J. Fee   D. Genovese

R. Healey   F. Masley   R. Stithem

J. Tucker   J. Murray   P. Rogowski

LUGE TEAM PERSONNEL
Ray Bateman, Somerville, New Jersey
  28th, doubles (with Frank Masley)
Donna Burke, Lake Placid, New York
  17th, women's singles
Susan Charlesworth, Lake Placid, New York
  women's singles, DNF.
Walter "Ty" Danco, Pepper Pike, O.
  21st, doubles (with Ray Dick Healey)
John Fee, Plattsburgh, New York
  14th, men's singles
Debra Genovese, Rockford, Illinois
  15th, women's singles
Richard Healey, Annandale, New Jersey
  21st, doubles (with Ty Danco)
Francis Masley, Newark, Delaware
  28th, doubles (with Ray Bateman)
Richard Stithem, Sterling, Colorado
  20th, men's singles
Jeffrey Tucker, Westport, Connecticut
  12th, men's singles

LUGE TEAM STAFF
Piotr Rogowski, Coach, New York, N.Y.
James Murray, Manager, Lakewood, Colo.

Speed Skating

Never in Olympic Games annals has one sport been so totally dominated by one individual. It is doubtful that it will even happen again, so forceful was its impact on the sporting community of the world that February in Lake Placid.

Eric Heiden's string of five gold medals in five events will rank as perhaps the all-time feat in Olympic history, bettering the achievements of such greats as Jessie Owens and Mark Spitz, among others. In addition, he was the first man to have entered all five speed skating events in any Olympic Winter Games.

The Madison, Wisconsin, youngster breezed through a field of talented skaters who were dead-set on taking his laurels away each day. Starting with the 500-meter sprint and ending with the grueling 10,000 meters, Heiden was equal to the challenge time after time. It was compared by some experts, trying vainly to compare it with something in track and field, like a 100-meter sprinter winning the dashes, then coming in first in the six-mile run as well. It simply hasn't been done before in sports.

Heiden gave notice of what was to come on February 15 in the 500 meters, the opening race on the Olympic card. He trailed Soviet world and Olympic record holder Evgenjy Kulikov at the 350-meter mark. But on the last curve, Eric switched to his afterburner and blazed past the Russian to win by half-a-second. It signalled the start of the greatest attack on the record book in Olympic history.

It all began to fall in place then for Eric. Olympic records in the 1000 meters, the 1500 meters, the 5000 meters, then finally, the day arrived for the demanding 10,000 meters, a race that some thought he could simply not win. He surely could not have that much energy left in that great body.

But again Heiden proved them wrong, in fact he went out and blitzed through a good field so quickly that he had his gold medal press conference halfway through the sixteen heats after setting a new world record by over six seconds with a clocking of 14:28.13. The impossible had been achieved, and with shocking ease.

On the flip side of the coin was sister Beth Heiden, who, like Eric, had been pasted all over the covers of various sporting magazines ahead of the Games, as well as the cover of Time. She was rated the favorite, perhaps unfairly, in as many as four of the women's events. The pressure and the attention turned into an albatross that the 20-year-old could not handle, and it showed.

Beth managed only a bronze medal in the final event, the women's 3000 meters, and reacted emotionally at a press conference following that event, telling the press that she felt pressured by them and not able to skate for herself.

Not so bad, however, for plucky Leah Poulos Mueller, who almost gave up the sport following the '76 Games at Innsbruck when she married teammate Peter Mueller and the couple felt that there was money for only one to continue. However, both got jobs through the USOC Job Opportunities Program and stayed on.

At Lake Placid, she finished second in the 500 meters to Karin Enke of East Germany, and second to Soviet star Natalia Petruseva in the 1000 meters to wrap up her fine career with the pair of silver medals to take back to Wisconsin.

The rest of the story was not so glamorous for the USA speed skating team, which had been tabbed for as many as 20 medals alone by some pre-Games prognostications in the media. Not a single skater besides the Heidens and Ms. Mueller managed to crack the top three and carry home a medal.

SPEED SKATING TEAM PERSONNEL

Jim Chapin, St. Louis, Missouri
  24th, men's 500 meters
Mary Docter, Madison, Wisconsin
  12th, women's 1500 meters
  6th, women's 3000 meters
Sarah Docter, Madison, Wisconsin
  23rd, women's 500 meters
  14th, women's 1000 meters
  13th, women's 1500 meters
  10th, women's 3000 meters
Beth Heiden, Madison, Wisconsin
  7th, women's 500 meters
  5th, women's 1000 meters
  7th, women's 1500 meters
  3rd, women's 3000 meters
Eric Heiden, Madison, Wisconsin
  1st, men's 500 meters
  1st, men's 1000 meters
  1st, men's 1500 meters
  1st, men's 5000 meters
  1st, men's 10,000 meters
Erik Henriksen, Champaign, Illinois
  Did Not Compete
Dan Immerfall, Madison, Wisconsin
  5th, men's 500 meters
Kim Kostron, St. Paul, Minnesota
  Did Not Compete
Craig Kressler, Midland, Michigan
  11th, men's 1000 meters
  18th, men's 1500 meters
  18th, men's 5000 meters
  DNF, men's 10,000 meters
Leah Mueller, Dousman, Wisconsin
  2nd, women's 500 meters
  2nd, women's 1000 meters
Peter Mueller, Dousman, Wisconsin
  5th, men's 1000 meters
Connie Paraskevin, Detroit, Michigan
  Did Not Compete
Mike Plant, West Allis, Wisconsin
  Did Not Compete
Tom Plant, West Allis, Wisconsin
  17th, men's 1500 meters
Nancy Swider, Park Ridge, Illinois
  Did Not Compete
Kent Thometz, Minnetonka, Minnesota
  Did Not Compete
Dr. Michael Woods, S. Milwaukee, Wis.
  7th, men's 5000 meters
  4th, men's 10,000 meters

SPEED SKATING STAFF

Peter Schotting, Coach, Milwaukee, Wis.
Dianne Holum, Coach, Madison, Wisconsin
Bill Cushman, Manager, St. Paul, Minnesota

TEAM PERSONNEL

J. Chapin   M. Docter   S. Docter

B. Heiden   E. Heiden   E. Henriksen

D. Immerfall   K. Kostron   C. Kressler

L. Mueller   P. Mueller   C. Paraskevin

M. Plant   T. Plant   N. Swider

K. Thometz   M. Woods

B. Cushman   D. Holum   P. Schotting

U.S. Summer Olympic Teams

Archery

TEAM PERSONNEL
Judi Adams, 20, Phoenix, Arizona
Lynette Johnson, 23, Glendale, Arizona
Scott Kertson, 18, Phoenix, Arizona
Darrell Pace, 23, Cincinnati, Ohio
Coach: Dwight Nyquist, Seattle, Wash.
Manager: Harold Kremer, Atlanta, Georgia

Results of Olympic Trials
Oxford, Ohio May 19-22, 1980
Ladies Division (52 entries):
1. Judi Adams 2,565 (#1 FITA round 1,272, #2 FITA Round 1,293)
2. **Lynette Johnson 2,523 (#1 round 1,257, #2 1,266)
3. Irene Daubenspeck 2,505 (#1 round 1,273, #2 round 1,232)
4. *Luann Ryon 2,485 (#1 round 1,255, #2 round 1,230)
5. Ruth Rowe 2,474 (#1 round 1,257, #2 round 1,217)
6. Robin Wools 2,429 (#1 round 1,222, #2 round 1,207)
7. Melanie Soltysik (#1 round 1,220, #2 round 1,202) 2,422
8. Cindy Vezzetti (#1 round 1,225, #2 round 1,197) 2,422
9. Michelle Frank 2,414 (#1 round 1,212, #2 round 1,202)
10. Carole Clark 2,407 (#1 round 1,219, #2 round 1,188)
11. Nancy Myrick 2,395 (#1 round 1,207, #2 round 1,188)
(*) 1976 Olympic champion
(**) 1979 Pan American champion

Men's Division (73 entries):
1. *Darrell Pace 2,572 (#1 FITA Round 1,306, #2 FITA round 1,266)
2. Scott Kertson 2,549 (#1 round 1,207, #2 round 1,279)
3. Richard McKinney 2,537 (#1 round 1,280, #2 round 1,257)
4. Ed Eliason 2,522 (#1 round 1,254, #2 round 1,268)
5. Tom Stevenson, Jr. 2,509 (#1 round 1,267, #2 round 1,242)
6. Richard Bednar 2,508 (#1 round 1,262, #2 round 1,246)
7. Henry Churchill 2,507 (#1 round 1,257, #2 round 1,250)
8. Larry Smith 2,458 (#1 round 1,250, #2 round 1,235)
9. Douglas Brothers 2,481 (#1 round 1,260, #2 round 1,231)
10. Robert Ryder, Jr. 2,469 (#1 round 1,222, #2 round 1,247)
11. **Rodney Baston 2,458 (#1 round 1,226, #2 round 1,232)
(*) 1976 Olympic champion
(**) 1979 Pan American champion

TEAM PERSONNEL

J. Adams   L. Johnson   S. Kertson

D. Pace   H. Kremer   D. Nyquist

Pre-Olympic International Competition
V Target Championship of the Americas
Melgar, Colombia June 6-7, 1980
Ladies Division:
1. Luann Ryon, USA 1,294 (one FITA Round only); 2. *Lynette Johnson, USA 1,268; 3. *Judi Adams, USA 1,263; 4. Irene Daubenspeck, USA 1,248.

Team: 1. USA 3,815; 2. Canada; 3. Mexico.

Men's Division:
1. Ed Eliason, USA 1,285 (one FITA round only); 2. Tom Stevenson, USA 1,278; 3. *Darrell Pace, USA 1,265; 4. *Scott Kertson, USA 1,260.

Team: 1. USA 3,828; 2. Canada.

(*) Members 1980 USA Olympic Team

Athletics (Track & Field)

TEAM PERSONNEL

Colin Anderson, 28, Golden Valley, Minnesota (Discus)

Duncan Atwood, 24, Seattle, Washington (Javelin)

Willie Banks, 24, Los Angeles, California (Triple Jump)

Andy Bessette, 27, Vernon, Connecticut (Hammer Throw)

Doug Brown, 28, Eugene, Oregon (Steeplechase)

Dick Buerkle, 32, Atlanta, Georgia (5,000m)

James Butler, 20, Stillwater, Oklahoma (200m)

Gregory Caldwell, 23, Los Angeles, California (Triple Jump)

Anthony Campbell, 20, Carson, California (110 Hurdles)

Matt Centrowitz, 25, Eugene, Oregon (5,000m)

Bob Coffman, 29, Houston, Texas (Decathlon)

Dedy Cooper, 24, Richmond, California (110 Hurdles)

Fred Dixon, 30, Placentia, California (Decathlon)

Boris Djerassi, 28, Raynham, Massachussetts (Hammer Throw)

Benji Durden, 28, Stone Mountain, Georgia (Marathon)

Michael Durkin, 27, Chicago, Illinois (1,500m)

Marco Evoniuk, 22, Longmont, Colorado (50-k Walk)

Rod Ewaliko, 26, Seattle, Washington (Javelin)

Allan Feuerbach, 32, Los Gatos, California (Shotput)

Benn Fields, 25, Salisbury Mills, New York (High Jump)

Stanley Floyd, 19, Putney, Georgia (100m)

Herman Frazier, 26, Tempe, Arizona (Relays)

Gregory Fredericks, 30, Boalsburg, Pennsylvania (5,000m)

Willie Gault, 19, Griffin, Georgia (Relays)

Harvey Glance, 23, Auburn, Alabama (100m)

Bill Green, 19, Palo Alto, California (400m)

John Gregorek, 20, Northport, New York (Steeplechase)

Kyle Heffner, 25, Richardson, Texas (Marathon)

James Heiring, 23, San Bernardino, California (20-k Walk)

Tomas Hintnaus, 22, San Jose, California (Pole Vault)

James Howard, Jr., 20, Alvin, Texas (High Jump)

Paul Jordan, 24, Houston, Texas (Triple Jump)

Bruce Kennedy, 29, San Jose, California (Javelin)

Steve Lacy, 24, Madison, Wisconsin (1,500m)

Melvin Lattany, 20, Brunswick, Georgia (100m)

David Lee, 21, University City, Missouri (400m Hurdles)

Carl Lewis, 19, Willingboro, Jew Jersey (Long Jump)

John McArdle, 23, Eugene, Oregon (Hammer)

TEAM PERSONNEL

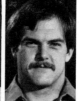

C. Anderson   W. Banks   A. Bessette

G. Caldwell   A. Campbell   M. Centrowitz

B. Djerassi   B. Durden   M. Durkin

S. Floyd   H. Frazier   G. Fredericks

J. Gregorek   K. Heffner   J. Heiring

William McChesney, 21, Eugene, Oregon (5,000m)

Walter McCoy, 21, Tallahassee, Florida (400m)

Henry Marsh, 26, Salt Lake City, Utah (3,000m Steeplechase)

Edwin Moses, 24, Mission Viejo, California (400m Hurdles)

Larry Myricks, 24, Tallahassee, Florida (Long Jump)

Renaldo Nehemiah, 21, Scotch Plains, New Jersey (110m Hurdles)

Daniel O'Connor, 28, Westminster, California (50-k Walk)

Nat Page, 23, Evanston, Illinois (High Jump)

Donald Paige, 23, Marcy, New York (800m)

Lee Palles, 24, Mobile, Alabama (Decathlon)

Ben Plucknett, 26, San Jose, California (Discus)

TEAM PERSONNEL

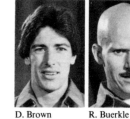

D. Brown   R. Buerkle   J. Butler

R. Coffman   D. Cooper   F. Dixon

M. Evoniuk   A. Feuerbach   B. Fields

W. Gault   H. Glance   W. Green

T. Hintnaus   J. Howard   P. Jordan

John Powell, 33, Cupertino, California (Discus)

Dan Ripley, 26, Bishop, California (Pole Vault)

James Robinson, 25, Oakland, California (800m)

Alberto Salazar, 21, Wayland, Massachussetts (1,000m)

Anthony Sandoval, 26, Los Alamos, New Mexico (Marathon)

Peter Schmock, 23, Cupertino, California (Shotput)

Carl Schueler, 24, Silver Springs, Maryland (50-k Walk)

Steve Scott, 24, Tempe, Arizona (1,500m)

Todd Scully, Jr., 31, Blacksburg, Virginia (20-K Walk)

Willie Smith III, 24, Auburn, Alabama (400m)

TEAM PERSONNEL

 S. Lacy
 M. Lattany
 D. Lee

 L. Myricks
 R. Nehemiah
D. O'Connor

J. Robinson
A. Salazar
A. Sandoval

 C. Virgin
 J. Walker
 L. Walker

 J. Carnes
 E. Cunliffe
 R. Griak

TEAM PERSONNEL

 C. Lewis
 J. McArdle
 W. McChesney

 N. Page
 D. Paige
 L. Palles

 C. Schueler
 S. Scott
T. Scully

 C. Wiley
 B. Williams
R. Williams

 S. Huntsman
 R. Newland
 J. Santos

TEAM PERSONNEL

 W. McCoy
 H. Marsh
E. Moses

 B. Plucknett
J. Powell
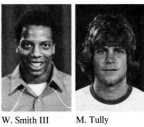 D. Ripley

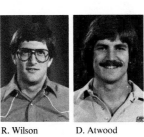 P. Shmock
W. Smith III
M. Tully

 R. Wilson
 D. Atwood

 S. Simmons
 T. Tellez
 W. Williams

Frederick Taylor, 22, Houston, Texas (200m)
Michael Tully, 23, Long Beach, California (Pole Vault)
Craig Virgin, 24, Lebanon, Illinois 10,000m)
James Walker, 22, Atlanta, Georgia (400m Hurdles)
Larry Walker, 37, Canoga Park, California (20-k Walk)
Clifford Wiley, 24, Houston, Texas (200m)
Mac Wilkins, 29, Soquel, California (Discus)
Barton Williams, 23, Vallejo, California (400m Hurdles)
Randy Williams, 26, Los Angeles, California (Long Jump)
Randy Wilson, 23, Ankeny, Iowa (800m)

Head Coach: Jimmy Carnes, Gainesville, Florida
Assistant Coach: Stan Huntsman, Knoxville, Tennessee
Assistant Coach: Jim Santos, Hayward, California
Assistant Coach: Tom Tellez, Houston, Texas
Assistant Coach: Willie Williams, Tucson, Arizona
Head Manager: Robert Newland, Eugene, Oregon
Assistant Manager: Ernie Cunliffe, Colorado Springs, Colorado
Assistant Manager: Roy Griak, Minneapolis, Minnesota
Assistant Manager: Steve Simmons, San Jose, California

Summaries U.S. Olympic Trials, Eugene, Oregon, June 21-29, 1980

100 Meters (10.26 sec.):
1. Stanley Floyd, Auburn T.C.; 2. Harvey Glance, Auburn T.C. 10.27; 3. Mel Lattany, Univ. of Georgia 10.30; 4. Carl Lewis, Univ. of Houston 10.32; 5. Willie Gault, Univ. of Tennessee 10.33; 6. Steve Williams, Athletic Attic 10.36; 7. Houston McTear, Muhammad Ali T.C. 10.43; 8. Jerome Deal, Univ. of Texas at El Paso 10.57.

200 Meters (20.49 sec.):
1. James Butler, Oklahoma State; 2. Clifford Wiley, D.C. International 20.54; 3. Fred Taylor, Philadelphia Pioneers 20.70; 4. LaMonte King, Stars and Stripes T.C. 20.73; 5. Willie Gault, Univ. of Tennessee 20.82; 6. Dwayne Evans, Arizona State 20.83; 7. Mark Duper, Northwestern Louisiana State 20.91; 8. Otis Melvin, Muhammad Ali T.C. 21.16.

Olympic Trials (continued)

400 Meters (45.85 sec.):
1. Bill Green, Univ. S. California; 2. Willie Smith, Auburn T.C. 45.97; 3. Walter McCoy, Athletic Attic, 46.06; 4. Herman Frazier, Philadelphia Pioneers 46.16; 5. Tony Darden, Philadelphia Pioneers 46.41; 6. Anthony Blair, Univ. of Tennessee 46.57; 7. Charles Oliver, Florida T.C. 46.64; 8. Albert Shorts, Mccabi T.C. 46.78.

800 Meters (1:44.53):
1. Don Paige, Athletic Attic 1:44.53; 2. James Robinson, Inner City A.C. 1:45.58; 3. Randy Wilson, Athletic Attic 1:45.82; 4. Mark Enyeart, Pacific Coast Club 1:46.05; 5. James DeRienzo, New York A.C. 1:46.19; 6. David Mack, Univ. of Oregon 1:46.67; 7. William Martin, Iona College 1:46.86. Johnny Gray, Santa Monica T.C., did not finish.

1,500 Meters (3:35.15):
1. Steve Scott, Sub-4 T.C. (Trials Record. Previous record 3:36.47 Rick Wohlhuter, 1976); 2. Steve Lacy, S. California. Striders 3:36.23; 3. Mike Durkin, Chicago T.C. 3:38.04; 4. Todd Harbour, Baylor 3:38.14; 5. (tie) Richard Harris, Colorado State and Craig Masback, New York Pioneer Club 3:38.46; 7. Jim Spivey, Indiana Univ. 3:42.30; 8. Kevin Ryan, Bowling Green State 3:46.04.

5,000 Meters (13:30.62):
1. Matt Centrowitz, Oregon T.C.; 2. Dick Buerkle, New York A.C. 13:31.90; 3. Bill McChesney, Univ. of Oregon 13:34.42; 4. Jerald Jones, Santa Monica T.C. 13:34.71; 5. Don Clary, Oregon T.C. 13:38.48; 6. Daniel Dillon, Greater Boston T.C. 13:41.58; 7. Steve Ortiz, USLA 14:14.01; 8. Douglas Padilla, B.Y.U. 14:19.80; 9. Marty Liquori, Athletic Attic 14:22.0.

10,000 Meters (27:45.61):
1. Craig Virgin, Front Runner T.C. (Olympic Trials record. Previous record 27:55.45 Frank Shorter, 1976); 2. Greg Fredericks, Brook T.C. 28:03.44; 3. Alberto Salazar, Greater Boston T.C. 28:10.42; 4. Jeff Wells, Athletics West 28:12.82: 5. Mike Buhmann, Frank Shorter Racing Team 28:12.99; 6. Thomas Wysocki, Silver State T.C. 28:19.56; 7. Steve Ortiz, UCLA 28:27.39; 8. Tony Sandoval, Athletics West 28:29.94.

20-Kilometer Race Walk (1:27.12):
1. (tie) Marco Evoniuk, Frank Shorter Racing Team and James Heiring, Southern California Road Runners; 3. Daniel O'Connor, New York A.C. 1:29.05; 4. Todd Scully, Shore A.C. 1:30.28; 5. Larry Walker, Tobias Striders 1:31.06; 6. Carl Schueler, Potomac Valley Seniors 1:31.17; 7. Joseph Berendt, U.S. Army 1:35.32; 8. Alan Price, Potomac Valley Seniors 1:36.36.

50-Kilometer Race Walk (3:59:34):
1. Carl Schueler; 2. Marco Evonuik, Frank Shorter Racing Team 4:00:30; 3. Dan O'Connor, New York A.C. 4:11:03; 4. Jim Heiring, Southern California Road Runners 4:12:37; 5. Vince O'Sullivan 4:17:57; 6. Wayne Glusker 4:23:44; 7. Tom Dooley 4:26:15; 8. Dennis Reilly 4:35.50.

110-Meter Hurdles (13.26):
1. Renaldo Nehemiah, DC International; 2. Dedy Cooper, Bay Area Striders 13:39; 3. Anthony Campbell, Muhammad Ali T.C. 13.44; 4. Dan Lavitt, Pacific Coast Club 13.56; 5. Wayne Mason, Cincinnati 13.60; 6. Jeffrey Bruce, Washington State T.C. 13.86; 7. Reggie Towns, Univ. of Tennessee 13.87; 8. Eugene Miller, Auburn T.C. 13.94.

400-Meter Hurdles (47.90:
1. Edwin Moses, Utopian International (Trials record. Previous record, Moses 48.22, 1976); 2. James Walker, Auburn T.C. 49.04; 3. (tie) David Lee, Univ. of Southern Illinois and Bart Williams, Stars and Stripes 49.34; 5. James King, Maccabi T.C. 49.49; 6. Richard Greybehl, Pacific Coast Club 50.10; 7. Nate Lundy, Univ. of Indiana 50.37; 8. Andre Phillips, Muhammad Ali T.C. (no time).

3,000-Meter Steeplechase (8:15.68):
1. Henry Marsh (American record. Previous record 8:19.3 Doug Brown, 1978); 2. Doug Brown, Athletics West 8:20; 3. John Gregorek, New York A.C. 8:21.32; 4. Kenneth Martin 8:26.72; 5. Randy Jackson, Univ. of Wisconsin 8:28.87; 6. Dan Heikkinen, Univ. of Michigan 8:29.46; 7. Mike Roche, Greater Boston T.C. 8:32.34; 8. Tom Hunt, Univ. of Arizona 8:35.3.

High Jump (7-5).
1. Benn Fields, Philadelphia Pioneers; 2. Nathaniel Page, 7-3 3/4; 3. James Howard, Texas A&M 7-3 3/4; 4. Mike Lattany, Michigan 7-2 1/2; 5. Lt. James Barrineau, U.S. Army 7-2 1/2; 6. Robert Berry; Indiana Univ. 7-2 1/2; 7. (tie) Ken Glover, Eastern Kentucky St. and Jeff Woodard, Univ. of Alabama, 7-2 1/2.

Long Jump (27-2):
1. Larry Myricks, Athletic Attic, (Trials record. Previous record 26-6½ Ralph Boston, 1968) 2. Carl Lewis, Univ. of Houston 26-3 1/2w; 3. Randy Williams, Maccabi T.C. 26-1 3/4; 4. Larry Doubley, Maccabi T.C. 25-11 3/4; 5. Greg Artis, Middle Tennessee State 25-11 1/2; 6. Arnie Robinson, San Diego, California 25-11w; 7. Jason Grimes, Univ. of Tennessee 25-7 1/2w; 8. LaMonte King, Stars and Stripes 25-5 1/2.

Triple Jump (55-1 1/2):
1. Willie Banks, American Council of Athletics; 2. Paul Jordan, Houston Athletic Club 53-2¼; 3. Greg Caldwell, Star and Stripes T.C. 53-2½; 4. James Butts, Muhammad Ali T.C. 53-2¼; 5. William Lloyd, U.S. Army 53-1 3/4; 6. Chip Benson, UCLA 53- 0 1/4; 7. Vince Parette, Colorado Flyers 52-8 3/4; 8. Robert Cannon, Univ. of Indiana 52-5 1/4.

Pole Vault (18-4 1/2):
1. Tom Hintnaus, Univ. of Oregon; 2. Dan Ripley, Pacific Coast Club, 3. Mike Tully, New York A.C. 18-2 1/2; 4. Steve Smith, American Council of Athletics 18- 2 1/2; 5. Billy Olson, Abilene Christian 18-0 1/2; 6. Terry Porter, Houston Athletics T.C., 18-0 1/2; 7. Jon Switzer, Univ. of Oregon 17-6 3/4; 8. Doug Bockmiller, West Valley T.C. 17-6 3/4.

Shotput (68-4):
1. Peter Schmock, So. California Striders; 2. Al Feuerbach, Athletics West, 68-3 3/4; 3. Colin Anderson, Chicago T.C., 68-0 1/4; 4. Brian Oldfield, 67-4 1/4; 5. Ian Pyka. San Jose Stars 66-9 1/2; 6. Dave Laut, Athletics West 66-6 3/4; 7. Sam Walker, Athletic Attic 66-4 1/2; 8. Steve Summers, Maccabi T.C. 66-4.

Discus Throw (225-4):
1. Mac Wilkins, Athletics West; 2. John Powell, San Jose Stars, 223-1; 3. Ben Plucknett, South Central T.C., 218-2; 4. Al Oerter, New York A.C. 215-1; 5. Stan Cain, Athletic Attic 210-11; 6. Ken Stadel, Athletics West 208-2; 7. Tim Scott, Texas A&M, 196-8; 8. Jay Silvester, Orem, Utah 196-11.

Javelin Throw (291-0):
1. Rod Ewaliko, Athletics West (Trails record. Previous record 281-1, Bill Schmidt, 1976); 2. Bruce Kennedy, San Jose Stars 274-5; 3. Duncan Atwood, Athletics West 271-3; 4. Tom Petranoff, Southern California Striders 271-3; 5. Curtis Ransford 269-3; 6. Bob Roggy, Athletics West 262-5; 7. Bill Schmidt, Athletic Attic 250-8; 8. Scott Sorchik, Bruce T.C., New York 248-11.

Hammer Throw (232-10):
1. Andy Bessette, New York A.C.; 2. John McArdle, Oregon T.C. 230-11; 3. Boris Djerassi, New York A.C. 230-8; 4. David McKenzie 225-10; 5. Rick Buss, Stanford T.C. 225-6; 6. Peter Galle, Maccabi T.C.; 7. Dwight Midies 216-4; 8. Edward Burke, San Jose Stars 214-8.

Decathlon (8,184 points):
1. Bob Coffman, Houston Athletics T.C.; 2. Lee Palles, Athletic Attic 8,159; 3. Fred Dixon, Southern California Striders 8,154; 4. John Crist, Greensboro Pacers 8,053; 5. Tony Allen-Cooksey, Terre Haute T.C., 7,791; 6. Al Hamlin, Sam Adams Multi Events T.C., 7,720; 7. Jim Howell, Houston Athletics T.C., 7,709; 8. Rob Baker, Hi Plains T.C., 7,651; 9. Wes Herbst, Reno, Nevada, 7,616; 10. Brian Mondschien, Philadelphia Pioneers 7,600.

Marathon (2:10:18.6):
1. Tony Sandoval, Athletics West; 2. Benji Durden, Stone Mountain, Georgia 2:10.40.3; 3. Kyle Heffner, Club Adidas 2:10.54.1; 4. Ron Tabb, Portland, Oregon 2:12.39; 5. Jeff Wells, Athletics West 2:13.16; 6. Kevin McCarey, Athletics West 2:13.17; 7. Randy Thomas, Greater Boston T.C. 2:13.40; 8. Gordon Minty 2:13.53.9.

Athletics (Track & Field) (Women)

TEAM PERSONNEL

Jodi Anderson, 22, Los Angeles, California (Pentathlon & Long Jump)

Lynne Anderson, 27, Golden Valley, Minnesota (Discus)

Roberta Belle, 21, Baltimore, Maryland (Relays)

Jeanette Bolden, 20, Los Angeles, California (Relays)

Alice Brown, 19, Altadena, California (100m)

Julie Brown, 25, San Diego, California (800m, 1,500m)

Robin Campbell, 21, Palo Alto, California (800m)

Chandra Cheeseborough, 21, Jacksonville, Florida (100m, 200m)

Sharon Dabney, 22, Philadelphia, Pennsylvania (Relays)

Mary Decker, 21, Eugene, Oregon (1,500m)

Benita Fitzgerald, 19, Woodbridge, Vermont (100m Hurdles)

Gwen Gardner, 19, Los Angeles, California (400m)

Paula Girven, 22, Dale City, Virginia (High Jump)

Pam Greene, 26, Mesa, Arizona (200m)

Lorna Griffin, 24, Huntington Beach, California (Discus)

Marlene Harmon, 17, Thousand Oaks, California (Pentathlon)

Karen Hawkins, 23, Houston, Texas (200m)

Stephanie Hightower, 22, Louisville, Kentucky (100m Hurdles)

Denean Howard, 15, Granada Hills, California (400m)

Sherri Howard, 18, Granada Hills, California (400m)

Francie Larrieu, 27, Waco, Texas (1,500m)

Carol Lewis, 16, Willingboro, New Jersey (Long Jump)

Kathy McMillan, 22, Raeford, North Carolina (Long Jump)

Madeline Manning Mims, 32, Tulsa, Oklahoma (800m)

Brenda Morehead, 22, Toledo, Ohio (100m)

Mary Osborne, 19, Billings, Montana (Javelin)

Louise Ritter, 22, Denton, Texas (High Jump)

Kate Schmidt, 26, Coquitlam, British Columbia (Javelin)

Maren Seidler, 29, Los Gatos, California (Shotput)

Karin Smith, 25, Venice, California (Javelin)

Pamela Spencer, 22, Northridge, California (High Jump)

Kim Thomas, 20, Queens Village, New York (Relays)

Ann Turbyne, 23, Waterville, Maine (Shotput)

Linda Waltman, 23, Mansfield, Texas (Pentathlon)

Diane Williams, 19, Chicago, Illinois (Relays)

Canzetta Young, 18, Beaver Falls, Pennsylvania (100m Hurdles)

TEAM PERSONNEL

J. Anderson   L. Anderson   R. Belle

B. Fitzgerald   G. Gardner   P. Greene

C. Lewis   K. McMillan   M. M. Mims

K. Thomas   A. Turbyne   L. Waltman

E. Dennis   K. Foreman   V. Plihal

Head Coach: Ken Foreman, Seattle, Washington

Assistant Coach: Edward Temple, Nashville, Tennessee

Assistant Coach: Dave Rodda, Long Beach, California

Head Manager: Dr. Evie Dennis, Denver, Colorado

Assistant Manager: Virginia Plihal, Tyndall, South Dakota

TEAM PERSONNEL

J. Bolden   A. Brown   R. Campbell

L. Griffin   K. Hawkins   S. Hightower

B. Morehead   M. Osborne   K. Schmidt

D. Williams   C. Young   J. Brown

D. Rodda   E. Temple

U.S. Olympic Trials
Official Summaries

100 Meters (11.32):
1. Alice Brown, Naturite T.C.; 2. Brenda Morehead, Tennessee State 11.43;
3. Chandra Cheeseborough, Tennessee State 11.45; 4. Jodi Anderson, Naturite T.C. 11.52; 5. Diane Williams, Michigan State 11.61; 6. (tie) Jeanette Bolden, Naturite T.C. and Michaele Glover, Willingboro T.C., 11.65; 8. Florence Griffith, Naturite T.C. 11. 70.

TEAM PERSONNEL

C. Cheeseborough   S. Dabney   M. Decker

D. Howard   S. Howard   F. Larrieu

M. Seidler   K. Smith   P. Spencer

Olympic Trials (cont's)

200 Meters (22.70):
1. Chandra Cheeseborough, Tennessee Tigerbelles; 2. Karen Hawkins, Texas Southern Univ., 23.04; 3. Pamela Greene, Mesa, Arizona, 23.21; 4. Florence Griffith, 23.32; 6. Kelia Bolton, Milbrae Lions T.C., 23.42; 7. Cheryl Gilliam, Michigan State 23.82. Alice Brown, withdrew.

400 Meters (51.48):
1. Sherri Howard, Muhammad Ali T.C. (Trials record. Previous record 51.79 Debra Sapenter, 1976); 2. Gwen Gardner, Los Angeles Mercurette 51.68; 3. Denean Howard, Muhammad Ali T.C. 51.70; 4. Sharon Dabney, Clippers T.C. 52.00; 5. Roberta Belle, D.C. International, 52.67; 6. Kim Thomas, N.Y. Police Athletic League 52.75; 7. Pat Jackson, Prairie View T.C. 53.20; 8. Kelia Bolton, Milbrae Lions T.C. 53.34.

800 Meters (1:58.30):
1. Madeline Manning Mims, Oral Roberts Univ. T.C., (Trials record. Previous record 1:59.9 Madeline Manning, 1976); 2. Julie Brown, Naturite T.C. 2:00.96; 3. Robin Campbell, Stanford T.C. 2:01.23; 4. Delisa Walton Knoxville T.C., 2:01.93; 5. Leann Warren, Univ. of Oregon 2:02.80; 6. Essie Kelley, Prairie View T.C. 2:03.17; 7. Joetta Clark, Atoms T.C., New York, 2:03.83; 8. Kim Gallagher, Willingboro T.C. (no time).

1,500 Meters (4:04.91):
1. Mary Decker, Athletics West (Trials record. Previous record 4:07.32 Cyndy Poor, 1976) 2. Julie Brown, Naturite T.C. 4:07.13; *3. Leann Warren, Univ. of Oregon 4:15.16; 4. Francie Larrieu, Pacific Coast Club, 4:15.32; 5. Linda Goen, UCLA 4:16.86; 6. Brenda Webb, Knoxville T.C. 4:17.52; 7. Cindy Bremser, Wisconsin United 4:17.89; 8. Maggie Keyes 4:18.38.

100-Meter Hurdles (12.90):
1. Stephanie Hightower, Ohio State, (Trials record. Previous record 13.00 Deby LaPlante, 1980 Trials Heats); 2. Benita Fitzgerald, Univ. of Tennessee 13.11; 3. Candy Young, Ryans Angels, 13.30; 4. Lori Dinello 13.52; 5. Pamela Page, Univ. of Missouri 13.65; 6. Linda Weekly, Texas Southern 13.75; 7. Debra Deutsch, Shore A.C. 14.00. Mrs. Debra LaPlante, Station KCBQ TC., did not finish.

Pentathlon (4,697 pts.):
1. Jodi Anderson, Naturite T.C.; 2. Marilyn King, Millbrae Lions 4,199*; 3. Mrs. Linda Waltman, Texas T.C. 4,191**; 4. Marlene Harmon, Naturite T.C., 4,189**; 5. Cindy Gilbert 4,080; 6. Joan Russell, Sam Adams, Multi Events T.C., 4,066; 7. Susan Brownell, Univ. of Virginia 4,037; 8. Theresa Smith, Sportswest 4,000.

High Jump (6-1 1/4):
1. Louise Ritter, Texas Woman's Univ. 6-1 1/4; 2. Paula Girven, Univ. of Maryland 6-1 1/4; 3. Pam Spencer, Naturite T.C. 6-0; 4. Lyn Grosswiller, Naturite T.C. 6-0; 5. Joni Huntley, Sheridan, Oregon, 5-11; 6. Coleen Rienstra, Sun Devils Sports Foundation, 5-11; 7. Wendy Markum, Wisconsin United 5-11; 8. Sue McNeal 5-9 3/4.

Long Jump (22-11 1/2):
1. Jodi Anderson, Naturite TC (American record. Previous record 22-7 1/2, Miss Anderson); 2. Kathy McMillian, Tennessee Tigerbelles 22-2 1/2; 3. Carol Lewis Willingsboro, New Jersey, T.C. 21-6 1/4 w 4. Lorraine Ray 20-11 1/2w; 5. Gwen Loud, L.A. Mercurettes 20-10 1/2; 6. Pat Johnson, Wisconsin United 20-10 1/2; 7. Sandy Crabtree, Club International 20-8 1/2w; 8. Jackie Joyner, E. St. Louis Rollers 20-4w.

Shotput (58-9 1/2):
1. Maren Seidler, San Jose Stars; 2. Ann Turbyne, Gilly's Gymnasium 56-8; *3. Lorna Griffin, American Council of Athletics 52-1 1/2; 4. Sandy Burke, Northeaster Univ. 51-7; 5. Mary Jacobson, Oregon T.C. 50-3 1/2; 6. Susan Thornton, Knoxville T.C. 49-9 3/4; 7. Emily Dole, Club International 49-5 3/4; 8. Melody Rose, Muhammad Ali T.C. 48-6 1/4.

Discus Throw (197-6):
1. Lorna Griffin, American Council of Athletics (Trials record. Previous record 192-8 Griffin in qualifying round); 2. Lynn Winbigler Anderson, Oregon T.C. 184-11; *3. Lisa Vogelsang, American Council of Athletics 176-0; 4. Denise Wood 175-8; 5. Leslie Deniz 175-0; 6. Julia Hansen, Sportswest 171-8; 7. Jan Svendsen 170-3; 8. Julie Car, Sun Devil Sports Federation 167-9.

Javelin Throw (208-5):
1. Karin Smith, American Council of Athletics; 2. Kate Schmidt, Pacific Coast Club 207-4; 3. Mary Osborne, Stanford T.C. 181-3; 4. Jeanne Eggart, Sportswest 169-11; 5. Patty Kearney, Oregon T.C. 166-3; 6. Jackie Nelson, Club International 159-10; 7. Lynda Hughes 158-8; 8. Sally Harmon, Univ. of Oregon 154-9.

(*) Performances in this meet and others by these individuals do not meet the qualifying standards to enter the Olympic Games.

(**) Met qualifying standard for Olympic Games at a meet following the Olympic Selection.

Basketball (Men)

TEAM PERSONNEL
Mark Aguirre, 20, Chicago, Illinois
Rolando Blackman, 21, Brooklyn, N.Y.
Sam Bowie, 19, Lebanon, Pennsylvania
Michael Brooks, 21, Philadelphia, Pa.
Bill Hanzlik, 22, Beloit, Wisconsin
Alton Lister, 21, Dallas, Texas
Rodney McCray, 18, Mt. Vernon, New York
Isiah Thomas, 19, Chicago, Illinois
Darnell Valentine, 21, Wichita, Kansas
Danny Vranes, 21, Salt Lake City, Utah
Buck Williams, 20, Rocky Mount, North
   Carolina
Al Wood, 22, Gray, Georgia

Head Coach: Dave Gavitt, Providence, R.I.
Assistant Coach: Larry Brown, Los Angeles,
   California
Manager: Joe Vancisin, Branford, Conn.

June 16, 1980 — Los Angeles
US Olympians (97)
Aguirre, DePaul 7 1-3 15, Brooks, LaSalle 6
6-7 18, Bowie, Kentucky 3 0-0 6, Blackman,
Kansas St. 3 0-0 6, Thomas, Indiana 4 2-3 10,
Vranes, Utah 4 0-0 8, Wood, N.C. 4 0-0 8,
Lister, Arizona St. 4 0-0 8, Valentine, Kansas
3 0-0 6, Williams, Maryland 5 2-3 12,
Hanzlik, Notre Dame 0 0-0 0, McCray,
Louisville 0 0-0 0. Totals 43 11-16 97.

NBA Stars (84)
Cooper, 5 0-0 10, Johnson, 6 1-3 13, Washington 7 1-4 15, Buckner 2 0-0 4, Gervin 8 0-2
16, Lucas 6 2-2 14, Shumate 0 0-0 0, P.
Smith 0 0-0 0, R. Smith 2 0-0 4, Theus
3 2-2 8.
Totals 39 6-14 84.

Halftime — US 46, NBA 36. Fouled out —
none. Total fouls — Olympians 17, NBA 20.
A-2,611.

June 18, 1980 — Phoenix
US Olympians (97)
Aguirre 6 1-3 13, Brooks 4 2-2 10,
Bowie 7 2-2 16, Blackman 2 2-3 6, Thomas
3 0-0 6, Valentine 2 2-3 6, Vranes 3 0-0 6,
Wood 8 1-3 17, Lister 1 0-0 2, Williams 2 3-3
7, Hanzlik 2 1-2 5, McCray 1 1-2 3.
Totals: 41 15-23 97.

NBA Stars (66)
Robinson 5 0-0 10, Olberding 1 0-0 2, Lanier
4 0-0 8, Gale 2 1-2 5, Johnson 3 4-4 10,
Heard 3 0-0 6, Macy 3 0-0 6, Shumate 4 2-4
10, Reid 4 1-3 9.
Totals: 29 8-13 66.

Halftime — Olympic team 45, NBA 38.
Total fouls — NBA 22, Olympians 21.
A-11,168.

TEAM PERSONNEL

M. Aguirre

R. Blackman

S. Bowie

R. McCray

I. Thomas

D. Valentine

L. Brown

D. Gavitt

J. Vancisin

June 20, 1980 — Seattle
US Olympians (76)
Aguirre 2 4-4 8, Brooks 3 2-2 8, Bowie 5 4-9
14, Blackman 5 2-3 12, Thomas 5 2-3 12,
Wood 3 0-0 6, Hanzlik 1 0-0 2, Williams
2 0-0 4, Vranes 1 0-0 2, Lister 0 0-0 0,
Valentine 4 0-0 8, McCray 0 0-0 0.
Totals: 31 14-21 76.

NBA All-Stars (78)
J. Johnson 3 2-2 8, Russell 2 3-5 7, Sikma
3 0-0 6, Hollins 1 2-2 4, Theus 1 0-0 2,
Natt 4 2-2 10, Westphal 8 3-4 19, Nater 2
2-2 6, Walker 2 0-0 4, Richardson 1 0-0 2,
Paultz 1 0-0 2, Brown 2 0-0 4, Short 2 0-0 4.
Totals: 32 14-17 78.

Halftime: NBA 40, Olympians 35.
Att: 10,192

June 22, 1980 — New York
US Olympians (77)
Aguirre 2 4-7 8, Brooks 6 8-12 20, Bowie 4
5-8 13, Blackman 2 0-0 4, Thomas 4 0-0 8,
Vranes 2 2-2 6, Wood 5 2-4 12, Lister 0 0-0 0,
Valentine 1 2-2 4, Williams 0 2-2 2, Hanzlik
0 0-0 0, McCray 0 0-0 0.
Totals: 26 25-37 77.

NBA Stars (75)
English 7 2-3 16, Shelton 2 6-12 10, Webster
4 1-4 9, Richardson 8 2-3 18, Sobers 3 0-0 6,
Johnson 3 2-3 8, Dunleavy 1 0-0 2,
van Breda Kolff 1 0-0 2, Archibald 0 0-0 0,
Carr 2 0-0 4.
Totals: 31 13-23 75.

Halftime: NBA 34, US Olympians 30 Fouled
out — none. Total fouls — Olympians 20,
NBA Stars 23. A-6,477.

TEAM PERSONNEL

M. Brooks

B. Hanzlick

A. Lister

D. Vranes

B. Williams

A. Wood

June 23, 1980 — Indianapolis
US Olympians (82)
Aguirre 3 6-7 12, Brooks 5 3-9 13, Bowie 4
0-0 8, Blackman 6 0-0 12, Thomas 3 3-4 9,
Hanzlik 1 0-1 2, Lister 0 0-0 0, Valentine 4
2-3 10, Vranes 4 3-6 11, Williams 0 1-3 1,
Wood 1 2-2 4.
Totals: 31 20-35 82.

NBA Stars (76)
Wedman 3 2-2 8, Bantom 2 1-3 5, Robisch
2 5-6 9, Knight 5 2-2 12, Johnson 3 2-4 8,
Bridgeman 5 0-0 10, Hill 0 0-0 0, Round-
field 4 5-9 13, Ford 1 0-0 2, Mix 1 0-0 2,
Gilmore 3 1-4 7.
Totals: 29 18-30 76.

Halftime Score: NBA 42, Olympians 34.
Fouled out — Thomas, Ford. Total fouls —
Olympians 20, NBA 25. A-10,109.

June 29, 1980 — Greensboro, N.C.
US Olympians '80 (81)
Aguirre 6 0-0 12, Blackman 4 0-0 8, Bowie
6 0-0 12, Brooks 5 0-0 10, Hanzlik 1 0-0 2,
Lister 0 0-0 0, McCray 0 0-0 0, Thomas 3 7-7
13, Valentine 0 0-0 0, Vranes 3 2-3 8,
Williams 0 3-5 3, Wood 6 1-3 13.
Totals: 34 13-18 81

US Olympians '76 (77)
Ford (Kansas City) 3 3-6 9, Dantley (Utah)
5 1-3 11; Davis (Phoenix) 7 0-0 14, Buckner
(Milwaukee) 2 0-2 4, May (Chicago) 4 4-9 12,
Armstrong (no team) 1 1-3 3, LaGarde
(Dallas) 2 1-3 5, Hubbard (Detroit) 3 0-0 6,
Kupchak (Washington) 5 3-3 13.
Totals: 32 13-29 77

Halftime Score: 1980 Olympic Team 47,
1976 Olympic Team 33
Fouled out — Buckner ('76) Total Fouls —
'80 Team 22, '76 Team 20 A-7,029.

Basketball (Women)

TEAM PERSONNEL

Carol Blazejowski, 23, Fairview, New Jersey
Denise Curry, 20, Davis, California
Anne Donovan, 18, Ridgewood, New Jersey
Tara Heiss, 23, Bethesda, Maryland
Kris Kirchner, 20, New Providence, New
  Jersey
Debra Miller, 19, Bronx, New York
Cindy Noble, 21, Clarksburg, Ohio
Lataunya Pollard, 19, E. Chicago, Indiana
Jill Rankin, 21, Phillips, Texas
Rosie Walker, 22, Emerson, Arkansas
Holly Warlick, 22, Knoxville, Tennessee
Lynette Woodard, 20, Wichita, Kansas

Head Coach: Sue Gunter, Nacogdoches,
  Texas
Assistant Coach: Pat Head, Seymour,
  Tennessee
Manager: Lea Plarski, Alton, Illinois

WORLD OLYMPIC QUALIFICATION TOURNAMENT FOR WOMEN'S BASKETBALL
Varna, Bulgaria from May 5 to 15, 1980

First Round
Group "A":
Cuba 98 — Japan 75; Poland 46 — Japan 40; Cuba 63 — Poland 62.

Group "B":
*Bulgaria 81 — China 80; Netherlands 107 — Nigeria 33; China 122 — Nigeria 44; Bulgaria 74 — Netherlands 66; China 67 — Netherlands 55; Bulgaria 151 — Nigeria 52.

(*) The score at the end of regular playing time was 71-71.

Group "C":
Korea 70 — Mexico 54; Yugoslavia 64 — Great Britain 56; Great Britain 70 — Mexico 55; Yugoslavia 70 — Korea 69; Yugoslavia 58 — Mexico 56; Korea 78 — Great Britain 65.

TEAM PERSONNEL

C. Blazejowski

D. Curry

A. Donovan

C. Noble

L. Pollard

J. Rankin

S. Gunter

P. Head

L. Plarski

Group "D":
Czechoslovakia 69 — France 60; Brazil 84 — Ireland 72; Czechoslovakia 88 — Brazil 60; France 98 — Ireland 50; France 65 — Brazil 64.

Group "E":
United States 68 — Australia 57; United States 109 — Hungary 79; Hungary 76 — Australia 62.

Group "F":
Italy 63 — Romania 56; Canada 56 — Germany Fed. Rep. 53; Romania 61 — Germany Fed. Rep. 52; Italy 59 — *Canada 57; Italy 62 — Germany Fed. Rep. 50; Canada 96 — Romania 66.

(*) The score at the end of regular playing time was 55-55.

TEAM PERSONNEL

T. Heiss

K. Kirchner

D. Miller

R. Waker

H. Warlick

L. Woodard

Semi-Finals
Group "A":
Cuba 64 — Italy 55; Bulgaria 79 — Poland 78; Canada 66 — China 51; China 85 — Cuba 78; Italy 68 — Poland 54; Bulgaria 65 — Canada 64; Poland 64 — China 58; Italy 82 — Bulgaria 81; Cuba 77 — Canada 68; Canada 67 — Poland 66; China 62 — Italy 60; Bulgaria 81 — Cuba 80.

Group "B":
United States 104 — France 58; Czechoslavakia 74 — Korea 67; Yugoslavia 65 — Hungary 64; Hungary 66 — Czechoslovakia 60; Korea 81 — France 63; United States 85 — Yugoslavia 84; Korea 98 — United States 88; Hungary 69 — France 64; Czechoslovakia 58 — Yugoslavia 56; Yugoslovia 69 — France 54; France 87 — Korea 71; United States 102 — Czechoslovakia 66.

Finals
United States 76 — Bulgaria — 75; France 85 — Poland 79; Czechoslovakia 75 — China 72; Canada 77 — Korea 71; Korea 61 — China 59; Canada 73 — Czechoslovakia 72; Cuba 87 — Hungary 81; Yugoslavia 65 — Italy 58; Italy 60 — Hungary 53; Cuba 80 — Yugoslavia 76.

Classification:

      I — United States of America
            (qualified)
     II — Bulgaria (qualified)
    III — Cuba (qualified)
     IV — Yugoslavia (qualified)
      V — Italy (qualified)
     VI — Hungary
    VII — Canada
   VIII — Czechoslovakia
     IX — Korea
      X — People's Republic of China
     XI — France
    XII — Poland

Boxing

TEAM PERSONNEL

Jackie Beard, 18, Jackson, Tennessee (Bantamweight)

James Broad, 22, Wildwood, New Jersey (Heavyweight)

Johnny Bumphus, 19, Nashville, Tennessee (Lightweight)

Charles Carter, 22, Santa Monica, California (Middleweight)

Don Curry, 18, Ft. Worth, Texas (Welterweight)

Joe Manley, 21, Ft. Braff, North Carolina (Lightweight)

Lee Roy Murphy, 22, Chicago, Illinois (Light Heavyweight)

Richard Sandoval, 19, Pomona, California (Flyweight)

Robert Shannon, 17, Edmonds, Washington (Light Flyweight)

James Shuler, 21, Philadelphia, Pennsylvania (Light Middleweight)

Bernard Taylor, 23, Knoxville, Tennessee (Featherweight)

Head Coach: Pat Nappi, Syracuse, New York

Assistant Coach: Dick Pettigrew, Norfolk, Virginia

Manager: Ed Silverglade, Trenton, New Jersey

US OLYMPIC FINAL SELECTION BOXING TRIALS
At the Omni, Atlanta, Georgia
June 16-21, 1980

Light Flyweight — 106 Pounds
Quarter-finals: Steven McCrory (GGAA) dec. Ronald Freeman (West) 5-0; Tommy Ayers (AAU) dec. Jesse Benavides (AAU) 5-0; Michael Caruthers (USA) won by medical disqualification over Alex Silva (AAU); Robert Shannon (AAU) dec. Inocenio Ventura (USMC) 5-0.

Semi-finals: Ayers (AAU), Cincinnati dec. McCrory (GGAA), Detroit 3-2; Shannon (AAU) Edmonds, Washington Dec. Caruthers (USA), Nashville 5-0.

Final Round: SHANNON dec. Ayers 3-2.

Flyweight — 112 Pounds
Quarter-finals: Pinky Rivera (AAU) dec. Tyrone Stewart (AAU) 3-2; Richard Sandoval (AAU) dec. Barry Houseman (West) 5-0; Jerome Coffee (GGAA) dec. George Killian (USMC) 5-0; Randy King (East) dec. Billy Smith (AAU) 5-0.

Semi-finals: Sandoval (AAU), Pomona dec. Rivera (AAU), San Jose; Coffee (GGAA), Nashville dec. King (East).

Final Round: SANDOVAL dec. Coffee 5-0

TEAM PERSONNEL

J. Beard   J. Broad   J. Bumphus

L. Murphy   R. Sandoval   R. Shannon

P. Nappi   R. Pettigrew

Bantamweight — 119 Pounds
Quarter-finals: Myron Taylor (GGAA) won by R.S.C. in 2:14 3rd round over Aaron Smith (USN); Harold Petty (AAU) dec. Steve Cruz (AAU) 3-2; Jackie Beard (AAU) won by R.S.C. in 1:31 of 1st over Sammy Fuentz (West); Kelvia Seabrook (AAU) drew a bye.

Semi-finals: Petty (AAU), St. Louis won by disqualification over Taylor (GGAA), Philadelphia in 1:18 of 3rd; Beard (AAU), Jackson, Tenn dec. Seabrook (AAU), Charlotte 5-0.

Final Round: BEARD dec. Petty 4-1

Featherweight — 125 Pounds
Quarter-finals: Hector Camacho (AAU) dec. Shelton LeBlanc (East) 4-1; Irving Mitchell (USA) dec. David Percifield (AAU) 5-0; Bernard Taylor (GGAA) dec. Orlando Johnson (AAU) 5-0; Clifford Gray (AAU) dec. Elichi Jumawan (West) 5-0.

Semi-finals: Mitchell (USA) dec. Camacho (AAU), New York 3-2; Taylor (GGAA) Knoxville dec. Gray (AAU) Bounton Beach, Florida 5-0.

Final Round: TAYLOR dec. Mitchell.

TEAM PERSONNEL

C. Carter   D. Curry   J. Manley

J. Shuler   B. Taylor

Lightweight — 132 Pounds
Quarter-finals: Joe Manley (USA) dec. Vincent Releford (AAU) 4-1; Arnold Wells (AAU) dec. Henry Hughes (AAU) 5-0; Frankie Randall (East) dec. Delio Palacious (West) 5-0; Robin-Blake (AAU) dec. Melvin Paul (GGAA) 5-0.

Semi-finals: Manley (USA), Detroit dec. Wells (AAU) Davison, Mich.; Randall (East) Morristown, Tenn. dec. Blake (AAU), Levelland, Texas.

Final Round: MANLEY dec. Randall

Light Welterweight — 139 Pounds
Quarter-finals: George Haynes, USMC dec. Darrel Robinson (West); Ronnie Shields (AAU) dec. James Mitchell (USA) 4-1; Johnny Bumphus (AAU) dec. Darryl Anthony (AAU) 5-0; Terry Silver (GGAA) dec. Harry Arroyo (AAU)

Semi-finals: Shields (AAU) won R.S.C. 3rd round over Haynes (USMC) Camp Lejeune; Bumphus won a referee disqualification in 3rd over Silver (GGAA), Louisville.

Final Round: BUMPHUS dec. Shields, 5-0.

Welterweight — 147 Pounds
Quarter-finals: Eddie Green (USA) dec. Kelvin Burton (West) 5-0; Don Curry (GGAA) dec. Michael Wright (AAU) 5-0; David Moore (East) dec. Sean Pruitt (AAU) 3-2; Gene Hatcher (AAU) dec. John Jackson (AAU) 3-2.

Semi-finals: Curry (GGAA), Fort Worth, dec. Green (USA) 4-1; Moore (East) Bronx dec. Hatcher (AAU), Fort Worth.

Final Round: CURRY dec. Moore 5-0.

Light Middleweight — 156 Pounds

Quarter-finals: Kenneth Styles (USMC) dec. Kenneth Butler (USA) 5-0; Michael Grogal (AAU) dec. Roosevelt Green (West) 4-1; James Shuler (GGAA) dec. Alfred Mays (AAU) 5-0; Donald Bowers (AAU) received a bye.

Semi-finals: Styles (USMC) Philadelphia dec. Grogan (AAU), Atlanta; Shuler (GGAA), Philadelphia dec. Bowers (AAU), Jackson, Tennessee.

Final Round: SHULER won by R.S.C. in 2:26 of 2nd round over Styles.

Middleweight — 165 Pounds

Quarter-finals: Andrew Schott (AAU) dec. Martin Pierce (AAU) 3-2; Randy Smith (AAU) won by disqualification over Harry Truman (GGAA); Charles Carter (West) dec William Trendley (AAU) 5-0; Scott Bryant (USA) dec. Charles Hannibal (East) 3-2.

Semi-finals: Smith (AAU) Chicago dec. Schott (AAU) New Paltz, New York 5-0; Carter (West) Santa Monica dec. Bryant (USA) Louisville 5-0.

Final Round: CARTER dec. Smith 5-0.

Light Heavyweight — 178 Pounds

Quarter-finals: Alex DeLucia (West) won by R.S.C. in 1:27 of 1st round over Steve Westbrook (AAU); Elmer Martin (USN) drew bye; LeRoy Murphy (AAU) won by R.S.C. in 2:14 of 3rd over Bluford Spencer (AAU); Steve Eden (GGAA) also drew bye.

Semi-finals: Martin (USN) Vallejo, California, dec. DeLucia (AAU), Portland, Oregon, 5-0; Murphy (AAU) Chicago dec. Eden (GGAA) Cedar Rapids, Iowa 5-0.

Final Round: MURPHY (AAU) ko'd Martin in 56 seconds of 1st round.

Heavyweight — Unlimited (over 178 lbs.)

Quarterfinals: Marvis Frazier (AAU) dec. Mitchell Green (East) 5-0; James Broad (USA) ko'd Freddy Guzman (AAU) 1:18 of 1st round; Chris McDonald (AAU) dec. Curtis Jackson (West) 5-0; Michael Arms (GGAA) dec. Joe Ballard (AAU) 5-0.

Semi-finals: Broad (USA) Wildwood, New Jersey ko'd Frazier (AAU), Philadelphia in 21 secs. of 1st round; McDonald (AAU) Tiverton, R.I. dec. Arms (GGAA), Madison, Wisconsin

Final Round: BROAD dec. McDonald 3-2.

Canoe-Kayak

TEAM PERSONNEL

Bruce Barton, 23, Homer, Michigan (K-2 1000m)
Gregory Barton, 20, Homer, Michigan (K-1 500m, 1000m)
Theresa DiMarino, 20, Alexandria, Virginia (K-1, K-2)
Linda Dragan, 27, Washington, D.C. (K-Res)
David Gilman, 25, Riverside, California (K-2, 500m)
Jay Kearney, 36, Lexington, Kentucky (C-Res)
Stephen Kelly, 29, Bronx, New York (K-Res)
Leslie Klein, 25, Concord, Massachusetts (K-2)
Charles Lyda, 28, Olympic Valley, California (C-Res)
Angus Morrison, 28, Bryson, North Carolina (C-2, 500m)
Roland Muhlen, 37, Cincinnati, Ohio (C-2 500m, 1000m)
John Plankenhorn, 25, Lombard, Illinois (C-1, C-2 500m, 1000m)
Terry Streib, 16, Bristol, Indiana (K-Res)
Ann Turner, 23, St. Charles, Illinois (K-1, K-2)
Jon Van Cleave, 34, Laguna Beach, California (K-1, K-2, K-4)
Andreas Weigand, 34, Fountain Valley, California (C-1, C-2, 1000m)
Terry White, 24, Arlington, Vermont (K-2, 500m)

Coach: Andy Toro, El Cerrito, California
Assistant Coach: Sperry Rademarker, Floral City, Florida
Manager: Howard Turner, St. Charles, Ill.

T. Streib

A. Turner

J. Van Cleave

S. Rademaker

A. Toro

H. Turner

TEAM PERSONNEL

B. Barton   G. Barton   T. DiMarino

L. Dragan   D. Gilman   J. Kearney

S. Kelly   L. Klein   C. Lyda

A. Morrison   R. Muhlen   R. Plankenhorn

A. Wiegand

Cycling

TEAM PERSONNEL
Les Barczewski, 23, West Allis, Wisconsin
 (Track)
Robert Cook, 22, Englewood, Colorado
 (Road)
Bruce Donaghy, 21, Wescoville,
 Pennsylvania (Track)
Thomas Doughty, 28, Hobart, Indiana
 (Road)
Brent Emery, 22, Milwaukee, Wisconsin
 (Track)
Mark Gorski, 20, Itasca, Illinois (Track)
David Grylls, 22, Gross Pointe, Michigan
 (Track)
Greg LeMond, 19, Carson City, Nevada
 (Road)
Leonard Nitz, 23, Flushing, New York
 (Track)
Thomas Schuler, 23, Downers Grove, Illinois
 (Road)
Douglas Shapiro, 20, Dix Hills, New York
 (Road)
Dale Stetina, 24, Indianapolis, Indiana
 (Road)
Wayne Stetina, 26, Schererville, Indiana
 (Road)
Danny Van Haute, 23, Chicago, Illinois
 (Track)
Andrew Weaver, 21, Gainesville, Florida
 (Road)

Track Coach: Edward Borysewicz, Colorado
 Springs, Colorado
Road Coach: Timothy Kelly, Eldorado
 Springs, Colorado
Assistant Coach: Carl Leusenkamp, Aloha,
 Oregon
Manager: Ed Burke, Iowa City, Iowa

OLYMPIC SELECTION TRIALS
**Selection Trials were conducted at San
Diego, May 5-8 1,000-Meter Time Trial:**
1. Brent Emery 1:09.8, 2. Eric Heiden 1:09.9.

4,000-Meter Individual Pursuit:
1. Leonard Nitz 4:47, 2. Dave Grylls 4:59,
3. John Beckman 5:02, 4. Vince Maggioni
5:09.

4,000-Meter Team Pursuit:
1. Leonard Nitz, Dave Grylls, Bruce
Donaghy, Danny Van Haute; 2. John
Beckman, Vince Maggioni, Brent Emery,
Dave Costelox.

Sprint:
1. Mark Gorski, 2. Les Barczewski. Leigh
Barczewski, four-time national champion,
did not compete.

ROAD RACING
Individual Time Trial

June 2, Lima, Ohio, 30km:
1. Andrew Weaver 37:03; 2. Tom Doughty
37:11; 3. Greg LeMond 37:40; 4. Hal Tozer
38:02; 5. Gerry Fornes 38:44; 6. Bob Cook
38:53; 7. Ian Jones 39:00; 8. Tom Schuler
39:02; 9. Scott Dorwart 39:02; 10. Dale
Stetina 39:03; 11. Davis Phinney 39:38; 12.
Wayne Stetina 39:42.

TEAM PERSONNEL

L. Barczewski   B. Donaghy   B. Emery

M. Gorski   D. Grylls   G. LeMond

D. Van Haute   A. Weaver

E. Burke   T. Kelly   C. Leusenkamp

E. Borysewicz

June 3, Lima, Ohio, 177km:
1. Greg LeMond; 2. Dale Stetina; 3. Doug
Shapiro; 4. Tom Schuler; 5. Wayne Stetina;
6. Steve Pyle; 7. Bob Cook; 8. Keith Vierra;
9. Hal Tozer; 10. Calvin Trampleasure;
11. John Cassidy; 12. Mark Hetzer.

Team Time Trial

June 5, Lima, Ohio, 80km:
1. W. Stetina, Schuler, Tom Doughty, A.
Weaver 1:51.19; 2. Kent Bostick, Jeff
Bradley. B. Cook, Chris Carmichael 1:53.57;
3. H. Tozer, S. Pyle, Tom Bronznowski,
D. Shapiro 1:55.52; 5. I. Jones, G. Fornes,
D. Phinney, S. Dorwart 1:55.55.

Diving

TEAM PERSONNEL

R. Ableman   B. Bungum   D. Burgering

M. Neyer   C. Potter   C. Seufert

G. Louganis   K. Machemer   A. McGrath

D. Kimball   R. O'Brien   B. Robbins

B. Weinstein

TEAM PERSONNEL
Randy Ableman, 21, Cedar Rapids, Iowa
 (Platform)
Brian Bungum, 24, Austin, Texas (Platform)
Dave Burgering, 26, San Juan Capistrano,
 California (Springboard)
Greg Louganis, 20, Mission Viejo, California
 (Springboard, Platform)
Kevin Machemer, 21, Ann Arbor, Michigan
 (Springboard)
Amy McGrath, 18, Louisville, Kentucky
 (Platform)
Megan Neyer, 18, Ashland, Kentucky
 (Springboard, Platform)
Cynthia Potter, 29, Dallas, Texas
 (Springboard)

Equestrian

TEAM PERSONNEL

Washington Bishop, 24, Middlebury,
  Virginia (3-Day)
Norman Dello Joio, 24, S. Salem, New York
  (Jumping)
Lendon Gray, 31, Dixmont, Maine
  (Dressage)
Conrad Homfeld, 28, Petersburg, Virginia
  (Jumping)
Katie Monahan, 26, Upperville, Virginia
  (Jumping)
J. Michael Plumb, 40, Chesepeake City,
  Maryland (3-Day)
Terry Rudd, 29, New Hope, Pennsylvania
  (Jumping)
Melanie Smith, 30, Stonington, Connecticut
  (Jumping)
Karen Stives, 29, Dover, Massachusetts
  (3-Day)
Gwen Elaine Stockebrand, 25, Santa Rosa,
  California (Dressage)
Torrance Watkins, 31, Boyce, Virginia
  (3-Day)
John Winnett, 51, Tuxedo Park, New York
  (Dressage)
James Wofford, 35, Upperville, Virginia
  (3-Day)
Linda Zang, 22, Davidsonville, Maryland
  (Dressage)

Manager: Maj. Gen. Jonathan Burton,
  Wenham, Massachusetts
Jumping Coach: Bert de Nemethy, Far Hills,
  New Jersey
Dressage Coach: Melle Van Bruggen,
  Blenheim, New Zealand
3-Day Event Coach: Jack LeGoff,
  Hamilton, Massachusetts

Diving

Chris Seufert, 23, Ambler, Pennsylvania
  (Springboard)
Barb Weinstein, 22, Cincinnati, Ohio
  (Platform)

Coach: Dick Kimball, Ann Arbor, Michigan
Coach: Ron O'Brien, Mission Viejo,
  California
Manager: Bryan Robbins, Dallas Texas

1980 U.S. OLYMPIC DIVING TRIALS
June 27 - July 1
Austin, Texas

Women's Springboard (June 27-28):
1. Megan Neyer, Mission Viejo, California
746.280; 2. Cynthia Potter, Dallas, Texas
704.685; 3. Chris Seufert, Ann Arbor,
Michigan 702.015; 4. Jennifer Chandler,
Mission Viejo, California 688.920; 5. Kelly
McCormick, Mission Viejo, California
683.040; 6. Carrie Finneran, Columbus,
0. 663.975.

Men's Springboard (June 28-29):
1. Greg Louganis, Mission Viejo, California
940.260; 2. Dave Burgering, Mission Viejo,
California 912.885; 3. Kevin Machemer,
Ann Arbor, Michigan 872.910; 4. Brian
Bungum, Austin, Texas 868.230; 5. Jim
Kennedy, Knoxville, Tennessee 865.860; 6.
Mike Finneran, Columbus, 0. 851.085.

TEAM PERSONNEL

W. Bishop   N. Dello Joio   L. Gray

M. Smith   K. Stives   G. Stockebrand

L. Zang

J. Burton   J. LeGoff   B. DeNemethy

M. Van Bruggen

Women's Platform (June 29-30):
1. Megan Neyer, Mission Viejo, California
620.205; 2. Barb Weinstein, Cincinnati, 0.
578.565; 3. Amy McGrath, Louisville,
Kentucky 559.635; 4. Kit Salness, Mission
Viejo, California 557.550; 5. Cynthia Potter,
Dallas, Texas 556.230; 6. Christine Loock,
Dallas, Texas 554.685.

Men's Platform (June 30 - July 1):
1. Greg Louganis, Mission Viejo, California
916.320; 2. Randy Ableman, Mission Viejo,
California 850.680; 3. Brian Bungum,
Austin, Texas 846.720; 4. Mark Virts,
Austin, Texas 844.200; 5. Bruce Kimball,
Ann Arbor, Michigan 822.285; 6. Kent
Vosler, Columbus, 0. 786.960.

TEAM PERSONNEL

K. Monahan   M. Plumb   T. Rudd

T. Watkins   J. Winnett   J. Wofford

Results of Trials' Competitions
At Blue Ridge:
1. Watkins (Poltroon); 2. Bishop (Taxi);
3. Plumb (The Shlek).

At Lexington:
1. Watkins (Poltroon); 2. Plumb (Better
and Better); 3. Plumb (Laurenson);
5. Wofford (Carawich); 6. Stives (The Saint);
7. Bishop (Taxi); 8. Watkins (Severo).

At Ships Quarters:
2. Watkins (Poltroon); 3. Wofford (Carawich); 4. Plumb (Laurenson); 5. Plumb
(Better and Better); 7. Stives (The Saint).

Show Jumping
Results of the Trials' Competitions
American Invitational:
2. Rudd (Fat City); 3. Homefeld (Balbuco);
5. Smith (Calypso); 7. Matz (Jet Run);
8. Brown (Number One Spy).

Charlotte:
1. Holmfeld (Balbuco); 2. Dello Joio
Allegro); 3. Rudd (Fat City); 4. Murphy
(Tuscaloosa); 5. Smith (Calypso); 6. Dello
Joio (Johnny's Pocket); 7. Monahan
(Silver Exchange).

Valley Forge:
1. Holmfeld (Balbuco); 2. Rudd (Fat City);
3. Monahan (Silver Exchange); 4. Dello Joio
(Johnny's Pocket); 6. Rudd (Semi Tough);
7. Smith (Calypso); 8. Dello Joio (Allegro).

Garden State:
2. Smith (Val de Loire); 4. Monahan (Silver
Exchange); 5. Rudd (Fat City).

Dressage
Results of Trials' Competition
Semi-Final at Flintridge, California:
1. Stockebrand (Bao).

Semi-Final at Gaithersburg, Maryland:
1. Zang (Fellow Traveler) 2. Winnett
(Leopardi); 3. Master (Dahlwitz); 4. Gray
(Beppo); 5. Master (La Paloma); 7. Goad
(Shine-o-Bit).

Finals at Gladstone, New Jersey
1. Winnett (Leopardi); 2. Stockebrand
(Boa); 3. Gray (Beppo); 4. Zang (Fellow
Traveler); 5. Howard (Bull Market);
6. Master (Dahlwitz).

Fencing

TEAM PERSONNEL

Jana Angelakis, 18, Peabody, Massachusetts (Women's Foil)

Gay D'Asaro, 25, San Jose, California
(Women's Foil)

Nikki Franke, 29, Philadelphia, Pennsylvania
(Women's Foil)

Timothy Glass, 24, Houston, Texas (Epee)

Elaine Ingram, 34, Denver, Colorado
(Women's Foil)

Stacey Johnson, 24, San Jose, California
(Women's Foil)

Wayne Johnson, 31, Vancouver, Washington (Epee)

Stan Lekach, 33, East Moriches, New York
(Sabre)

Thomas Losonczy, 27, New York, New
York (Sabre)

Michael Marx, 22, Portland, Oregon
(Men's Foil)

Gregory Massialas, 24, San Jose, California
(Men's Foil)

*Robert Nieman, 32, San Antonio, Texas
(Epee)

John Nonna, 32, Pleasantville, New York
(Men's Foil)

Alex Orban, 40, Hackensack, New Jersey
(Sabre)

Paul Pesthy, 42, San Antonio, Texas (Epee)

Phillip Reilly, 28, New York, New York
(Sabre)

Mark Smith, 24, East Point, Georgia
(Men's Foil)

Peter Westbrook, 28, New York, New York
(Sabre)

Captain: Jack Keane, E. Brunswick, N.J.
Coach: Csaba Elthes, New York, New York
Coach: Yves Auriol, Beaverton, Oregon
Manager: Marius Valsamis, Brooklyn, N.Y.
Armorer: Joseph Byrnes, Elizabeth, N.J.

*Also a member of Modern Pentathlon Team

TEAM PERSONNEL

J. Angelakis   E. Cheris   G. D'Asaro

W. Johnson   S. Lekach   T. Losonczy

    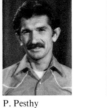
J. Nonna   A. Orban   P. Pesthy

J. Byrnes   Y. Auriol   C. Elthes

TEAM PERSONNEL

N. Franke   T. Glass   S. Johnson

M. Marx   G. Massialas   R. Nieman

P. Reilly   M. Smith   P. Westbrook

J. Keane   M. Valsamis

Field Hockey (Women)

I.F.W.H.A. WORLD CHAMPIONSHIPS, 1979
(Results were used in selecting the USA to compete in the 1980 Olympic Games)

Pool Play
USA 3, New Zealand 0
USA 11, Fiji 1
USA 3, India 2
USA 1, Australia 3

Quarter-Final Round
USA 2, England 1

Semi-Final Round
USA 0, West Germany 1 (triple overtime)

Final Round — First Place Game
The Netherlands 3, West Germany 1

Third Place Game
USA 1, Australia 0

Final Standings:
1. The Netherlands, 2. West Germany,
3. USA, 4. Australia, 5. Wales, 6. England,
7. Scotland, 8. Canada, 9. New Zealand,
10. Argentina, 11. Ireland, 12. Japan,
13. India, 14. Fiji, 15. Trinidad, 16. Hong Kong, 17. Bermuda, 18. Zambia.

TEAM PERSONNEL
Elizabeth Anders, 28, Norristown, Pa.
Elizabeth Beglin, 23, Philadelphia, Pa.
Gwen Cheeseman, 28, West Chester, Pa.
Denise Desautels, 25, Rockport, Mass.
Jill Grant, 27, Benton Harbor, Michigan
Sheryl Johnson, 22, Cupertino, California
Christine Larson, 24, Chestnut Hill, Mass.
Susan Marcellus, 21, Somerset, Mass.
Anita Miller, 29, Irvine, California
Leslie Milne, 23, Darien, Connecticut
Charlene Morett, 22, Aldan, Pennsylvania
Diane Moyer, 22, Laureldale, Pennsylvania
Karen Shelton, 22, Ocean View, New Jersey
Julie Staver, 28, Palmyra, Pennsylvania
Judy Strong, 20, W. Hatfield, Mass.
Nancy White, 22, McLean, Virginia

Head Coach: Vonnie Gros, West Chester,
  Pennsylvania
Assistant Coach: Will van Beaumont,
  St. Louis, Missouri
Manager: Margery Watson, Kimberton
  Pennsylvania

TEAM PERSONNEL

E. Anders

E. Beglin

G. Cheeseman

TEAM PERSONNEL

D. Desaultels

J. Grant

S. Johnson

C. Larson

S. Marcellus

A. Miller

L. Milne

C. Morett

D. Moyer

K. Shelton

J. Staver

J. Strong

N. White

V. Gros

W. Van Beaumont M. Watson

Gymnastics (Men)

TEAM PERSONNEL

P. Cahoy

B. Conner

R. Gallimore

L. Gerard

J. Hartung

P. Vidmar

M. Wilson

F. Allen

W. Meade

TEAM PERSONNEL

Phil Cahoy, 19, Omaha, Nebraska
Bart Conner, 22, Morton Grove, Illinois
Ron Galimore, 21, Tallahassee, Florida
Larry Gerard, 25, Lincoln, Nebraska
Jim Hartung, 20, Omaha, Nebraska
Peter Vidmar, 19, Los Angeles, California
Mike Wilson, 23, Rowlett, Texas

Head Coach: Francis Allen, Lincoln, Nebraska
Assistant Coach: William Meade, Carbondale, Illinois

OLYMPIC TRIALS

Men's Competition All-Around:
1. Bart Conner 115.200, 2. Jim Hartung 114.300, 3. Peter Vidmar 112.50, 4. Ron Galimore 114.100, 5. Phil Cahoy 112.550, 6. Larry Gerard 112.400, 7. Mike Wilson 112.300.
   Also, 8. Tim LaFleur 111.700, 9. Casey Edwards 111.500, 10. Wallace Miller 110.800, 11. Tom Hardin 110.300, 12. Kevin Praby 110.250, 13. Breck Grigas 110.100, 14. Mitch Gaylord 109.650.

Gymnastics (Women)

TEAM PERSONNEL

L. Collins

M. Frederick

K. Johnson

B. Kline

A. Koopman

J. McNamara

T. Talavera

E. Weaver

P. Ziert

TEAM PERSONNEL

Luci Collins, 16, Inglewood, California
Marcia Frederick, 17, North Haven, Connecticut
Kathy Johnson, 20, Stone Mountain, Georgia
Beth Kline, 14, Covina, California
Amy Koopman, 13, Northbrook, Illinois
Julianne McNamara, 14, Danville, California
Tracee Talavera, 13, Walnut Creek, California

Head Coach: Ernestine Weaver, Gainesville, Florida
Assistant Coach: Paul Ziert, Norman, Oklahoma
Pianist: Carol Stabisevski, Arlington, Texas

OLYMPIC TRIALS

Women's Competition All-Around:
1. Tracee Talavera 76.950, 2. Kathy Johnson 76.550, 3. Marcia Frederick 76.150, 4. Luci Collins 76.100, 5. Amy Koopman 75.800, 6. (tie) Beth Kline and Julianne McNamara 75.450.
   Also, 8. Lisa Zeis 75.200, 9. Jackie Cassello 75.000, 10. Kelly Garrison 74.650, 11. Sharon Shapiro 74.400, 12. Lynn Lederer 74.250, 13. Gigi Ambandos 73.900, 14. Jeanine Creek 73.750, 15. (tie) Kelly Gallagher and Tracy Curtis 73.600, 17. Amy Wilson 73.250, 18. Suzie Van Slyke 73.150, 19. Trina Tinti 72.950.

Judo

TEAM PERSONNEL

J. Goldstein

T. Martin

K. Nakasone

M. Santa Maria

S. Seck

M. Swain

M. Tudela

N. Yonezuka

F. Fullerton

P. Maruyama

TEAM PERSONNEL

Jesse Goldstein, 26, Toms River, New Jersey (Heavyweight)
Tommy Martin, 23, Stockton, California (189 Lbs.)
Keith Nakasone, 24, Cupertino, California (132 Lbs.)
Mitchell Santa Maria, 28, Roselle Park, New Jersey (Open)
Steven Seck, 24, Venice, California (156 Lbs.)
Michael Swain, 19, Bridgewater, New Jersey (143 Lbs.)
Miguel Tudela, 25, Alhambra, California (209 Lbs.)
Nicky Yonezuka, 16, Watchung, New Jersey (172 Lbs.)

Head Coach: Major Paul Maruyama, USAF Monument, Colorado
Manager: Frank Fullerton, El Paso, Texas

Modern Pentathlon

TEAM PERSONNEL

M. Burley   J. Fitzgerald   D. Gleneck

R. Nieman

TEAM PERSONNEL

Michael Burley, 27, Berea, Ohio
John Fitzgerald, 32, San Antonio, Texas
Dean Glenesk, 22, San Antonio, Texas
Robert Nieman, 32, San Antonio, Texas

Olympic Selection Trials Competitions
First Pentathlon Competition
March 19, 1980 San Antonio, Texas
1. Michael Burley 5,567.82 points; 2. Robert Nieman 5,550.27; 3. N. Glenesk 5,479.82; 4. John Fitzgerald 5,460.42; 5. D. Glenesk 5,332.85; 6. Losey 5,280.70; 7. McCormick 5,231.24; 8. H. Cain 5,225.10; 9. Withers 5,5156.85; 10.5, 138.73.

Second Pentathlon Competition
April 23, 1980 San Antonio, Texas
1. Burley 5,632.86; 2. N. Glenesk 5,553.57; 3. Losey 5,329.34; 4. Fitzgerald 5,281.46; 5. Brynestad 5,327.51; 6. Nieman 5,205.59; 7. Withers 5,192.76; 8. McCormick 5,131.43; 9. Helmick 5,099.65; 10. D. Glenesk 5,084.03.

Third Pentathlon Competition (also the Senior National Championships)
May 28, 1980 San Antonio, Texas
1. Fitzgerald 5,555; 2. Burley 5,402; 3. D. Glenesk 5,382; 4. Nieman 5,362; 5. Losey 5,306; 6. Driggs 5,243; 7. Beres and N. Glenesk 5,210; 9. M. Storm 5,196; 10. Withers 5,191.

Final Standings Based on Best Score in March or April Competitions plus "double" the point total in the National Championships, and those total points divided by three.
1. Fitzgerald 5,523.47; 2. Burley 5,478.95; 3. Nieman 5,424.75; 4. D. Glenesk 5,382.28; 5. N. Glenesk 5,324.52; 6. Losey 5,313.78; 7. Driggs 5,198.78; 8. Withers 5,191.58; 9. H. Cain 5, 151.70; 10. M. Storm 5,136.32.

Rowing (Men)

TEAM PERSONNEL

Chris Allsopp, 25, Palo Alto, California (Quad)
Charles Altekruse, 21, Columbia, S.C. (8's)
Bill Belden, 31, Paoli, Pennsylvania (Single Sculls)
Fred Borchelt, 26, Arlington, Virginia (Pairs with Coxswain)
Mark Borchelt, 29, Arlington, Virginia (Pairs with Coxswain)
John Carababas, 24, Grosse Pt. Park, Michigan (Pairs without Coxswain)
Dick Cashin, 27, Cambridge, Massachusetts (8's)
John Chatzky, 23, Scarsdale, New York (8's)
Steve Christensen, 23, Dayton, Ohio (8's)
Sean Colgan, 24, Ardmore, Pennsylvania (8's)
Tom Darling, 22, Swampscott, Mass. (4 with Coxswain)
James Dietz, 31, New Rochelle, New York (4 with Coxswain)
Bruce Epke, 24, Wilmington, Delaware (4 without Coxswain)
Bob Espeseth, 27, Champaign, Illinois (Spare)
John Everett, 25, S. Easton, Massachusetts (8's)
Tom Hazeltine, 25, Seattle, Washington (Spare)
Tom Howes, 24, Arlington, Massachusetts (Quad)
Tom Hull, 23, Seattle, Washington (4 without Coxswain)
Bruce Ibbetson, 27, Tustin, California (8's)
Bob Jaugstetter, 32, Cambridge, Massachusetts (4 with Coxswain)
David Kehoe, 23, Seattle, Washington (4 with Coxswain)
Steve Kiesling, 21, New Haven, Connecticut (Spare)
Brad Lewis, 25, Corona del Mar, California (Quad)
Walter Lubsen, 25, Arlington, Virginia (Spare)
Mark O'Brien, 23, Mt. Clemons, Michigan (Pair without Coxswain)
Paul Prioleau, 22, Piedmont, California (Four with Coxswain)
Bill Purdy, 23, Liverpool, New York (Spare)
Dan Sayner, 26, Annapolis, Maryland (Four without Coxswain)
Kurt Somerville, 23, Wellesley, Massachusetts (8's)
Phil Stekl, 24, Middletown, Connecticut (4 with Coxswain)
John Terwilliger, 22, Ben Lomond, California (4 without Coxswain)

TEAM PERSONNEL

C. Alsopp   C. Alterkruse   F. Borchelt

R. Espeseth   J. Everett   T. Hazeltine

W. Purdy   D. Sayner   K. Somerville

R. Dressigacker   P. Gardner   A. Meislahn

John Van Blom, 32, Long Beach, California (Double Sculls)
Chris Wells, 26, Alexandria, Virginia (Pair with Coxswain)
Chris Wood, 27, Allston, Massachusetts (Quad)
Thomas Woodman, 24, Beaverton, Oregon (8's)

Assistant Coach: Richard Bell, Detroit, Michigan
Assistant Coach: Peter Gardner, Hanover, New Hampshire
Assistant Coach: Findley Meislahn, Ithaca, New York
Assistant Coach: Vincent Ventura, Detroit, Michican
Sculling Coach: Mike Vespoli, New Haven, Connecticut
Manager: Peter Zandbergen, Omaha, Nebraska
Boatman: Richard Dreissigacker, Morrisville, Vermont

TEAM PERSONNEL

M. Borchelt   J. Carababas   R. Cashin

T. Howes   T. Hull   B. Ibbetson

P. Stekl   J. Terwilliger   J. Van Blom

M. Vespoli   P. Zandbergen

PRE—OLYMPIC COMPETITION
The Henley Royal Regatta
July 2-6, 1980

Grand Challenge Cup for 8's with Coxswain:
U.S. Olympic 8 outrowed New Zealand by
1½ lengths.

Prince Philip Cup for 4's with coxswain:
U.S. Olympic shell outrowed Yale/Potomac
British Columbia, by 1⅔ lengths.

Double Sculls Cup:
Canada (Patrick Walter and Bruce Ford)
won by two lengths over USA (CHRIS
ALSOPP and CHRIS WOOD).

**Stewards Challenge Cup for fours without
coxswain:** USA outrowed New Zeland by
two lengths.

Silver Goblet for pairs without coxswain:
USA (MARK and FRED BORCHELT)
outrowed British pair "easily."

TEAM PERSONNEL

J. Chatzky   S. Christensen   S. Colgan

R. Jaugstetter   D. Kehoe   S. Kiesling

C. Wells   C. Wood

The Lucerne International Regatta
Women's Events
Saturday June 14, 1980
Coxed Fours: USA 4th; Pairs without
Coxswain: USA (FLANAGAN and
THAXTON) 2nd; Eights with Coxswain:
USA 2nd behind East Germany by four
tenths of a second; Single sculls; JOAN
LIND, USA was second behind the East
Germany sculler; Double Sculls: USA (THE
GEER SISTERS) placed 2nd, while another
USA double (WARNER, NORELIUS) was
4th; Quadruple Sculls with coxswain: USA
was 4th.

Sunday June 15, 1980
Coxed Fours: USA was 3rd; Pairs without
coxswain: USA finished .5 seconds behind
East Germany; Eights with Coxswain USA
defeated East Ger. by .72 seconds, a first in
USA rowing history (men or women);
Single Sculls: JOAN LIND, USA, trailed the
Canadian sculler by .06 secs.; Double Sculls:
USA trailed East Germany by 2 secs.;
Quadruple Sculls with Coxswain: USA was
third.

Recapitulation:
German Democratic Republic won 10 of 12
events; The USA won one, placed second in
seven and third in three, and wound up
fourth in the other race.

TEAM PERSONNEL

T. Darling   J. Dietz   B. Epke

B. Lewis   M. O'Brien   P. Prioleau

Men's Events
8's: 2nd to East Germany, Saturday and
Sunday losing by about a length each time;
4's without coxswain: DNQ Saturday, 8th
Sunday; Pair with coxswain: USA 4th
Saturday, 3rd Sunday; Pairs without cox-
swain: DNQ; Single sculls: No USA
entry either day; double sculls: 8th Saturday,
7th Sunday; Quadruple Sculls: DNQ
Saturday, 5th on Sunday; 4's with coxswain:
USA 5th, 6th on Saturday; 5th, 7th on
Sunday. East Germany won 11 first, Finland
won the single sculls both days, and West
Germany captured the quadruple sculls
on Saturday and then finished 2nd to East
Germany on Sunday.

The Rotterdam International Regatta
Men's Events
The USA swept the river on Saturday except
for the single sculls and quadruple sculls.
HAZELTINE placed 2nd in the lightweight
single sculls. On Sunday the "8" set a course
record by 02.57 secs. The same men's crews
won on Sunday.

Women's Events
The ladies won five gold and JOAN LIND
was beaten by New Zeland in the single
sculls. On the following day Ms. Lind
avenged the defeat of the previous day, the
double sculls placed first while the pairs
without coxswain finished 2nd and the
quadruple sculls with coxswain came in 4th.

Recapitulation:
The USA flotilla enjoyed great success in
the three international regattas. The Men's
eight climaxed their successes with a victory
in the Grand Challenge at Henley and the
women's "8" scored a first for USA rowing
by defeating the East German "8" on
Sunday at Lucerne. Joan Lind remains as
one of the great scullers in the world.

Rowing (Women)

TEAM PERSONNEL
Valerie Barber, 24, West Dover, Vermont
Hope Barnes, 21, Manchester, Mass.
Carol Bower, 24, Manhattan Beach, Cal.
Carol Brown, 27, Lake Forest, Illinois
Christina Cruz, 23, N. Fond Du Lac, Wis.
Anita DeFrantz, 27, Princeton, New Jersey
Karla Drewsen, 22, Greenwich, Connecticut
Jean Flanagan, 23, Killingworth, Conn.
Charlotte Geer, 25, West Fairlee, Vermont
Julia Geer, 27, West Fairlee, Vermont
Virginia Gilder, 22, New York, New York
Carrie Graves, 27, Spring Green, Wisconsin
Jan Harville, 28, Seattle, Washington
Holly Hatton, 32, Philadelphia, Pa.
Elizabeth Hills, 26, Hingham, Mass.
Kathleen Keeler, 23, Chevy Chase, Maryland
Elizabeth Kent, 24, Philadelphia, Pa.
Joan Lind, 27, Long Beach, California
Anne Marden, 22, Concord, Massachusetts
Peggy McCarthy, 24, Madison, Wisconsin
Valerie McClain, 24, Oakland, California
Christy Norelius, 23, Bellevue, Washington
Mary O'Connor, 23, West Haven, Conn.
Jan Palchikoff, 29, Santa Ana, California
Kelly Rickon, 20, San Diego, California
Patricia Spratlen, 24, Seattle, Washington
Nancy Storrs, 30, Philadelphia, Pa.
Cathleen Thaxton, 23, San Diego, California
Susan Tuttle, 23, Middletown, Connecticut
Nancy Vespoli, 25, New Haven, Connecticut
Anne Warner, 25, Lexington, Mass.

Head Manager: Peter Lippett, San Francisco, California
Coach: Kris Korzeniowski, Lawrenceville, New Jersey
Coach: Nathaniel Case, West Haven, Connecticut
Coach: Robert Ernst, Washington
Coach: Thomas McKibbon, Newport, Beach, California

TEAM PERSONNEL

C. Bower

C. Brown

C. Cruz

J. Geer

J. Harville

H. Hatton

J. Lind

A. Marden

P. McCarthy

J. Palchikoff

K. Rickon

P. Spratlen

N. Vespoli

A. Warner

N. Case

R. Ernst

P. Lippett

TEAM PERSONNEL

A. DeFrantz

J. Flanagan

C. Geer

E. Hills

K. Keeler

E. Kent

V. McClain

K. Norelius

M. O'Connor

N. Storrs

C. Thaxton

S. Tuttle

T. McKibbon

Shooting

Official World Records
(Recognized by the International Shooting Union (UIT) January 1, 1980)

Free Rifle — 300 meters
3 x 40 shots
1160 LONES WIGGER, JR., USA 1978 Seoul, South Korea. 4,602 USA Team, 1966 Wiesbaden, West Germany

40 shots Standing
379 LONES WIGGER, JR., USA 1972 Munich.

40 shots Kneeling
392 LONES WIGGER, JR., USA 1977 Mexico City

Standard Rifle — 300 meters
3 x 20 shots
577 DAVID KIMES, USA 1978 Seoul. 2,281 USA Team 1978 Seoul.

Small-bore Rifle — 50 meters
3 x 40 shots
4,656 USA Team, 1973 Mexico City

40 shots Prone
400 JOHN WRITER, USA 1974 Thun. 1,595 USA Team, 1973 Mexico City.

40 shots Standing
385 MARGARET MURDOCK, 1975 Mexico. 1,508 USA Team, 1974 Thun.

40 shots Kneeling
1,563 USA Team, 1973 Mexico City.

World Shooting Records
Centre-Fire Pistol 25 Meters
597 T.D. SMITH III, USA, 1963 Sao Paulo. 2,353 USA Team, 1971 California

Trap Shooting (150 birds)
586 USA Team, 1977 Mexico City.

Skeet Shooting (200 birds; Team 150 birds)
199 J. CLEMMONS. USA 1977 Mexico City. 586 USA Team, 1977 Mexico City, 586 USA Team, 1979 Montecatini.

Automatic Trap (200 birds; Team 150 birds)
191 ROBERT GREEN, USA 1979 San Juan. 563 USA Team, 1979 San Juan.

Ladies World Records
Standard Rifle — 50 meters

60 shots Prone
598 MARGARET MURDOCK, USA, 1974 Thun

Air Rifle — 10 meters
40 shots
391 KAREN MONEZ, USA, 1979 Seoul.

Olympic Selection Trials
(First two finishers in each event qualified for the Olympic Team)
Olympic Trials
Running Game Target, Ft. Benning, Georgia May 7-9, 1980
1. Randy Stewart 1,703; 2. Martin Edmondson 1,698; 3. Robert Partridge 1,688; 4. Louis Michael Theimer 1,686; 5. Robert George 1,686; 5. John Anderson 1,683; 7. Donald Harmon 1,673; 8. Todd Bensley 1,664; 9. Tom Pool 1,664; 10. Randy Hicks 1,659.

TEAM PERSONNEL

T. Anderson | D. Clark | S. Collins

B. Goldsby | D. Hamilton | T. Howard

R. Stewart | L. Wigger

J. Berry | W. Pullum | J. Sizemore

Clay Pigeon, San Antonio, Texas, June 2-6, 1980
1. Ernest Neel 392; 2. Terry Howard 389; 3. Peter Piffath, Jr. 385; 4. Walter Zobell 384; 5. D. Wenner 382; 6. (tie) Kenneth Blasi, and G. Bogner 381; 8 (tie) Frank Tamburelli and Robert Kalwas 379; 10. Dudley Coleman 378.

Skeet Shooting, San Antonio, Texas, May 27-30, 1980
1. (tie) Dean Clark and Matthew Dryke 392; 3. (tie) John Satterwhite, Carl Poston, A. Iruarrizaga 389; 6. Al Leverett 388; 7. Al Mullins 387; 8. (tie) Burl Branham and David Stilley 385; 10. Richard Boss 383.

"English Match," Phoenix, Arizona, June 13-15, 1980
1. David Kimes 1,785; 2. (tie) Boyd Goldsby and Lones Wigger, Jr. 1,784; 4. (tie) Roderick Fitz-Randolph, Jr. and William Beard 1,781; 6. (tie) Dennis Dingman and Ronald Butterman 1,779; 8. (tie) Gary Andrade, Lanny Bassham, David Boyd 1,778.

TEAM PERSONNEL

M. Dryke | M. Edmondson | R. Fitz-Randolph

D. Kimes | E. Neel | S. Reiter

Smallbore Rifle, Three-position, Phoenix, Arizona, June 16-18, 1980
1. Lones Wigger, Jr. 3,475; 2. Roderick Fitz-Randolph, Jr. 3,467; 3. Karen Monez 3,460; 4. Lanny Bassham 3,454; 5. Philip Whitworth 3,449; 6. Edward Etzel 3,441; 7. Boyd Goldsby 3,438; 8. (tie) Ray Carter and David Kimes 3,436; 10. William Beard 3,433.

Free Pistol, Phoenix, Arizona June 8-10, 1980
1. Steve Reiter 1,653; 2. Donald Hamilton 1,652; 3. Donald Nygord 1,650; 4. Jimmie Dorsey 1,641; 5. Melvin Makin 1,640; 6. Erich Buljung 1,639; 7. Charles McCowan 1,636; 8. Eugene Ross 1,632; 9. Martin Buehler 1,631; 10. Jerry Wilder 1,629.

Rapid Fire Pistol, Phoenix, Arizona June 8-10, 1980
1. Steven Collins 1,762; 2. (tie) *Terry Anderson and Darius Young 1,757; 4. Melvin Makin 1,756; 5. Allyn Johnson 1,755; 6. Waymond Alvis 1,754; 7. John McNally 1,752; 8. (tie) J. Timmerman and Carl Shrader 1,750; 10. Samuel Baiocco 1,747.
(*) Olympic Team member.

TEAM PERSONNEL

Terence Anderson, 35, New Orleans,
Louisiana (Rapid Fire Pistol)
Dean Clark, 20, Ft. Benning, Georgia
(Skeet)
Steven Collins, 18, Sanborn, New York
(Rapid Fire Pistol)
Matthew Dryke, 21, Ft. Benning, Georgia
(skeet)
Martin Edmondson, 36, Ft. Benning,
Georgia (Running Game)
Rod Fitz-Randolph, 21, Palm Beach
Florida (Small Bore, 3-Pos.)
Boyd Goldsby, 33, Little Rock, Arkansas
(English Match)
Donald Hamilton, 50, Kingston, Mass.
(Free Pistol)
Terry Howard, 36, Mascoutah, Illinous
(Trap)
David Kimes, 39, Monterey Park, California
(English Match)
Ernest Neel, 34, Ft. Benning, Georgia (Trap)
Steve Reiter, 38, Daly City, California
(Free Pistol)
Randy Stewart, 28, Columbus, Georgia
(Running Game)
Lones Wigger, 42, Ft. Benning, Georgia
(Small Bore, 3-Pos.)

Team Manager: Bill Pullum, Ft. Benning,
Georgia
Assistant Manager: Joseph Berry, Lorton,
Virginia
Gunsmith: James Sizemore, Phoenix City,
Alabama

Soccer

Olympic Qualifying Tournament

FIRST ROUND
USA vs. Mexico
Game No. 1 at Leon, Mexico — Mexico 4,
USA 0 (May 23, 1979)

Game 2 at East Rutherford, New Jersey —
Mexico 2, USA 0 (June 3, 1979). USA was
eliminated, but protested to the International
Amateur Football Federation (FIFA) that
Mexico had used players ineligible for
Olympic Games competition. The protest
was upheld and the USA was reinstated.

USA vs. Bermuda
Game No. 1 at Hamilton, Bermuda —
USA 3, Bermuda 0. (Scoring for USA
PESA in 9th minute of game, DAVIS in
68th, DIBERNARDO in 77th) December 2,
1979.

Game No. 2 at Ft. Lauderdale, Florida —
USA 5, Bermuda 0. (Scoring for USA
L. NANCHOFF in 32nd minute, DAVIS in
60th, VILLA in 67th, DAVIS in 71st, G.
NANCHOFF in 82nd) Dec. 6, 1979. Thus
USA advanced to the Second Round.

Game No. 1 at Orlando, Florida — USA 2,
Surinam 1 (USA Scoring EBERT in 23rd
minute, MORRONE in 71st) March 16,
1980.

Game No. 2 at San Jose, C.R. USA 1,
Costa Rica 0 (USA scoring MORRONE in
30th minute) March 20, 1980.

Game No. 3 at Edwardsville, Illinois —
USA 1, Costa Rica 1 (USA scoring EBERT
in 22nd minute) March 25, 1980.

Game No. 4 at Paramribo, Surinam —
USA 2, Surinam 4 (USA scoring PESA in
51st minute, GEE in 75th minute)

CONCACAF Final Standings
*Costa Rica 2-1-1; **USA 2-1-1; Surinam
1-3-0.
(*) Costa Rica placed first on basis of ''goal
difference'' (goals scored minus goals scored
against).
(**) USA qualified for the 1980 Olympic
Games, but was replaced by Cuba in
Moscow as the second CONCACAF repre-
sentative, joining Costa Rica.

TEAM PERSONNEL

P. Arnautoff   T. Clark   D. Gee

J. Hayes   B. McKeon   J. Morrone

D. Salvemini   P. VanDerBeck

W. Chyzowych   R. Gansler   K. Lamm

TEAM PERSONNEL
Peter Arnautoff, 28, San Francisco,
California
Tony Bellinger, 21, Dallas, Texas
Tim Clark, 21, Burnsville, Minnesota
Paul Coffee, 23, Buffalo Grove, Illinois
Angelo Di Bernardo, 24, Woodbridge, New
Jersey
Don Ebert, 21, Florissant, Missouri
Darryl Gee, 18, Columbia, Maryland
John Hayes, 19, Florissant, Missouri
Ty Keogh, 22, San Diego, California
Adolphus Lawson, 22, St. Albans, New
York
Bill McKeon, 18, Florissant, Missouri
Joe Morrone, 21, Storrs, Connecticut
Louis Nanchoff, 23, Atlanta, Georgia
Njego Pesa, 23, Elmhurst, New York
Dan Salvemini, 23, Danville, California
Perry Van Der Beck, 20, Tampa, Florida
Greg Villa, 23, Ballwin, Missouri

Head Coach: Walt Chyzowych, King of
Prussia, Pennsylvania
Assistant Coach: Robert Gansler, Glendale,
Wisconsin
Manager: Kurt Lamm, New York, New York

Swimming (Men's)

NATIONAL LONG COURSE CHAMPIONSHIPS
(First three in each of The Olympic Events selected for the Olympic Team)
AR = American Record; * 1976 Olympic Champion; WR = World Record.

MEN'S SWIMMING SUMMARIES

100m Freestyle
1. Rowdy Gaines, Gainesville, Florida 50.19 AR; 2. Chris Cavanaugh, Saratoga, California 50.26; 3. Kris Kirchner, Austin, Texas 51.21; 4. *Jim Montgomery, Dalls, Texas 51.32; 5. Greg Kraus, Dallas, Texas 51.41; 6. Gary Schatz, Austin, Texas 51.52; 7. Scott Findorff, Madison, Wisconsin 51.57; 8. Andy Schmidt, Houston, Texas 51.66.

200m Freestyle:
1. Gaines 1:50.02; 2. Richard Thornton, Moraga, California 1:51.05; 3. Bill Forrester, Gainesville, Florida 1:51.06; 4. David Larson, Gainesville, Florida 1:51.79; 5. Todd Trowbridge, Pleasant Hill, California 1:52.28; 6. Doug Northway, Tucson, Arizona 1:52.29; 7. Montgomery 1:52.81; 8. Bill O'Brien, O'Brien, Houston, Texas 1:52.85.

400m Freestyle:
1. Mike Bruner, Los Altos, California 3:52.19; 2. *Brian Goodell, Mission Viejo, California 3:52.99; 3. Brian Roney, Woodland Hills, California 3:56.10; 4. Tony Bartle, New Haven, Connecticut 3:56.21; 5. Bari Weick, Tucson, Arizona 3:56.39; 6. Kent Martin, Austin, Texas 3:56.72; 7. O'Brien 3:58.30; 8. John Hillencamp, Gainesville, Florida 4:02.48

1,500m Freestyle:
1. Bruner 15:19.8; 2. Dave Sims, Joliet, Illinois 15:25.9; 3. Ron Neugent, Wichita, Kansas 15:27.6; 4. Weick 15:13.0; 5. *Goodell 15:34.7; 6. Monte Weaver 15:34.9; 7. Roney 15:35.7; 8. James Lorys, Portland, Oregon 15:37.5.

100m Backstroke:
1. Peter Rocca, Orinda, California 56.64; 2. Bob Jackson, San Jose, California 56.78; 3. Rick Carey, Mt. Kisco, New York 56.93; 4. Clay Britt, Fairfax, Virginia 57.15; 5. Steven Barnicoat, Mission Viejo, California 57.40; 6. David Marsh, Miami, Florida 57.78; 7. John Engs, Reno, Nevada 58.00; 8. Jesse Vassallo, Mission Viejo 58.28

200m Backstroke:
1. Barnicoat 2:01.06; 2. Rocca 2:01.34; 3. Vassallo 2:02.11; 4. Carey 2:02.79; 5. Jackson 2:03.17; 6. Engs 2:04.38; 7. Jamie Fowler, Mission Viejo 2:05.01; 8. Tom Roemer, Univ. of Iowa 2:06.38

100m Breaststroke:
1. Steve Lundquist, Jonesboro, Georgia 1:02.89 AR; 2. Bill Barrett, Alpherette, Georgia 1:03.04; 3. John Hencken, Sunnyvale, California 1:03.82; 4. Rick Meador, Austin, Texas 1:04.24; 5. John Moffet, Fullerton, California 1:04.38; 6. Roger Lager, Mill Valley, California 1:04.46; 7. Greg Higginson, Cincinnati, Ohio 1:04.49; 8. David Lundberg, Walnut Creek, California 1:04.74.

200m Breaststroke:
1. Glenn Mills, No. Ridgeville, Ohio 2:18.78; 2. Moffet 2:18.79; 3. Hencken 2:19.09; 4. Barrett 2:19.93; 5. John Simons, Scottsdale, Arizona, 2:20.68; 6. Higginson 2:20.75; 7. Meador 2:22.38; 8. Nick Nevid, Austin 2:23.13.

100m Butterfly:
1. William Paulus, Austin, Texas 54.34; 2. Matt Gribble, 54.51; 3. Mike Bottom 54.97; 4. Jim Halliburton 54.98; 5. Steve Smith, Gainesville, Florida 55.07; 6. Joe Bottom, Walnut Creek, California 55.17; 7. (tie) Sam Franklin and Jeff Stuart 55.54.

200m Butterfly:
1. Craig Beardsley, Harrington Park, New Jersey 1:58.46; 2. Bruner 1:59.13; 3. Forrester 1:59.40; 4. O'Brien 1:59.77; 5. Dennis Baker, Portland, Oregon 2:00.26; 6. Bartle 2:00.72; 7. Float 2:00.95; 8. Steve Gregg, Wilmington, Delaware 2:00.98.

400m Individual Medley:
1. Vassallo 4:21.51; 2. Simons 4:24.74; 3. Float 4:25.19; 4. Neugent 4:26.74; 5. David Santos 4:28.27; 6. Chuck Bauman 4:28.67; 7. Ed Ryder, Mission Viejo 4:29.39; 8. Kyle Miller, Gainesville, Florida 4:31.29.

TEAM PERSONNEL
Stephen Barnicoat, 18, Mission Viejo, California (200 backstroke)
William Barrett, 20, Alpherette, Georgia (200 breaststroke)
Craig Beardsley, 19, Harrington Park, N.J. (200 butterfly)
Michael Bottom, 24, Santa Ana, California (100 butterfly)
Michael Bruner, 24, Los Altos, California (200 butterfly, 400 & 1,500 freestyle)
Rick Carey, 17, Mt. Kisco, New York (100 backstroke)
Christopher Cavanaugh, 18, Saratoga, California (100 freestyle)
Jeffrey Float, 20, Sacramento, California (400 individual medley)
William Forrester, 22, Hilton Head, S.C. (200 freestyle, 200 butterfly)
Ambrose Gaines, 21, Winter Haven, Florida (100, 200 freestyle)
Brian Goodell, 21, Mission Viejo, California (400 freestyle)
Matt Gribble, 18, Miami, Florida (100 butterfly)
John Hencken, 26, Sunnyvale, California (100,200 breaststroke)
Robert Jackson, 23, San Jose, California (100 backstroke)
Kris Kirchner, 21, Austin, Texas (100 freestyle)
David Larson, 21, Jessup, Georgia (relays)
Stephen Lundquist, 19, Jonesboro, Arkansas (100 breaststroke)
Glenn Mills, 18, No. Ridgeville, Ohio (200 breaststroke)
John Moffet, 16, Newport Beach, California (200 breaststroke)
Ron Neugent, 20, Wichita, Kansas (1,500 freestyle)
William Paulus, 19, Fort Worth, Texas (100 butterfly)
Peter Rocca, 22, Orinda, California (100, 200 backstroke)
Brian Roney, 20, Woodland Hills, California (400 freestyle)
John Simons, 19, Scottsdale, Arizona (400 individual medley)
Richard Thornton, 21, Morage, California (200 freestyle)
David Sims, 17, Joliet, Illinois (1,500 freestyle)
Jesse Vassallo, 19, Mission Viejo, California (200 backstroke, 400 individual medley)

(Staff for both men's and women's teams)
Head coach: George Haines, San Jose, Cal.
Assistant Coach: Paul Bergen, Austin, Texas
Assistant Coach: Donald Gambril, Tuscaloosa, Alabama
Assistant Coach: Dennis Pursely, Cincinnati, Ohio
Assistant Coach: Randy Reese, Gainesville, Florida
Assistant Coach: Mark Schubert, Mission Viejo, California
Head Manager: George T. Breen, Philadelphia, Pennsylvania
Assistant Manager: Linda Burton, Glendale, Arizona
Assistant Manager: Pokey Watson Richarson, Honolulu, Hawaii

TEAM PERSONNEL

T. Baxter   S. Barnicoat   W. Barrett

T. Caulkins   C. Cavanaugh   S. Elkins

K. Kirchner   E. Kinkead   D. Larson

W. Paulus   S. Rapp   P. Rocca

J. Vassallo   C. Woodhead

P. Bergen   G. Breen   L. Burton

TEAM PERSONNEL

C. Beardsley   M. Bottom   M. Bruner

W. Forrester   A. Gaines   B. Goodell

K. Linehan   S. Lundquist   M. Meagher

B. Roney   J. Simons   D. Sims

D. Gambril   G. Haines   D. Pursley

TEAM PERSONNEL

L. Buese   R. Carey   K. Carlisle

J. Hencken   R. Jackson   L. Jezek

G. Mills   J. Moffet   R. Neugent

J. Sterkel   S. Thayer   R. Thornton

R. Reese   P. Richardson   M. Schubert

Swimming (Women's)

WOMEN'S SWIMMING SUMMARIES

100m Freestyle:
1. Sippy Woodhead, Riverside, California 56.57; 2. Jill Sterkel, Hacienda Heights, California 56.61; 3. Susan Thayer, Winter Haven, Florida 56.81; 4. Marybeth Linzmeier, Mission Viejo, California 56.99; 5. Sue Habernig, Mission Viejo, California 57.19; 6. Lisa Buese, Louisville, Kentucky 57.82; 7. Stephanie Elkins, Indianapolis, Indiana 57.88; 8. Heather Strang, Lansing, Michigan 58.41.

200m Freestyle:
1. Woodhead 1:59.44; 2. Linzmeier 2:01.02; 3. Mary T. Meagher, Louisville, Kentucky 2:01.45; 4. Kimberly Linehan, Sarasota, Florida 2:01.80; 5. Elkins 2:01.94; 6. Buese 2:03.22; 7. Michelle Amen, Mission Viejo 2:04.41; 8. Gwen Cross, Rockledge, Florida 2:04.47.

400m Freestyle:
1. Linehan 4:07.77; 2. Woodhead 4:08.17; 3. Elkins 4:11.58; 4. Linzmeier 4:11.92; 5. Karin LaBerge, Doylestown, Pennsylvania 4:14.18; 6. Linda Thompson, Phoenix, Arizona 4:14.31; 7. Sherri Hanna, Mission Viejo, California 4:15.52; 8. Linda Irish, Austin, Texas 4:17.94.

800m Freestyle:
1. Linehan 8:27; 2. Woodhead 8:30.3; 3. Linzmeier 8:32.6; 4. Sherri Hanna, Mission Viejo 8:37.1 5. Elkins 8:39.4; 6. LaBerge 8:39.5; 7. Laura Campanzo, City of Industry, California 8:42.5; 8. Linda Irish Austin, Texas 8:44.8.

100m Backstroke:
1. Linda Jezek, Mission Viejo 1:03.16; 2. Susan Walsh, Hamburg, New York 1:03.18; 3. Kim Carlisle, Cincinnati, Ohio 1:03.53; 4. Libby Kinkead, Wayne, Pa. 1:03.76; 5. Theresa Andrews, Towson, Maryland 1:03.85; 6. Joan Pennington, Austin, Texas 1:04.03; 7. Diane Johanningman, Cincinnati 1:04.65; 8. Darci Bodner, North Huntingdon, Pennsylvania 1:04. 88.

200m Backstroke:
1. Jezek 2:14.52; 2. Libby Kinkead, Wayne Pennsylvania 2:15.65; 3. Pennington 2:16.22; 4. Carlisle 2:16.39; 5. Walsh 2:16.85; 6. Bodner 2:17.22; F. Dian Girard, Austin, Texas 2:17.94; 8. Meg McCully, St. Petersburg, Florida 2:20.85.

100m Breaststroke:
1. Tracy Caulkins, Nashville, Tennessee 1:10.40 AR; 2. Terri Baxter, Palo Alto, California 1:12.42; 3. Susan Rapp, Alexandria, Virginia 1:12.93; 4. Kim Rodenbaugh, Cincinnati 1:12.97; 5. Kathy Smith, Bellevue, Washington 1:13.10; 6. Patty Waters, Miami, Florida 1:13.57; 7. Kathy Treible, Gainesville, Florida 1:13.65; 8. Kim Alsobrook, Mission Viejo 1:13.80.

200m Breaststroke:
1. (tie) Caulkins and Baxter 2:34.66; 3. Rapp 2:35.08; 4. Smith 2:37.21; 5. Polly Winde, Towson, Maryland 2:37.30; 6. Treible 2:37.45; 7. Torry Blazey, Gainesville, Florida 2:38.46; 8. Rhodenbaugh 2:38.87.

100m Butterfly:
1. Mary T. Meagher, Louisville, Kentucky 59.41; 2. Caulkins 1:00.75; 3. Lisa Buese, Louisville, Kentucky 1:01.75; 4. Johanningman 1:01.33; 5. Sterkel, 1:01.67; 6. Laurie Lehner, Ft. Lauderdale, Florida 1:01.76; 7. Hogshead 1:02.09; 8. Pennington 1:02.57.

200m Butterfly:
1. Meagher 2:06.37 WR; 2. Hogshead 2:11.07; 3. Linehan 2:11.57; 4. Thompson 2:11.70; 5. Johanningman 2:12.48; 6. Betsy Rapp, Alexandria, Virginia 2:13.96; 7. Mayumi Yokoyama, City of Industry, California 2:14.32; 8. Buese 2:15.45.

400m Individual Medley:
1. Caulkins 4:40.61 AR; 2. Hogshead 4:47.81; 3. LaBerge 4:49.61; 4. Anne Tweedy, Santa Barbara, California 4:50.39; 5. Pennington 4:54.68; 6. Bonnie Glascow, Baltimore, Maryland 4:58.61; 7. Sue Heon, Pittsburgh, Pennsylvania 4:58.81 Diane Ursin, Mission Viejo, disqualified.

TEAM PERSONNEL

Terri Baxter, 15, Palo Alto, California (100, 200 breaststroke)

Lisa Buese, 17, Louisville, Kentucky (100 butterfly)

Kimberly Carlisle, 19, Cincinnati, Ohio (100 backstroke)

Tracy Caulkins, 17, Nashville, Tennessee (100, 200 breaststroke, 100 butterfly, 400 individual medley)

Stephanie Elkins, 17, Indianapolis, Indiana (400 freestyle)

Nancy Hogshead, 18, Jacksonville, Florida (200 butterfly, 400 individual medley)

Linda Jezek, 20, Los Altos, California (100, 200 backstroke)

Elizabeth Kinkead, 15, Wayne, Pennsylvania (200 backstroke)

Karin LaBerge, 16, Doylestown, Pennsylvania (400 individual medley)

Kimberly Linehan, 17, Sarasota, Florida (400, 800 freestyle, 200 butterfly)

Marybeth Linzmeier, 17, Mission Viejo, California (200, 800, relay freestyle)

Mary T. Meagher, 15, Louisville, Kentucky (100, 200 butterfly, 200 freestyle)

Joan Pennington, 20, Austin, Texas (200 backstroke)

Susan Rapp, 15, Alexandria, Virginia (200 breaststroke)

Jill Sterkel, 19, Hacienda Heights, California (100 freestyle)

Susan Thayer, 17, Winter Haven, Florida (100 freestyle)

Susan Walsh, 18, Hamburg, New York (100 backstroke)

Cynthia (Sippy) Woodhead, 16, Riverside, California (100, 200, 400, 800 freestyle)

For coaches and managers refer to listings under Men's Team Personnel.

Volleyball (WOMEN)

NORTH CENTRAL AMERICA AND THE CARIBBEAN VOLLEYBALL CONFEDERATION (NORCECA)
(Olympic Qualifying Tournament)
Havana, Cuba April, 1979
Results of Matches Played by USA
National Team
vs. Mexico, 3-2 (13-15, 15-11, 9-15, 15-11, 15-5)
vs. Guatemala, 3-0 (15-0, 15-0, 15-0)
vs. Dominican Republic, 3-0 (15-2, 15-3, 15-4)
vs. Bahamas, 3-0 (15-0, 15-3, 15-0)
vs. Canada, 3-0 (15-6, 15-2, 15-5*)
vs. Cuba, 1-3 (6-15, 15-10, 9-15, 12-15**)

Final Standings — 1. Cuba**, 2. USA*, 3. Mexico, 4. Canada, 5. Dominican Republic, 6. Bahamas, 7. Guatemala.

(*) This victory guaranteed a second place finish, at worst, and qualification for the Olympic Tournament since Cuba had previously qualified by winning the 1979 world championship.
(**) This game had no bearing on qualification for 1980 Olympic Games because USA had already clinched a place in the Olympic Tournament by defeating Canada in the penultimate game of the round-robin tournament.

TEAM PERSONNEL
Janet Baier, 24, Washington, Missouri
Carolyn Becker, 21, Bellflower, California
Laurel Brassey, 26, San Diego, California
Rita Crockett, 22, DeRidder, Louisianna
Patty Dowdell, 26, Houston, Texas
Laurie Flachmeier, 23, Garland, Texas
Debbie Green, 22, Westminster, California
Flo Hyman, 26, Inglewood, California
Debbie Landreth, 23, Tempe, Arizona
Diane McCormick, 30, Charleroi, Pa.
Terry Place, 22, Redondo Beach, California
Sue Woodstra, 23, Sacramento, California

Head Coach: Dr. Arie Selinger
Assistant: Toshiaki Yoshida
Manager: Ruth Becker

TEAM PERSONNEL

J. Baier   C. Becker   L. Brassey

R. Crockett   P. Dowdell   L. Flachmeier

D. Green   F. Hyman   D. Landreth

D. McCormick   T. Place   S. Woodstra

R. Becker   A. Salenger   T. Yoshida

Water Polo

TEAM PERSONNEL

C. Dorst   G. Figueroa   S. Hamann

(Row labels)
E. Lindroth   A. McDonald   K. Robertson

P. Schnugg   P. Schroeder   J. Siman

J. Svendsen   J. Vargas

K. Lindgren   M. Nitzkowski   T. Sayring

TEAM PERSONNEL

Chris Dorst, 24, Atherton, California
Gary Figueroa, 23, Coasta Mesa, California
Steve Hamann, 30, San Jose, California
Eric Lindroth, 28, Costa Mesa, California
Andrew McDonald, 24, Orinda, California
Kevin Robertson, 21, Santa Ana Heights, California
Peter Schroeder, 21, Santa Barbara, California
John Siman, 27, Long Beach, California
Jon Svendsen, 26, Oakland, California
Joe Vargas, 24, Hacienda Heights, California

Coach: Monte Nitzkowski, Huntington Beach, California
Assistant Coach: Kenneth Lindgren, Huntington Beach, California
Manager: Terry Sayring, Manhattan Beach, California

Wrestling (Free-Style)

TEAM PERSONNEL

John Azevedo, 23, Patterson, California
(125.5 lbs.)
Chris Campbell, 25, Ames, Iowa (180.5 lbs.)
Russ Hellickson, 32, Oregon, Wisconsin
(220 lbs.)
Lee Kemp, 23, Madison, Wisconsin
(163 lbs.)
Randy Lewis, 21, Rapid City, South Dakota
(136.5 lbs.)
Gene Mills, 21, Pompton Lakes, New Jersey
(114.5 lbs.)
Ben Peterson, 30, Watertown, Wisconsin
(198 lbs.)
Bob Weaver, 21, Easton, Pennsylvania
(105.5 lbs.)
Greg Wojciechowski, 29, Toledo, Ohio
(Heavyweight)
Chuck Yagla, 26, Iowa City, Iowa
(149.5 lbs.)

Coach: Dan Gable, Iowa City, Iowa
Assistant Coach: Stan Dziedzic, Lincoln,
Nebraska

1980 FINAL OLYMPIC TRIALS
Freestyle Wrestling
June 20-22
Brockport State College
Brockport, New York

105.5 Pounds:
1. Bob Weaver (NYAC, Easton, Pa.), 2. Bill
Rosado (Sunkist Kids, Tempe, Ariz.),
3. Rich Salamone (NYAC, Rochester, N.Y.).

Results: Salamone dec. Rosado, 14-12;
Rosado dec. Salamone, 16-8; Salamone
pinned Rosado, 1:38; Weaver pinned
Salamone, :28; Weaver by injury forfeit
over Salmone; Weaver dec. Rosado, 9-6;
Weaver pinned Rosado, 3:21.

114.5 Pounds:
1. Gene Mills (NYAC, Pompton Lakes,
N.J.), 2. Ed Knecht (Sunkist Kids, Tempe,
Ariz.) 3. Bill DePaoli (NYAC, California,
Pa.), 4. Tom Dursee (NYAC, Levittown,
N.Y.).

Results: Mills pinned DePaoli, 2:25; Mills
dec. Knecht, 16-3; Mills pinned Knecht, 4:47.

125.5 Pounds:
1. John Azevedo (Sunkist Kids, Bakers-
field, Cal.), 2. Nick Gallo (NYAC, Deer
Park, N.Y.), 3. Mark Mangianti (Sunkist
Kids, Tempe, Ariz.), 4. Jack Reinwand
(Wisconsin W.C., Madison, Wis.).

Results: Mangianti dec. Azevedo, 7-4; Gallo
dec. Reinwand, 13-5; Azevedo by injury
forfeit over Mangianti; Gallo dec.
Reinwand, 12-6; Mangianti injured and
could not continue after first day; Reinwand
withdrew after loss to Gallo; Azevedo, 5-2; .
Gallo, 5-4; Gallo dec. Azevedo, 5-2;
Azevedo dec. Gallo, 4-3.

TEAM PERSONNEL

J. Azevedo   C. Campbell   R. Hellickson

L. Kemp   R. Lewis   G. Mills

B. Peterson   B. Weaver   G. Wojciechowski

C. Yagla

S. Dziedzic   D. Gable

136.5 Pounds:
1. Randy Lewis (Hawkeye W.C., Rapid
City, S.D.), 2. Tim Cysewski (Hawkeye
W.C., Iowa City, Iowa), 3. Ricky Dellagatta
(NYAC, Lexington, Ky.)

Results: Cysewski pinned Dellagatta,
1:28; Cysewski dec. Dellagatta, 22-3; Lewis
dec. Dellagatta, 17-14; Lewis dec. Dellagatta,
15-6; Lewis dec. Cysewski, 6-3; Cysewski
dec. Lewis, 13-4; Lewis dec. Cysewski, 3-2.

149.5 Pounds:
1. Chuck Yagla (Hawkeye W.C., Iowa City,
Iowa), 2. Andy Rein (Wisconsin W.C.,
Stoughton, Wis.), 3. Phil Anglim (Buckeye
W.C., Columbus, Ohio), Jim Humphrey
Oklahoma Underdogs, Norman, Okla.)

Results: Humphrey dec. Anglim, 7-4;
Yagla dec. Rein, 12-7; Humphrey dec.
Anglim, 7-2; Yagla pinned Rein, 8:49; Yagla
pinned Humphrey, 5:27, Rein pinned
Anglim, 3:31; Yagla pinned Humphrey,
4:44, Rein pinned Anglim, 7:20; Rein by
forfeit over Humphrey, Yagla pinned
Anglim, 1:43; Rein by forfeit over
Humphrey; Yagla pinned Anglim, 2:38.

163 Pounds:
1. Lee Kemp (Wisconsin W.C., Madison
Wis.); 2. Dave Schultz (Oklahoma
Underdogs, Palo Alto, Cal.), 3. Grant Smith
(Wisconsin W.C., DeForest, Wis.).

Results: Kemp dec. Smith, 13-0; Kemp dec.
Schultz, 5-4; Kemp dec. Schultz, 7-4.

180.5 Pounds:
1. Chris Campbell (Cyclone W.C., Ames,
Iowa), 2. John Peterson (Athletes in
Action, Hawaiian Gardens, Cal.), 3. Ed
Banach (Hawkeye W.C., Port Jervis, N.Y.).

Results: Banach dec. Campbell, 15-7;
Campbell dec. Banach, 7-4; Campbell dec.
Banach, 15-8; Banach pinned Peterson,
1:31; Peterson dec. Banach, 10-5;
Campbell won in a tiebreaker over Peterson
(8-8); Campbell dec. Peterson, 7-4.

198 Pounds
1. Ben Peterson (Wisconsin W.C., Water-
town, Wis.), 2. Laurent Soucie (Wisconsin
W.C., Milwaukee, Wis.), 3. Roy Baker
(NYAC, Plainview, N.Y.), 4. Charlie
Gadson (Cyclone W.C., Ames, Iowa).

Results: Soucie dec. Baker, 6-4; Peterson
dec. Gadson, 11-8; Soucie dec. Baker, 7-2;
Peterson pinned Gadson, 1:37; Soucie dec.
Gadson, 5-4; Peterson dec. Baker, 8-1;
Gadson dec. Soucie, 8-0; Peterson dec.
Baker, 10-3; Peterson dec. Soucie, 5-2;
Baker won in a tiebreaker over Gadson (3-3);
Soucie dec. Peterson, 5-4; Baker won in a
tie-breaker over Gadson (6-6); Peterson dec.
Soucie, 5-4.

220 Pounds:
1. Russ Hellickson (Wisconsin W.C.,
Oregon, Wis.), 2. Mike Evans (Unattached,
Joliet, Ill.).

Results: Hellickson pinned Evans, 5:03;
Hellickson dec. Evans, 17-5.

Heavyweight
1. Greg Wojciechowski (Toledo Area W.C.,
Toledo, Ohio), 2. Bruce Baumgartner
(NYAC, Haledon, N.J.).

Results: Wojciechowski dec. Baumgartner,
6-3; Wojciechowski dec. Baumgartner,
9-4.

Wrestling (Greco-Roman)

TEAM PERSONNEL

Jeff Blatnick, 23, Schenectady, New York (Heavyweight)
Dan Chandler, 28, Minneapolis, Minnesota (180.5 lbs.)
Mark Fuller, 19, Auburn, California (105.5 lbs.)
Brian Gust, 31, Lakeville, Minnesota (125.5 lbs.)
Mark Johnson, 24, Rock Island, Illinois (198 lbs.)
John Matthews, 28, Flint, Michigan (163 lbs.)
Thomas Minkel, 30, Mount Pleasant, Michigan (149.5 lbs.)
Daniel Mello, 27, Bakersfield, California (136.5 lbs.)
Brad Rheingans, 26, Appleton, Minnesota (220 lbs.)
Bruce Thompson, 28, Rosemont, Minnesota (114.5 lbs.)

Coach: Lee Allen, El Granada, California
Assistant Coach: Major Wayne Baughman, USAF, Colorado Springs, Colorado

1980 FINAL OLYMPIC TRIALS
Greco-Roman Wrestling
June 26-28
Brockport State College
Brockport, New York

105.5 Pounds
1. Mark Fuller (San Francisco Peninsula Grapplers, Auburn, Cal.), 2. T.J. Jones (U.S. Navy, Coronado, Cal.), 3. Scott Revis (Eugene, Ore.).

Results: Fuller dec. Revis, 11-6; Fuller by forfeit over Revis; Jones by forfeit over Revis, twice; Fuller dec. Jones, 9-5; Fuller dec. Jones, 15-3.

114.5 Pounds:
1. Bruce Thompson (Rosemont, Minn.), 2. John Hartupee (Michigan Wrestling Club, Mt. Pleasant, Mich.), 3. Todd Rosenthal (Moline, Ill.).

Results: Thompson dec. Hartupee, 26-6; Thompson pinned Hartupee, 8:49; Hartupee by tiebreaker over Rosenthal, 8-8; Hartupee dec. Rosenthal, 9-7; Thompson pinned Rosenthal, 4:43; Thompson pinned Rosenthal, 4:05.

125.5 Pounds:
1. Brian Gust (Lakeville, Minn.), 2. Rob Hermann (U.S. Navy, San Diego, Cal.), 3. Frank Famiano (Adirondack Three-Style Wrestling Club, Schenectady, N.Y.).

Results: Gust dec. Famiano, 14-5; Gust dec. Famiano, 31-3; Gust dec. Hermann, 17-4; Gust by tiebreaker over Hermann, 10-10; Hermann dec. Famiano, 11-4; Hermann dec. Famiano, 14-5.

TEAM PERSONNEL

J. Blatnick   D. Chandler   M. Fuller

B. Gust   M. Johnson   J. Matthews

D. Mello   T. Minkel   B. Rheingans

B. Thompson

L. Allen   W. Baughman

136.5 Pounds:
1. Dan Mello (U.S. Marine Corps, Quantico, Va.), 2. John Hughes (Minneapolis, Minn.), 3. Larry Nugent (Ashland, Ore.)

Results: Mello dec. Nugent, 16-1; Mello pinned Nugent, 7:10; Mello dec. Hughes, 20-5; Mello dec. Hughes, 10-5; Hughes dec. Nugent, 9-4; Hughes dec. Nugent, 7-4.

149.5 Pounds:
1. Tom Minkel (Michigan Wrestling Club, Mt. Pleasant, Mich.); 2. Dave Butler (U.S. Navy, San Diego, Cal.); 3. Chris Benintende (U.S. Navy, El Cajon, Cal.).

Results: Minkel dec. Butler, 12-6; Butler pinned Minkel, 1:22; Minkel dec. Butler, 7-6; Butler dec. Benintende, 10-3; Butler dec. Benintende, 11-6; Minkel dec. Benintende, 10-3; Minkel dec. Benintende, 7-4.

163.0 Pounds:
1. John Matthews (Michigan Wrestling Club, Mt. Pleasant, Mich.); 2. Dave Schultz (Oklahoma Undergods, Palo Alto, Cal.); 3. Jim Andre (Minneapolis, Minn.).

Results: Matthews dec. Andre, 14-0; Matthews dec. Andre, 8-1; Schultz dec. Andre; Schultz dec. Andre; Matthews dec. Schultz, 4-2; Matthews dec. Schultz, 4-2.

180.5 Pounds:
1. Dan Chandler (Minneapolis, Minn.); 2. Phil Lanzatella (Adirondack Three-Style Wrestling Club, Rochester, N.Y.); 3. Keith Fisher (Wisconsin Wrestling Club, Waupaca, Wis.).

Results: Chandler pinned Fisher, 1:14; Chandler pinned Fisher, 2:59; Chandler dec. Lanzatella, 8-1; Chandler dec. Lanzatella, 8-1; Lanzatella pinned Fisher, 3:23; Lanzatella by tiebreaker over Fisher, 9-9.

198.0 Pounds:
1. Mark Johnson (Hawkeye Wrestling Club, Iowa City, Iowa; 2. Laurent Soucie (Wisconsin Wrestling Club, Milwaukee, Wis.); 3. Mike Houck (Minnesota Wrestling Club; Minneapolis, Minn.).

Results: Johnson dec. Soucie, 6-2; Johnson dec. Soucie, 8-3; Johnson dec. Houck, 11-7; Johnson by tiebreaker over Houck, 8-8; Soucie dec. Houck, 10-4; Soucie pinned Houck, 2:06.

220.0 Pounds:
1. Brad Rheingans (Minnesota Wrestling Club; Appleton, Minn.); 2. Greg Gibson (U.S. Marine Corps, Quantico, Va.); 3. Ron Carlisle (U.S. Marine Corps, Quantico, Va.).

Results: Rheingans dec. Gibson, 5-3; Rheingans dec. Gibson, 7-1; Rheingans by passivity over Carlisle; Rheingams by injury over Carlisle; Gibson dec. Carlisle, 16-4; Gibson by passivity over Carlisle.

Heavyweight:
1. Jeff Blatnick (Adirondack Three-Style Wrestling Club, Schenectady, N.Y.), 2. Carl Dambman (Athletes In Action, Philadelphia, Pa.); 3. Tom Zupancic (Michigan Wrestling Club; Indianapolis, Ind.).

Results: Blatnick by passivity over Zupancic; Blatnick by passivity over Zupancic; Blatnick pinned Dambman, 3:48; Blatnick pinned Dambman, 1:09; Dambman dec. Zupancic, 6-5; Dambman by passivity over Zupancic.

Weightlifting

1980 NATIONAL AAU SENIOR WEIGHTLIFTING CHAMPIONSHIPS
(Also served as Olympic Final Selection Trials)
(*) Indicates 1980 Olympic Team Selection

114-Pound Weight Class:
1. Leslie Sewall 402 pounds; 2. Brian Miyamoto 391 pounds; 3. Mark Kappes 369 pounds.

123-Pound Weight Class:
1. Joe Widdell 463 pounds; 2. Richard Palmer 452 pounds; 3. Ronald Crawley 441 pounds.

132-Pound Weight Class:
1. Philip Sanderson 535 pounds; 2. Gerald Fukuoka 507 pounds; 3. Bill Leblanc 490 pounds.

148¾-Pound Class:
1. *Cal Schake 639 pounds (American record); 2. James Benjamin 595 pounds; 3. Donnie Warner 584 pounds.

165¼-Pound Class:
1. Myron Davis 656 pounds; 2. Fred Lowe 639 pounds; 3. Curt White 628 pounds.

181¾-Pound Class:
1. *Michael Karchut 722 pounds; 2. *Michael Cohen 717 pounds; 3. Tom Hirtz 711 pounds.

198¼-Pound Class:
1. *James Curry, Jr. 744 pounds; 2. *Joe Puleo 728 pounds; 3. *Luke Klaja 722 pounds.

220-Pound Class:
1. *Brian Derwin 799 pounds; 2. *Guy Carlton 794 pounds; 3. *Kurt Setterburg 772 pounds.

242-Pound Class:
1. *Mark Cameron 821 pounds; 2. *Bob Giordano 805 pounds; 3. Mario Martinez 766 pounds.

Super Heavyweight, over 242 pounds:
1. *Tom Stock 865 pounds; 2. *Jerome Hannan 849 pounds; 3. Joe Dube 777 pounds.

TEAM PERSONNEL
Mark Cameron, 28, Middletown, Rhode Island (242 lbs.)
Guy Carlton, 26, LaPlace, Illinois (220 lbs.)
Michael Cohen, 22, Savannah, Georgia (181 lbs.)
James Curry, Jr., 27, Berkeley, California (198 lbs.)
Brian Derwin, 29, Cresskill, New Jersey (220 lbs.)
Bob Giordano, 29, Belleville, New Jersey (242 lbs.)
Jerome Hannan, 27, Levittown, Pensylvania (super heavyweight)
Michael Karchut, 36, Calumet City, Illinois (181.5 lbs.)
Luke Klaja, 27, Jacksonville, Oregon (198 lbs.)

TEAM PERSONNEL

M. Cameron   G. Carlton   M. Cohen

J. Curry   B. Derwin   B. Giordano

J. Hannan   M. Karchut   L. Klaja

J. Puleo   C. Schake   K. Setterberg

T. Stock

J. Schmitz   D. Smith

Joe Puleo, 37, Grosse Pointe Woods, Michigan (198 lbs.)
Cal Schake, 22, Butler, Pennsylvania (148 lbs.)
Kurt Setterburg, 29, Masury, Ohio (220 lbs.)
Tom Stock, 28, Belleville, Illinois (super heavyweight)

Head Coach: James Schmitz, San Francisco, California
Manager: Richard Smith, York, Pa.

Yachting

TEAM PERSONNEL

J. Bertrand   H. Bossett   R. Davis

M. Duane   N. Fowler   R. Haines

J. Kent   M. Loeb   E. Trevelyan

H. Arnold   C. Eichenlaub   C. Kober

R. Mairs   S. Merrick

TEAM PERSONNEL
Ron Anderson, 28, Sausalito, California
Steve Benjamin, 24, Oyster Bay, New York
John Bertrand, 24, San Rafael, California
Henry Bossett, 29, Pt. Pleasant Beach, N.J.
Bill Buchan, 45, Bellevue, Washington
Rod Davis, 25, Seal Beach, California
Marshall Duane, 24, Delray Beach, Florida
Neal Fowler, 25, Easton, Connecticut
Robbie Haines, Jr., 26, Coronado, California
Jeff Kent, 24, Weymouth, Massachussetts
Michael Loeb, 28, New Haven, Connecticut
Ed Trevelyan, 24, Coronado, California

Coach: Dr. Homer Arnold, Austin, Texas
Manager: Sam Merrick, Washington, D.C.
Assistant Manager: Chuck Kober, Long Beach, California
Boatwright: Carl Eichenlaub, San Diego, California
Meteorologist: Robert Mairs, Edgewater, Maryland.

Olympians received their special Gold Medals at the Capitol.

OLYMPIC HONORS PROGRAM

By Mike Moran

It's doubtful that any nation, or its national Olympic committee, has ever done as much in the way of recognition. And all this for a team that stayed home while the rest of the world partied in Moscow yet . . .

The United States Olympic Committee, ever mindful of the achievements of its athletes in becoming Olympians, plus the long years of training and dedication, took it upon itself to recognize the 500 and some athletes with an Olympic Honors Program in Washington, D.C., July 26-30. It was a five-day period that will live forever in the hearts of the athletes and the Olympic staff, who must have had a myriad of thoughts running through their heads on July 30 as they received Congressional medals on the steps of the Capitol, while thousands of miles away the Games went on without them in Moscow.

The USOC's effort was not designed to make the athletes forget what had happened to them. The boycott was still a sobering reality.

The Honors Program came about because the USOC wanted the athletes to have, even for just a day, the recognition of an entire nation, and the recognition that goes with achieving the status of an Olympian. And the USOC wanted it to be a fun experience that could be shared by friends and family, too. For a few days in the summer of 1980, it was fun, and it gave an entire Olympic Team the chance to really get to know each other, a unique experience.

There was a little talk about Moscow, but most of the conversation centered on the future, and what would happen in 1984. American athletes who saw their final chance at Olympic competition waxed philosophical about helping the next generation develop and get its chance. Others said they came to Washington to make sure the same thing never happened again. It seemed that a new spirit was born among the American athletes in Washington, and that perhaps in the midst of all the turmoil that a newer and stronger foundation was forged for America's Olympic future.

If you looked closely at the medal ceremony on July 30, you could see a multitude of emotions on the faces of the athletes as they stepped up to receive the gold-plated medals from USOC officers. The almost adolescent faces of the women gymnasts, and lined and creased faces of the veteran shooters, and the fresh faces of the swimmers and basketballers. It was all there, and each had their own private thoughts on that broiling summer day in Washington. Some would be back, some would not, others will be upstaged by younger athletes with more skills in 1984.

But the only truly somber moment in five days of sometimes casual and relaxed happenings and spectacular entertainment came on July 30 at the Capitol ahead of the medals ceremony when President Jimmy Carter descended the steps to the strains of "Hail to the Chief," to speak to the American athletes.

"If our Olympic Team had been in Moscow these past days, with all the pageantry and spectacle, it would have been impossible for us credibly to maintain our continuing effort to seek freedom in Afghanistan," Carter told the Olympians and their guests.

"No matter what else we had done, no matter what other step we had taken, our participation would have sent an unmistakable message — to the Soviet government, to the Soviet people and the people all over the world. That message would have been like this: The United States may not like the idea of aggression, but when it comes down to it, we are willing to join the parade as if nothing had happened. For the sake of world peace, we cannot allow such a message to be conveyed," said Carter.

Later, when the athletes journeyed to the White House and a reception and buffet dinner with the Carters on the South Lawn, the President told the athletes that "You have honored me by letting me shake your hand. You have done more to uphold the Olympic ideal than any other group of athletes in American history. I thank you from the bottom of my heart."

After Carter departed the Capitol steps, the American athletes stepped forward, team by team, individual by individual, to have the beautiful gold-plated medals draped on their necks by the officers of the United States Olympic Committee, which had sponsored and funded the five-day ceremonies in appreciation of the athletes and their achievements.

Following the two-hour ceremony, during which several of the over-heated athletes dunked themselves in the nearby fountain to cool off, athletes Madeline Manning Mims (track and field) and Bob Nieman (fencing and modern pentathlon) spoke for the team.

"We are honored and proud to receive this award from the American people," said the 32-year-old Manning Mims, who in 1968 won an Olympic gold medal at Mexico City in the 800 meters. She then urged the American public and the athletes to "unite in perpetuating the true spirit of the Olympic movement."

Olympian swimmer Donna de Verona was the master of ceremonies for the medal ceremony at the Capitol, and delivered a stirring and timely message to the athletes and their families, plus the American public, pleading for their support of amateur athletics in the nation over the years to come.

The Olympians were then treated to a special parade in TourMobiles around the vast expanse of the Washington Mall, past the monuments, past the memorials and in front of thousands of cheering Americans who obviously held a special place in their hearts for

With the Carters at the White House.

this most unusual collection of Olympic athletes — the most unique team in American history.

Later that night, the team was hosted by the Carters at the White House on the South Lawn, along with its guests. There was music, there was a reception line in which the President greeted each of the athletes and then posed for a team picture with them, there was food and drink, and there was laughter and there was thought.

The evening, and the gala week, was capped by a gorgeous and colorful show for the Olympians at the Kennedy Center's Concert Hall.

On the roster were show business names like singers Patti LaBelle, Andy Gibb, and the Lennon Sisters, plus Peter Marshall (of the "Hollywood Squares" TV show) and his group, Chapter Five, comedian Jamie Farr of the TV series M-A-S-H, acress-singer Irene Cara (fresh from the hit movie "Fame"), and master of ceremonies Leonard Nemoy, the "Star Trek" actor who played Mr. Spock in the now-famous series, and who gave a stirring dramatic reading for the Olympians on the life of Abraham Lincoln.

The entertainers donated their time and talents to honor the Olympians, and the exciting show was put together by Sheldon Saltman, president of 20th Century Fox Sports, along with producers Andre Tayir and Tennyson Flowers.

At the end of the dramtic evening, two hundred of the Olympic athletes

trooped onto the stage to join the entertainers in the last number as the show closed. At that point, tears flowed freely down the cheeks of the athletes and their families and friends who had made the trip to Washington to be with them.

They knew the curtain was coming down, and it was to be the end of a lifetime dream for many of them. Certainly a good number would be back to try to win a berth on the 1984 Olympic Team, but for many it was over. For others, young still, there are better athletes waiting in the wings to steal their spot in '84. That's the American way.

But on this night, in the Nation's Capitol, they were heroes all, and they clung to each other one last time as the evening ended.

THE WEEK IN WASHINGTON REVISITED

Though the medals ceremony, the White House reception, and the Kennedy Center show highlighted the final day of the USOC's Olympic Honors Program, there were a series of noteworthy events and parties for the athletes which took place from July 26-29 which were a major success. Here's a rundown on what our Olympic athletes took part in on their journey to Washington:

- A mammoth country and western party at the beautiful Smokey Glen Farm near Gaithersburg, Maryland, thrown by Levi Strauss & Co., the

Senator Gary Hart

outfitters of the 1980 Olympic and Pan American Games Teams. Levi spared nothing in this fabulous party, including importing two of the now-famous mechanical bull machines features in the hot movie "Urban Cowboy." Levi's also threw in barbequed ribs, chicken, corn on the cob, drinks and ice cream, then a spectacular evening of entertainment under the stars featuring Country and Western song star Red Steagle and a giant fireworks show. (Levi's also outfitted the Olympians in complete Western gear and leisure wear, along with some luggage and two sets of warmups. The colorful red shirts, jeans, belt buckles, scarves and western hats worn by the athletes to the Capitol and to the White House came from Levi's, too.)

- A "Washington After Dark" bus tour, with stops at the Lincoln Memorial, Iwo Jima Monument, Jefferson Memorial and Washington Monument. Then, a garden party in historic Gerogetown at the home of Mrs. Carol Shapiro, the Prospect House, featuring carloads of ice cream and drinks, plus live music.

- A fresh seafood dinner at Hogate's Restaurant on the water, where the restaurant staff lined up and gave the Olympic Team a ten-minute standing ovation as they arrived and were seated in the establishment.

- An evening and special performance at the Ford Theatre for the Olympic Team of "Joseph and the Amazing Technicolor Dreamcoat," then a party at the Marriott-Twin Bridges Hotel (USOC & Team Headquarters) with the cast of the show.

- A gala catered dinner at the venerable Museum of History and Technology of the Smithsonian Institution amongst the displays of autos, trains, engines, steamships and assorted artifacts from America's past.

- A refreshing and lively two-hour special parade and concert for the Olympians at the U.S. Marine Barracks, with the U.S. Marine Band performing. It got a standing ovation from the athletes and staff for a great show.

But in the end, the nice thing was that the families, the girlfriends, the boyfriends, aunts, uncles, brothers and sisters, could be in Washington to see it all with the Olympic athletes. One by one they paid tribute to the USOC for honoring the kids, and for wanting them to feel special, which they are.

The only athletes not able to attend were the Olympic swimmers, who were chosen during the national long-course championships at Irvine, Cal., the same week. However, the USOC hosted the swimmers August 4-5-6 in Washington anyway, and the group got its own "mini-program" featuring a night at the National Theatre, another party at Prospect House in Georgetown, a White House reception with President Carter, and its own medal ceremony at the White House, with USOC Vice-President Joel Ferrell, Jr., doing the honors. It was capped off by a special dinner at the Capital in the Mike Mansfield Room, with a segment of the U.S. Marine Band playing music during the meal.

It ended the historic chain of events which began in early January when President Carter first revealed to a nationwide television audience his feelings about not sending a team to Moscow in July, setting off a dramatic, controversial, and sometimes bitter struggle between politics and sports in America, the likes of which had never been seen before.

Perhaps the struggle has molded American sports purpose into a solid weld, and perhaps there will be changes in the Olympic Games and in the Olympic Movement in the world.

But if you listened carefully to the kids in Washington, if you listened to the whispers and the shouts, and if you looked past the anger, frustration, divided opinion and the tears on the cheeks — you could see a new sense of dedication and desire on those young faces, and a new message.

I wouldn't miss Los Angeles in 1984 for a six percent home loan or free gasoline for the rest of my life.

Bob Nieman and Madeline Manning Mims respond for the Olympians at the Capitol Ceremony.

The Last Day